CONTENTS

RATINGS & PRICES

Ratings

Our rating system is unlike those found in other guides (most of which tell you nothing more helpful than that expensive restaurants are, as a general rule, better than cheap ones).

What we do is to compare each restaurant's performance – as judged by the average ratings awarded by reporters in the survey – with other restaurants in the same price-bracket.

This approach has the advantage that it helps you find – whatever your budget for any particular meal – where you will get the best 'bang for your buck'.

The following qualities are assessed:

F — Food
S — Service
A — Ambience

The rating indicates that, *in comparison with other restaurants in the same price-bracket*, performance is…

❶ — Exceptional
❷ — Very good
❸ — Good
④ — Average
⑤ — Poor

Prices

The price shown for each restaurant is the cost for one (1) person of an average three-course dinner with half a bottle of house wine and coffee, any cover charge, service and VAT. Lunch is often cheaper. With BYO restaurants, we have assumed that two people share a £5 bottle of off-licence wine.

Telephone number – all numbers should be prefixed with '020' if dialling from outside the London area.

Map reference – shown immediately after the telephone number.

Rated on Editors' visit – indicates ratings have been determined by the Editors personally, based on their visit, rather than derived from the survey.

Website – the first entry in the small print (after any note about Editors' visit)

Last orders time – listed after the website (if applicable); Sunday may be up to 90 minutes earlier.

Opening hours – unless otherwise stated, restaurants are open for lunch and dinner seven days a week.

Credit and debit cards – unless otherwise stated, Mastercard, Visa, Amex and Maestro are accepted.

Dress – where appropriate, the management's preferences concerning patrons' dress are given.

Special menus – if we know of a particularly good value set menu we note this (e.g. "set weekday L"), together with its formula price (FP) calculated exactly as in 'Prices' above. Details change, so always check ahead.

HOW THIS GUIDE IS WRITTEN

Survey

This guide is based on our 18th annual survey of what Londoners think of their restaurants; it is by far the largest annual survey of its type. Since 1998, we have also surveyed restaurant-goers across the rest of the UK. The out-of-town results are published in our national 'Restaurant Guide' (formerly called 'UK Restaurants') published in association with Rémy Martin Fine Champagne Cognac. This year the total number of reporters in our combined London/UK survey, conducted mainly online, exceeded 8,000, and, between them, they contributed some 85,000 individual reports.

How we determine the ratings

In most cases, ratings are arrived at statistically. This essentially involves 'ranking' the average rating each restaurant achieves in the survey – for each of food, service and ambience – against the average ratings of the other establishments which fall in the same price-bracket. A few restaurants – usually those which have opened after the survey began – are rated by ourselves, as editors, personally. To emphasise the personal (non-democratic) basis of such assessments, we include a small-print note – "Rated on Editors' visit".

How we write the reviews

The tenor of each review is broadly determined by the ratings of the establishment concerned (which we derive as described above). We also pay some regard to the proportion of positive nominations (such as for 'favourite restaurant') compared to negative nominations (such as for 'most overpriced'). To explain why a restaurant has been rated as it has, we extract snippets from survey comments ("enclosed in double quotes"). A short review cannot possibly reflect all the nuances from, sometimes, several hundred reports, and what we try to do is to illustrate the key themes which emerge.

Editors' visits

We have – anonymously and at our own expense – visited almost all the restaurants listed in this book. As noted above, in the case of a few restaurants which open in the months before the guide goes to press, we use these experiences not only to inform our review but also as the basis of the ratings awarded. More generally, however, our personal views about any particular restaurant are irrelevant: the reviews we write (and ratings the guide awards) reflect our best analysis of the survey responses.

Richard Harden   **Peter Harden**

Editors' note

"Pétrus"

The restaurant referred to in this guide as "Pétrus"
is the establishment run by Marcus Wareing at the
Berkeley Hotel. At about the time of the publication of
this guide, that restaurant will cease to be a member of
the Gordon Ramsay group, and the Berkeley lease will
be taken over by Marcus Wareing personally.

At the time of writing, it is unclear whether – once the
Gordon Ramsay group is no longer involved – the
restaurant will continue to be called Pétrus, or whether
it will be called Marcus Wareing at the Berkeley (or
perhaps some other name).

SURVEY MOST MENTIONED

These are the restaurants which were most frequently mentioned by reporters. (Last year's position is given in brackets.) An asterisk* indicates the first appearance in the list of a recently-opened restaurant.

1   J Sheekey (1)
2   Chez Bruce (2)
3   The Wolseley (3)
4   Hakkasan (5)
5   Gordon Ramsay (6)
6   Bleeding Heart (4)
7   Scott's (24)
8   Pétrus (12)
9   Le Gavroche (11)
10 The Ivy (7)

11 La Poule au Pot (9)
12 La Trompette (18)
13 Arbutus (13)
14 Oxo Tower (8)
15 Galvin Bistrot de Luxe (16)
16 Le Caprice (15)
17 Andrew Edmunds (10)
18 Zuma (22)
19 The Square (26)
20 Gordon Ramsay at Claridge's (14)

21 Yauatcha (19)
22 The Anchor & Hope (27)
23 Wild Honey*
24 The Cinnamon Club (23)
25 Locanda Locatelli (20)
26 Benares (-)
27 Tom Aikens (25)
28 maze (21)
29 Le Café Anglais*
30 L'Atelier de Joel Robuchon (32)

31 Roka (-)
32 Moro (29)
33 The River Café (32)
34 Amaya (28)
35 The Ledbury (-)
36 The Don (30)
37 Roussillon (40)
38 St John (36)
39= St Alban (35)
39= Zafferano (-)

SURVEY NOMINATIONS

Top gastronomic experience

1   Gordon Ramsay (1)
2   Chez Bruce (2)
3   Pétrus (4)
4   Le Gavroche (3)
5   La Trompette (9)
6   Tom Aikens (5)
7   L'Atelier de Joel Robuchon (6)
8   The Square (-)
9   maze (7)
10 J Sheekey (-)

Favourite

1   Chez Bruce (1)
2   Le Caprice (5)
3   J Sheekey (3)
4   La Trompette (6)
5   The Wolseley (2)
6   The Ivy (4)
7   Moro (7)
8   Pétrus (-)
9   Galvin Bistrot de Luxe (9)
10 Gordon Ramsay (8)

Best for business

1   The Wolseley (1)
2   The Don (3)
3   Bleeding Heart (2)
4   The Square (6)
5   1 Lombard Street (5)
6   Coq d'Argent (4)
7   The Ivy (9)
8   The Goring Hotel (-)
9   Galvin Bistrot de Luxe (-)
10 Rhodes 24 (10)

Best for romance

1   La Poule au Pot (1)
2   Andrew Edmunds (2)
3   Bleeding Heart (3)
4   Chez Bruce (4)
5   Clos Maggiore (9)
6   Le Caprice (5)
7   Restaurant (7)
8   Pétrus (-)
9   Café du Marché (6)
10 J Sheekey (-)

Best breakfast/brunch

1 The Wolseley (1)
2 Ground Floor (3)
3 Roast (-)
4 Electric Brasserie (10)
5 Cecconi's (-)
6 High Road Brasserie (-)
7 Simpsons-in-the-Strand (5)
8 Tapa Room (9)
9 Chelsea Bun Diner (-)
10 The Ritz Restaurant (-)

Best bar/pub food

1 The Anchor & Hope (1)
2 The Gun (5)
3 The Narrow*
4 The Anglesea Arms (3)
5 The Engineer (5)
6 The Eagle (2)
7 Thomas Cubitt (7)
8 The Ladbroke Arms (-)
9 Churchill Arms (10)
10 The Havelock Tavern (4)

Most disappointing cooking

1 Oxo Tower (1)
2 The Ivy (2)
3 Gordon Ramsay at Claridge's (3)
4 The Wolseley (4)
5 Le Café Anglais*
6 Tom Aikens (5)
7 Gordon Ramsay (-)
8 Wild Honey*
9 Cipriani (10)
10 Skylon*

Most overpriced restaurant

1 Oxo Tower (1)
2 Cipriani (3)
3 Gordon Ramsay (9)
4 Gordon Ramsay at Claridge's (4)
5 The River Café (6)
6 Hakkasan (7)
7 The Ivy (8)
8 L'Atelier de Joel Robuchon (-)
9 Sketch, Lecture Room (-)
10 Tom Aikens (-)

SURVEY HIGHEST RATINGS

FOOD

SERVICE

£80+

	FOOD		SERVICE
1	Pétrus	1	Pétrus
2	Gordon Ramsay	2	Gordon Ramsay
3	Le Gavroche	3	Le Gavroche
4	Bacchus	4	The Ritz Restaurant
5	The Capital Restaurant	5	Pied à Terre

£60-£79

1	Zuma	1	The Goring Hotel
2	The Ledbury	2	Roussillon
3	Kai Mayfair	3	The Ledbury
4	One-O-One	4	J Sheekey
5	Roussillon	5	Scott's

£45-£59

1	Chez Bruce	1	Chez Bruce
2	La Trompette	2	Michael Moore
3	Morgan M	3	Oslo Court
4	Roka	4	Le Caprice
5	Yauatcha	5	La Trompette

£35-£44

1	Jin Kichi	1	Upstairs Bar
2	Sushi-Say	2	Lamberts
3	Barrafina	3	Isarn
4	Bombay Palace	4	Sushi-Say
5	Lamberts	5	Caraffini

£34 or less

1	Ragam	1	Uli
2	New Tayyabs	2	Hot Stuff
3	Dinings	3	Fresco
4	Babur Brasserie	4	Yming
5	Pham Sushi	5	Golden Hind

AMBIENCE

1 The Ritz Restaurant
2 Pétrus
3 Le Gavroche
4 Gordon Ramsay
5 Galvin at Windows

1 Les Trois Garçons
2 Winter Garden
3 Petersham Nurseries
4 Rules
5 The Goring Hotel

1 La Poule au Pot
2 Julie's
3 Crazy Bear
4 Clos Maggiore
5 Belvedere

1 Andrew Edmunds
2 Holly Bush
3 Champor-Champor
4 A Cena
5 The Swan

1 Gordon's Wine Bar
2 Rebato's
3 Bar Italia
4 Babur Brasserie
5 Bincho Yakitori

OVERALL

1 Pétrus
2 Gordon Ramsay
3 Le Gavroche
4 The Ritz Restaurant
5 Pied à Terre

1 The Ledbury
2 J Sheekey
3 The Goring Hotel
4 Scott's
5 Roussillon

1 Chez Bruce
2 La Trompette
3 Le Caprice
4 Petersham Hotel
5 Clos Maggiore

1 Lamberts
2 Upstairs Bar
3 Barrafina
4 A Cena
5 Il Bordello

1 Babur Brasserie
2 Flat White
3 Hot Stuff
4 Rebato's
5 Uli

SURVEY BEST BY CUISINE

These are the restaurants which received the best average food ratings (excluding establishments with a small or notably local following).

Where the most common types of cuisine are concerned, we present the results in two price-brackets. For less common cuisines, we list the top three, regardless of price.

For further information about restaurants which are particularly notable for their food, see the cuisine lists starting on page 246. These indicate, using an asterisk*, restaurants which offer exceptional or very good food.

British, Modern

£45 and over		Under £45	
1	Chez Bruce	1	Lamberts
2	Bacchus	2	The Anglesea Arms
3	The Glasshouse	3	Tom Ilic
4	Petersham Nurseries	4	Phoenix Bar & Grill
5	Notting Hill Brasserie	5	Inside

French

£45 and over		Under £45	
1	Pétrus	1	Upstairs Bar
2	Gordon Ramsay	2	Galvin Bistrot de Luxe
3	La Trompette	3	Fig
4	Le Gavroche	4	Cellar Gascon
5	The Ledbury	5	Rosemary Lane

Italian/Mediterranean

£45 and over		Under £45	
1	Assaggi	1	Latium
2	Quirinale	2	A Cena
3	Enoteca Turi	3	Il Bordello
4	Locanda Locatelli	4	Oliveto
5	Riva	5	Spacca Napoli

Indian

£45 and over		Under £45	
1	Rasoi Vineet Bhatia	1	New Tayyabs
2	Amaya	2	Babur Brasserie
3	Zaika	3	Bombay Palace
4	The Painted Heron	4	Kastoori
5	Veeraswamy	5	Hot Stuff

Chinese

£45 and over
1. Kai Mayfair
2. Yauatcha
3. Hunan
4. Princess Garden
5. Hakkasan

Under £45
1. Mandarin Kitchen
2. Pearl Liang
3. The Four Seasons
4. Yming
5. Singapore Garden

Japanese

£45 and over
1. Zuma
2. Roka
3. Umu
4. Sumosan
5. Ubon

Under £45
1. Jin Kichi
2. Dinings
3. Sushi-Say
4. Pham Sushi
5. Kurumaya

British, Traditional
1. St John
2. Scott's
3. The Anchor & Hope

Vegetarian
1. Kastoori
2. Roussillon
3. The Gate

Burgers, etc
1. Ground
2. Haché
3. Eagle Bar Diner

Pizza
1. Il Bordello
2. Oliveto
3. Pizza Metro

Fish & Chips
1. Two Brothers
2. Golden Hind
3. Fish Club

Thai
1. Sukho Thai Cuisine
2. Amaranth
3. Churchill Arms

Fusion
1. Ubon
2. Tsunami
3. Archipelago

Fish & Seafood
1. One-O-One
2. J Sheekey
3. Mandarin Kitchen

Greek
1. Vrisaki
2. Daphne
3. Retsina

Spanish
1. Barrafina
2. Moro
3. Cambio de Tercio

Turkish
1. Mangal Ocakbasi
2. Cyprus Mangal
3. Gem

Lebanese
1. Fresco
2. Beirut Express
3. Al Sultan

TOP SPECIAL DEALS

The following menus allow you to eat in the restaurants concerned at a significant discount when compared to their evening à la carte prices.

The prices used are calculated in accordance with our usual formula (i.e. three courses with house wine, coffee and tip).

Special menus are by their nature susceptible to change – please check that they are still available.

Weekday lunch

£65+	Gordon Ramsay	**£35+**	L'Anima
	The Ritz Restaurant		L'Autre Pied
			The Avenue
£60+	Le Gavroche		Babylon
	L'Oranger		Bistro 190
	Rib Room		Blue Elephant
			Chez Bruce
£55+	The Greenhouse		The Cinnamon Club
	Ikeda		Clos Maggiore
	Pétrus		Le Colombier
	Rhodes W1 Restaurant		Il Convivio
	Winter Garden		L'Etranger
			Foliage
£50+	Ambassade de l'Ile		The Glasshouse
	Aubergine		Hibiscus
	The Capital Restaurant		Incognico
	Cipriani		L'Incontro
	The Landau		Morgan M
	Pied à Terre		Notting Hill Brasserie
	Restaurant		One-O-One
	Roussillon		Oslo Court
	Theo Randall		Brasserie
	Toto's		Patterson's
			Quilon
£45+	Bibendum		Ransome's Dock
	Boxwood Café		Red Fort
	Dorchester Grill		Sketch, Lecture Room
	Galvin at Windows		Le Suquet
	Gordon Ramsay at		Sumosan
	Claridge's		Thomas Cubitt
	Maze Grill		Trinity
	Mosaico		La Trompette
	Nahm		
	Orrery	**£30+**	L'Aventure
	Pearl		Awana
	Rasoi Vineet Bhatia		Axis
	The Square		La Bouchée
	Tom Aikens		Brasserie St Quentin
			Carpaccio's
£40+	Apsleys		Cheyne Walk Brasserie
	Bentley's		Daphne's
	Bonds		Enoteca Turi
	The Fifth Floor		L'Escargot
	5 Cavendish Square		L'Escargot (Picasso Rm)
	Kai Mayfair		Joe Allen
	Launceston Place		Kiku
	The Ledbury		Little Italy
	Locanda Ottomezzo		Lucio
	Mint Leaf		Michael Moore
	1901		Momo
	Petersham Hotel		Moti Mahal
	Poissonnerie de l'Avenue		Notting Grill
	Skylon		Papillon
	Tamarind		Pissarro's

	La Poule au Pot		Vino Rosso
	Sargasso Sea		Vivat Bacchus
	Timo		The Wharf
	La Trouvaille		Wild Honey
	Vanilla		Wódka

£25+	Arbutus	£20+	Arancia
	Arturo		La Cage Imaginaire
	Benares		Chez Patrick
	The Brackenbury		Daphne
	Café du Jardin		Eriki
	Camino		Il Falconiere
	Cantina del Ponte		Gastro
	Chez Kristof		Hazuki
	The Depot		Inaho
	The Farm		The Palmerston
	Fish Hook		Potemkin
	The Forge		Tentazioni
	Franklins		
	Frantoio	£15+	Bistro Aix
	Frederick's		Galicia
	Galvin Bistrot de Luxe		Greig's
	Phoenix Bar & Grill		Kolossi Grill
	Rosemary Lane		El Pirata
	Sam's Brasserie		
	San Lorenzo Fuoriporta	£10+	Mandalay
	The Terrace in the Fields		Sagar

Pre/post theatre (and early evening)

£50+	Lindsay House		Criterion Grill
	Theo Randall		L'Escargot
			L'Escargot (Picasso Rm)
£45+	The Landau		Joe Allen
			Orso
£40+	Red Fort		The Portrait
	Tamarind		San Lorenzo Fuoriporta
			La Trouvaille
£35+	L'Autre Pied		Wild Honey
	Franco's		
	Galvin at Windows	£25+	Arbutus
	Incognico		Café du Jardin
	Indigo		Chez Kristof
	Brasserie		The Forge
	Zaika		Frederick's
			Mon Plaisir
£30+	Albannach		Tuttons
	Baltic		Wódka
	Bord'Eaux		
	Brasserie St Quentin	£20+	Christopher's

Sunday lunch

£50+	The Ledbury	£35+	Hix Oyster & Chop House
£45+	Bibendum		
	Cheyne Walk Brasserie	£25+	Chez Patrick
	Notting Hill Brasserie		Village East
£40+	Babylon	£15+	Galicia
	Chez Bruce		
	L'Etranger		
	The Ivy		
	Paternoster Chop House		
	Roast		

THE RESTAURANT SCENE

A peculiar year

This year, we record 111 new openings (see page 20). This is a little below the normal range of openings – 120 to 142 – which has generally prevailed in this millennium. Macro-economic considerations aside, the figure may to an extent be a reaction to the previous year, when we registered an above-normal-range (and record) 158 openings.

Closings (p21) are 'normal'. At 71, this year, they are in fact down on last year (89), and just a fraction ahead of the mid-60s figures of the two years before that. In accordance with their normal cycle, we had expected closures to rise this year. It has been suggested, however, that restaurant owners may currently be reluctant to sell up, in what they perceive as a weak market for their premises.

Pétrus takes the lead...

For the first time this millennium, London has a clear new best restaurant at the top end of the market. Last year, the signs were mixed, with *Pétrus* a whisker ahead overall, but *Gordon Ramsay* still leading for food (if not by the same margin as in former years). No longer. For food, for service, and overall, *Pétrus* now clearly leads (see pages 12 and 13).

...as Ramsay's empire slides further

Ratings at the flagship *Gordon Ramsay* restaurant this year were undercut by a rising proportion of negative survey reports. While the restaurant (just) held on to its lead for Top Gastronomic Experience nominations (p10), it also ranked – for the first time – in the top 10 for Most Disappointing Cooking (p11), and rose to number 3 in Most Overpriced nominations (p11).

The out-gunning of *Gordon Ramsay* by his former lieutenant's restaurant, *Pétrus*, shows how deep the cracks that began to show in Ramsay's empire last year are starting to run. At Ramsay's other 'name'-place, at *Claridges*, standards are now in serious decline, with the survey rating the food in the bottom quarter of restaurants in its price bracket.

There have been other setbacks too. One restaurant, *La Noisette,* had to close for want of business, and two of the four grand hotels tenancies which originally enabled Ramsay so quickly to achieve 'critical mass' (at the Connaught and Berkeley) were, for whatever reason, not renewed.

Perhaps most telling, however, are the very poor standards evident at the Ramsay group's most recent openings aimed at the mass market – *The Warrington*, *The Devonshire Arms*, and *Foxtrot Oscar*. Roughly one report in three on each of these places is as the 'most disappointing' meal of the year, and many of these reports suggest a startling lack both of inspiration and of basic management. If 'little people' opened such places, they would be hard-pushed to survive for a year.

Gordon Ramsay has made quite a name dishing out harsh advice to struggling restaurateurs. The time has come, perhaps, for him to take a large dose of his own medicine.

Market trends

The following seem to us the trends of the moment:

● Not since the Entente Cordiale, has London seemed to hold such interest for the French, with the arrival not only of three star French chefs – Alain Ducasse and Hélène Darroze from Paris, and Jean Christophe Ansanay-Alex (*Ambassade de L'Ile*) from Lyons, but also of an outpost of one of the City of Light's most happening 'scenes' (*Buddha Bar*). The reaction to all three of the 'haute' openings has been somewhat mixed, illustrating how – at the top end – success in France is no instant ticket to creating a hit here.

● Echoing an even more pronounced trend in New York, the classic Gallic bistro/brasserie format is currently popular.

● Although there is the occasional lavish oriental début (such as the respective Yau brothers' *Aaya* and *Sake no Hana*) – and also the *Buddha Bar* – much of the interest at the higher end of the market is in 'plain vanilla' establishments in the traditional – French and Italian – restaurant cuisines.

● 'Proud-to-be-British,' however, continues to evolve as a recognised – and even quite fashionable – restaurant and gastropub cuisine (rather than just being something for the tourists). *Hix Oyster Bar & Chop House* and the relaunch of *Quo Vadis* are among leading examples.

● There is a small but emerging school of upmarket restaurants – such as *Bacchus* and *Texture* – which are trying to introduce genuinely new tastes and indeed, textures, to London's diners-out.

● The City – twenty years ago a restaurant desert – is now emerging as a restaurant destination in its own right. It suddenly seems natural for fashionable central/westerly restaurants – such as the *Cinnamon Club*, *Manicomio*, *Kazan* and *Mint Leaf* – to open a City offshoot.

● The City's eastern fringes, in particular Shoreditch, are further emerging as the trendiest area in town.

Every year, we select what seem to us to be the ten most significant openings of the preceding 12 months. This year, our selection is as follows:

Aaya	Hélène Darroze
L'Anima	Hix Oyster & Chop House
Le Café Anglais	The Landau
Cha Cha Moon	maze Grill
Dehesa	Texture

Prices

The average price of dinner for one at establishments listed in the guide is £40.11. Prices have on average risen by 4.7% in the past 12 months. As was the case last year, this rise is, for all practical purposes at the same rate as retail prices.

OPENINGS AND CLOSURES

EATING IN LONDON FAQs

How should I use this guide?

This guide can be used in many ways. You will often wish to use it to answer practical queries. These tend to be geographical – where can we eat near…? To answer such questions, the Maps (from page 301) and Area Overviews (from page 266) are the place to start. The latter tell you all the key facts about the restaurants – perhaps dozens – in a particular area in the space of a couple of pages.

But what if you'd like to be more adventurous and seek out new places purely for interest's sake or for a truly special occasion? That's the main point of this brief section – to give you a handy overview of London's dining scene, and also some thoughts as to how you can use the guide to lead you to eating experiences you might not otherwise have found (or perhaps even contemplated).

What makes London special?

Until recently, most people would have said that it was the internationalism of London's restaurants that was their most eye-catching feature. Indeed, the joke was that if you were going to eat well, the only certainty was that you wouldn't – except for breakfast, perhaps – be eating English.

That's no longer really true: as a complement to the hotch-potch of cuisines which remains a key strength of the city – there aren't many cuisines you can't eat here well – there are now some definably English restaurants of real note too.

Of non-indigenous cuisines, the ones in which London, as a legacy of empire, excels are those of the Indian subcontinent. Indeed, the concentration of diverse restaurants within this category within a relatively small area makes London arguably the world's leading 'Indian' restaurant city. (The poorest-served cuisine until recently was Chinese, but – even here – there are now signs of progress.)

Which is London's best restaurant?

As in most major cities the 'best' restaurants are still by and large French, and the best grand French restaurant in town, currently by a fair margin, is Marcus Wareing's *Pétrus*. Also at a very high level is the Chelsea flagship of the UK's best-known chef, *Gordon Ramsay*, and – if you're looking for the sort of dinner Escoffier might recognise as such – *Le Gavroche*. The best all-round mid-price restaurants are *Chez Bruce* (again Londoners' favourite destination this year) and its sibling *The Ledbury*.

London now – in *Bacchus* – also has a restaurant of note for its high level 'molecular gastronomy', in the style of Spain's El Bulli. For further best restaurant suggestions, consult the double-page spread on pages 10 and 11.

What's 'in' at the moment?

The days when the scene was small enough to have only a handful of 'in' restaurants have passed. Nowadays, the question is rather: 'in' with whom? For the Dolce Vita crowd, the place of the moment is still – whatever its other failings – *Cipriani*. The media still regard *The Ivy* as something of a canteen, but *Scott's* is starting to establish itself as the all-purpose see-and-be-seen destination. The fashion world is still somewhat taken with *Sketch* and *Momo*. *The Wolseley* is the 'café' to be seen at (especially for breakfast). *J Sheekey* – and in particular *Le Caprice* – are 'in' with people who feel that being 'in' is trying a bit too hard.

For younger City and international types, the all-round appeal of orientals such as *Zuma*, *Roka*, *Hakkasan* and *Yauatcha* remain very strong. If it's true to its Parisian form the *Buddha Bar* – opening around the time this guide is published – will join that club.

I'm not fussed about 'scenes' – where can I get a good meal at reasonable cost?

The best tip of all – and this may become even more so if recession bites – is to lunch rather than dine. If you do, you can experience some of London's grandest restaurants – and they don't come much grander than *Le Gavroche* – for less than many lesser restaurants charge for dinner. See the list of suggestions on pages 16 and 17.

One of the greatest successes of recent times has been *Arbutus* – right in the heart of Soho – where the formula has always been conceived with good value in mind. Some other Gallic restaurants – pre-eminently *Galvin Bistro de Luxe* and *Racine* – offer a top-quality product, but at prices which leave the customer happy.

For sheer upper-middle market value, the family of restaurants put together by Nigel Platts-Martin is impossible to beat. *Chez Bruce* has made itself into a modern legend, and *La Trompette*, *The Glasshouse* and *The Ledbury* – all a little way from the centre – are worthy stablemates to it. If you're looking for decent upper-middle market value in the West End, names worth considering include *Le Caprice*, *Clos Maggiore* and *Latium*.

The names above, however, are just the beginning. Look through the Area Overviews beginning on page 266. These should enable you to find value – wherever in town you're looking and whatever your budget – for any occasion.

And for the best of British?

As we suggested earlier, British food, until quite recently, was largely reserved for tourists. The Roast Beef of Old England still is. If that's what you're looking for, head for *Simpson's-on-the-Strand* for the full tourist experience, or *Rules* for a rather more agreeable one.

In just the last few years, though, restaurants with more

intelligent and wholehearted roots in native culinary traditions have become very fashionable. (This is often painted as some kind of renaissance, but in truth there never was a golden era of British Restaurant Cooking.)

The pioneer establishment of the new-wave Brits – which long seemed to be crying in the wilderness – was *St John*. But over the last few years the trend – often conflated with 'gastropub' cooking in many people's minds – has become mainstream. Restaurants proper which may be said to be strongly influenced by the style include *Magdalen*, *Great Queen Street*, *Hereford Road* and – most recently and most modishly – *Hix Oyster Bar & Grill*.

What are gastropubs?

It's difficult to talk about London restaurants, especially of the more British sort, without talking about gastropubs. These are essentially bistros in the premises of former pubs. They come, though, in a variety of styles. What many people think of as the original gastropub (*The Eagle*, 1991) still looks – to this day – very much like a pub with a food counter. At the other end of the scale, however, the 'pub' element is almost redundant, and the business is really just a restaurant housed in premises that happen once to have been a pub. Perhaps the most striking example is Belgravia's new *Pantechnicon Rooms*, where the upstairs room is every bit as grand as many a gentleman's club.

The best gastropubs are generally not in the West End. The central-ish location of the *Anchor & Hope*, on the South Bank, is no doubt part of the reason for its bonkers popularity. Hammersmith and its environs, for some reason, have a particular concentration, with the *Anglesea Arms* the stand-out performer. Out east, near Canary Wharf, the equivalent is the *Gun*.

Isn't London supposed to be a top place for curry?

London, as noted above, has a reasonable claim to being the world's top Indian restaurant city. At the top end, leading lights such as *Rasoi Vineet Bhatia*, *Amaya*, *The Painted Heron*, *Benares* and *Zaika* are pushing back the frontiers, but – perfectly reasonably – charge the same as equivalent restaurants with European cuisines. What's therefore more exciting in terms of value is the vast range of subcontinental restaurants where you can still have a knock-out meal for the sort of prices you're hardly ever likely to find if you eat European-style.

Two of the best of the budget subcontinentals – both, in fact, Pakistani – are *New Tayyab* and the *Lahore Kebab House*. There are, however, so many good Indian places in almost all parts of town – often well away from the West End – that it's impossible to list them here. To find these, search out the asterisked restaurants in the Indian and Pakistani lists commencing on pages 260 and 263 respectively.

There's supposed to a recession coming. Any tips?

●The top tip, already noted, is to lunch not dine. If you're a visitor, you'll find that it's better for your wallet, as well as your digestion, to have your main meal in the middle of the day. In the centre of town, it's one of the best ways you can be sure of eating 'properly' at reasonable cost. See the spread on pages 16 and 17.

●Think ethnic – for a food 'experience' at modest cost, you'll almost always be better off going Indian, Thai, Chinese or Vietnamese (to choose four of the most obvious cuisines) than French, English or Italian. The days when there was any sort of assumption that ethnic restaurants were – in terms of comfort, service and décor – in any way inferior to European ones is long gone.

●Try to avoid the West End. That's not to say that, armed with this book, you shouldn't be able to eat quite well in the heart of things, but you'll almost certainly do better outside the Circle Line. Many of the best and cheapest restaurants in this guide are easily accessible by tube. Use the maps at the back of this book to identify restaurants near tube stations on a line that's handy for you.

●If you must dine in the West End, try to find either pre-theatre (generally before 7.30 pm) or post-theatre (generally after 10 pm) menus. You will generally save at least the cost of a cinema ticket, compared to dining à la carte. Many of the more upmarket restaurants in Theatreland do such deals. For some of our top suggestions, see page 17.

●Use this book! Don't take pot luck, when you can benefit from the pre-digested views of thousands of other diners-out. Choose a place with a ❶ or ❷ for food, and you're very likely to eat much better than if you walk in somewhere on spec. And once you have decided that you want to eat within a particular area, use the Area Overviews (starting on p266) to identify the restaurants that are offering top value.

●Visit our website, www.hardens.com for the latest reviews, and restaurant news.

DIRECTORY

Comments in "double quotation-marks" were made by reporters.

Establishments which we judge to be particularly notable have their NAME IN CAPITALS.

A Cena TW1 £40 ❷⓿❷
418 Richmond Rd   8288 0108   1–4A
Locals "absolutely love" this "comfortable" St Margaret's Italian, near Richmond Bridge – "the food just gets better", and you get a "great welcome" too. / www.acena.co.uk; 10.30 pm; closed Mon L & Sun D; booking: max 6, Fri & Sat.

Aaya W1 NEW £52 ❷❷❷
66-70 Brewer St   7319 3888   3–2D
From Alan Yau's brother Gary, a path-breaking restaurant, bringing high-quality Japanese fare (including top-quality sushi) and striking design values to Soho; it's no bargain, but standards on our early-days visit were uniformly very high. / Rated on Editors' visit; www.aaya.com; 11.30 pm, Sun 10.30 pm.

The Abbeville SW4 £33 ④④❷
67-69 Abbeville Rd   8675 2201   10–2D
A "casual" Clapham hang-out, with a "quiet" location and "great" atmosphere – the cooking, though, is "hit-and-miss". / www.theabbeville.com; 10.30 pm.

Abeno WC1 £34 ❷❸④
47 Museum St   7405 3211   2–1C
"A pleasant change, and good fun" – the okonomiyaki (a Japanese omelette/pancake) are "weird but delicious", at this "friendly" outfit, near the British Museum; the staff are "good with children" too. / www.abeno.co.uk; 10 pm.

Abeno Too WC2 £32 ❸❷❸
17-18 Great Newport St   7379 1160   4–3B
"Quirky and fun", this Theatreland stand-by is handily-sited for a "quick" and "authentic" okonomiyaki (a Japanese omelette/pancake); on the downside, the place can "get a bit hot and crowded". / 11 pm; no booking.

The Abingdon W8 £45 ❸❷❸
54 Abingdon Rd   7937 3339   5–2A
On a quiet Kensington corner, this "lively" former boozer continues to tick all the boxes of those looking for a "fun" and "cosy" bite; the snug booths at the back are particularly popular. / www.theabingdonrestaurant.com; 11 pm, Mon 10.30 pm, Sun 10pm.

Abokado WC2 £15 ❷❸④
160 Drury Ln   7242 5600   4–2D
"For a quick, interesting and healthy lunch" – this "clean and fresh" small chain excites rave reviews for its "nice juices, smoothies and wraps". / www.abokado.com; 7.30 pm; closed Sat & Sun.

About Thyme SW1 £40 ❸❷④
82 Wilton Rd   7021 7501   2–1B
"Convenient for Victoria Station", this "good Pimlico local" offers "a really warm welcome" and "good-value" Spanish/French food; the occasional doubter, however, finds the formula "a tad pretentious". / www.aboutthyme.co.uk; 11 pm.

L'Absinthe NW1 NEW £35 ❸❷❷
40 Chalcot Rd   7483 4848   8–3B
Jean-Christophe Slowik's "busy" new bistro may have finally broken the jinx on this Primrose Hill corner site (most recently, the Black Truffle, RIP); it serves up ultra-traditional Gallic fare at very keen prices. / 10.30 pm, Sun 9.30 pm; closed Mon.

Abu Zaad W12   £17   ❷④❸
29 Uxbridge Rd   8749 5107   7–1C
*"Incredibly tasty kebabs and mezze are served at "shockingly
inexpensive" prices, at this "very authentic" Syrian café,
near Shepherd's Bush Market; no booze, but "lovely juices".*
/ www.abuzaad.co.uk; 11 pm.

The Academy W11   £36   ❸②❸
57 Princedale Rd   7221 0248   6–2A
*"For a relaxed bite" in a "pub-with-food", "you won't find much
better" than this "welcoming" and "hype-free" Holland Park local.*
/ www.academybar.com; 10.30 pm, Sun 9 pm; no Amex.

L'Accento Italiano W2   £40   ❸④❸
16 Garway Rd   7243 2201   6–1B
*It's hard to believe this small and "plain" Bayswater Italian was
a foodie hot spot when it opened in the early '90s, but it remains
"a good-value neighbourhood place that rarely disappoints".*
/ www.laccentorestaurant.co.uk; 11 pm; closed Sun.

Acorn House WC1   £43   ❸④④
69 Swinton St   7812 1842   8–3D
*"Extreme eco-friendliness" is the mantra at this year-old training
restaurant, in the King's Cross "wasteland" – "the food is good and
the ethos is great, but the prices are a touch extravagant".*
/ www.acornhouserestaurant.com; 10 pm; closed Sun.

Adam Street WC2   £56   ❸❸❷
9 Adam St   7379 8000   4–4D
*"Non-members have to pay £10 extra for lunch, and a surprising
number do", at this civilised club's dining room, in an intriguing
cellar off the Strand; the food "doesn't vary much, but is well put
together".* / www.adamstreet.co.uk; L only (open for D to members only),
closed Sat & Sun.

Adams Café W12   £26   ❸0❸
77 Askew Rd   8743 0572   7–1B
*"A favourite local haunt", in Shepherd's Bush, especially notable for
its "friendly" service; by day, it's a greasy spoon, but at night
it transforms into a BYO Tunisian café, serving "an interesting array
of N African dishes" (including "delicious tajines").* / 11 pm;
closed Sun.

Addendum
Apex City Of London Hotel EC3   £53   ❸❸④
1 Seething Ln   7977 9500   9–3D
*The food at this City dining room can be surprisingly "fresh" and
interesting; shame its "slightly weird" location – in the middle of an
hotel – seems to discourage a wider following.* / www.apexhotels.co.uk;
9.30 pm; closed Sat & Sun; set always available £40 (FP).

Addie's Thai Café SW5   £26   ❷0❷
121 Earl's Court Rd   7259 2620   5–2A
*Near Earl's Court tube, an "authentic" café, hailed by its small fan
club as a "top value-for-money Thai".* / www.addiesthai.co.uk; 11 pm;
closed Sat L & Sun L; no Amex.

Admiral Codrington SW3 £42 ④❸❸
17 Mossop St 7581 0005 5–2C
Some things never change, and you still get a very "Chelsea crowd"
at the "lively" pub/dining room known to Hoorays everywhere
as 'The Cod'; both menu and prices, though, sometimes seem
to have ideas above their station. / www.theadmiralcodrington.co.uk;
11pm, Sun 10.30pm.

The Admiralty
Somerset House WC2 £47 ⑤④④
Strand 7845 4646 2–2D
With "such a quirky setting" – in London's greatest public palazzo
– these small dining rooms "should be great"; so "bland" is the
food, though, and so "dire" the service, that the overall impression
is sometimes "like school". / www.theadmiraltyrestaurant.com; 10.30 pm;
closed Sun D.

Afghan Kitchen N1 £19 ❷❸④
35 Islington Grn 7359 8019 8–3D
"A fantastic little place", on Islington Green – "ideal for a quick
bite", it serves a short and "simple" menu of "interesting and well-
prepared dishes" in a slightly IKEA-esque setting; "the staff seem
friendlier of late". / 11 pm; closed Mon & Sun; no credit cards.

Aglio e Olio SW10 £33 ❷④❸
194 Fulham Rd 7351 0070 5–3B
"Outstanding pasta at affordable prices" makes for "very consistent
good value", at this "fun" and "noisy" Italian "gem", near the
Chelsea & Westminster Hospital. / 11.30 pm.

Agni W6 £28 ❷❷④
160 King St 8846 9191 7–2C
"Amazing, fresh, clean Indian" dishes – "as cheap as chips" –
win many fans for this "stark" outfit, opposite Hammersmith Town
Hall; there's a vague feeling, though, that it's "gone downhill"
of late. / www.agnirestaurant.com; 11 pm; D only.

Al Duca SW1 £40 ④❸④
4-5 Duke of York St 7839 3090 3–3D
A "straightforward" modern Italian in St James's, long known as a
"reliable" destination and "a bit of a bargain for the area";
its "noisy" setting can seem "corporate", though, and the food has
become more "standard" of late. / www.alduca-restaurant.co.uk; 11 pm;
closed Sun.

Al Forno £29 ④❷❷
349 Upper Richmond Rd, SW15 8878 7522 10–2A
2a King's Rd, SW19 0510 5710 10 2B
"A Wimbledon Town favourite that's always packed to the rafters";
this "hectic" old-fashioned Italian serves tasty "slabs of pizza"
(and other fare), and it's "great fun", too – "especially in a group"
or with kids. / SW15 11 pm; SW19 11.30 pm.

Al Hamra W1 £45 ④⑤⑤
31-33 Shepherd Mkt 7493 1954 3–4B
Inside seating is "very tight", so "get an outside table if you can",
if you visit this "busy" Lebanese veteran in Shepherd Market;
the food is often "good", but staff attitude is "hit-and-miss".
/ www.alhamrarestaurant.co.uk; 11.30 pm.

Al Sultan W1 £39 ❷❸⑤
51-52 Hertford St   7408 1155   3–4B
No one doubts that this Shepherd Market Lebanese is an
"authentic" spot, and the food is "good" too – "you do pay Mayfair
prices for it", however, and the décor is "terrible".
/ www.alsultan.co.uk; 11 pm.

Al-Waha W2 £33 ❷❷❸
75 Westbourne Grove   7229 0806   6–1B
A "cosy" Bayswater Lebanese attracting steady praise for its
"delicious" food and "unvarying" standards.
/ www.alwaharestaurant.com; 11.30 pm; no Amex.

Alain Ducasse
Dorchester W1 £104 ④❸④
53 Park Ln   7629 8866   3–3A
"Not nearly up to Paris or Monte Carlo..." – the Gallic über-chef's
Mayfair opening has "fallen woefully short of expectations";
the food "tries hard to be flash", but just ends up "seriously
underpowered", and it comes at "wild" prices too.
/ www.alainducasse-dorchester.com; 10 pm; closed Mon, Sat L & Sun; jacket.

Alastair Little W1 £58 ④❸⑤
49 Frith St   7734 5183   4–2A
"Nothing is hopelessly lacking", but there's "nothing very inspiring"
either nowadays about this "weirdly bright" '80s survivor, in Soho –
a "casual" sort of place where the cuisine is "decent" enough,
but still a let-down for those who remember its "historic" rôle in the
'Modern British' revolution. / 11.30 pm; closed Sat L & Sun.

Alba EC1 £47 ❸❷④
107 Whitecross St   7588 1798   9–1B
"Helpful" service and a "wide range of Italian wines at low mark-
ups" are key strengths – especially for business customers – of this
low-key veteran, "tucked-away" near the Barbican; its Piedmontese
cuisine is "safe", but "not exciting". / www.albarestaurant.com; 11 pm;
closed Sat & Sun; set dinner £31 (FP).

Albannach WC2 £52 ⑤⑤④
66 Trafalgar Sq   7930 0066   2–3C
It has "a superb selection of whiskies" and "competent" food,
but reporters still often think this large and very central Scottish
bar/restaurant one to "avoid" – at the "enormous" prices,
it "should be better in every respect". / www.albannach.co.uk; 10.15 pm;
closed Sun; set pre theatre £32 (FP).

The Albemarle
Brown's Hotel W1 £67 ④④④
Albemarle St   7493 6020   3–3C
Rocco Forte Hotels rarely seem to get their dining rooms spot-on,
and this newly-revamped "traditional" bastion, in Mayfair, is no
exception; its "spacious" layout is "great with clients", but while
fans praise its "perfect British fare", rather too many critics think
it "a waste of money". / www.roccofortecollection.com; 10.30 pm.

The Albion N1   £38   ④❷❷
10 Thornhill Rd   7607 7450   8–3D
"Eating outdoors is a must", say summer visitors to this jazzed-up Islington boozer, which is particularly known for its "lovely" garden; reports on the food remain mixed (but "pre-ordered suckling pig for large parties" gets a consistent thumbs-up). / www.the-albion.co.uk; 10 pm.

Ali Baba NW1   £21   ❷❸④
32 Ivor Pl   7723 5805   2–1A
Behind a Marylebone take-away, this unique front-room-style place offers simple but "unbeatable" Egyptian dishes – not least "exceptional shish kebabs" – that are "amazing value for money"; BYO. / midnight; no credit cards.

Alisan HA9   £29   ❶❷④
The Junction, Engineers Way, Wembley   8903 3888   1–1A
"Impressive" dim sum comes at a notably "low cost", at this "spacious and airy" modern Cantonese, right by Wembley Stadium. / www.alisan.co.uk; Mon-Thu 11 pm, Fri & Sat 11.30 pm, Sun 10.30 pm.

All Star Lanes   £36   ④⑤④
Victoria Hs, Bloomsbury Pl, WC1   7025 2676   2–1D
Whiteley's, 6 Porchester Gdns, W2   7313 8363   6–1C
Old Truman Brewery, 3 Dray Walk, E1   awaiting tel   9–1D
For "geek-chic" types, these "upmarket bowling venues" can be "great fun"; their "US diner-style" food, however, seems to be on the slide – likewise the "hopeless" service. / www.allstarlanes.co.uk; WC1 10.30 pm, Fri & Sat midnight, Sun 9 pm.

Alloro W1   £50   ❷❷❸
19-20 Dover St   7495 4768   3–3C
Cooking that's "well-polished" and "not too expensive" makes this "very professional" Italian restaurant (and bar) a "dependable" Mayfair destination, especially for a business lunch. / www.alloro-restaurant.co.uk; 10.30 pm; closed Sat L & Sun.

Alma SW18   £37   ④④④
499 Old York Rd   8870 2537   10–2B
"A mean burger" is the culinary highlight nowadays at this Wandsworth rugger-buggers' boozer; the cooking "was better in years gone by", but no one much seems to care. / www.thealma.co.uk; 10.30 pm, Sun 9 pm.

The Almeida N1   £45   ④❸④
30 Almeida St   7354 4777   8–2D
A "welcome re-fit" has begun to boost ratings at this D&D-group fixture, near the eponymous Islington theatre; reports, though, have still been up-and-down – perhaps because the place "can't decide if it's posh-French or useful-local". / www.almeida-restaurant.co.uk; 10.30pm, Sun 9pm.

Alounak   £27   ❸④④
10 Russell Gdns, W14   7603 1130   7–1D
44 Westbourne Grove, W2   7229 0416   6–1B
A Persian duo offering a "pretty basic", but "incredibly cheap", BYO formula, and where "heavenly, freshly-baked flat breads" and "consistently excellent kebabs" are the menu stars. / 11.30 pm; no Amex.

Amano £29 ❷④❸
The Blue Fin Building, 20 Sumner St, SE1   7234 9530   9–4B
More London Pl, (off Weavers Lane), SE1   7407 9751   9–4D
Potters Field, SE1   7407 9759   9–4D
Victor Wharf, Clink St, SE1   7234 0000   9–3C
*World-famous in SE1 – a really impressive mini-group
of café/diners serving a "great choice of sandwiches, soups and
salads" (and, at the Potters Field branch, top pizza too).*
/ www.amanocafe.com.

Amaranth SW18 £25 ❷❸❸
346 Garratt Ln   8874 9036   10–2B
*This "simple Earlsfield BYO" is always "packed" ("you need to book
most evenings"), thanks to its "real" Thai food at "unbeatable-
value" prices. / 10.30 pm; D only, closed Sun; no Amex.*

Amato W1 £28 ❸❸❸
14 Old Compton St   7734 5733   4–2A
*Now under the same ownership as Richoux, this ever-busy Soho
pâtisserie retains a devoted following for its "very good coffee and
sandwiches" (and "the best hot chocolate in town" too).*
/ www.amato.co.uk; Mon-Sat 10 pm, Sun 8 pm; no booking.

Amaya SW1 £56 ❶❷❷
Halkin Arc, 19 Motcomb St   7823 1166   5–1D
*"Cutting-edge", "exotic" and "subtle" Indian cuisine elicits waves
of rave reports on this "swish" Belgravia hot spot; "the tapas
format could seem faddish, but here it really works".*
/ www.amaya.biz; 11.15 pm, Sun 10.15 pm.

Ambassade de l'Ile SW7 🆕 £90 ④④④
117/119 Old Brompton Rd   7373 7774   5–2B
*Offshoot of a starry restaurant in Lyons, this ambitious South
Kensington newcomer (on the site of Lundum's, RIP) is a puzzling
affair in every way; our early-days lunchtime visit found notably up-
and-down food, and décor – black shag-pile and all – so bizarre
that it was impossible to work out who the place is supposed
to appeal to. / Rated on Editors' visit; www.ambassadedelile.com; 10 pm;
closed Sun; set weekday L £51 (FP).*

Ambassador EC1 £36 ❸❷❸
55 Exmouth Mkt   7837 0009   9–1A
*"The sort of reliable local everyone should have" – this "friendly"
two-year-old offers "unpretentious", "seasonal" food and
"interesting wine"; the service is "fabulous" too.*
/ www.theambassadorcafe.co.uk; 10.15 pm; closed Sun D.

Amerigo Vespucci E14 £43 ④❸④
25 Cabot Sq   7513 0288   11–1C
*This "good, old-fashioned trattoria" (a rare "non-chain" Canary
Wharf option) is "one of the oldest eateries hereabouts, and still
one of the best" ("... of a bad bunch"). / www.amerigovespucci.co.uk;
11.30 pm; closed Sat L & Sun.*

Anarkali W6 £28 ❷❷④
303 King St   8748 1760   7–2B
*"Not much changed over many years" – this "friendly", if slightly
"gloomy", Hammersmith veteran is "still a cut above many
Indians". / www.anarkalirestaurant.co.uk; midnight, Sun 11.30 pm.*

The Anchor & Hope SE1 £35 ❶❸❸
36 The Cut 7928 9898 9–4A
"The Holy Grail of gastropubs" – this *"mobbed"* Waterloo boozer
strikes the *"perfect balance"* between *"wonderfully earthy"* British
cooking and *"unpretentious, even ordinary surroundings"*; the wait
can admittedly be *"excruciating"*, but it's *"worth it"*. / 10.30 pm;
closed Mon L & Sun D; no Amex; no booking.

ANDREW EDMUNDS W1 £38 ❸❷❶
46 Lexington St 7437 5708 3–2D
"Rickety" but *"wonderfully snug"*, this Soho townhouse *"has a
certain je-ne-sais-quoi"* that makes it unbelievably popular,
especially for a *"dream date"*; the *"simple"* food is *"no gastronomic
tour de force"*, but – like the *"fascinating wine list"* – it offers
"great value". / 10.30 pm; no Amex; booking: max 6.

Angelus W2 £60 ❸❸④
4 Bathurst St 7402 0083 6–2D
Ex-sommelier Thierry Tomasin's Bayswater pub-conversion hasn't
quite lived up to the launch *"hype"* – fans do find it a
"sophisticated" sort of place with *"fabulous"* wine, but critics note
only *"cramped"* conditions and *"average"* standards overall.
/ www.angelusrestaurant.co.uk; 11 pm; closed Mon.

The Anglesea Arms SW7 £31 ④④❷
15 Sellwood Ter 7373 7960 5–2B
An *"old-fashioned"* pub in the heart of South Kensington, with a
terrace that's mobbed on sunny days; it has no real gastro-
pretensions, but does a *"great Sunday roast"*.
/ www.angleseaarms.com; 10 pm.

The Anglesea Arms W6 £38 ❶❸❷
35 Wingate Rd 8749 1291 7–1B
"It's worth waiting for a table", at this *"superb"* gastropub *"classic"*,
near Ravenscourt Park, where the *"freshly-chalked"* menu delivers
"mouthwatering" dishes; incredibly – for those who remember the
bad old days – service *"is actually pretty good"* too. / Tue-Sat
10.30 pm, Sun & Mon 10 pm; no Amex; no booking.

Anglo Asian Tandoori N16 £24 ❷❶④
60-62 Stoke Newington Church St 7254 3633 1–1C
In Stoke Newington, a *"good-quality Indian of long standing"*;
attractions include *"great food"* and *"staff who never forget
a face"*. / www.angloasian.co.uk; 11.45 pm.

L'Anima EC2 NEW £52 ❷❶❷
1 Snowden St 7422 7000 9–1D
For our money, one of the best openings of recent times –
this Italian newcomer, behind Broadgate, offers deft cooking
(from Francesco Mazzei, ex-St Alban) in a minimalist setting of a
design-quality rarely seen in London; in the early days, service was
charming too. / Rated on Editors' visit; www.lanima.co.uk; 10.30 pm; closed
Sat & Sun; set weekday L £38 (FP).

Annie's £37 ④❸❶
162 Thames Rd, W4 8994 9080 1–3A
36-38 White Hart Ln, SW13 8878 2020 10–1A
"Boudoirish" décor has helped these *"casual"* and *"obliging"*
west London hang-outs win quite a following; brunch is *"always
reliable"*, but, more generally, the food *"lacks wow-factor"*. / W4
10 pm, SW13 11 pm.

Antipasto & Pasta SW11 £32 ❸❸❷
511 Battersea Park Rd   7223 9765   10–1C
"This isn't the best Italian locally", but on "half-price evenings" –
which is "most nights" – this Battersea local offers a "very good
deal". / 11.30 pm; need 4+ to book.

Aperitivo W1 £35 ❸❷④
41 Beak St   7287 2057   3–2D
"A fun and reliable" Soho spot, serving "interesting", "tapas-style"
Italian bites; "they've packed in more tables, so it's less stylish than
it was", however – "when the after-work crowd's in, the noise can
be unbearable". / www.aperitivo-restaurants.com; 11 pm; closed Sun.

Apostrophe £14 ❷❸❷
16 Regent St, SW1   7930 9922   3–3D
10 Grosvenor St, W1   7499 6511   3–2B
20/20 Opt' Store, 216 Tott' Ct Rd, W1   7436 6688   2–1C
23 Barrett St, W1   7355 1001   3–1A
40-41 Great Castle St, W1   7637 5700   3–1C
215 Strand, WC2   7427 9890   4–2D
42 Gt Eastern St, EC2   7739 8412   9–1D
3-5 St Bride St, EC4   7353 3704   9–2A
With their "ultra-fresh sarnies" and "outstanding coffee" – not to
mention "the best hot chocolate" – these "pricey alternatives
to Pret" still "take some beating". / www.apostropheuk.com; L &
afternoon tea only, Barrett St 8pm; no Amex; no booking.

Apsleys
Lanesborough Hotel SW1 NEW £75 ④❷❸
1 Lanesborough Pl   7333 7254   5–1D
The conservatory of Hyde Park Corner's landmark luxury hotel
emerged this year from a lavishly OTT revamp (from leading
US designer Adam Tihany); despite its new Anglo-Saxon name,
the food is rustic Italian, and – though competent enough – rather
overshadowed by the setting and the service. / www.apsleys.co.uk;
11 pm; booking: max 12; set weekday L £42 (FP), set always available
£45 (FP).

Aquasia
Wyndham Grand SW10 £52 ④❸❸
Chelsea Harbour   7300 8443   5–4B
A Riviera-style setting "overlooking the marina" creates
an almost "holiday-like" ambience at this Chelsea Harbour hotel,
whose "discreet and quiet" style particularly suits business;
also "great for Sunday brunch". / www.wyndham.com; 10.30 pm.

Arancia SE16 £31 ❷❷❷
52 Southwark Park Rd   7394 1751   11–2A
"A totally unexpected cosy oasis, in deepest Bermondsey" –
this "fantastic" and "personal" Italian serves up "honest" food
at "ridiculously cheap" prices. / www.arancia-london.co.uk; 11 pm; closed
Mon & Sun D; set weekday L £20 (FP).

ARBUTUS W1 £42 ❷❷❸
63-64 Frith St   7734 4545   4–2A
"An utterly winning formula"; "adventurous" and "hearty" cooking
and "fabulous wine sold in 25cl carafes" – all at "fair" prices –
make this "confident" Soho two-year-old one of the West End's top
foodie hot spots; the "bustling" setting, though, suffers from
"awkward" proportions. / www.arbutusrestaurant.co.uk; 10.45pm,
Sun 9.30 pm; set weekday L £27 (FP), set pre-theatre £29 (FP).

Archduke Wine Bar SE1 £39 ⑤⑤④
Concert Hall Approach, South Bank 7928 9370 2–3D
Thanks to its "convenient" South Bank location, this dated wine bar (in the arches of Hungerford Railway Bridge) is usually "crowded"… despite its "lousy" service and its "disappointing" food. / www.thearchduke.co.uk; 11 pm; closed Sat L & Sun.

The Arches NW6 £36 ⑤❸❷
7 Fairhazel Gdns 7624 1867 8–2A
Who cares if the food is "very average"? – it's the "amazingly good-value wine list" which draws fans to this "unpretentious" Swiss Cottage bistro. / 10.30 pm; no Amex.

Archipelago W1 £49 ❷①①
110 Whitfield St 7383 3346 2–1B
A "most bizarre" menu (including "zebra, locust, gnu, peacock and scorpion") is only part of the "truly memorable" – and "romantic" – formula of this "Bohemian-quirky" den, near the Telecom Tower; the food is "not just strange for the sake of it", though – indeed, it's often "brilliant". / www.archipelago-restaurant.co.uk; 10.30 pm; closed Sat L & Sun.

The Ark W8 £46 ④④❸
122 Palace Gardens Ter 7229 4024 6–2B
"Catch it on a good night", and you may find "high-quality" Italian food at this "unassuming" shack, which – in its various incarnations over the years – has long been a "cosy" feature, near Notting Hill Gate; ordinary nights, though, are "average". / www.ark-restaurant.com; 11 pm; closed Mon L & Sun.

Ark Fish E18 £35 ❷❷④
142 Hermon Hill 8989 5345 1–1D
"It's worth the wait for a table", say fans of this South Woodford chippy, which offers "tasty" fare in "huge" portions. / www.arkfishrestaurant.co.uk; Tue-Thu 9.45 pm, Fri & Sat 10.15 pm, Sun 8.45 pm; closed Mon; no Amex.

L'Artista NW11 £30 ❸⑤④
917 Finchley Rd 8731 7501 1–1B
A "manic and squashed" (and family-friendly) Golder's Green stalwart, near the tube; service is "erratic", but the pizza is "great", and the other Italian fare is "light on cost, but heavy on portions". / 11.30 pm.

L'Artiste Musclé W1 £38 ④❸❷
1 Shepherd Mkt 7493 6150 3–4B
"Save the fare on the Eurostar", and head instead to this "crowded" and "very French-run-down-style" bistro, in Shepherd Market – it serves "enjoyable rather than amazing" scoff that's "very cheap… for Mayfair". / 11 pm.

Arturo W2 £42 ④❷❸
23 Connaught St 7706 3388 6–1D
A "discreet" Bayswater Italian praised for its "dark and interesting" interior and "high-quality" cooking; sceptics, though, find it "such a shame that a place with so much potential fails to deliver". / www.arturorestaurant.co.uk; 10 pm; set weekday L £25 (FP).

Asadal WC1 £40 ❸④⑤
227 High Holborn   7430 9006   2–1D
"Hidden-away under Holborn tube", this subterranean two-year-old
offers "a good introduction to Korean food", serving up some
"tasty" and "good-value" dishes (most of them barbecued at the
table). / www.asadal.co.uk; 11 pm.

Asia de Cuba
St Martin's Lane Hotel WC2 £82 ④④❷
45 St Martin's Ln   7300 5588   4–4C
"It certainly has a pulse", but that's the only real plus nowadays
of this once-oh-so-trendy dining room, on the fringe of Covent
Garden – service is so-so, and its "Asian-Cuban, sharing" cuisine
can come out "weird instead of interesting". / www.stmartinslane.com;
midnight, Thu-Sat 12.30 am, Sun10.30 pm.

Ask! Pizza £27 ⑤④④
Branches throughout London
Odd to recall that this pizza multiple once seemed a serious
pretender to PizzaExpress's crown – its branches remain "buzzy"
enough, but service is "distinctly indifferent" nowadays, and the
food can be plain "dire". / www.askcentral.co.uk; 11 pm; some booking
restrictions apply.

ASSAGGI W2 £59 ❶❶❸
39 Chepstow Pl   7792 5501   6–1B
"The best Italian in London, bar none"; implausibly located above
a pub, this "plain" Bayswater dining room may be "noisy" and
"cramped", but Nino Sassu's "fabulous" food, and the "wonderful"
service make it one of the hottest tickets in town. / 11 pm; closed Sun;
no Amex.

Les Associés N8 £34 ❸❷❷
172 Park Rd   8348 8944   1–1C
A "little bit of France in Crouch End", occupying the "comfortable"
front room of a house; sceptics say its "traditional" Gallic fare
is "unmemorable", but more reporters find it "terrific", certainly
given the "incredibly low prices". / www.lesassocies.co.uk; 10 pm;
Tue-Sat D only, closed Mon & Sun D.

Atami SW1 £60 ❸❸④
37 Monck St   7222 2218   2–4C
With its "delicious" Japanese food (somewhat à la Nobu),
this smart yearling "attracts a young trendy crowd, as well as the
business fraternity" – in the "dead area" which is Westminster,
that's no small achievement! / www.atami-restaurant.com; 10.30 pm;
closed Sat L & Sun.

L'ATELIER DE JOEL ROBUCHON WC2 £80 ❷④❷
13-15 West St   7010 8600   4–2B
"Wow!"; most reporters are still "blown away" by the
"extraordinary" (if "tiny") dishes and the "sexy" décor of the
famous French chef's Theatreland jewel; service of late has been
very "average", though, and bills can be "apocalyptic".
/ www.joel-robuchon.co.uk; 10.30 pm.

The Atlas SW6 £34 ❷❸❷
16 Seagrave Rd   7385 9129   5–3A
"Gourmet pub food" draws a big fan club to this backstreet boozer, near Earl's Court 2; it's also a *"cosy"* place (and has *"a great terrace for summer days"*). / www.theatlaspub.co.uk; 10.30 pm; closed Sun D; no booking.

Atma NW3 £41 ❷❷❸
106c Finchley Rd   7431 9487   8–2A
New owners seem to have done nothing to dent the appeal of this *"unsung hero"*, in Belsize Park – it is *"on a different level from most Indian restaurants in terms of quality and presentation"*. / www.atmarestaurants.com; 11 pm; closed Mon.

Atrium SW1 £40 ⑤⑤⑤
4 Millbank   7233 0032   2–4C
The hugely complacent dining room adjacent to Parliament's media centre *"feels like a mid-budget hotel lounge"*; this year's BEST report? – *"unexciting, and a huge disappointment"*. / www.atriumrestaurant.com; 9.30 pm; closed Sat & Sun.

Aubaine £43 ④⑤④
4 Heddon St, W1   7440 2510   3–2C
260-262 Brompton Rd, SW3   7052 0100   5–2C
With their *"long queues"*, *"rude"* staff and *"overpriced"* fare, these fashionably-located bakeries-cum-bistros can seem like some sort of *"ghastly caricature"* of *"see-and-be-seen"* London life; *"A1 cakes"*, though. / SW3 10 pm – W1 11 pm; W1 closed Sun.

Aubergine SW10 £98 ❸❸④
11 Park Wk   7352 3449   5–3B
What's up at this suddenly *"fading"* Chelsea dining room? – there are still many fans who acclaim William Drabble's food as *"sublime"*, but there are also reports of *"a sad decline"*, and of *"surprisingly bad"* service. / www.auberginerestaurant.co.uk; 11 pm; closed Sat L & Sun; no jeans or trainers; set weekday L £54 (FP).

Aurora W1 £36 ❸❷❶
49 Lexington St   7494 0514   3–2D
Can't get into Andrew Edmunds (opposite)? – this *"pretty little place"* (complete with cute courtyard) is also supremely *"charming"* and likewise well-suited to romance; it also offers *"good-value"* fare from *"an interesting short menu"*. / Mon & Tues 10 pm, Wed - Sun 10.30 pm; closed Sun.

Automat W1 £46 ④④❸
33 Dover St   7499 3033   3–3C
A *"noisy"* and *"overpriced"* burger joint, popular with *"Eurobrats"*, or *"in a posy way, quite a fun place"*? – if you want to form your own view on this swanky Mayfair diner, brunch is probably the best way to start. / www.automat-london.com; 11 pm; closed Sat D & Sun D.

L'Autre Pied W1 NEW £52 ❷❸④
5-7 Blandford St   7486 9696   2–1A
"A great addition to Marylebone eating" – this offshoot of Pied à Terre serves up *"adventurous"* and often *"stunning"* dishes; it has, however, inherited the awkward former Blandford Street (RIP) site, and can similarly seem *"devoid of atmosphere"*. / www.lautrepied.co.uk; 11 pm, Sun 9.30 pm; set weekday L & pre-theatre £35 (FP).

L'Aventure NW8   £53   ❷❷❶
3 Blenheim Ter   7624 6232   8–3A
"For that special meal", Catherine Parisot's "traditional" St John's Wood charmer – with its "cosy interior in winter and lovely summer terrace" – makes a famously "romantic" choice; its Gallic fare is "delicious" and "unfussy" too. / 11 pm; closed Sat L & Sun; set weekday L £34 (FP).

The Avenue SW1   £55   ❹❹❹
7-9 St James's St   7321 2111   3–4D
Fans love the "bright" and "airy" interior of this "NYC-style" eatery in St James's, which is undoubtedly "a lively place for a business lunch"; doubters find it "jaded" and "very noisy", though, and the menu is "very standard". / www.danddlondon.com; midnight; closed Sat L & Sun; set weekday L £39 (FP).

Awana SW3   £52   ❷❷❸
85 Sloane Ave   7584 8880   5–2C
In the heart of Chelsea, this "modern and glamorous" Malaysian restaurant has gathered quite a following for its "tasty" fare; some reporters, though, feel that "unless you've got money to burn, the only way to enjoy it is one of those half price-offers". / www.awana.co.uk; Mon-Wed 11 pm, Thu-Sat 11.30 pm, Sun 10.30 pm; set weekday L £30 (FP).

Axis
One Aldwych Hotel WC2   £55   ❹❸❹
1 Aldwych   7300 0300   2–2D
"Nothing actively bad, just very ordinary for the price" – it's a real shame that the recent revamp has done so little to restore reporters' affection for this smart and airy Covent Garden basement; as a "perfect fall-back for business entertaining", though, it undoubtedly has its uses. / www.onealdwych.com; 10.45 pm, Sat 11.30 pm; closed Sat L & Sun; set weekday L £34 (FP).

Babur Brasserie SE23   £32   ❶❷❶
119 Brockley Rise   8291 2400   1–4D
"You just don't expect restaurants of this quality deep in SE London suburbia" – this "classy" modern Indian, in Honor Oak Park, offers "wonderfully original" cuisine and "exceptional" service. / www.babur.info; 11.30 pm.

Babylon
Kensington Roof Gardens W8   £61   ❹❹❶
99 Kensington High St   7368 3993   5–1A
"Visit on a spring day, and stroll around the gardens" on the 8th floor! – to catch this "beautiful" Kensington eyrie at its best; service "means well but lacks polish", however, and the food varies. / www.virgin.com/roofgardens; 11 pm; closed Sun D; set weekday L £36 (FP), set Sun L £42 (FP).

Bacchus N1   £82   ❷❷❹
177 Hoxton St   7613 0477   1–2C
"El Bulli comes to London", at this "daring", year-old pub-conversion; Nuño Mendes "doesn't get the press he deserves" for his "really exciting" creations, that are "experimental without being pretentious" – perhaps it's got something to do with the "dodgy" Hoxton location. / www.bacchus-restaurant.co.uk; midnight; D only, closed Sun.

Il Bacio £31 ❸❸❷
61 Stoke Newington Church St, N16   7249 3833   1–1C
178-184 Blackstock Rd, N5   7226 3339   8–1D
*"Cheap, cheerful, and with great pizzas" – pretty much the whole
story on these "invariably busy" north London Sardinians.
/ www.ilbaciohighbury.co.uk; N5 & N16 11 pm; N5 Mon-Fri L - N16 Mon L;
no Amex.*

Back to Basics W1 £42 ❶❷④
21a Foley St   7436 2181   2–1B
*A "cramped" Fitzrovia bistro which "never fails to please", thanks
to its "brilliant" fish and seafood, served "in unusual combinations"
– "get there early for the best choice". / www.backtobasics.uk.com;
10.30 pm; closed Sun; set always available £27 (FP).*

Baker & Spice £36 ❷④④
54-56 Elizabeth St, SW1   7730 3033   2–4A
47 Denyer St, SW3   7589 4734   5–2D
75 Salusbury Rd, NW6   7604 3636   1–2B
20 Clifton Rd, W9   7266 1122   8–4A
*"A veritable smorgasbord" of "lovely, lovely" delights awaits,
at these de luxe bakery/delis (where seats at the communal tables
are most sought-after for brunch); "price is an issue" however –
they're "unbelievable!" – as is the "slow" and "snooty" service.
/ www.bakerandspice.com; 6.30 pm, Sun 4.30 pm; closed D; no Amex;
no bookings.*

Balans £34 ⑤❸❷
34 Old Compton St, W1   7439 3309   4–2A
60 Old Compton St, W1   7439 2183   4–3A
239 Old Brompton Rd, SW5   7244 8838   5–3A
214 Chiswick High Rd, W4   8742 1435   7–2A
187 Kensington High St, W8   7376 0115   5–1A
*These "hip", gay-friendly diners make an "easy-going" stand-by
at any time of day; the food "has really declined in recent years",
but breakfast remains a "strong point". / www.balans.co.uk; varies from
midnight to 6 am, 34 Old Compton St 24 hrs; some booking restrictions apply.*

Balfour WC1 NEW £34 ④④❸
75-77 Marchmont St   7713 6111   8–4C
*"A pleasant, informal atmosphere" is perhaps the high point of this
new "Italian bistro", near Russell Square; the food
is "straightforward" (with the "interesting specials" being a better
bet than the "more mundane main menu").*

Baltic SE1 £45 ❸④❷
74 Blackfriars Rd   7928 1111   9–4A
*"Wonderful vodka" helps fuel a "hip" and "happy" vibe at this
"bright" bar/restaurant, near Southwark Tube; it offers
a "surprisingly reasonable" twist on central European food,
but service seems increasingly "hapless". / www.balticrestaurant.co.uk;
11.15 pm, Sun 10.15 pm; set pre theatre £30 (FP).*

Bam-Bou W1 £45 ❸❸❶
1 Percy St   7323 9130   2–1C
*"There's always a good buzz", at this "dark" and "decadent"
Fitzrovia townhouse, which is decked out in "French Indo-Chinese"
style; its oriental fare is "fresh and extremely tasty", but the
"superb cocktails" are arguably an even greater attraction.
/ www.bam-bou.co.uk; 11 pm; closed Sat L & Sun; booking: max 6.*

The Banana Leaf Canteen SW11   £30   ②②②
75-79 Battersea Rise   7228 2828   10–2C
"An absolute gem"; this "oriental canteen", in Battersea, wins a loud cheer from reporters as an "excellent cheap and cheerful option". / 11 pm; need 6+ to book.

Bangkok SW7   £31   ❸②④
9 Bute St   7584 8529   5–2B
"I've been going since 1972, and still not found another Thai I prefer!"; it "may not look much", but this South Kensington canteen – the UK's original Thai – "survives virtually unchanged", with its "charming" service and "invariably fresh and tasty" cooking. / 10.45 pm; closed Sun; no Amex.

Bank Westminster
St James Court Hotel SW1   £45   ⑤④④
45 Buckingham Gate   7630 6644   2–4B
Given the thin pickings near Victoria, this "airy" bar/brasserie wins support as "a handy local option", and in particular as "a business lunch venue"; its "stereotypical" cooking, though, often seems "disappointing and overpriced". / www.bankrestaurants.com; 10.30 pm; closed Sat L & Sun.

Banners N8   £32   ④❸❶
21 Park Rd   8348 2930   1–1C
The "absolutely massive breakfasts" at this "buzzy", "fun" and "child-friendly" Crouch End hang-out are something of an institution; at other times it offers an "eclectic" menu, and an experience that's "not always cheap but definitely cheerful". / 11.30 pm, Fri midnight; no Amex.

Baozi Inn WC2 NEW   £16   ④④❸
25 Newport Ct   7287 6877   4–3B
From the Bar Shu people, a tightly-packed new Chinatown bistro specialising in the cuisine of northern China; it's certainly very cheap, but our early-days visit suggested that its dishes are something of an acquired taste. / Rated on Editors' visit; 10 pm; no credit cards.

Bar Bourse EC4   £50   ④❸④
67 Queen St   7248 2200   9–3C
A comfortable City basement – "nothing particularly special, but an OK place for a business lunch". / www.barbourse.co.uk; L only, closed Sat & Sun.

Bar Estrela SW8   £25   ④④❷
111-115 South Lambeth Rd   7793 1051   10–1D
"You really feel like you're abroad", when you've made the trip to this "excellent" and "lively" bar – "the best in Vauxhall's Little Portugal" – which serves up "solid" food in "generous" portions. / midnight.

Bar Italia W1   £18   ④❸❶
22 Frith St   7437 4520   4–2A
The food will never win any awards, but fans say this "lively" 24/7 "classic" does "London's best espresso"; it's "a great spot for watching Italian football matches", or to see "Soho low-life" passing by. / open 24 hours, Sun 3 am; no booking.

Bar Shu W1 £38 ❷④④
28 Frith St 7287 6688 4–3A
*"Mouth-tinglingly thrilling Sichuan food" – "hot! hot! hot!" –
"gets everybody talking", at this "authentic" Soho two-year-old;
even though waiters wear "special agent-style" headphones,
however, the service is "indifferent and slow". / www.bar-shu.co.uk;
11 pm.*

Barcelona Tapas £33 ④④❸
481 Lordship Ln, SE22 8693 5111 1–4D
1 Beaufort Hs, St Botolph St, EC3 7377 5111 9–2D
24 Lime St, EC3 7929 2389 9–2D
13 Well Ct, EC4 7329 5111 9–2B
*A tapas chain, with four rather disparate branches; all please
most reporters most of the time, not least with a "good selection
of Spanish wines". / www.barcelona-tapas.com; 10 pm,Fri 10.30,Sat
11.30 pm; all City branches closed Sat & Sun.*

Barnes Grill SW13 £45 ⑤④④
2-3 Rock's Ln 8878 4488 10–1A
*The "simple" burgers and steaks at AWT's rather suburban-style
grill "would be OK… if they weren't so seriously overpriced",
and the whole style of the operation strikes some reporters
as "pretentious". / www.awtrestaurants.com; 10.30 pm; closed Mon L.*

The Barnsbury N1 £41 ❷❸❸
209-211 Liverpool Rd 7607 5519 8–2D
*"Fab and filling" food, "a lovely garden", "accommodating" staff
and "a good range of beers on tap" – all features which help make
this "friendly" Islington boozer a "great neighbourhood pub".
/ www.thebarnsbury.co.uk; 10 pm.*

Barrafina W1 £42 ❶❶❷
54 Frith St 7813 8016 4–2A
*"Faultless!… except they need more seats!" – the Hart brothers'
year-old Barcelona-inspired tapas bar may be "cramped" and
"busy", but its "awesome" dishes have made it one of the top
survey raves of recent years; "it's worth the wait".
/ www.barrafina.co.uk; 11 pm; closed Sun; no booking.*

Basilico £30 ❷❷④
690 Fulham Rd, SW6 0800 028 3531 10–1B
26 Penton St, N1 0800 093 4224 8–3D
515 Finchley Rd, NW3 0800 316 2656 1–1B
175 Lavender Hill, SW11 0800 389 9770 10–2C
178 Upper Richmond Rd, SW14 0800 096 8202 10–2B
*"Standard-to-exotic toppings" – plus "very thin and delicious bases"
– make the pizzas of this popular chain "by far the best of the
take-aways". / www.basilico.co.uk; midnight; no booking.*

Bayee Village SW19 £32 ❸❶❸
24 High St 8947 3533 1–4A
*"A fine Chinese restaurant", in the heart of Wimbledon Village;
it can seem a mite "overpriced", and some regulars say last year's
refurb "robbed it of character", but fans find the new style "lovely",
"quiet" and "relaxed". / www.bayee.co.uk; 11 pm.*

Beach Blanket Babylon £65 ⑤⑤❶
45 Ledbury Rd, W11   7229 2907   6–1B
19-23 Bethnal Green Rd, E1   7749 3540   1–2D **NEW**
*Stick to the "divine" cocktails, at these "stunning" Gothic hang-outs
(now in Shoreditch, as well as Notting Hill) – try to eat, and you
risk "clueless" service and nosh that's "disappointing" and "hugely
overpriced". / 11 pm.*

Beauberry House
Belair Park SE21 £48 ⑤④❸
Gallery Rd, Dulwich Village   8299 9788   1–4C
*This beautiful Grade I-listed house, by Belair Park, is "worth it for
the setting"; while the strenuously contemporary Franco-Japanese
fusion cuisine has "potential", though, its realisation is far too "hit-
and-miss". / www.beauberryhouse.co.uk; 10.30 pm; closed Mon & Sun D.*

Bedford & Strand WC2 £42 ❸❷❷
1a Bedford St   7836 3033   4–4D
*A "really imaginative" wine list is the top draw to this "surprise
find", in a basement just off the Strand; it's emerging, though, as a
good all-round "hide-out", with "competent" bistro fare, "intelligent"
service and a "lively" (if "crammed") atmosphere.
/ www.bedford-strand.com; 11 pm; closed Sat L & Sun.*

Bedlington Café W4 £22 ❸❸④
24 Fauconberg Rd   8994 1965   7–2A
*"Very much a local dive" – this long-established Chiswick caff still
offers pretty "reliable" Thai fare; "despite being licensed, they let
you BYO". / 10 pm; closed Sun L; no credit cards.*

The Beehive W1 **NEW** £32 ❷❸④
126 Crawford St   7486 8037   2–1A
*In Marylebone, an interesting re-working of the gastropub concept
– more like an informal continental restaurant – by leading
restaurateur Claudio Pulze; the food was good on our early-days
visit, but it's difficult to predict how this hard-to-categorise venture
will prosper. / Rated on Editors' visit.*

Beirut Express £35 ❷④⑤
65 Old Brompton Rd, SW7   7591 0123   5–2B
112-114 Edgware Rd, W2   7724 2700   6–1D
*The name says it all, at this "great" and "quick" Lebanese chain,
where you get an "overload" of "delicious" kebabs, salads and
juices, all at "unbelievable" prices. / W2 2am, SW7 midnight;
W2 no credit cards.*

Beiteddine SW1 £40 ❸❷④
8 Harriet St   7235 3969   5–1D
*A "very pleasant" Lebanese stalwart, where "everything tastes
fresh"; "tucked-away off Sloane Street", its "unfancy" style seems
increasingly at odds with its ever-ritzier location.
/ www.beiteddinerestaurant.com; midnight.*

Bel Canto EC3 **NEW**
1 Minster Ct   no tel   9–3D
*On the City site formerly known as Simply Gladwin's (RIP), this late-
2008 newcomer is promising to replicate the operatic song-with-
your-supper format that sustains no fewer than three such outlets
in Paris.*

Belgo £35 ④④❸
50 Earlham St, WC2 7813 2233 4–2C
72 Chalk Farm Rd, NW1 7267 0718 8–2B
"Its heyday may be long gone", but fans still *"love the moules/frites"* and the *"enormous list of unusual beers"*, at this once-pioneering – and still *"buzzing"* – *"industrial-chic"* chain; its critics, though, continue to find it *"very average"* nowadays.
/ www.belgo-restaurants.com; NW1 Mon-Thu 11 pm, Fri-Sat 11.30 pm, Sun 10 pm – WC2 Mon-Fri 11pm, Sat 11.30pm, Sun 10.30pm.

Bellamy's W1 £62 ❸②❸
18-18a Bruton Pl 7491 2727 3–2B
Gavin Rankin's *"posh"* Mayfair mews brasserie has a *"personal feel"* and *"charming"* staff, even if – for such a *"smart"* location – seating is quite *"cheek-by-jowl"*; critics find the food *"expensive and unexciting"*, but the more general view is that it's *"very enjoyable"*.
/ www.bellamysrestaurant.co.uk; 10.15 pm; closed Sat L & Sun.

Belvedere W8 £50 ❸❸❶
Holland Pk, off Abbotsbury Rd 7602 1238 7–1D
"A wonderful setting among the peacocks" is not the only plus point of this *"beautiful"* and *"glamorous"* Art Deco-styled favourite, within Holland Park – generally speaking, food and service are *"hard to fault"* too. / www.belvedererestaurant.co.uk; 10 pm; closed Sun D.

Benares W1 £65 ❷❷❸
12 Berkeley Hs, Berkeley Sq 7629 8886 3–3B
Thanks to his *"fantastically subtle"* cuisine, Atul Kochar's *"sophisticated"* Mayfair Indian is *"going from strength to strength"* – it also offers *"efficient and helpful"* service, in a *"beautifully-designed"* (if *"slightly impersonal"*) space. / www.benaresrestaurant.com; 10.30 pm; set weekday L £28 (FP).

Bengal Clipper SE1 £35 ❷④④
Shad Thames 7357 9001 9–4D
It's a shame that *"erratic"* (sometimes *"dismissive"*) service has suddenly begun to erode support for this grand and spacious South Bank Indian; the food – as ever – is *"very good"*.
/ www.bengalclipper.co.uk; 11.30 pm.

Benihana £53 ④④⑤
37 Sackville St, W1 7494 2525 3–3D
77 King's Rd, SW3 7376 7799 5–3D
100 Avenue Rd, NW3 7586 9508 8–2A
"Friendly chefs juggling knives" provide some distraction from the *"bland"* and *"hugely overpriced"* oriental fodder dished up at this teppan-yaki chain; children *"love it"*, but too many reporters find it very *"tired"*. / www.benihana.co.uk; 10.30 pm.

Benja W1 £44 ❷❶❸
17 Beak Street 7287 0555 3–2D
"Set over a number of small floors", this dinky Soho yearling has a *"lovely atmosphere"*, and serves some *"very good"* Thai food too.
/ www.benjarestaurant.com; 10.45 pm; closed Sun.

Bentley's W1 £61 ❷❸❸
11-15 Swallow St   7734 4756   3–3D
"The oyster-bar has a great buzz", say fans of Richard Corrigan's
revived Mayfair stalwart, and it makes a "fun" venue for some
"classic seafood" (not least at the al fresco tables on the newly-
pedestrianised street); service can "lapse", though, and the
relatively "subdued" and "pricey" first-floor dining room attracts
more mixed reports. / www.bentleysoysterbarandgrill.co.uk; midnight;
booking: max 12; set weekday L £43 (FP).

Bento NW1 £25 ❸❸④
9 Parkway   7482 3990   8–3B
A simple Japanese café, in Camden Town, that does an "efficient
bento lunch", and offers general "good value". / bentocafe.co.uk.

Benugo £14 ④❸❷
14 Curzon St, W1   7629 6246   3–4B
23-25 Gt Portland St, W1   7631 5052   3–1C
V&A Museum, Cromwell Rd, SW7   7581 2159   5–2C
BFI Southbank, Belvedere Rd, SE1   7401 9000   2–3D
116 St John St, EC1   7253 3499   9–1A
82 City Rd, EC1   7253 1295   9–1C
For "super sandwiches and pies", this fast-food chain has "cracked
the formula"; its more ambitious branches (at the V&A and BFI),
however, have yet to measure up – they may have "interesting"
locations (the V&A is "stunning"), but the "brasserie" fare
is "nothing special". / www.benugo.com; 4 pm - 9.30 pm; W1 & EC1
branches closed Sat & Sun; W1 & EC1 branches, no credit cards.

Beotys WC2 £47 ④❸④
79 St Martin's Ln   7836 8768   4–3B
The Frangos family's "welcoming" and "quirky" Theatreland
stalwart offers a "unique" Franco-Greek menu in a comfortably
"old-fashioned" setting; its tiny reporter base is split between those
who consider it to be a "national treasure" and those who find
it "disappointing". / http://www.covent-garden.co.uk/beotys/; 11.30 pm;
closed Sun.

Bermondsey Kitchen SE1 £41 ❸④④
194 Bermondsey St   7407 5719   9–4D
A handy bistro stand-by which generally (if not invariably) pleases
reporters, in particular with its "excellent cooked breakfasts".
/ www.bermondseykitchen.co.uk; 10.30 pm; closed Sun D.

Bertorelli's £40 ⑤⑤⑤
11-13 Frith St, W1   7494 3491   4–2A
19-23 Charlotte St, W1   7636 4174   2–1C
37 St Martin's Ln, WC2   7836 5837   4–4C
44a Floral St, WC2   7836 3969   4–2D
15 Mincing Ln, EC3   7283 3028   9–3D
1 Plough Pl, EC4   7842 0510   9–2A
A "dull" and "disappointing" Italian chain, where "some nights are
like 'Pop Idol' for the World's Worst Waiter"; "I used to visit
regularly, but I don't think I'll bother again…" / www.santeonline.co.uk;
9.30 pm-11 pm; WC2 & Charlotte St closed Sun, EC3 & EC4 closed
Sat & Sun.

Best Mangal W14 £24 ❷❷❷
104 North End Rd 7610 1050 7–2D
"It may look like an ordinary Turkish place, but you often have to book", at this "friendly" establishment, near West Kensington tube; it serves "unbeatable" kebabs, "freshly cooked on a charcoal BBQ in front of you". / midnight; no Amex.

The Betjeman Arms
St Pancras International NW1 NEW £38 ④④⑤
Pancras Rd 7923 5440 8–3C
Staff with a notably positive attitude added life to our early-days visit to this Identikit gastropub newcomer, by the platforms for the Eurostar; service was slow, though, and the food seemed designed to reinforce continentals' negative preconceptions about our national cuisine. / Rated on Editors' visit; www.geronimo-inns.co.uk/thebetjemanarms/; 11 pm, Sun 10.30 pm.

Bevis Marks EC3 £60 ❸❸④
4 Heneage Ln 7283 2220 9–2D
This City venture benefits from a "beautiful" and "bizarrely peaceful" location, in a conservatory "lean-to" attached to the side of the UK's oldest synagogue; the contemporary kosher food is rarely less than "decent", and occasionally "exceptional". / www.bevismarkstherestaurant.com; 8 pm; closed Fri D, Sat & Sun.

Beyoglu NW3 £26 ❸❸④
72 Belsize Ln 7435 7733 8–2A
In Belsize Park, a Turkish restaurant where the food is "very good and reliable", but service is sometimes "hit-and-miss". / www.beyoglu.co.uk; 11 pm; no Amex or Maestro.

Bianco Nero W6 NEW £42 ④④④
206-208 Hammersmith Rd 8748 0212 7–2C
It may have a horribly "downmarket" location ("right on Hammersmith Broadway"), but fans insist this is a "splendid" Italian newcomer; the monochrome interior is arguably a bit "'80s", though, and "even if the food is average-to-good, it's quite pricey". / www.bianconerorestaurants.com; 10 pm; closed Sat L & Sun.

Bibendum SW3 £67 ❸❷❷
81 Fulham Rd 7581 5817 5–2C
This "very comfortable" and "lovely" first-floor Brompton Cross veteran – which "looks at its best for lunch" – has "sharpened up its act" of late; its modern Gallic cuisine, however, is still somewhat eclipsed by the "brilliant" (if "pricey") wine list. / www.bibendum.co.uk; Mon-Fri 11 pm, Sat 11.30 pm, Sun 10.30 pm; booking: max 12; set brunch, weekday L & Sun L £46 (FP).

Bibendum Oyster Bar SW3 £40 ❸❸❷
Michelin Hs, Fulham Rd 7589 1480 5–2C
For a "spur of the moment" treat – "a glass of champagne and a shellfish platter" still slips down very nicely, at this "fun" café, off the foyer of Chelsea's Conran Shop. / www.bibendum.co.uk; 10.30 pm.

Big Easy SW3 £50 ❸❸❷
332-334 King's Rd 7352 4071 5–3C
This "lively" and – if you're near the "fab live music" –
loud "American-style" hang-out serves up "huge portions" of "great
seafood", plus "excellent steak, ribs and BBQ chicken"; it's very
much "priced for Chelsea", though. / www.bigeasy.uk.com; 11.30 pm,
Fri & Sat 12.30 am.

Bincho Yakitori £34 ❷❷❶
16 Old Compton St, W1 7287 9111 4–2A **NEW**
Oxo Tower, Barge House St, SE1 7803 0858 9–3A
"Forget the 8th-floor 'Oxo Tower'" – "for half the money, you get
double the satisfaction", on the second floor of the South Bank
landmark; it's a "crowded but fun" venue with "amazing" views,
and serving "succulent" Japanese skewers (and other "tapas-like"
dishes); the new Soho offshoot seems the palest of imitations.

Bistro 1 £23 ❹❷❸
27 Frith St, W1 7734 6204 4–3A
75 Beak St, W1 7287 1840 3–2D
33 Southampton St, WC2 7379 7585 4–3D
"The food isn't gourmet, but for central London it's a bargain",
at this "cramped" Mediterranean/Turkish chain, which makes
a very "useful" stand-by, thanks not least to its "jolly and brisk"
service. / www.bistro1.co.uk; 11.30 pm.

Bistro Aix N8 £45 ❸❹❸
54 Topsfield Pde, Tottenham Ln 8340 6346 8–1C
This "cute" Gallic bistro, in Crouch End, is a "cosy, intimate and
dependable" sort of place, that's "good value" too (especially
"during the week"); service, though, can be "erratic".
/ www.bistroaix.co.uk; 11 pm; closed Mon, Tue-Fri D only, Sat & Sun open
L & D; set weekday L £17 (FP).

Bistro 190
Gore Hotel SW7 £50 ❹❸❸
190 Queen's Gate 7584 6601 5–1B
After years in the doldrums, this "lovely, bright and airy" bistro, in a
characterful townhouse hotel, looks at last to be "Improving";
"it's perfect pre-Albert Hall". / www.gorehotel.com; 11.30 pm;
set weekday L £35 (FP).

Bistrotheque E2 £44 ❸❷❷
23-27 Wadeson St 8983 7900 1–2D
"Hard to find" but "worth the schlep to E2" – this "hip" hang-out
in an "arty/industrial bit of Bethnal Green" is particularly tipped for
its "great weekend brunch" (as well as its drag cabarets and
a "cool downstairs bar"); the "simple" food is "not groundbreaking,
but reasonably priced". / www.bistrotheque.com; 10.45 pm; closed
weekday L.

Black & Blue £44 ❸❸④
90-92 Wigmore St, W1   7486 1912   3–1A
105 Gloucester Rd, SW7   7244 7666   5–2B
215-217 Kensington Church St, W8   7727 0004   6–2B
205-207 Haverstock Hill, NW3   7443 7744   8–2A
1-2 Rochester Walk, SE1   7357 9922   9–4C
"Quality" steaks, burgers and salads have won a big fan club for this "honest" steakhouse chain; it's rather a "bog-standard" formula, though, and its food rating drifted this year.
/ www.blackandblue.biz; 11 pm, Fri & Sat 11.30 pm; SE1 & W1 11 pm; no booking.

Blah! Blah! Blah! W12 £30 ❸❸④
78 Goldhawk Rd   8746 1337   7–1C
"Carnivores don't miss their meat", at this BYO "veggie haven", near Goldhawk Road tube, where the dishes are "creative" and "well thought-out". / www.gonumber.com/2524; 10.30 pm; closed Sun; no credit cards.

Blakes
Blakes Hotel SW7 £104 ⑤④❷
33 Roland Gdns   7370 6701   5–2B
"Dark", "decadent", "discreet"… and "ridiculously overpriced", this datedly luxurious South Kensington basement is still – for its small fan club – "the most romantic place in town"; standards are "variable", though, and it inspires much less interest than once it did. / www.blakeshotels.com; 10.45 pm.

BLEEDING HEART EC1 £49 ❷❷❷
Bleeding Heart Yd, Greville St   7242 8238   9–2A
"Hidden-away in an historic courtyard", near Holborn, this amazingly popular "all-rounder" – which comprises tavern, bistro and restaurant – is a "surefire winner" for business or romance; its "veeeery French" staff deliver "admirable" dishes and "splendid" wine in "dimly-lit" and "rustic" surroundings. / www.bleedingheart.co.uk; 10 pm; closed Sat & Sun.

Blue Elephant SW6 £52 ❸❷⓪
4-6 Fulham Broadway   7385 6595   5–4A
"For the full Thai experience" ("orchid for the lady, and all"), you can't beat this "beautiful theme park" – complete with "bridges, streams, and foliage" – lurking "behind a dull facade" on Fulham Broadway; the cooking "has slipped in recent years… but I still don't see how any date could fail to be impressed". / www.blueelephant.com; midnight, Sun 10.30 pm; closed Sat L (except Stamford Bridge match days); set weekday L £36 (FP).

Blue Jade SW1 £31 ❸❶④
11 Hugh St   7828 0321   2–4B
"Totally reliable" and "always welcoming" – a useful Thai corner spot, hidden-away in the back streets of Pimlico. / 11 pm; closed Sat L & Sun.

Bluebird SW3 £58 ⑤⑤⑤
350 King's Rd   7559 1000   5–3C
"What a waste of a prime location"; a year after its recent re-launch, this Chelsea landmark is once again a pin-up for all the "dire" values many reporters still associate with the Conran (now D&D) name – "substandard" food, "terrible" service and "hideous" prices. / www.bluebird-restaurant.co.uk; 10.30 pm.

Bluebird Café SW3 £38 ⑤⑤⑤
350 King's Rd 7559 1000 5–3C
*"Overpriced", "awful", "rubbish" – this "cramped and chaotic"
D&D-group operation, with its many pavement tables, monstrously
exploits its prime Chelsea real estate. / www.bluebird-restaurant.co.uk;
10 pm, Sun 5 pm; no booking.*

**Blueprint Café
Design Museum SE1** £48 ④④❷
28 Shad Thames, Butler's Wharf 7378 7031 9–4D
*"Wonderful views over the Thames" are the stand-out attraction
at this bright D&D-group operation, on the South Bank; as ever,
Jeremy Lee's fans insist his "seasonal" food is "delicious", but the
continuing survey consensus is that it's "rather ordinary".
/ www.blueprintcafe.co.uk; 10.45 pm; closed Sun D.*

Bob Bob Ricard W1 NEW
1 Upper James St no tel 3–2D
*Set to open in late-2008, this somewhat eccentric-sounding British
bar/brasserie – on the Soho site formerly known as Circus, RIP –
promises to offer an all-day (and much of the night) formula which,
if they get it right, could make it quite a destination.*

Bodean's £36 ④④④
10 Poland St, W1 7287 7575 3–1D
Fulham Broadway, SW6 7610 0440 5–4A
169 Clapham High St, SW4 7622 4248 10–2D
*"A super-finger-lickin" good "meat-fest"; fans say these American
joints are "THE place in London for ribs" (and "great if you go on
a burnt ends day"); service is "patchy", though, and standards
strike critics as generally "uninspiring". / www.bodeansbbq.com; 11 pm.*

La Bodeguita del Medio W8 £38 ❸④❶
47 Kensington Ct 7938 4147 5–1A
*There are "tasty" Cuban tapas – "a nice change from the familiar
Spanish range" – and "the Mojitos are fab", at this improving
Latino bar/restaurant, in a cute alley off Kensington High Street.
/ www.bdelmlondon.com; 11 pm.*

Bohème Kitchen & Bar W1 £42 ④④❸
19 Old Compton St 7734 5656 4–2A
*"Great" hamburgers are the menu highlight, but it's the "happening
atmosphere in the heart of Soho" that packs 'em in at this loungey
and "fun" bar/diner. / www.bohemekitchen.co.uk; midnight, Sun 10.30 pm.*

Boiled Egg & Soldiers SW11 £24 ❸④④
63 Northcote Rd 7223 4894 10–2C
*"It's heaving with scrummy mummies" (and buggies), but this
Battersea café is also dazzlingly popular with singletons
as "the perfect place for a lazy brunch" – "arrive early for a table".
/ L & afternoon tea only; no Mastercard or Amex; no booking.*

Boisdale SW1 £65 ④❸❷
13-15 Eccleston St 7730 6922 2–4B
*"For a boisterous, big-eating, big-drinking meal" – complete with
"great steaks", "a fab selection of whiskies", "super jazz" and
"a sensational cigar terrace" – this "clubby", Scottish-themed
Belgravia haunt may well be the place… if you can overlook the
fact that it's "a wee bit over-priced", that is. / www.boisdale.co.uk;
11.15 pm; closed Sat & Sun; set dinner £41 (FP).*

Boisdale of Bishopsgate EC2 £48 ❸❸❸
202 Bishopsgate, Swedeland Ct   7283 1763   9–2D
This "well-spaced" City basement put in a stronger showing this year (and some fans now claim it's "better than Belgravia"); the food's "great" ("apart from being Scottish", that is), and majors in "top-notch" steaks and "sublime haggis" (plus a lighter menu in the bar above). / www.boisdale.co.uk; 9.30 pm; closed Sat & Sun.

Bombay Bicycle Club £35 ❷❷❸
128 Holland Park Ave, W11   7727 7335   6–2A
3a Downshire Hill, NW3   7435 3544   8–2A
95 Nightingale Ln, SW12   8673 6217   10–2C
For a "smart curry", the "still very atmospheric" Wandsworth original of this Indian chain has long been "worth a trip"; all branches inspire positive reports, however, not least for their "superb take-aways"; as this guide was going to press, the chain was acquired by Tiffinbites. / www.thebombaybicycleclub.co.uk; 11 pm; D only ex NW3, Sun open L & D.

Bombay Brasserie SW7 £55
Courtfield Close, Gloucester Rd   7370 4040   5–2B
One of London's path-breaking quality Indians – this Raj-scale South Kensington institution was still achieving "first-rate" standards when it closed for a major refurb in mid-2008 – we trust that it will re-emerge stronger than ever. / www.bombaybrasserielondon.com; 11.30 pm.

Bombay Palace W2 £44 ❶❷④
50 Connaught St   7723 8855   6–1D
"Shame about the setting" – "a big box of a room with hotel décor"; this "seriously under-rated" venture, north of Hyde Park, has "charming and professional" service, and its "classic" Indian cuisine has been "consistently fantastic over many years". / www.bombay-palace.co.uk; 11.30 pm.

Bonds
Threadneedles Hotel EC2 £58 ❸④④
5 Threadneedle St   7657 8088   9–2C
A heart-of-the-City dining room, praised by fans for its "calm" style, "slick" service and "classy" food, but dismissed by critics for being "seriously unremarkable and overpriced" – so, all-in-all, "not a bad business stalwart" then! / www.theetoncollection.com/restaurants/bonds/; 10 pm; closed Sat & Sun; set weekday L £40 (FP).

Bord'Eaux
Grosvenor House Hotel W1 NEW £50 ❸❷⑤
Park Ln   7399 8460   3–3A
With its "confused menu" and "aircraft hangar" proportions, this new Gallic brasserie is a perfect example of just how 'wrong' hotel-restaurants can be; bizarrely, the food and service are actually quite good, so the place has its uses as a Mayfair business rendezvous. / www.bord-eaux.com/; 10.30 pm, 11 pm Fri & Sat; set pre theatre £34 (FP).

Il Bordello E1 £42 ❷❶❶
75-81 Wapping High St   7481 9950   11–1A
"Huge and fabulous portions of every kind of Italian food" – not least "unbeatable pizzas" – help win the usual rave reviews for this notably "professional" Wapping fixture, which is "always packed" and "buzzing". / 11 pm; closed Sat L.

The Botanist SW1 NEW £48 ④④❸
7 Sloane Sq   7730 0077   5–2D
On a Sloane Square corner, an elegant but tightly-packed new brasserie from the Martin brothers (of 'Gun' fame); location has ensured instant popularity, but on our early-days visit standards were humdrum. / Rated on Editors' visit; www.thebotanistsloanesquare.com; 10.30 pm.

La Bouchée SW7 £46 ❸❸❷
56 Old Brompton Rd   7589 1929   5–2B
"Oozing romance", this "cramped" and "rustic" candlelit bistro, in South Kensington, "really feels like France"; it's "not exactly cheap", but it is "good value". / www.boudinblanc.co.uk; 11 pm; set dinner & weekday L £31 (FP).

Le Bouchon Bordelais SW11 £44 ④❸❸
5-9 Battersea Rise   7738 0307   10–2C
"Only come here if you are having the Chateaubriand" – this rather old-fashioned Gallic bar/bistro, in Battersea, otherwise often seems to "lack spark". / 11 pm.

Le Bouchon Breton E1 NEW
Horner Building, Old Spitalfields Mkt   08000 191704   9–2D
A Gallic brasserie, on quite a scale, scheduled to open in Shoreditch around the publication date of this guide; it's backed by the same team as Battersea's long-established Bouchon Bordelais – let's hope standards here are a bit more consistent!

Boudin Blanc W1 £50 ❷❸❷
5 Trebeck St   7499 3292   3–4B
"Just like a little piece of France" – this "super" bistro in Shepherd Market offers "fantastic" food, in a "crowded" and "noisy" setting with "bags of atmosphere"; nicely-located outside tables make it "great outdoors in summer" too. / www.boudinblanc.co.uk; 11 pm.

Boulevard WC2 £36 ④❸❸
40 Wellington St   7240 2992   4–3D
"A useful stand-by for a pre-theatre dinner" – this "consistent" brasserie is a "value-for-money" destination, if hardly an exciting one. / www.boulevardbrasserie.co.uk; midnight.

The Boundary E2 NEW
2-4 Boundary St   no tel   9–1D
Sir Terence Conran may be disengaging from his famous restaurant group (now called D&D London), but he's not hung up his restaurateur's cap yet; this latest project in which he's involved is a restaurant with rooftop bar and grill, scheduled to open in Shoreditch in late-2008; there will also be a café/foodstore (The Albion).

Bowler Bar & Grill SW3 £45 ❸❸④
2a Pond Pl   7589 5876   5–2C
On a sidestreet site that's proved "tricky" for a succession of operators, this Chelsea yearling is making something of a name for its "great steaks and sauces"; it "seems to be popular" – fingers crossed it's going to last... / www.bowlerbarandgrill.co.uk; 11.30 pm; closed Mon, Tue-Fri L only, Sat open L & D, closed Sun.

Boxwood Café
The Berkeley SW1 £62 ❸❸④
Wilton Pl   7235 1010   5–1D
It's "expensive" – particularly for a so-called 'café' – but fans say
this Ramsay-group venture is a "reliable" Knightsbridge destination
(especially for business); service "can be up-and-down", though,
and the oddly-configured setting is "a bit clinical".
/ www.gordonramsay.com/boxwoodcafe; 11 pm; booking: max 8; set weekday L
£46 (FP).

The Brackenbury W6 £41 ④❸❸
129-131 Brackenbury Rd   8748 0107   7–1C
"Year after year", this Hammersmith neighbourhood favourite
delights reporters with its "intimate" style, "sensible" food and
"reasonable" prices (plus a "nice terrace" too); the cooking,
however, "has deteriorated" of late. / www.thebrackenbury.com; 11 pm;
closed Sat L & Sun D; set weekday L £26 (FP), set dinner £30 (FP).

Bradley's NW3 £47 ④④④
25 Winchester Rd   7722 3457   8–2A
This ambitious local restaurant has a "somewhat bizarre" location
– in a Swiss Cottage sidestreet – but is "ideal pre/post-Hampstead
Theatre"; it has an "interesting" menu and "serene" style,
but "needs a bit of a tweak" to hit its full potential.
/ www.bradleysnw3.co.uk; 11 pm; closed Sun D.

Brady's SW18 £26 ❸❷❸
513 Old York Rd   8877 9599   10–2B
"Traditional fish 'n' chips" (or healthier grills), plus "old-fashioned
puds", typically make for "a happy crowd of eaters", at this
"simple", family-run chippy-cum-fish-bistro in Wandsworth; of late,
however, "quality has been a little variable". / 10.30 pm; closed
Mon L & Sun; no Amex; no booking.

La Brasserie SW3 £46 ④④❷
272 Brompton Rd   7581 3089   5–2C
"Great people-watching" is the highlight of the weekend brunches
for which this "typically French" Brompton Cross veteran
is particularly known; at other times the food can often
be "disappointing". / www.labrasserielondon.co.uk; 11 pm; no booking,
Sat L & Sun L.

Brasserie James SW12 🆕 £38 ❷❸❸
47 Balham Hill   8772 0057   10–2C
Near Clapham South, an extremely competent new local restaurant
from a former head chef of Quaglino's, offering no-nonsense Gallic
fare that – on our early-days visit – almost invariably satisfied;
it was already pretty busy too. / Rated on Editors' visit;
www.brasseriejames.com.

Brasserie Roux
Sofitel St James SW1 £58 ❸❸❸
8 Pall Mall   7968 2900   2–3C
A "good all-rounder" – just off Trafalgar Square – of particular note
as an "elegant" setting for an "outstanding-value pre-theatre
menu", and also as a "great place for a business lunch".
/ www.sofitelstjames.com; 11 pm.

Brasserie St Jacques SW1 NEW £46 ④④④
33 St James's St 7839 1007 3–4C
*An upmarket Gallic brasserie, launched in St James's in the summer
of 2008, on the 'difficult' site which was formerly Fiore (RIP); it got
off to a notably uneven start – let's hope its (very experienced)
backers can pull it round. / Rated on Editors' visit;
www.brasseriestjacques.co.uk; 11 pm, Sun 10 pm.*

Brasserie St Quentin SW3 £46 ❸❸④
243 Brompton Rd 7589 8005 5–2C
*This "rather staid" (but "friendly") Gallic brasserie, in Knightsbridge,
is past its glory days, but still has fans for its "consistent" cooking
at "reasonable" prices. / www.brasseriestquentin.co.uk; 10.30 pm;
set weekday L & pre-theatre £31 (FP).*

Brew Wharf SE1 £41 ❸④❶
Brew Wharf Yd, 1 Stoney St 7378 6601 9–4C
*A South Bank beerhall – occupying an impressively "light and airy"
series of railway arches – where "simple well-cooked food"
is "matched by great beer". / www.brewwharf.com; 9.30 pm; closed
Sun D.*

Brick Lane Beigel Bake E1 £6 ❷④⑤
159 Brick Ln 7729 0616 1–2D
*"So cheap, so moreish" – this 24/7 East End legend has beigels
"second to none" (not least the "fantastic salt beef ones"); it may
look "dull" but "at 2 am, it feels amazing". / open 24 hours; no credit
cards; no booking.*

The Bridge SW13 £37 ④④④
204 Castelnau 8563 9811 7–2C
*"No longer the interesting gastropub it used to be" – a number
of reporters lament the decline of this "once-excellent"
establishment, near Harrods Village, where the garden now
sometimes seems "the only redeeming feature".
/ www.thebridgeinbarnes.com; midnight.*

Brilliant UB2 £35 ❷❸④
72-76 Western Rd 8574 1928 1–3A
*Deep in Southall, this large Punjabi stalwart "lives up to its name",
offering "absolutely wonderful food for the price"; the ambience
"can vary", though – "it depends on which Bollywood movie is on
the screens". / www.brilliantrestaurant.com; 11.30 pm, Fri & Sat midnight;
closed Mon, Sat L & Sun L; booking: weekends only.*

Brinkley's SW10 £41 ④④❸
47 Hollywood Rd 7351 1683 5–3B
*"Very reasonably-priced wine" and a "great garden" are the high
points at John Brinkley's "very Chelsea-sceney" hang-out; "we call
it Crinkleys: it's always full of 35+ Chelsea girls and past-it public
school boys". / www.brinkleys.com; 11 pm; closed weekday L.*

Britannia W8 £38 ④④❸
1 Allen St 7937 6905 5–1A
*Revamped a couple of years ago, this attractive and "well-located"
pub (off Kensington High Street) is consistently praised by locals;
the food is not art, but it is "good enough".
/ www.britanniakensington.co.uk; 11 pm.*

FSA

La Brocca NW6 £32 ❸❸❷
273 West End Ln 7433 1989 1–1B
*"Still going strong" – this "intimate and buzzy basement" is a
"trusted" stand-by for many a West Hampstead local, thanks to its
"great basic pizzas and pastas", and its "tasty" Italian specials.*
/ www.labrocca.co.uk; Sun-Thu 10.30 pm, Fri & Sat 11 pm; booking: max 8.

Brompton Quarter Café SW3 £42 ⑤⑤④
223-225 Brompton Rd 7225 2107 5–2C
*"Convenience for a light snack" does win some positive reports for
this "light and luminous" room, near Harrods; it's a "noisy" place,
though, with sometimes "awful" service, and a menu that can
be realised "with all the skill of a motorway café".*
/ www.bromptonquartercafe.com; 10.30 pm.

The Brown Dog SW13 £42 ❸❸❸
28 Cross St 8392 2200 10–1A
*This "great little pub", tucked away in Barnes's 'Little Chelsea',
is "a real local asset", with "imaginative" food and "pleasant" staff;
tables, though, are "just too close together for comfort".*
/ www.thebrowndog.co.uk; 10 pm.

Browns £37 ④④④
47 Maddox St, W1 7491 4565 3–2C
82-84 St Martin's Ln, WC2 7497 5050 4–3B
9 Islington Grn, N1 7226 2555 8–3D
Butler's Wharf, SE1 7378 1700 9–4D
Hertsmere Rd, E14 7987 9777 11–1C
8 Old Jewry, EC2 7606 6677 9–2C
*Fans of this well-known bar/brasserie chain say it's "a fun stand-by",
which serves "decent" staples; it has numerous 'foes', though,
who think standards overall are just "the worst".*
*/ www.browns-restaurants.com; 10 pm-11 pm; W1 4pm Sun; EC2 closed
Sat & Sun; need 5+ to book, early eve & Sat.*

Brula TW1 £43 ❸❷❷
43 Crown Rd 8892 0602 1–4A
*This "very Left Bank" bistro describes itself as a 'restaurant
du quartier', and – with its "lovely" staff, and its "more-than-
competent" Gallic food – "the inhabitants of this part
of St Margarets are indeed lucky to have it". / www.brula.co.uk;
10.30 pm.*

Brunello
Baglioni Hotel SW7 £70 ④❸❸
60 Hyde Park Gate 7368 5700 5–1B
*The departure of the former chef seems to have had no effect
on this wackily-luxurious Kensington design-hotel – for Italian fare
that's no more than "decent", however, it remains a "dizzyingly
expensive" place to eat. / www.baglionihotellondon.com; 10.45 pm.*

Buchan's SW11 £40 ❸④❸
62-64 Battersea Bridge Rd 7228 0888 5–4C
*"At the south end of Battersea Bridge", this long-established,
Scottish-themed wine bar wins consistent praise as "a reliable
local". / www.buchansrestaurant.co.uk; 10.45 pm.*

54

Buddha Bar WC2 NEW
8 Victoria Embankment   3371 7777   2–2D
*Opening under Westminster Bridge (near the Savoy) as this guide
goes to press, a lavish oriental offshoot of a perennially-popular
Parisian bar/restaurant. / www.buddhabar-london.com.*

Buen Ayre E8 £39 ❷❸❷
50 Broadway Mkt   7275 9900   1–2D
*"Authentic, unreconstructed and unpretentious" – this "happy and
buzzy" Argentinean 'parillada', in Hackney, "pulls in punters from
far and wide", thanks to its "tremendous" steaks, served "at a
fraction of the typical London price". / www.buenayre.co.uk; 10.30 pm;
closed weekday L.*

The Builders Arms SW3 £39 ④④❷
13 Britten St   7349 9040   5–2C
*A "particularly cosy atmosphere" maintains the popularity of this
"always-buzzing" Chelsea pub, despite service that's "hit-and-miss"
and food that's "rather average"; (well, it is a Geronimo Inn).
/ www.geronimo-inns.co.uk; 10 pm, Sun 9 pm; no booking.*

The Bull N6 £48 ④④④
13 North Hill   0845 456 5033   1–1C
*A smart Highgate spot that "can't decide whether it's a restaurant
or a pub" – either way, some reporters feel it charges "sky-high
prices for ordinary food". / www.inthebull.biz; 10.30 pm; closed Mon L.*

Bumpkin £43 ❷❷❷
102 Old Brompton Rd, SW7   no tel   5–2B NEW
209 Westbourne Park Rd, W11   7243 9818   6–1B
*This "rustic" Notting Hill hang-out – a "crowded" brasserie,
plus "cosy" upstairs restaurant – is "as much like a real country
place as Harrods is like a farm shop"; its "funky" style and "sturdy"
comfort fare are winning over the critics, though, and a South
Kensington offshoot opens in late-2008. / www.bumpkinuk.com.*

Buona Sera £34 ④❸❸
289a King's Rd, SW3   7352 8827   5–3C
22 Northcote Rd, SW11   7228 9925   10–2C
*These useful Italians "continue to dish up some good-value staples";
the Chelsea branch (with its quirky "bunk bed-style" tables)
is "always fun" – the "large and noisy" original is a "long-standing"
Nappy Valley "favourite". / midnight; SW3 closed Mon L.*

Busaba Eathai £28 ❷❸❷
106-110 Wardour St, W1   7255 8686   3–2D
8-13 Bird St, W1   7518 8080   3–1A
22 Store St, WC1   7299 7900   2–1C
*"The queues out the door tell their own story"; these "superior
versions of Wagamama" are "cool" places, which offer "fresh" and
"strongly-flavoured" Thai dishes at large communal tables – let's
hope the formula survives the dreaded national 'roll out', scheduled
to commence in late-2008. / 11 pm, Fri & Sat 11.30 pm, Sun 10 pm;
W1 no booking; WC1 need 12+ to book .*

Bush Bar & Grill W12 £38 ⑤④④
45a Goldhawk Rd   8746 2111   7–1C
*"Great bar, but on no account eat here" – the damning verdict
on the cavernous eating area of this Beeb hang-out, hidden down
an alleyway in Shepherd's Bush. / www.bushbar.co.uk; 11 pm; closed
Sun D.*

Butcher & Grill £48 ④⑤⑤
39 Parkgate Rd, SW11 7924 3999 5–4C
33 High St, SW19 8879 3845 10–2B **NEW**
It has an "interesting" concept (with butcher's shop attached),
but this "bustling" Battersea grill – with its "slow" service, "bland"
décor and "pricey" fare – has "little to recommend it"; only too
natural, then, that Wimbledon was selected as the location for the
recently-opened second branch!

Butcher's Hook SW6 £38 ❸❷❷
477 Fulham Rd 7385 4654 5–4A
This "rustic"-looking gastropub is a "good, solid performer",
opposite Stamford Bridge; "avoid it on match days… unless you're
a Chelsea fan that is". / www.thebutchershook.co.uk; 10.30 pm; no Amex.

Butlers Wharf Chop House SE1 £50 ⑤⑤❸
36e Shad Thames 7403 3403 9–4D
"Lovely views of the river and Tower Bridge" are – increasingly –
the only saving grace of this D&D-group bar/restaurant; service
is ever more "slack", and the "traditional British" fare is too often
"the worst". / www.chophouse.co.uk; 10.45 pm.

La Buvette TW9 £42 ④❷❸
6 Church Walk 8940 6264 1–4A
"A tranquil location in the heart of Richmond" (off a church yard)
and an "intimate" atmosphere still win praise for this "classic
French bistro" (a sibling to St Margaret's Brula); the food "hasn't
maintained its original standards", however, although the "excellent
set lunch" is still worth seeking out. / www.brula.co.uk; 10.30 pm.

Byron W8 **NEW** £26 ❸❸❷
222 Kensington High St 7361 1717 5–1A
With its "mouthwatering" burgers (and "yummy courgette chips
too"), this "posh" new diner, by the entrance to Holland Park,
has been a "welcome" addition to Kensington; its "cleverly-designed
interior" helps create "a real buzz", too. / www.byronhamburgers.com;
Mon-Thu 11 pm, Fri-Sat 11.30, Sun 10.30 pm.

C&R Cafe W1 £28 ❷⑤④
3-4 Rupert Ct 7434 1128 4–3A
Lost "in a Chinatown back alley", "a Malaysian café with brilliant
food" – it may be "basic", but it's "a great place for expats missing
the taste of home". / 11 pm.

The Cabin SW6 £39 ❸❷❷
125 Dawes Rd 7385 8936 10–1B
"The closest thing we have to 'Cheers'", this "homely" and
"relaxed" bar/diner, in deepest Fulham, is "an-all round good local
place", serving "great burgers" and grills.
/ www.thecabinbarandgrill.co.uk; 10.30 pm; D only, ex Sun open L & D;
no Amex.

Café 209 SW6 £23 ④❷❶
209 Munster Rd 7385 3625 10–1B
"Joy lives up to her name" – and is "a real giggle" too – at the
"tightly-packed" Fulham BYO Thai over which she presides;
"the food's not top class, but you can guarantee a good night".
/ 10.30 pm; D only, closed Sun, closed Dec; no Amex.

Le Café Anglais
Whiteley's W2 £48 ❸❹❸

8 Porchester Gdns 7221 1415 6–1C

It's been "much-hyped", but Rowley Leigh's large new Art Deco-style brasserie is undoubtedly an "elegant" and "airy" space that's given "a very necessary culinary boost to Bayswater"; service is often "inept", though, and realisation of the long and enticing menu is somewhat up-and-down. / www.lecafeanglais.co.uk.

Café Bohème W1 £39 ❹❹❷

13 Old Compton St 7734 0623 4–2A

Plus ça change…, at this "crowded" bar/bistro, in the heart of Soho; despite a major refurbishment, its "great, buzzy atmosphere" is pretty much unchanged, and the Gallic fare is still "not the point". / www.cafeboheme.co.uk; 3 am, Sun 12 pm; booking: max 7.

Café des Amis WC2 £42 ❹❸❸

11-14 Hanover Pl 7379 3444 4–2D

A "handy" but "rather boring" veteran, right by the Royal Opera House, with "dreary" food and sometimes "dilatory" service; curiously, though, the basement bar is a brilliant "bolt hole", offering "wonderful wine and perfect cheese". / www.cafedesamis.co.uk; 11.30 pm; closed Sun; set always available £30 (FP).

Café du Jardin WC2 £44 ❹❹❹

28 Wellington St 7836 8769 4–3D

"Dependable, but not stunning", this "well-located" Covent Garden corner restaurant can only actively be recommended for its fixed-price menus (lunch and pre/post-theatre). / www.lecafedujardin.com; Midnight, Sun 11 pm; set weekday L & pre-theatre £28 (FP).

Café du Marché EC1 £45 ❷❷❶

22 Charterhouse Sq 7608 1609 9–1B

This "tucked-away" Smithfield stalwart is, as always, "hard to fault on any level"; "top-notch, French provincial cooking", "friendly but efficient" staff and its "lovely, rustic style" make it "a tip-top choice for business or romance". / www.cafedumarche.co.uk; 10 pm; closed Sat L & Sun; no Amex.

Café Emm W1 £27 ❹❷❷

17 Frith St 7437 0723 4–2A

"Expect to queue after 7.30 pm", for this "fantastic little place" in Soho – a younger crowd loves its "dependable, if not stunning", food, and its "good-value" prices. / www.cafeemm.com; 10.30 pm, Fri-Sat 11.30 pm; no Amex; no booking after 6.30 pm.

Café España W1 £26 ❹❸❷

63 Old Compton St 7494 1271 4–3A

"A cheap but interesting option", in the heart of Soho – an "always-bustling", "slightly shabby" and "Bohemian" small caff, serving "tasty" dishes in "portions so big, they almost belie the description 'tapas'". / 10 pm; no Amex; no booking.

Café in the Crypt
St Martin's in the Fields WC2 £23 ④④❷
Duncannon St 7766 1158 2–2C
On balance, reporters feel this large crypt-cafeteria has been "improved" by the huge St Martin-in-the-Fields redevelopment project; the food is still nothing special, but fans tip this as a "great-value pit stop, in the heart of the West End".
/ www.stmartin-in-the-fields.org; Sun 6 pm, Mon-Tue 7.30 pm, Wed-Sat 10 pm; no Amex; no booking.

Café Japan NW11 £29 ❶③④
626 Finchley Rd 8455 6854 1–1B
You don't go to this "cramped" café, opposite Golder's Green station, for its looks, but for its "sensational sushi" at "amazing prices" – even so, "it'd be nice if they revamped".
/ www.cafejapan.co.uk; 10 pm; closed Mon, Tue, & Wed L-Fri L; no Amex.

Café Laville W2 £36 ④❸❷
453 Edgware Rd 7706 2620 8–4A
"The view's sublime, the food ordinary", at this inviting-looking café, cutely perched above the canal in Little Venice. / 11 pm, Sun 10 pm; no Amex.

Café Lazeez W1 £38 ❸❸❸
21 Dean St 7434 9393 4–2A
Often overlooked nowadays (despite a location in the heart of Soho), this modern Indian still wins praise from diehard fans for food that's "good, and cheaper than its nearby oppo".
/ www.cafelazeez.com; 11.30pm; closed Sun.

Café Med NW8 £38 ④④④
21 Loudon Rd 7625 1222 8–3A
This "popular" pub-style operation in St John's Wood (effectively part of the Med Kitchen chain) is "not the best place in the world", but it makes "an adequate spot for a quick meal". / 11 pm.

Café Pacifico WC2 £37 ⑤⑤④
5 Langley St 7379 7728 4–2C
Fans say it's "worth the queue", for the "fun" atmosphere (and "good cocktails") at this Covent Garden Tex/Mex veteran; critics, though, just find it "dated, noisy and formulaic".
/ www.cafepacifico-laperla.com; 11.45 pm.

Café Rouge £32 ⑤⑤④
Branches throughout London
Optimists see "signs of improvement" at this "dire" and "formulaic" high street chain – too often, however, it still seems like "a terrible imitation of a French brasserie". / www.caferouge.co.uk; 11 pm.

Café Spice Namaste E1 £44 ❶❷❸
16 Prescot St 7488 9242 11–1A
A "marvellous and subtle range of textures, spicing and flavours" has long been the hallmark of Cyrus Todiwala's east-City Indian, still frequently nominated as "the best in London"; "warm and efficient service" helps add charm to its "bright and quirky" interior.
/ www.cafespice.co.uk; 10.30 pm; closed Sat L & Sun.

Caffè Caldesi W1 £51 ④❸④
15-17 Marylebone Ln   7935 9226   2–1A
This "less formal" offshoot of Caldesi has "characterful" service and
an "attractive" bar, praised for its "gorgeous, fresh Italian food";
the more "formal" upstairs, however, can be "disappointing".
/ www.caldesi.com; 10.30 pm; closed Sun.

Caffè Nero £13 ④❸❸
Branches throughout London
"You need three Starbucks to get the same kick", say fans of this
popular café multiple; the scoff is basic, though – "it's all about the
coffee". / 7 pm -11 pm, City branches earlier; most City branches closed all
or part of weekend; no credit cards; no booking.

Caffé Vergnano £8 ❷❷❷
62 Charing Cross Rd, WC2   7240 8587   4–3B
Royal Festival Hall, SE1   7921 9339   2–3D
Coffee "worthy of Milan" and "wonderful hot chocolate" are the
twin highlights of this emerging chain – everything else is by
the bye.

La Cage Imaginaire NW3 £35 ④❸❸
16 Flask Walk   7794 6674   8–1A
Cutely tucked-away in a picturesque Hampstead lane, this "old-
fashioned" Gallic spot still strikes fans as "glorious" – detractors,
though, can find it a mite "pretentious". / 11 pm; set weekday L
£23 (FP).

Caldesi W1 £53 ❸❸④
15-17 Marylebone Ln   7935 9226   3–1A
Even regulars concede this "understated" Marylebone Tuscan can
be "variable"; at best it offers "sophisticated" cooking and "a very
hospitable welcome" – at worst, "disappointingly average food" and
an "off-hand" attitude. / www.caldesi.com; 11 pm; closed Sat L & Sun.

Cambio de Tercio SW5 £46 ❶❶❷
161 Old Brompton Rd   7244 8970   5–2B
"You can't go wrong", at this "fun" Earl's Court Spaniard, where the
"authentic but innovative" food is amongst the "best in town",
certainly of its type; it's matched by a "really interesting" wine
list too. / www.cambiodetercio.co.uk; 11.30 pm.

Camden Brasserie NW1 £39 ④❸⑤
9-11 Jamestown Rd   7482 2114   8–3B
An innocuous institution that's had "no atmosphere" since its
unhappy re-location a few years ago; it still makes a useful stand-by
for some reporters, even if "the only dish you can really rave about
is the chips". / www.camdenbrasserie.co.uk; 11 pm.

Camerino W1 £48 ❸❸④
16 Percy St   7637 9900   2–1C
After a heady start, this Fitzrovia Italian quickly slipped into
obscurity; its small fan club says its food is "always good", and that
it "should be more popular". / www.camerinorestaurant.com; 11 pm;
closed Sat L & Sun.

Camino N1 £42 ❸❸❸
3 Varnishers Yd, Regent Quarter 7841 7331 8–3C
*"Down an all-too-easily-missed alleyway by King's Cross",
this "chilled" Hispanic yearling is "a ray of light" in a still-dismal
area; fans vaunt its "quality" fare (in both bar and restaurant),
but sceptics fear it's "trying to be too clever". / www.barcamino.com;
11 pm; set weekday L £26 (FP).*

Canteen £35 ④④④
Royal Festival Hall, SE1 0845 686 1122 2–3D
Crispin Pl, Old Spitalf'ds Mkt, E1 0845 686 1122 9–1D
*Shame this "great concept" – elegant diner-style operations,
promising the "idyll of quick, fresh and classic British cuisine" –
is being so poorly realised; the food is increasingly "mediocre",
and the staff "seem to be recruited from planet Dizzy".
/ www.canteen.co.uk; E1 11 pm - SE1 11 pm; no booking weekend L.*

Cantina del Ponte SE1 £41 ⑤⑤④
Butler's Wharf Building, 36c Shad Thames 7403 5403 9–4D
*"Truly appalling" service continues – as it has for the last decade! –
to undermine appreciation of this potentially "fun" Thames-sider
(owned by the D&D group); its Italian fare is "remarkably
uninteresting" too. / www.cantina.co.uk; 11 pm, Sun 10 pm; set weekday L
£25 (FP).*

Cantina Italia N1 £34 ❸❸❸
19 Canonbury Ln 7226 9791 8–2D
*The name says it all about this north-Islington pizza 'n' pasta stop
– a "regular indulgence" for a small fan club. / 11 pm, Fri & Sat
11.30 pm; D only, ex Sun open L & D; no Amex.*

Cantina Vinopolis
Vinopolis SE1 £47 ④④❸
1 Bank End 7940 8333 9–3C
*"They could hardly fail to have an interesting wine list" –
this "buzzy" venue is, after all, part of the South Bank's museum
of wine; it has an "atmospheric" (railway arch) location too, but the
brasserie fare is "overpriced", and service "could be improved".
/ www.cantinavinopolis.com; 10.30 pm; closed Sun.*

Il Cantuccio di Pulcinella SW11 £29 ❸❶④
143 St John's Hill 7924 5588 10–2C
*"A very good, no-nonsense Italian", in Wandsworth, with a
particular reputation for pizza… and, "with Mama always sitting
in the corner", you feel this is "the genuine article" too.
/ www.ilcantucciodipulcinella.co.uk; 11 pm; Mon-Thu D only, Fri-Sun open
L & D; no Amex.*

Cape Town Fish Market W1 £40 ④④⑤
5 & 6 Argyll St 7437 1143 3–1C
*This large, luridly-lit South African import, near Oxford Circus,
brings a sort of upmarket Angus Steak House style to the
consumption of fish and seafood; some reporters "love the
concept", but there's also quite a school of thought that it's
"disappointing all round". / www.ctfm.com; 11pm, Fri-Sat Midnight.*

THE CAPITAL RESTAURANT
CAPITAL HOTEL SW3   £82   ❷❷④

22-24 Basil St   7589 5171   5–1D

Eric Chavot's "beautifully realised" cuisine "can be compared with the best in London", but the atmosphere of this small and "quiet" Knightsbridge hotel dining room divides reporters – fans find it "discreet" and "personal", but for critics it's just rather "austere"; "outstanding value lunch". / www.capitalhotel.co.uk; 10 pm; no jeans; set weekday L £51 (FP).

LE CAPRICE SW1   £55   ❷❶❶

Arlington Hs, Arlington St   7629 2239   3–4C

The "sheer class" of this resurgent '80s "classic", near the Ritz, still "ticks all the boxes" for its army of fans; the service is "the slickest in town", the food is "simply great" ("with no gimmicks"), and the décor, though rather dated, "somehow still looks sophisticated". / www.caprice-holdings.co.uk; midnight.

Caraffini SW1   £42   ❸❶❷

61-63 Lower Sloane St   7259 0235   5–2D

An "honest" and still-"vivacious" Italian old-timer, near Sloane Square, which – thanks to its "exceptional" service and "no-frills", "classic" cooking – maintains a huge fan club. / www.caraffini.co.uk; 11.30 pm; closed Sun.

Caramel SW1   £31   ④④❸

77 Wilton Rd   7233 8298   2–4B

"Exactly what's needed for any breakfast situation" is to be found on the "extensive" menu of this Pimlico café/diner – it's "a very good local, but just too popular". / 11 pm; closed Mon D & Sun D.

Caravaggio EC3   £49   ④④⑤

107-112 Leadenhall St   7626 6206   9–2D

"One of the worst examples of fleecing the City lunch market" – this "bog-standard" Italian is not without fans, but more vociferous are critics who dismiss it as "hugely overpriced". / www.etruscarestaurants.com; 10 pm; closed Sat & Sun.

Carluccio's Caffè   £30   ④④❸

Branches throughout London

"Taken a dive, since the big man stepped back"; this "bright" and "buzzy" chain of Italian deli-cafés – no longer owned by Antonio & Priscilla Carluccio – "used to be a reliable fallback, but is now just deeply mediocre". / www.carluccios.com; 11 pm; no booking weekday L.

Carnevale EC1   £34   ❸❸④

135 Whitecross St   7250 3452   9–1B

A "great veggie, hidden-away near the Barbican" that pleases most of (if not quite all) those who have truffled it out; its small premises can seem "romantic" too. / www.carnevalerestaurant.co.uk; 11 pm; closed Sat L & Sun; no Amex.

Carpaccio's SW3   £51   ⑤④❸

4 Sydney St   7352 3433   5–2C

It has an "enviable location" and is "still very buzzy", but this "typical" Chelsea Italian has become "a victim of its own success" – its fare is "formulaic" and priced "way above its station". / www.carpacciorestaurant.co.uk; 11.30 pm; closed Sun; set weekday L £31 (FP).

The Carpenter's Arms W6 NEW   £38   ❸④④
91 Black Lion Ln   0871 8741 8386   7–2B
*It's already hard to get a booking at this gastropub newcomer,
hidden-away in an obscure bit of Hammersmith; fans say it has
been "a great addition to W6", but there's also a school of thought
that it's "over-rated" – "decent, but not as good as others nearby".
/ 11 pm, Sun 9.30 pm; no Amex.*

Castello SE16   £27
192-196 Jamaica Rd   7064 4631   11–2A
*This popular Bermondsey Italian – with a particular name for its
"tasty pizza" – changed hands towards the end of our survey year,
so no rating is appropriate; we're told, though, that the chef has
stayed on. / 11 pm; closed Mon, Sat L & Sun.*

Catch
Andaz Hotel EC2 NEW   £62   ④④④
40 Liverpool St   7618 7200   9–2D
*Formerly called Fishmarket, this "awkwardly-shaped" fish
specialist remains broadly unchanged – it offers "good"
to "average" fare, at notably 'City' prices. / www.andaz.com; 10.15 pm;
closed Sat & Sun.*

Cây Tre EC1   £31   ❷❷④
301 Old St   7729 8662   9–1B
*Redecoration has led to improvements across the board at this
"great local Vietnamese", near Hoxton Square, which continues
to offer "amazing food at incredibly cheap prices".
/ www.vietnamesekitchen.co.uk; 11 pm, Fri-Sat 11.30 pm, Sun 10.30 pm.*

Cecconi's W1   £55   ❸❸❷
5a Burlington Gdns   7434 1500   3–3C
*Not only a hit "with the hedge fund set" – Nick Jones's "bustling"
Italian brasserie is becoming a truly "useful" linchpin of modern
Mayfair life (from breakfast onwards); the food – perhaps
surprisingly – "is quite good too"! / www.cecconis.co.uk; 1am, Sun
midnight.*

Cellar Gascon EC1   £38   ❸❷❸
59 West Smithfield Rd   7600 7561   9–2B
*This "budget version of Club Gascon" is a "cool" bar with
a "very buzzy" style; its food, though, inspires less excitement than
the "hard-to-beat" list of SW France wines. / www.cellargascon.com;
midnight; closed Sat & Sun.*

Centrepoint Sushi WC2   £23   ❷❷❷
20-21 St Giles High St   7240 6147   4–1B
*"Extremely fresh, tasty and good-value sushi" makes it worth
seeking out this "friendly" operation, above an oriental
supermarket, right by Centrepoint. / www.cpfs.co.uk; 10.30 pm;
closed Sun.*

Le Cercle SW1   £45   ❶❸❷
1 Wilbraham Pl   7901 9999   5–2D
*"Grazing is taken to a new level", at Club Gascon's groovy Belgravia
basement offshoot – its "absolutely thrilling French tapas and
beautifully matched wines" are now even better than its famous
City-fringe sibling's. / www.lecercle.co.uk; 11 pm; closed Mon & Sun.*

Cha Cha Moon W1 NEW £18 ❷❷❷
15-21 Ganton St 7297 9800 3–2C
*From Wagamama-creator Alan Yau, a hotly-awaited new oriental
'format', of which this elegantly-styled Soho canteen is the
first example; at launch prices – £3.50 for every dish, mainly
noodles and dim sum – it was a bargain, but it's not clear how long
this pricing will last.* / Rated on Editors' visit; 11.30 pm.

Chakalaka SW15 £37 ❸❸④
136 Upper Richmond Rd 8789 5696 10–2B
*A "South African-themed" venture, in East Putney, whose "varied"
menu – with a "focus on quirky meats" – helps make it a
"fun place to spend the evening".* / www.chakalakarestaurant.com;
10.45 pm.

Chamberlain's EC3 £60 ④④④
23-25 Leadenhall Mkt 7648 8690 9–2D
*Few report on this City fish restaurant, whose best tables are semi-
al fresco (within Leadenhall Market); such as there are suggest it's
a "reliable" place... but then, at the prices, it should be.*
/ www.chamberlains.org; 9.30 pm; closed Sat & Sun.

Chamomile NW3 £21 ❸❷❸
45 England's Ln 7586 4580 8–2B
*"You could spend all day here reading the paper", but this Belsize
Park café is "no longer just a breakfast place", and now offers
an "enterprising" menu all day (but not into the evening).* / 6 pm;
L only; no Amex.

Champor-Champor SE1 £43 ❷❷❶
62 Weston St 7403 4600 9–4C
*"Down a dingy sidestreet behind Guy's Hospital", a "fabulously
eccentric" destination – with its "sweet" staff, and "Malay-fusion"
cuisine that's "packed full of flavours", it can make a "wonderful"
discovery for first-time visitors.* / www.champor-champor.com; 10.15 pm;
closed Mon L, Tue L, Wed L, Sat L & Sun; booking: max 12.

The Chancery EC4 £48 ❷❸④
9 Cursitor St 7831 4000 9–2A
*A "discreet" location – "tucked-away behind Chancery Lane" –
helps this "high-quality" but "nondescript" corner spot to "fulfill
a City-lunch need", especially for the "nearby legal eagles".*
/ www.thechancery.co.uk; 10.30 pm; closed Sat & Sun; set dinner £31 (FP).

The Chapel NW1 £32 ❸❸❷
48 Chapel St 7402 9220 6–1D
*A long-established (1995) gastropub, just off Edgware Road, which
still offers "consistently good and imaginative food", and at
"reasonable prices" too.* / www.thechapellondon.com; 11 pm.

Chapter Two SE3 £40 ❷❶❸
43-45 Montpelier Vale 8333 2666 1–4D
*"Worth a trip to Blackheath" – this "classy" basement operation
offers "rich and sophisticated cooking at unusually low prices";
it's "getting better" too, and supporters say it's "catching up with its
Bromley sibling, Chapter One".* / www.chaptersrestaurants.co.uk;
10.30 pm, Fri-Sat 11 pm.

Le Chardon £38 ④④❸
65 Lordship Ln, SE22   8299 1921   1–4D
32 Abbeville Rd, SW4   8673 9300   10–2D **NEW**
"A bubbling French bistro with crammed tables, in an ex-butchers shop" in East Dulwich; some dishes can seem "a bit amateurish", but "stick to the Gallic staples" and all should be well; (this year it added a new offshoot in Clapham). / www.lechardon.co.uk.

Charles Lamb N1 £29 ❸❸❷
16 Elia St   7837 5040   8–3D
"A great find in the back streets behind the Angel" – this year-old gastropub offers a "friendly" atmosphere and "reliable" food, and at "fair" prices too. / www.thecharleslambpub.com; 9.30 pm; closed Mon L, Tue L & Sun D; no Amex; no booking.

Charlotte's Place W5 £40 ④❸❸
16 St Matthew's Rd   8567 7541   1–3A
With its leafy location by Ealing Common, this cute-looking local certainly "has potential", and "its special offers are good value"; at full prices, though, not all reporters are convinced that it 'stacks up'. / www.charlottes.co.uk; 10.30 pm; no Amex.

The Chelsea Brasserie
Sloane Square Hotel SW1 £49 ④④④
7-12 Sloane Sq   7881 5999   5–2D
This "smart" operation was relaunched not long after it opened, and does win praise as "a much needed addition to the square"; especially "for the price", though, its standards still seem no more than "routine". / www.chelsea-brasserie.co.uk; 10.30 pm.

Chelsea Bun Diner SW10 £25 ❸❸④
9a Lamont Rd   7352 3635   5–3B
"Huge menu, great prices... you can't go wrong" – London's top "hang-over-cure" breakfast maintains the high profile of this "American diner-style" greasy spoon, at World's End; BYO. / www.chelseabun.co.uk; midnight, Sun 10 pm; no Amex; no booking, Sat & Sun.

Cheyne Walk Brasserie SW3 £60 ❸❸❷
50 Cheyne Walk   7376 8787   5–3C
"There's a great vibe", at this "beautiful" Gallic hang-out in Chelsea, where "you can watch your food being cooked on the open charcoal grill"; it's undoubtedly "expensive", but most people feel it's "worth it". / www.cheynewalkbrasserie.com; 10.30 pm; closed Mon L & Sun D; set weekday L £31 (FP), set Sun L £46 (FP).

CHEZ BRUCE SW17 £56 ❶❶❷
2 Bellevue Rd   8672 0114   10–2C
"Relaxed, not a temple" – that's the whole joy of Bruce Poole's "unpretentious" foodie Mecca, by Wandsworth Common, which is yet again Londoners' No. 1 favourite haunt; "unshowy, but beautiful" food and "wonderful" wine are served up by "unbelievably helpful" staff, and all "without an OTT price tag". / www.chezbruce.co.uk; 10.30 pm; booking: max 6 at D; set weekday L £37 (FP), set Sun L £41 (FP).

Chez Gérard £41 ⑤⑤④
Thistle Hotel, 101 Buck' Palace Rd, SW1 7868 6249 2–4B
31 Dover St, W1 7499 8171 3–3C
8 Charlotte St, W1 7636 4975 2–1C
119 Chancery Ln, WC2 7405 0290 2–2D
45 Opera Ter, Covent Garden, WC2 7379 0666 4–3D
9 Belvedere Rd, SE1 7202 8470 2–3D
64 Bishopsgate, EC2 7588 1200 9–2D
14 Trinity Sq, EC3 7480 5500 9–3D
1 Watling St, EC4 7213 0540 9–2B
*"A bad experience", "too awful for words", "the worst ever"… –
despite food that's often an "embarrassment", this uninspired
steak/frites chain is still surprisingly frequently tipped
as "convenient for business"! / www.chezgerard.co.uk; 10 pm-11.30 pm;
City branches closed all or part of weekend.*

Chez Kristof W6 £46 ④④❸
111-115 Hammersmith Grove 8741 1177 7–1C
*Largely thanks to its "lively" style, Jan Woroniecki's packed
Hammersmith hang-out has a more-than-local fan club; "iffy"
service, and "disappointing" food have led to up-and-down reports
of late, but an optimist insists the place is now "back on form".
/ www.chezkristof.co.uk; 11.15 pm, Sun 10 pm; set weekday L & pre-theatre
£26 (FP).*

Chez Liline N4 £43 ❷④⑤
101 Stroud Green Rd 7263 6550 8–1D
*Eye-poppingly spicy fish that's "as good as it gets" has long made
this inauspicious-looking Mauritian spot an unlikely find in "out-of-
the-way" Finsbury Park; some former fans, though, feel it has been
"resting on its laurels" of late. / 11 pm; closed Sun L.*

Chez Lindsay TW10 £37 ❸❸❸
11 Hill Rise 8948 7473 1–4A
*"A lovely little Breton restaurant near Richmond Bridge"; it's a
"reliable and cosy" spot, where the highlights are "great crêpes"
and "a nice selection of ciders". / www.chezlindsay.co.uk; 11 pm;
no Amex.*

Chez Marcelle W14 £26 ❶④⑤
34 Blythe Rd 7603 3241 7–1D
*"Like Fawlty Towers, but with great food"; Marcelle's "one-woman
show", behind Olympia, is a "delightfully chaotic" place, where
"lovingly-prepared" Lebanese fare is served up for "a pittance".
/ 10 pm; closed Mon, Tue-Thu D only,Fri-Sun open L & D; no credit cards.*

Chez Patrick W8 £39 ❸❷❸
7 Stratford Rd 7937 6388 5–2A
*"Simple, high-quality, beautifully-cooked" fish and seafood dishes
and an "involved" owner – the two big pluses of this Gallic venture,
in a quiet Kensington backwater; it inspires the odd 'off' report,
though. / www.chezpatrickinlondon.co.uk; 11 pm; closed Sun D; set weekday
L £22 (FP), set Sun L £25 (FP).*

Chi Noodle & Wine Bar EC4 £22 ❸❷❷
5 New Bridge St 7353 2409 9–2A
*"Far better than Wagamama" – this "buzzing" and "friendly"
family-run oriental makes a "good spot for lunch, or a quick bite
after work". / www.chinoodle.com; 10.30 pm; closed Sat & Sun.*

Chiang Mai W1   £30   ❸④⑤
48 Frith St   7437 7444   4–2A
*"You don't go for the surroundings", to this grungy Soho veteran;
fans still say its north Thai food "makes it worthwhile", but reports
nowadays are few and mixed.* / 11 pm; closed Sun L.

Chicago Rib Shack SW1 NEW   £38   ⑤⑤④
145 Knightsbridge   7591 4664   5–1D
*After a ten-year gap, this tacky Knightsbridge institution has now
been revived (on the tricky site that was Mocoto, RIP) –
fans insist it offers "more than nostalgia" but, for too many critics,
"disappointment reigns supreme".* / www.thechicagoribshack.co.uk/;
11 pm.

Chimes SW1   £29   ④❸❸
26 Churton St   7821 7456   2–4B
*It would be hard to think of somewhere more "studiedly un-glitzy"
than this age-old Pimlico 'pie house', which has survived for
a quarter of a century on its "decent" and "fairly-priced" pies,
beer and cider.* / www.chimes-of-pimlico.co.uk; 10.15 pm, Sun 9.15 pm.

China Boulevard on the River SW18   £37   ❷④④
1 The Boulevard, Smugglers Way   8871 3881   10–2B
*In an out-on-a-limb riverside development, near Wandsworth
Bridge, this large oriental is "always packed with Chinese
customers" (perhaps why "staff don't always understand English");
"dim sum is the main reason to visit".* / www.chinaboulevard.com;
11 pm; no Maestro.

China Tang
Dorchester Hotel W1   £75   ④④❸
53 Park Ln   7629 9988   3–3A
*"Shame the food doesn't keep pace" with the "gorgeously opulent",
"'30s-Shanghai" décor of David Tang's "decadent" Mayfair
basement; it comes at "absurd" prices too.* / www.thedorchester.com;
midnight; set always available £30 (FP).

The Chinese Experience W1   £34   ❸❸④
118-120 Shaftesbury Ave   7437 0377   4–3A
*Service "cheerier than the Chinatown average" enlivens this
"slightly different" canteen, opposite the Curzon Soho; "excellent
dim sum" is part of the package that generally makes this
a "reliable" option for a "speedy" bite.* / www.chineseexperience.com;
11 pm.

Chisou W1   £40   ❷❶④
4 Princes St   7629 3931   3–1C
*The setting's "nondescript", but this "handily-located" Japanese
café, near Oxford Circus, serves up "beautiful sushi", and a range
of other "exciting" dishes, in a "wonderfully charming" way.*
/ www.chisou.co.uk; 10.30 pm; closed Sun.

Cho-San SW15   £39   ❷❸④
292 Upper Richmond Rd   8788 9626   10–2A
*"Like being in Japan" – this "homely", family-run Putney outfit may
be decked out in "slightly kitsch" style, but it offers "excellent
sushi", plus a "wide range of traditional staples", all at "exceptional
prices".* / 10.30 pm; closed Mon; no Amex.

Chop'd £11 ②④⑤
52 Curzon St, W1 7495 1014 3–3B
St Pancras International, NW1 7837 1603 8–3C
Unit 1 34 The North Colonnade, E14 3229 0087 11–1C
2 Horner Sq, Old Spitalfields Mkt, E1 7247 8757 9–1D
2 Leadenhall Mkt, EC3 7626 3706 9–2D
*"No more mayo-ridden, under-sized salads for me" – this small
chain is tipped for its "huge" and "fresh" portions of chopped
greenery, plus "great soups, coffee, breakfasts and juices". / L only.*

Chor Bizarre W1 £43 ②❸②
16 Albemarle St 7629 9802 3–3C
*It's "as much an experience as a meal" to eat at this "wackily-
furnished" Mayfair Indian; the "imaginative" cuisine is an attraction
in itself, though, making it all the more undeserved that the place
sometimes "seems empty". / www.chorbizarre.com; 11.30 pm; closed
Sun L.*

Chowki W1 £28 ④④④
2-3 Denman St 7439 1330 3–2D
*Monthly-changing, regional menus "keep things interesting", at this
"handy" and "relatively cheap" Indian pit stop, near Piccadilly
Circus; "it's let standards slip" of late, however, and some ex-fans
feel is "no longer worth it". / www.chowki.com; 11.30 pm.*

Choys SW3 £35 ❸②④
172 King's Rd 7352 9085 5–3C
*"Still good after 30 years" – this imperishable Chelsea stand-by
offers a "wide choice" of "better-than-average" Chinese fare.
/ midnight.*

Christopher's WC2 £55 ⑤④④
18 Wellington St 7240 4222 4–3D
*This potentially "amazing" Covent Garden American – reached via
the "sweeping" staircase of a beautiful townhouse – turns off many
reporters with its "plain" surf 'n' turf fare, its sometimes "surly"
service and its "outrageous" prices; Sunday brunch, however,
is "not to be missed". / www.christophersgrill.com; 11 pm, Sat-Sun
11.30 pm; booking: max 12; set pre theatre £24 (FP).*

Chuen Cheng Ku W1 £32 ④④④
17 Wardour St 7437 1398 4–3A
*"The hubbub of the trollies keeps the kids entertained" – "just grab
what you want when they reach your table" – at this Chinatown
leviathan, where weekend dim sum is an institution.
/ www.chuenchengku.co.uk; 11.45 pm*

Churchill Arms W8 £20 ②④❷
119 Kensington Church St 7792 1246 6–2B
*"You always know what to expect", at this "wonderful" annex to a
"traditional Notting Hill pub" – "heaving plates of Thai food",
served in a "cosy", if "cramped" and "chaotic", setting; "how do
they do it so cheaply?" / 10 pm; closed Sun D.*

Chutney SW18 £26 ❷⓿❸
11 Alma Rd 8870 4588 10–2B
*"A gem in the heart of Wandsworth" – this "fantastic" curry house
wins praise for its "lovely" service, and for its "delicious"
(if "not especially creative") cooking. / 11.30 pm; D only.*

Chutney Mary SW10 £54 ❷❷❷
535 King's Rd 7351 3113 5–4B
"Lovely modern Indian food with amazing spices" keeps this famous Chelsea-fringe "subcontinental pioneer" in London's foodie front-line; recently revamped, it has "very attractive" décor throughout, but "the conservatory is the best place to sit". / www.realindianfood.com; 11.15 pm, Sun 10 pm; closed weekday L; booking: max 12.

Chutneys NW1 £25 ❸④④
124 Drummond St 7388 0604 8–4C
A "great veggie Indian", near Euston, which has been "tried and tested over many years" – "it's a bit dull, but always reliable". / 11 pm; no Amex; need 5+ to book.

Ciao Bella WC1 £31 ❸❷❶
86-90 Lamb's Conduit St 7242 4119 2–1D
"A terrifically good-value old-fashioned Italian", in Bloomsbury, offering "huge" portions to "locals and tourists alike", in "very crowded" conditions – "don't expect the best food in the world", but otherwise "it's a riot". / www.ciaobellarestaurant.co.uk; 11.30 pm, Sun 10.30 pm.

Cibo W14 £42 ❷❷❸
3 Russell Gdns 7371 6271 7–1D
Sometimes seeming "quiet" nowadays, this once-fashionable Olympia Italian is still a firm favourite for its diehard fans, who praise its "high standards" and "reasonable prices". / www.ciborestaurant.net; 11 pm; closed Sun D.

Cicada EC1 £44 ❷❸❸
132-136 St John St 7608 1550 9–1B
Will Ricker's "trendy" Clerkenwell hang-out still delivers "fantastic", "Asian-fusion" tapas and a "fun" atmosphere – a "successful formula" it has maintained for over 10 years now. / www.rickerrestaurants.com; 11 pm; closed Sat L & Sun.

Cigala WC1 £46 ④❸④
54 Lamb's Conduit St 7405 1717 2–1D
Fans applaud this Hispanic corner-spot, in Bloomsbury, for its "really interesting" food (and "fascinating" Iberian wines); for critics, though, "it just doesn't zing". / www.cigala.co.uk; 10.45 pm, Sun 9.45 pm.

The Cinnamon Club SW1 £60 ❷❸❷
Old Westminster Library, Great Smith St 7222 2555 2–4C
"Wonderfully delicate" Indian cuisine has won renown for this former library – a much-needed "haven" of gastronomy in under-served Westminster; it's a "lovely" and "impressive" place, albeit in a style that's fairly "businessy". / www.cinnamonclub.com; 10.45 pm; closed Sun; no trainers; set dinner & weekday L £39 (FP).

Cinnamon Kitchen EC2 NEW
9 Devonshire Sq no tel 9–2D
First offshoot of the celebrated Cinnamon Club – this large new Indian restaurant is scheduled to open in late-2008, in the Devonshire Square development, near Liverpool Street. / www.cinnamonkitchen.co.uk.

Cipriani W1 £75 ⑤⑤④
25 Davies Street 7399 0500 3–2B
*"WAGs", "B-listers", "obnoxious Russians and their nieces",
"surgery-addicted women", "extreme Euros"… – the cavalcade
of "people-watching" at this otherwise "astonishingly bad" and
"wildly overpriced" Mayfair Venetian is "impossible to beat".*
/ www.cipriani.com; 11.45 pm; set weekday L £51 (FP).

City Café
City Inn Westminster SW1 £41 ❸❷④
30 John Islip St 7932 4600 2–4C
*It look's "a bit sterile", but this "efficient" and "comfortable"
Westminster dining room is something of a "secret bargain",
offering "surprisingly good food for an hotel, including some
imaginative dishes".* / www.citycafe.co.uk; 11 pm; set dinner £29 (FP).

City Miyama EC4 £48 ④④⑤
17 Godliman St 7489 1937 9–3B
*A stalwart City Japanese, where the "lively" sushi counter provides
some respite from an ambience that can otherwise be "deathly" –
most reporters confirm its "top-end" reputation for food, but it has
also sometimes seemed rather "tired" of late.* / www.miyama.co.uk;
9.30 pm; closed Sat D & Sun.

The Clarence SW12 £28 ❸④❸
90-92 Balham High Rd 8772 1155 10–2C
*"A good buzzing local", down Balham way, with "well-cooked" fare
and "friendly" service.* / www.capitalpubscompany.com; Midnight, Fri & Sat
1 am; no Amex.

Clarke's W8 £63 ❷❷❸
124 Kensington Church St 7221 9225 6–2B
*"Assured" cooking with "a high-quality, low-key simplicity" has long
been the "ethos" of Sally Clarke's Californian-inspired HQ,
near Notting Hill Gate; of late, however, it has "slipped a little".*
/ www.sallyclarke.com; 10 pm; closed Sun; booking: max 14.

The Clerkenwell Dining Room EC1 £48 ❸❸④
69-73 St John St 7253 9000 9–1B
*Fans of this "conventional" Farringdon spot say it's "under-rated",
and serves "tremendous" food; even supporters may concede,
though, that it's "possibly rather overpriced".* / www.theclerkenwell.com;
11 pm; closed Sat L & Sun.

Clifton E1 £22 ❷❷❸
1 Whitechapel Rd 7377 5533 9–2D
*"One of the best Brick Lane Indians" "a cut above in terms
of both food and atmosphere".* / www.cliftonrestaurant.com; midnight,
Sat & Sun 1am.

The Clissold Arms N2 NEW £38 ❸❸④
115 Fortis Grn 8444 4224 1–1C
*"The décor's a bit run-of-the-mill", but this newly-refurbished boozer
– linked with the glory days of The Kinks – is "a good all-round
gastropub" that's all the more welcome in the thin area around
Muswell Hill.* / 10 pm, Sun 9 pm; no Amex.

Clos Maggiore WC2 £55 ❷⓿⓿
33 King St   7379 9696   4–3C
"A perfect romantic haven in the midst of tourist-trap Covent
Garden"; it's the "lovely" conservatory and "phenomenal" wine
list ("like 'War & Peace'") which are the special attractions, but the
food can be "excellent" too. / www.closmaggiore.com; 10.45 pm,
Sat 11.15 pm, Sun 10 pm; closed Sat L & Sun L; set weekday L £39 (FP).

Club Gascon EC1 £60 ❷❷❸
57 West Smithfield   7796 0600   9–2B
"Paradise for foie gras lovers" – this "casual" foodie hot spot,
by Smithfield Market, is the place for a "hugely indulgent" meal
of "sumptuous and heart-stoppingly rich Gascon dishes", served
tapas-style; there's "a fascinating wine list from SW France" too.
/ www.clubgascon.com; 10 pm, Fri & Sat 10.30 pm; closed Sat L & Sun.

Club Mangia
The Punch Tavern EC4 £25 ❸❷❷
99 Fleet St   7353 6658   9–2A
A "comprehensive" self-service buffet makes this "atmospheric"
City pub a surprisingly well-rated lunch-stop (and breakfasts and
"evening platters" also earn praise). / www.punchtavern.com; 11.30 pm,
Thu & Fri midnight; closed Sat D & Sun.

Coach & Horses EC1 £39 ❸❷④
26-28 Ray St   7278 8990   9–1A
"In what seems like an unpromising location", in Farringdon,
this newly-extended gastropub wins praise for its "thoughtful" food
and "decent" service; as ever, though, the occasional reporter finds
it "over-rated". / www.thecoachandhorses.com; 11 pm; closed
Sat L & Sun D.

Cochonnet W9 £27 ❸❸❸
1 Lauderdale Pde   7289 0393   1–2B
"A lovely local bar and pizzeria", in Maida Vale, that's always
"very busy"; it has above-average wines too. / www.cochonnet.co.uk;
10.30, pizza until close at midnight.

Cock Tavern EC1 £22 ❸❷④
Smithfield Mkt   7248 2918   9–2A
From the early hours, "simply the best full English there is"
is served, with a pint, at this subterranean pub in the very heart
of Smithfield meat market. / 5 pm; closed Sat & Sun.

Cocoon W1 £52 ❸④❷
65 Regent St   7494 7600   3–3D
It may "look like a film set, with a crowd that behaves as if they're
film stars", but this sleekly-designed venue, near Piccadilly Circus,
does a fair job of offering "style AND substance" – not just with
"expert" cocktails, but with "good" oriental food too; prices,
though, are undeniably "sky high". / www.cocoon-restaurants.com; 1 am,
Sat 3 am; closed Sat L & Sun.

The Collection SW3 £60 ⑤⑤⑤
264 Brompton Rd   7225 1212   5–2C
"Everyone loves that tunnel entrance", but – thanks to its "awful
food and service" – this "Eurotrashy" Brompton Cross scene has
largely fallen off the map as anything other than a bar.
/ www.the-collection.co.uk; midnight; D only, closed Sun.

La Collina NW1   £35   ❸④④
17 Princess Rd   7483 0192   8–3B
*"Non-standard" Piedmontese dishes and an "unusual Italian wine
list" help make this Primrose Hill spot "a good-value option in a
pricey area". / 11 pm; closed weekday L.*

Le Colombier SW3   £47   ❸⓿❷
145 Dovehouse St   7351 1155   5–2C
*Thanks to its "no-nonsense" Gallic fare, this "civilised" bistro,
by Chelsea Square, is "always packed" – or perhaps it has more
to do with the "helpful and professional" service, and the quiet and
notably "attractive" terrace. / www.lecolombier-sw3.co.uk; 10.30 pm,
Sun 10 pm; set weekday L £35 (FP).*

Commander W2 NEW
47 Hereford Rd   7229 1503   6–1B
*Backed by some folk from Vancouver, this ambitious new deli-
restaurant (plus mini-conference centre) is set to open on an ever
more trendy Bayswater street, in late-2008.
/ www.commanderrooms.co.uk.*

Como Lario SW1   £42   ④❷❷
18-22 Holbein Pl   7730 2954   5–2D
*A "cramped", "old-school" and "reliable" Italian, hidden-away near
Sloane Square; it's "always busy". / www.comolario.uk.com; 11.30 pm;
closed Sun.*

Comptoir Gascon EC1   £46   ⓿❸❷
63 Charterhouse St   7608 0851   9–1A
*Discover "France on your doorstep", at this "uncannily good" spin-
off from Club Gascon – with its "hearty" fare and "unstarchy"
setting, it "mixes bistro simplicity with the refinement of its parent".
/ www.comptoirgascon.com; 10 pm, Thu & Fri 11 pm; closed Mon & Sun.*

The Contented Vine SW1   £42   ④❸④
17 Sussex St   7834 0044   5–3D
*A "relaxed" bistro, in the heart of Pimlico, with a "lovely terrace"
in summer; its "comfort food" is "not memorable", but comes
at "bargain prices". / www.contentedvine.com; 10.30 pm.*

Il Convivio SW1   £60   ❸❸❸
143 Ebury St   7730 4099   2–4A
*With its "inventive" cooking and "friendly" staff, this "dependable
high-level Italian", in Belgravia, strikes many reporters
as "an under-rated gem"; perhaps that's because the style of the
place – though "beautiful" to some – seems a little passé to others.
/ www.etruscarestaurants.com; 10.45 pm; closed Sun; set weekday L £36 (FP).*

Coopers Arms SW3   £40   ❸④❷
87 Flood St   7376 3120   5–3C
*A charming Chelsea back street boozer; it's no longer the culinary
hot spot it once was, but still "highly recommended for a Sunday
roast". / www.youngs.co.uk; 10 pm, Sun 9 pm.*

Coq d'Argent EC2 £58 ④④❸
I Poultry 7395 5000 9–2C
"The roof garden is fantastic on a summer evening", at the D&D group's 6th-floor bar/restaurant, by Bank (and it enjoys some "stunning" views too); it's a venue that "works well for business", despite "boring" food and sometimes "disorganised" service.
/ www.coqdargent.co.uk; 10 pm; closed Sat L & Sun D; set always available £45 (FP).

Cork & Bottle WC2 £35 ④④❶
44-46 Cranbourn St 7734 7807 4–3B
A supremely "cosy" and "timeless" basement "oasis", just off "seedy Leicester Square"; the food "doesn't seemed to have changed a jot since the '70s" – its main virtue is to "provide an excuse" to order from the "phenomenal wine list".
/ www.corkandbottle.net; 11.30 pm; no booking after 6.30 pm.

Costa's Fish Restaurant W8 £23 ❷❷❸
18 Hillgate St 7727 4310 6–2B
"As friendly as ever" – this veteran, Greek-run chippy near Notting Hill Gate wins a consistent thumbs-up from its small local fan club.
/ 10 pm; closed Mon & Sun; no credit cards.

Costa's Grill W8 £23 ④❸④
12-14 Hillgate St 7229 3794 6–2B
"Don't expect culinary fireworks", if you visit this "refreshingly unreconstructed" veteran Greek taverna; in the trendy environs of Notting Hill Gate, its "basic dishes with prices to match" come as something of a "relief". / www.costasgrill.com; 10.30 pm; closed Sun (closed 3 weeks in Aug).

Côte £35 ④❸④
124-126 Wardour St, W1 7287 9280 3–2D **NEW**
8 High St, SW19 8947 7100 10–2B **NEW**
24 Hill St, TW9 8948 5971 1–4A
Fans hail the "good basic French bistro fare" on offer at this Wimbledon chain-prototype (which now has Soho and Richmond offshoots); an "excellent-value set lunch" is of particular note.
/ www.cote-restaurants.co.uk.

Cottons £38 ④❸❷
55 Chalk Farm Rd, NW1 7485 8388 8–2B
70 Exmouth Mkt, EC1 7833 3332 9–1A
"Terrific cocktails" fuel the atmosphere at this fun duo of Caribbean Rhum Shacks, where "curried goat" is a highlight of the "colourful" fodder; "excellent in a group".
/ www.cottons-restaurant.co.uk; EC1 10.30 pm, Fri-Sat 11 pm; NW1 Mon-Fri L; EC1 Sat D; EC1 no Amex; EC1 no shorts, no trainers.

The Cow W2 £49 ❸④❸
89 Westbourne Park Rd 7221 0021 6–1B
Tom Conran's "characterful" Irish boozer on the Bayswater/Notting Hill border has an "always-crowded" downstairs bar, and a "cosy", upstairs dining room; the former is known for its "great seafood and Guinness" (though it's been more "average" of late) – the latter serves "a more upscale menu". / www.thecowlondon.co.uk; 10.30 pm; D only, Sun open L & D; no Amex.

Crazy Bear W1 £55 ❷❷❶
26-28 Whitfield St 7631 0088 2–1C
"Top-notch oriental-fusion food" and a "cosy" and "opulent" setting make for an ultra-"romantic" experience at this "fun and fashionable" oriental bar/restaurant, hidden-away in Fitzrovia; (in their different ways, the "manic" bar and "mirrored loos" are "great" too). / www.crazybeargroup.co.uk; 10.30 pm; closed Sat L & Sun; no shorts.

Crazy Homies W2 £35 ❷⑤❷
127 Westbourne Park Rd 7727 6771 6–1B
Tom Conran's "buzzy Mexican local", where "scatty" staff serve up "truly authentic food", and "lethal margaritas"; it's "always great fun". / www.crazyhomieslondon.co.uk; 10.30 pm; closed weekday L; no Amex.

Criterion Grill W1 £55 ④④❷
224 Piccadilly 7930 0488 3–3D
MPW's "remarkable" neo-Byzantine chamber, on Piccadilly Circus, seems to rely on its "glittering" looks to get by – "average" food and service can leave the overall experience seeming "soulless" and "overpriced". / www.whitestarline.org.uk; 11.30 pm; set pre theatre £33 (FP).

The Crown & Sceptre W12 £33 ❸❸❷
57 Melina Rd 8746 0060 7–1B
It may offer "excellent bistro fare", but "it's the atmosphere you really go for", say fans of this "real" pub in a Shepherd's Bush backstreet. / www.fullers.co.uk; 9.45 pm, Sun 9 pm.

Cruse 9 N1 NEW £37 ④④④
62-63 Halliford St 7354 8099 8–2D
A striking – but perhaps unatmospheric – new-build, at the north end of Islington; it's a brave venture, in contemporary brasserie style, but we'd have to agree with the the sole early-days reporter, who found standards "somewhat mixed". / www.cruse9.com; 11.30 pm.

Crussh £12 ❸❷④
1 Curzon St, W1 7629 2554 3–3B
BBC Media Village, Wood Ln, W12 8746 7916 6–2A
27 Kensington High St, W8 7376 9786 5–1A
One Canada Sq, E14 7513 0076 11–1C
Unit 21 Jubilee Pl, E14 7519 6427 11–1C
48 Cornhill, EC3 7626 2175 9–2C
6 Farringdon St, EC4 7489 5916 9–2A
"The freshest and healthiest of the chains"; it serves a "splendid array of quick bites" (and, of course, "fab" smoothies and juices). / www.crussh.com; 4.30 pm - 7 pm; some branches closed all or part of weekend; no credit cards.

Cumberland Arms W14 £35 ❸❷④
29 North End Rd 7371 6806 7–2D
This "decent" gastropub is all the more welcome in the thin area near Olympia; its menu is "ever-changing" and "reliable", and there are "good ales on tap" too. / www.thecumberlandarmspub.co.uk; 10.30 pm, Sun 10 pm.

Curve
London Marriott W' India Quay E14 £52 ❸❸⑤
52 Hertsmere Rd 7517 2808 11–1C
Shame about the "soulless" hotel-ambience; the fish, fresh from nearby Billingsgate, is often "great" at this "surprising" Canary Wharf "oasis". / www.marriothotel.co.uk; 10.30 pm, Sun 10 pm.

Cyprus Mangal SW1   £25   ❷❸⑤
45 Warwick Way   7828 5940   2–4B
An "excellent, no-frills" kebab house, with "prompt and friendly"
service, in the heart of Pimlico. / Sun-Thu midnight, Fri & Sat 1 am;
no Amex.

The Czechoslovak Restaurant NW6   £24   ④④④
74 West End Ln   7372 1193   1–1B
"It's a bit like eating in your auntie's front room", at this "old-
fashioned" Central European "throw-back", in a West Hampstead
émigrés' club; with its "warm and hearty" fodder and "brilliant
lagers", though, it's certainly "different".
/ www.czechoslovak-restaurant.co.uk; 10 pm; closed Mon, Tue-Fri D only,
Sat & Sun open L & D; no credit cards.

D Sum 2 EC4 NEW   £40   ❸❸④
14 Paternoster Row   7248 2288   9–2B
"A good choice of dim sum" helps this shiny newcomer near
St Paul's live up to its name; initial reports are few, but for
"business lunches or an after-work dinner", the place already has
its fans. / www.dsum2.com; 11 pm; closed Sat & Sun L.

Da Mario SW7   £36   ④❸❸
15 Gloucester Rd   7584 9078   5–1B
A "surprise find" in the thin area near the Albert Hall,
this "friendly", family-run Italian serves a "typical" menu, which
includes "great pizza and pasta"; try to stay out of the "soulless"
basement. / www.damario.co.uk; 11.30 pm.

Da Scalzo SW1 NEW
2 Ecclestone Pl   no tel   2–4B
A new venture from Enzo Scalzo, one-time principal shareholder
of Pâtisserie Valerie; comprising an art gallery, café and champagne
bar, it will open on the former Goya (RIP) site by Victoria Coach
Station in late-2008.

Dalchini SW19   £31   ❷❷❷
147 Arthur Rd   8947 5966   10–2B
An "interesting" menu – "Indian with a Chinese twist" –
and "friendly" service make this Wimbledon Park fixture
a "good bet"; "sit upstairs if you can". / www.dalchini.co.uk; 10.30 pm,
Fri & Sat 11 pm; no Amex.

Dans le Noir EC1   £56   ⑤❸④
29 Clerkenwell Grn   7253 1100   9–1A
You eat in "pitch black" (and are served by blind staff), at this
bizarre Clerkenwell two-year-old; your resulting "heightened
senses", may only emphasise how "poor" the food is, but some
reporters still feel "it's worth a trip for the experience alone".
/ www.danslenoir.com; 9.30 pm; D only.

Daphne NW1   £31   ❸❷❷
83 Bayham St   7267 7322   8–3C
A "homely" and "genuine" Camden Town taverna of long standing,
which still offers "reasonably-priced" Greek food and "a good night
out"; "nice roof terrace, too". / 11.30 pm; closed Sun; no Amex;
set weekday L £20 (FP).

Daphne's SW3 £48 ❷❷❷
112 Draycott Ave 7589 4257 5–2C
"Cosy", "friendly" and "atmospheric", this Knightsbridge Italian
is much better for being less trendy than it once was – you get
"surprisingly good food nowadays… and you can generally get
a table". / www.daphnes-restaurant.co.uk; 11.30 pm, Sun 10.30 pm; booking:
max 12; set weekday L £31 (FP).

Daquise SW7 £29 ❹❹❸
20 Thurloe St 7589 6117 5–2C
"More an institution than a restaurant" – this "unique", Polish
survivor, by South Kensington tube, dishes up "warming" and
"honest" fare in "a setting that looks like it was last decorated
in the '50s". / 11 pm; no Amex.

The Dartmouth Arms SE23 £35 ❸❸❸
7 Dartmouth Rd 8488 3117 1–4D
This "really good" converted boozer "brings the gastropub
experience to Forest Hill", and is enthusiastically acclaimed by the
locals. / www.thedartmoutharms.com; 10.30 pm, Sun 9 pm.

Daylesford Organics SW1 £40 ❹❷❶
44B Pimlico Rd 7881 8060 5–2D
"Lady Bamford knows her design", and reporters 'dig' the
"beautifully-finished, white marble and glass" look of her Pimlico
deli-café; it's at its best for breakfast or a cake – otherwise prices
can seem "unjustified"; a Notting Hill sibling is expected to open
in late-2008. / www.daylesfordorganic.com; 8 pm, Sun 5 pm.

De Cecco SW6 £36 ❸❸❹
189 New King's Rd 7736 1145 10–1B
Its fame no longer stretches beyond the borders of Parson's Green
(as once it did), but this "cheerful" institution still wins acclaim
as an "excellent neighbourhood Italian". / www.dececcorestaurant.com;
11 pm; closed Sun D.

Defune W1 £68 ❶❷⑤
34 George St 7935 8311 3–1A
"Truly exquisite" food (especially sushi) and "very gracious" service
help offset the "completely soulless" ambience of this Marylebone
stalwart; "take your trust fund", though – even fans say it's
"way overpriced". / 11 pm.

Dehesa W1 NEW £43 ❷❸❶
25 Ganton St 7494 4170 3–2C
It's not just the "lovely" interior which makes this "cool" spin-off
from Salt Yard a "fantastic addition" to Soho – its "affordable" and
"very enjoyable" Italian/Spanish tapas, and "delicious" wines too,
have transplanted very well. / www.dehesa.co.uk; 11 pm; closed Sun D;
no booking.

Del'Aziz SW6 £30 ❸❸❷
24-32 Vanston Pl 7386 0086 5–4A
"Feast your eyes on the mouthwatering cakes and pastries", at this
"fun", "bazaar"-like Middle Eastern deli/café, off Fulham Broadway
– an "unbeatable" spot "for a great breakfast-with-the-paper,
at the big wooden tables"; there's also an adjoining restaurant
(and deli spin-offs in Swiss Cottage and Bankside).
/ www.delaziz.co.uk; 10.30 pm.

Delfina Studio Café SE1 £45 ❷❶❸
50 Bermondsey St 7357 0244 9–4D
*An airy Bermondsey "art gallery-cum-restaurant", where it's
"a pleasure to eat", and where the "well-spaced" tables are well
suited to business-lunching; the "excellent" food has "a Kiwi slant",
and is matched by an "imaginative" and "good-value" wine list.*
/ www.thedelfina.org.uk; 10 pm; L only, except Fri when open L&D, closed
Sat & Sun.

Delfino W1 £36 ❷❸④
121 Mount St 7499 1256 3–3B
*A "tightly-packed" pizzeria that "always bustling", and "for a
reason" – "super, thin-crust pizza" that's "cheap, by Mayfair
standards".* / www.finos.co.uk; 11 pm; closed Sat L & Sun.

La Delizia Limbara SW3 £26 ❸④④
63-65 Chelsea Manor St 7376 4111 5–3C
*"A good local pizza place", in Chelsea (where such places are few
and far between); it offers a "daily-changing selection of pastas"
too.* / 11 pm; no Amex.

The Depot SW14 £42 ④④❷
Tideway Yd, Mortlake High St 8878 9462 10–1A
*"Brilliant river-views" ("if you sit by the window") buoy the
"pleasurable" ambience of this local favourite, near Barnes Bridge;
the rest of the package is "dependable but unexciting".*
/ www.depotbrasserie.co.uk; 11 pm, Sun 10.30 pm; set weekday L £27 (FP).

Le Deuxième WC2 £48 ④❸④
65a Long Acre 7379 0033 4–2D
*This "stark" Gallic restaurant, near the Royal Opera House,
is "justifiably popular" as a "quick and convenient" choice,
not least for business, and for the "reasonably-priced" pre-show
menu; this year, however, its ratings dipped a bit.*
/ www.ledeuxieme.com; midnight, Sun 11 pm; set always available £27 (FP).

Devonshire House W4 £42 ④⑤⑤
126 Devonshire Rd 7592 7962 7–2A
*"A generally poor addition to the Ramsay stable"; "amateurish"
and "unfriendly" service does nothing to soften the "sterile"
ambience of this Chiswick gastropub; the grub is "underwhelming"
too.* / www.gordonramsay.com/thedevonshire/; 11 pm, Sun 10.30 pm;
no Amex.

Devonshire Terrace EC2 NEW £42 ④❸④
Devonshire Sq 7256 3233 9–2D
*Near Liverpool Street, a large new bar/brasserie with many
al fresco (but not especially charmingly-situated) tables; we suspect
it will make a popular City lunch/after-work rendezvous, even if the
food on our early-days visit was unexciting.* / Rated on Editors' visit;
www.devonshireterrace.co.uk/; 11 pm; closed Sat & Sun.

Dexters £36 ④④❸
20 Bellevue Rd, SW17 8767 1858 10–2C
36-38 Abbeville Rd, SW4 8772 6646 10–2D NEW
*"Delicious" burgers are the highlight of the "predictable" scoff
at this low-key family chain; the Wandsworth branch enjoys "great
views across the common".*

dim T £28 ④④❸
32 Charlotte St, W1 7637 1122 2–1C
1a Hampstead Ln, N6 8340 8800 8–1B
3 Heath St, NW3 7435 0024 8–2A
Tooley St, SE1 7403 7000 9–4C
A "stylish"-looking oriental chain, where the pan-Asian dishes – majoring in dim sum – "may not be especially authentic, but they are tasty and cheap". / www.dimt.co.uk; 11 pm, NW3 Sat 11.30 pm; NW3 no booking 7.30 pm - 9.30 pm.

Diner £28 ④⑤❷
18 Ganton St, W1 7287 8962 3–2C
2 Jamestown Rd, NW1 7485 5223 8–3B **NEW**
128 Curtain Rd, EC2 7729 4452 9–1D
"The real American deal, in W1"; well, nearly – this Carnaby Street diner (also in Shoreditch and Camden Town) does offer "good burgers", "top milkshakes" and "great 'Happy Days'-style décor", but its "slow" service wouldn't pass muster Stateside. / www.thedinershoreditch.com; W1 12.30 am, Sun midnight - EC2 midnight, Sun & Mon 10.30 pm.

Dinings W1 £30 ❶❷❷
22 Harcourt St 7723 0666 8–4A
"Incredible"; make sure you "book ahead", if you want to sample this "delightful" Japanese, where the "amazing" sushi somehow transcends the location in a "weird" Marylebone "bunker". / 10.30 pm; closed Sat L & Sun.

Dish Dash SW12 £32 ④④❸
11-13 Bedford Hill 8673 5555 10–2C
A Balham Persian that's "nearly always full", despite a rather mixed performance of late; its Chelsea offshoot closed in the spring of 2008. / www.dish-dash.com; midnight.

Diwana Bhel-Poori House NW1 £21 ④⑤⑤
121-123 Drummond St 7387 5556 8–4C
In Euston's Little India, a "stalwart", '60s vegetarian canteen with a big name for its "great lunchtime buffet"; taking the long view, it's been "going downhill" for years, but no-corkage BYO is still a consolation. / 10.45 pm; need 10+ to book.

$ EC1 £37 ④⑤❸
2 Exmouth Mkt 7278 0077 9–1A
"Superb cocktails" and a "comfy, dark atmosphere" are the selling points of this "fun" Clerkenwell pub-conversion; apart from "good burgers", however, the food's "nothing special", and service is sometimes "non-existent". / www.dollargrills.com; 11 pm, Fri & Sat 11.30 pm, Sun 10pm.

The Don EC4 £47 ❷❶❷
20 St Swithin's Ln 7626 2606 9–3C
Near Bank, an "oasis of quality", widely tipped as "the best place for business in the City", thanks to its "relaxed" style, "well-executed" food, "superb" wine, and "attentive" staff; the cellar bistro is "more atmospheric" than the (recently-extended) upstairs. / www.thedonrestaurant.com; 10 pm; closed Sat & Sun; no trainers.

don Fernando's TW9 £33 ❸❷❷
27f The Quadrant   8948 6447   1–4A
*A big and "jolly" tapas bar, by Richmond Station, that "deservedly
has a great local reputation" for dishing up "good" dishes, "reliably
and fast". / www.donfernado.co.uk; 11 pm; no Amex; no booking.*

Don Pepe NW8 £35 ❸❸❷
99 Frampton St   7262 3834   8–4A
*London's oldest tapas bar, in an "out-of-the-way" spot, near Lord's
– "nothing beats this place if you want a really authentic Spanish
experience", and at reasonable prices too. / 11.30 pm; closed Sun.*

Donna Margherita SW11 £40 ❶❸❷
183 Lavender Hill   7288 2660   10–2C
*"An authentic neighourhood Italian for the Lavender Hill mob" –
this "casual" Neapolitan wins particular praise for its "fantastic
pizza and pasta". / www.donna-margherita.com; 11 pm, Sat & Sun
10.30 pm.*

Donzoko W1 £34 ❷④④
15 Kingly St   7734 1974   3–2C
*"Everything is in Japanese", at this "most authentic" Soho 'izakaya';
it is consistently praised for its "fantastic" and "unpretentious"
dishes, not least sushi that's "so fresh and cheap". / 10.15 pm; closed
Sat L & Sun.*

Dorchester Grill
Dorchester Hotel W1 £80 ④④⑤
53 Park Ln   7629 8888   3–3A
*"How can they get it so wrong?"; since a "ridiculous",
"mock Scottish" revamp a couple of years ago, this once-splendid
Mayfair chamber has gone from bad to worse – service
is lacklustre, and its "forgettable" food comes at "blistering" prices.
/ www.thedorchester.com; 11 pm, Sun 10 pm; no trainers; set weekday L
£46 (FP).*

Dover Street Restaurant & Bar W1 £47 ⑤④④
8-10 Dover St   7491 7509   3–3C
*At its best, this old Mayfair dive – one of the few in town to offer
"a mix of food, dancing and live music" – offers "a great night out",
but at its worst, the fare can be "frankly awful"; (an "excellent-
value lunch" has long been a top tip, but its future was uncertain
as this guide went to press). / www.doverstreet.co.uk; 2 am; closed
Sat L & Sun; no trainers.*

Dragon Castle SE17 £30 ❸❷❸
114 Walworth Rd   7277 3388   1–3C
*After a blazing start, this "cavernous" oriental in "drab" Elephant
& Castle has put in a more mixed performance this year – fans still
say it's "the best Chinese ever" (with "very good dim sum"),
but others only put it just "one notch up from average".
/ www.dragoncastle.eu; 11 pm, Fri 11.30 pm, Sun 10.30 pm.*

The Drapers Arms N1 £40 ❸❷❷
44 Barnsbury St   7619 0348   8–3D
*"A splendid pub in leafy Barnsbury", with "genuine" staff,
"a beautiful garden" and a "tranquil" dining room upstairs;
the cooking is "consistently good" too. / www.thedrapersarms.co.uk;
10 pm, Sun 9.30 pm; booking: max 8.*

Drones SW1
1 Pont St   7235 9555   5–1D
This once-celebrated Belgravia restaurant was sold in mid-2008, and closed; it was not possible, as this guide was going to press, to ascertain future plans.

The Drunken Monkey E1   £27   ❸❸❷
222 Shoreditch High St   7392 9606   9–1D
"Consistently good" dim sum makes this "funky" Shoreditch boozer a regular hit with reporters – it's such a "buzzy" place, though, that you "often can't hear yourself think".
/ www.thedrunkenmonkey.co.uk; 11.45 pm; closed Sat L.

The Duke of Cambridge N1   £42   ④④❸
30 St Peter's St   7359 3066   1–2C
This Islington gastropub is usually "packed" with a "trendy" crowd, drawn by its "warm" and "comfy" vibe, and its "all-organic" policy; the food's "unremarkable at the price", though, and service is really "not great". / www.sloeberry.co.uk; 10.30 pm, Sun 10 pm; no Amex.

Duke Of Sussex W4 NEW   £35   ❸④④
75 South Pde   8742 8801   7–1A
Fans hail a "wonderful restoration" of this Chiswick boozer, applauding its "wholesome", "Spanish-influenced" food, "knowledgeable" staff and "glorious back garden"; it doesn't wow everyone, though – the setting can seem "barn-like", and service "slow" or "over-familiar". / Midnight, Sun 11 pm; closed Mon L; no Amex.

Duke on the Green SW6   £44   ❸❸❸
235 New King's Rd   7736 2777   10–1B
A "stylish", year-old revamp of a big old boozer overlooking Parson's Green, liked by the locals for its "great atmosphere and pub food". / www.dukeonthegreen.co.uk; midnight, Sun 11.30 pm.

The Duke's Head SW15   £33   ❸❸❶
8 Lower Richmond Rd   8788 2552   10–1B
A "lovely airy dining room" with "amazing river views" is the star turn at this "friendly" (and "child-friendly") Putney landmark, which serves "really good, standard pub fare". / www.dukesheadputney.co.uk; 10.30 pm.

Durbar W2   £25   ❸④④
24 Hereford Rd   7727 1947   6–1B
A "sweet" and "old-fashioned" Bayswater curry house of 50 years' standing; sceptics say it's "pretty average", but most reporters give the thumbs-up to its menu of "tasty classics". / www.durbartandoori.co.uk; 11.30 pm; closed Fri.

E&O W11   £43   ❷❷❶
14 Blenheim Cr   7229 5454   6–1A
After all these years, Will Ricker's "frenetically buzzing" Notting Hill hang-out is "still happening" – its staff put "bags of energy and enthusiasm" into serving up "innovative" Pan-Asian fusion bites that are "bursting with flavour". / www.rickerrestaurants.com; 11 pm, Sun 10.30 pm; booking: max 6.

The Eagle EC1 £25 ❸④❷
159 Farringdon Rd 7837 1353 9–1A
This "funky" gastropub – London's first, 1992 – is, for its many devoted fans, "still the best"; "complacent" service has tested their loyalty over the years, though, and in truth the "gutsy" fare no longer stands out. / 10.30 pm; closed Sun D; no Amex; no booking.

Eagle Bar Diner W1 £31 ❷④❷
3-5 Rathbone Pl 7637 1418 4–1A
"Delicious" burgers, "great" cocktails and shakes that "ROCK" keep the "fun" vibe grooving along at this "clubby" diner, just north of Oxford Street; "it can be loud later on". / www.eaglebardiner.com; Mon-Wed 11 pm, Thu-Sat 1 am; closed Sun D; no Amex; need 6+ to book.

Ealing Park Tavern W5 £38
222 South Ealing Rd 8758 1879 1–3A
In "pretty barren" South Ealing, this "unpretentious" and "always-buzzing" gastroboozer has long stood out; it changed hands this year, however, so we've left it unrated. / www.ealingparktavern.com; 10 pm, Sun 9 pm; closed Mon L; booking: max 10.

Earl Spencer SW18 £36 ❷❸❷
260-262 Merton Rd 8870 9244 10–2B
"A beacon in a culinary desert"; this large, "lively" and "convivial" Southfields fixture is "just how a gastropub should be", and it offers "big portions" of "the best comfort food" – no wonder it's "always hard to get a table". / www.theearlspencer.co.uk; 10 pm, Sun 9.30 pm; no booking.

The East Hill SW18 £36 ❸❸❷
21 Alma Rd 8874 1833 10–2B
An "excellent" Wandsworth pub, praised for its "fun" and "buzzy" atmosphere, and its "honest fare"; no surprise that it "gets packed" ("especially during big sporting events"). / www.geronimo-inns.co.uk; Mon-Wed 10 pm, Thu-Sat 10.30 pm, Sun 8.30 pm.

The Easton WC1 £30 ❸❸❷
22 Easton St 7278 7608 9–1A
A "spacious and chilled" Aussie-influenced boozer, near Exmouth Market, that's "always a winner" – "the fare is simple, but always comes with a twist that makes it interesting". / 10 pm; closed Sat L; no Amex.

Eastway
Andaz Hotel EC2 NEW £46 ⑤⑤④
40 Liverpool St 7618 7400 9–2D
"Not much changed from when it was called Terminus" – this "noisy" brasserie, adjacent to Liverpool Street, remains "fairly standard" (except for its "enjoyable breakfast"). / www.andaz.com; 11 pm, Sat & Sun 10 pm; closed Sat L & Sun L.

Eat £11 ④④④
Branches throughout London
"Clever additions to the menu" – including "winning soups" and "delicious pies" – help win praise for this sarnies-'n'-more chain; its fans find it "a better alternative to Pret", but its overall ratings continue to trail the market leader. / www.eatcafe.co.uk; 4pm-8pm; most City branches closed all or part of weekend; no credit cards; no booking.

Eat & Two Veg £33 ④④④
50 Marylebone High St, W1   7258 8595   2–1A
291-293 Muswell Hl Broadway, N10   8883 4503   1–1C **NEW**
Most reports talk up the "good food" at "fair prices" offered by this "diner-like" Marylebone veggie (which has a new sibling in Muswell Hill) – for critics, though, it's still "not very inspiring". / www.eatandtwoveg.com.

The Ebury SW1 £45 ④⑤④
11 Pimlico Rd   7730 6784   5–2D
Potentially "a really nice venue", this large and "noisy" Pimlico bar/restaurant often just "comes over as rather self-satisfied" nowadays – hazards include "hit-and-miss" food and "unbelievably slow" service. / www.theebury.co.uk; 10.30 pm, Sun 10 pm.

Ebury Wine Bar SW1 £41 ④❸❸
139 Ebury St   7730 5447   2–4A
"Cosy" and "friendly" (if rather "dated") – this Belgravia veteran is never going to set the world on fire, but its bistro fare seemed more "reliable" again this year. / www.eburywinebar.co.uk; 10.15 pm; closed Sun L.

Eco £29 ❸④❸
144 Chiswick High Rd, W4   8747 4822   7–2A **NEW**
162 Clapham High St, SW4   7978 1108   10–2D
"Brilliant pizza", "so cheap", has made this Clapham fixture an institution (if a "deafeningly noisy" one); its new offshoot – hip, by Chiswick standards – is already "the best pizzeria in the area" (but why the "extraordinarily uncomfortable bench seating"?). / www.ecorestaurants.com; SW4 11 pm.

Ed's Easy Diner £23 ❸❷❷
12 Moor St, W1   7434 4439   4–2A
Trocadero, 19 Rupert St, W1   7287 1951   3–3D
15 Gt Newport St, WC2   7836 0271   4–3B
"If you're looking for '50s US nostalgia", nip in to one of these "retro" diners, which offer "a reliable burger", "excellent cheesy fries" and "a milkshake to die for". / www.edseasydiner.co.uk; Rupert St 10 pm, Fri & Sat midnight; Moor St 11.30 pm, Fri & Sat midnight; no Amex; no booking at weekends.

Edera W11 £49 ❸❸④
148 Holland Park Ave   7221 6090   6–2A
The Italian cooking is "solid" and "authentic" – but "expensive for what it is" – at this "neighbourhood" venture, in Holland Park. / 11 pm.

Edokko WC1 £42 ❶❶❸
50 Red Lion St   7242 3490   2–1D
Upstairs (the better option), it's "shoes off, and cross-legged at low tables", at this "authentically rickety" Japanese, off Holborn; it serves "some of the best sushi in town", with "impeccable style and grace", and at "good prices" too – particularly the "bargain set lunch". / 10 pm; closed Sat L & Sun; no Amex.

Efes £30 ❸❷④
1) 80 Gt Titchfield St, W1   7636 1953   2–1B
2) 175-177 Gt Portland St, W1   7436 0600   2–1B
Not much feedback nowadays on these large, faded, "cheap and cheerful" Turkish stalwarts, in Marylebone; for an inexpensive get-together, they're OK – it helps if you "love meat". / Gt Titchfield St 11.30 pm, Gt Portland St 1 am, Fri & Sat 3 am; Gt Titchfield St closed Sun.

Eight Over Eight SW3 £45 ❶❷❷
392 King's Rd   7349 9934   5–3B
It may be a "chic" Chelsea "scene", but Will Ricker's "buzzy" hang-out doesn't just trade on its "people-watching" possibilities – service is "friendly", and the fusion fare is "beautiful" and "delicious". / www.rickerrestaurants.com; 11 pm, Sun 10.30 pm; closed Sun L.

Ekachai £27 ❷④④
Southside Shopping Cntr, SW18   8871 3888   10–2B
9-10 The Arcade, Liverpool St, EC2   7626 1155   9–2D
For a "super-fast, super-cheap" meal near Liverpool Street, try this "brilliant" canteen, which offers "healthy" Chinese/Malaysian "noodles and curries". / www.ekachai.net; EC2 10 pm - SW18 10 pm, Fri & Sat 10.30 pm; EC2 closed Sat & Sun; minimum £10; minimum 3 people, dinner only.

The Electric Birdcage SW1 NEW £28 ❸❷❸
11 Haymarket   7839 2424   4–4A
A newly-opened cocktail bar, handily located in the heart of Theatreland; a comfortable (if OTT) place, it offers "good-quality bar food" (especially dim sum) at "reasonable prices". / www.electricbirdcage.com; 10.30 pm; closed Sat L & Sun; no trainers.

Electric Brasserie W11 £43 ❸④❷
191 Portobello Rd   7908 9696   6–1A
This "sexy" all-day brasserie has become a "humming" – and at times "unbearably noisy" – epicentre of Notting Hill life; it's no foodie haunt, but its "classic French fare" seems improved of late (and – if you "scramble for a table" – they do a "cool brunch"). / www.the-electric.co.uk; 10.45 pm.

Elena's L'Etoile W1 £51 ④❸❷
30 Charlotte St   7636 7189   2–1C
"The nearest place you'll find to old-school Paris" – this "timeless" Fitzrovia veteran can still be a "hugely enjoyable" destination, especially for business; standards, however, have seemed ever more "complacent" of late. / www.elenasletoile.co.uk, 10.30 pm, closed Sat L & Sun.

Elephant Royale
Locke's Wharf E14 £39 ❸❸❸
Westferry Rd   7987 7999   11–2C
It's the "lovely" riverside location at the tip of the Isle of Dogs which really makes this Thai restaurant "worthwhile"; its "expensive" food is "consistently good" too, though, and the interior, if tacky, is "lively" and "fun". / www.elephantroyale.com; Mon-Thu 11.30 pm, Fri & Sat midnight, Sun 11 pm.

11 Abingdon Road W8 £40 ❸❸④
11 Abingdon Rd 7937 0120 5–1A
*Fans of Sonny's Kensington spin-off say it has "become a favourite",
thanks to its "good-value" food and "competent" service; overall,
however, the modest feedback it inspires balances out somewhere
around "pleasant enough". / www.abingdonroad.co.uk; 10.45,
Sun 9.30pm.*

Elistano SW3 £42 ④④④
25-27 Elystan St 7584 5248 5–2C
*Fans still find this "noisy" Chelsea Italian "simpatico" ("especially
in summer when the tables spill out onto the street"); feedback
is still up-and-down, though, and critics say "it needs a new chef,
or at least a new attitude". / www.elistano.com; 10.30 pm; closed Sun D.*

The Elk in the Woods N1 £38 ❸❸❷
39 Camden Pas 7226 3535 8–3D
*"Spot-on" cocktails, "decent" wines and "trendy" styling help fuel
the "really cosy" vibe at this Islington hang-out; the food's "good"
too – "if from a somewhat limited menu" – especially "for brunch".
/ www.the-elk-in-the-woods.co.uk; 10.30 pm; no Amex.*

Emile's SW15 £37 ❷❶❷
96 Felsham Rd 8789 3323 10–2B
*A recent revamp has done nothing to dim the charms of Emile
Fahy's "very entertaining" Putney backstreet bistro, which
just "gets better and better with age"; "London's best beef
Wellington" is a perennial attraction, as is an "exceptional-value
wine list". / www.emilesrestaurant.co.uk; 11 pm; D only, closed Sun; no Amex.*

Emni N1 £35 ❸❸❸
353 Upper St 7226 1166 8–3D
*A "stylish" yearling, handily-sited near Angel tube, where
"welcoming" staff serve up "tasty" Indian grub.
/ www.emnirestaurant.com; 11 pm, Fri midnight; Mon-Thu D only, Fri-Sun open
L & D.*

The Empress of India E9 £39 ④④④
130 Lauriston Rd 8533 5123 1–2D
*An often "hectic" Victoria Park gastropub – "more like a restaurant
with a bar" – that's sometimes praised for its "good food
in pleasant surroundings"; standards, however, are much less
consistent than at its famous sibling, The Gun.
/ www.theempressofindia.com; 9.30 pm.*

The Engineer NW1 £43 ❸④❸
65 Gloucester Ave 7722 0950 8–3B
*This "bubbly" Primrose Hill gastropub has long been a fashionable
hang-out, and "on a summer day, there are few nicer places than
the garden"; the food is "not as good as used to be", though,
and the setting is starting to look a little "tired".
/ www.the-engineer.com; 11 pm, Sun 10.30 pm; no Amex.*

Enoteca Turi SW15 £49 ❷❷❸
28 Putney High St 8785 4449 10–2B
*It's not just the "phenomenal" all-Italian wine list that makes
it "worth the trip to Putney", to visit the Turi family's "cosy" and
"obliging" fixture – it also serves up "some of the best Italian
cooking in town". / www.enotecaturi.com; 11 pm; closed Sun; set weekday L
£32 (FP).*

The Enterprise SW3 £42 ❸❷❷
35 Walton St 7584 3148 5–2C
"A fun Chelsea local" – this "classy and buzzing bar" (in a former pub) remains a "reliable winner for lunch or dinner"; "you don't come here for the food", though – "you come for the comfortable overall package". / www.theenterprise.co.uk; 10.30 pm, Sun 10 pm; no booking, except weekday L.

Eriki NW3 £35 ❶❶❸
4-6 Northways Pde, Finchley Rd 7722 0606 8–2A
"Superb" regional cooking – with "subtle spicing and rich flavours" – wins applause for this Swiss Cottage Indian, and the service is "charming" too; a St John's Wood branch (RIP) never really got off the ground. / www.eriki.co.uk; 10.30 pm; set weekday L £21 (FP).

Esarn Kheaw W12 £24 ❶❸④
314 Uxbridge Rd 8743 8930 7–1B
The "amazing Northern Thai grub" at this low-key Shepherd's Bush café is some of the best in town; the place never seems to attract nearly the following it deserves. / www.esarnkheaw.co.uk; 11 pm; closed Sat L & Sun L; no Amex.

Esca SW4 £28 ❸❸❸
160a, Clapham High St 7622 2288 10–2D
"A wonderful deli", near Clapham Common tube, "with great sandwiches and puddings to die for". / www.escauk.com; 9 pm; no Amex.

L'Escargot W1 £50 ❷❷❷
48 Greek St 7437 2679 4–2A
This "classic" Soho "gem" remains an "impressive all-rounder", with "fine" décor, "very professional" service and notably "solid" Gallic cuisine; it's "perfect for a business lunch", and "tremendous value pre-theatre". / www.whitestarline.org.uk; 11.30 pm; closed Sat L & Sun; set weekday L & pre-theatre £33 (FP).

L'Escargot (Picasso Room) W1 £64 ❸❷❷
48 Greek St 7437 2679 4–2A
L'Escargot's small upstairs room offers "a quieter and more intimate" environment, and "a more elaborate menu" than below; it can sometimes be "superb", but at the higher prices it's easier to feel "disappointed" too. / www.whitestarline.org.uk; 11 pm; closed Mon, Sat L & Sun; set weekday L & pre-theatre £33 (FP).

Esenza W11 £46 ❸❸④
210 Kensington Park Rd 7792 1066 6–1A
This Notting Hill Italian may be "less buzzy" than its famous sibling, Osteria Basilico, but it "looks after its regulars well". / www.esenza.co.uk; 11.30 pm.

The Establishment SW6 NEW £40 ④④❸
45-47 Parson's Green Ln 7384 2418 10–1B
Fans say it's "a welcome addition to Parson's Green", but this "cool" new bar inspires mixed views on the food and service fronts; there's some agreement, though, that the music's "too loud". / www.theestablishment.com; Midnight, Sun 10.30 pm.

L'Etranger SW7 £61 ❸❸④
36 Gloucester Rd 7584 1118 5–1B
"Interesting French/Asian fusion fare" and a "brilliant but pricey wine list" make this South Kensington spot of some note; the food can be "hit-and-miss", though, and the atmosphere is sometimes "a bit of a let-down". / www.etranger.co.uk; 11 pm; closed Sat L; set weekday L £37 (FP), set Sun L £41 (FP).

Ev Restaurant, Bar & Deli SE1 £29 ④❸❸
97-99 Isabella St 7620 6191 9–4A
An "oasis of greenery under the railway arches", near Southwark Tube, creates a "fun" setting for this large and airy Tas-group operation, which serves "reliable" Turkish fare; its ratings generally, however, have drifted of late. / www.tasrestaurant.com; 11.30 pm.

Everest Inn SE3 £28 ❸❸④
39 Tranquil Vale 8852 7872 1–4D
"Amazing flavours" from a somewhat "unusual" Nepalese menu underpin the appeal of this "always-friendly and cosy" outfit, in Blackheath. / www.everestinn.co.uk; 11.30 pm, Fri & Sat midnight.

Eyre Brothers EC2 £50 ❷❷❸
70 Leonard St 7613 5346 9–1D
"Hearty" dishes and "keen" service win consistent praise for this "relaxed" Shoreditch Hispanic, especially as a "discreet" and "spacious" business venue; its "hip" styling, though, can sometimes seem a touch "clinical". / www.eyrebrothers.co.uk; 10.45 pm; closed Sat L & Sun.

Fabrizio EC1 £35 ❷❸⑤
30 Saint Cross St 7430 1503 9–1A
"A diamond, hidden-away in the backstreets of Farringdon" – this "friendly" and "rustic" Sicilian serves up some "amazing" food at "great-value" prices. / www.fabriziorestaurant.co.uk; 10 pm; closed Sat L & Sun.

Fairuz W1 £44 ❸❸④
3 Blandford St 7486 8108 2–1A
With its "fresh" mezze at "very reasonable prices", this "simple and unpretentious" Marylebone Lebanese still generally "hits the button"; some reports, however, suggest a "deterioration" of late. / www.fairuz.uk.com; 11 pm, Sun 10.30 pm.

Fakhreldine W1 £51 ❸④④
85 Piccadilly 7493 3424 3–4C
"Lovely Green Park views" and regular belly dancing "add spice" to a visit to this first-floor Lebanese, near the Ritz; fans laud its "decent cooking and good choice of wine" – critics just say it's "much too expensive". / www.fakhreldine.co.uk; midnight, Sun 11 pm.

Il Falconiere SW7 £39 ④❸⑤
84 Old Brompton Rd 7589 2401 5–2B
"Extremely good-value set deals" are the reason to seek out this "nostalgic, '70s-style" Italian, in South Kensington; the food is "basic", though, and the interior "very bland and dated". / www.ilfalconiere.co.uk; 11 pm; closed Sun; set weekday L £23 (FP).

La Famiglia SW10 £47 ❸❷❷
7 Langton St 7351 0761 5–3B
"It's not the height of gastronomy", but this veteran World's End Italian is still "hard to beat for a thoroughly enjoyable evening", and the food is "consistently good"; on a warm night, its garden is one of the nicest spots in Chelsea. / www.lafamiglia.co.uk; 11.45 pm.

The Farm SW6 £40 ④④❷
18 Farm Ln 7381 3331 5–3A
Visits to this trendy-looking Fulham gastroboozer seem rather a "lottery" nowadays; fans say the grub can be "delicious", but doubters find the style generally "pretentious". / www.thefarmfulham.co.uk; 10.30 pm, Sun 10 pm; set weekday L £25 (FP).

El Faro E14 £43 ❶❷❸
3 Turnberry Quay 7987 5511 11–2C
A "hidden gem" near Crossharbour DLR; it serves some "wonderful" and "authentic" Spanish dishes – including "outstanding tapas" – and has nice waterside tables too. / www.el-faro.co.uk; 11 pm; closed Sun D.

The Fat Badger W10 £41 ❸④❸
310 Portobello Rd 8969 4500 6–1A
This "lively" North Kensington boozer attracts rather mixed reports – its "simple, staple fare" strikes some reporters as having been "over-hyped", and "the staff can seem endearing or infuriating, depending on your mood". / www.thefatbadger.com; 10 pm, Fri-Sat 10.30 pm, Sun 9 pm.

Fat Boy's £27 ④❸④
33 Haven Grn, W5 8998 5868 1–2A
431-433 Richmond Rd, TW1 8892 7657 1–4A
68 High St, TW8 8569 8481 1–3A
10a-10b Edensor Rd, W4 8994 8089 10–1A
"For a good-value Thai meal" ("or cheap breakfast"), these "pleasant, out-of-the-way" west London cafés make a "no-nonsense" and "reliable" choice. / 11 pm.

Faulkner's E8 £30 ❷❸④
424-426 Kingsland Rd 7254 6152 1–1D
"It might not be London's best… but it's the best I've found"; this "stalwart" chippy in Dalston has "its own charm", and its "generous" portions of "un-greasy" fish 'n chips still set a "mightily high standard". / 10 pm; no Amex; need 8+ to book.

Feng Sushi £30 ④④④
26 Elizabeth St, SW1 7730 0033 2–4A
218 Fulham Rd, SW10 7795 1900 5–3B
101 Notting Hill Gate, W11 7727 1123 6–2B
21 Kensington Church St, W8 7937 7927 5–1A
1 Adelaide St, NW3 7483 2929 8–2B
13 Stoney St, SE1 7407 8744 9–4C
Royal Festival Hall, SE1 7261 0001 2–3D
Fans still praise these sushi cafés for their "reliable" fare – for a growing number of critics, though, they're just "average" and "overpriced". / www.fengsushi.co.uk; 11 pm, Sun-Wed 10 pm, SE1 Thu-Sat 10.30 pm; SE1 closed Sun.

The Fentiman Arms SW8 £34 ④④❷
64 Fentiman Rd 7793 9796 10–1D
A "lovely" gastropub for the Lambeth gentry, "hidden-away down a picturesque street"; reports are not quite consistent, but the food seems to be generally "well-cooked". / www.geronimo-inns.co.uk; 10 pm, Fri-Sat 10.30 pm, Sun 9 pm.

Fernandez & Wells £25 ❷❸❸
43 Lexington St, W1 7734 1546 3–2D
73 Beak St, W1 7287 2814 3–2D
These cracking Soho "media-crowd" cafés both offer "top-quality produce" – in 'Beak', it's "the best coffee in town" (plus breakfasts, buns and "sublime sarnies"), whereas in nearby 'Lexington' it's "interesting wine, good cured meats and cheeses". / Lexington 10 pm, Beak 7pm; Lexington, closed Sun.

Ffiona's W8 £45 ❸❶❶
51 Kensington Church St 7937 4152 5–1A
"If you get Ffiona onside", this "old-fashioned" Kensington fixture can offer a "unique and brilliant" experience; the "no-nonsense" bistro fare, though, plays second fiddle to the joys of la patronne "buzzing around the room". / www.ffionas.com; 11 pm, Sun 10 pm; D only, closed Mon; no Amex.

Fifteen Restaurant N1 £70 ④④④
15 Westland Pl 0871 330 1515 9–1C
Is Jamie finally getting his Hoxton project sorted? – a high proportion of reports still dismiss it as "pretentious" and "over-priced", but those who find the service "knowledgeable" and the Italian food "enjoyable" were rather more in evidence this year. / www.fifteenrestaurant.net; 9.30 pm; booking: max 6.

Fifteen Trattoria N1 £54 ❸❷❸
15 Westland Pl 0871 330 1515 9–1C
"The most reliable part of the Fifteen operation" – the cheaper ground floor of Jamie's Hoxton Italian has "enthusiastic" staff, and offers "robust" and "flavoursome" fare (including "brilliant" breakfasts) that generally lives up to the prices. / www.fifteen.net; 10 pm; booking: max 12.

The Fifth Floor Café
Harvey Nichols SW1 £43 ④④④
109-125 Knightsbridge 7823 1839 5–1D
If you're "armed with a Gucci wallet", the "frenetic" café, right next to the fifth-floor food hall of this Knightsbridge store, can be "lovely for a light lunch" – otherwise it's easy to take exception to its "excessive" prices. / www.harveynichols.com; 11 pm, Sun 5 pm; closed Sun D; no booking at L; set dinner £28 (FP).

The Fifth Floor Restaurant
Harvey Nichols SW1 £60 ④④④
109-125 Knightsbridge 7235 5250 5–1D
For those with long memories, it was "once so good", but this "unimaginative" fifth-floor Knightsbridge dining room offers standards verging on "rubbish" nowadays – not least its "average" but "expensive" cooking; "the best wine list", however, offers some consolation. / www.harveynichols.com; 11.30 pm; closed Sun D; set weekday L £41 (FP).

54 Farringdon Road EC1 NEW   £34   ❷❷❸
54 Farringdon Rd   7336 0603   9–1A
*The style may be "very odd" – "mixing Malaysian dishes with Gallic
classics" – but the really extraordinary thing about this "interesting"
Farringdon newcomer is... "it works!" / 11 pm; closed Sat L & Sun.*

Fig N1   £41   ❷❶❶
169 Hemingford Rd   7609 3009   8–3D
*"Terrific and adventurous" cooking – and "superlative service" too
– are making quite a name for this "wonderful little hide-away",
"tucked away in elegant Barnsbury". / www.fig-restaurant.co.uk;
10.15 pm, Sun 9 pm; D only, closed Sun-Tue.*

La Figa E14   £38   ❷❷❷
45 Narrow St   7790 0077   11–1B
*"Amazing pizza", "huge portions" and "very friendly staff" are
among the highlights which – by common consent – make this
Docklands spot "an absolutely stunning local Italian". / 11 pm,
Sun 10.30 pm.*

Fine Burger Company   £31   ❸④④
50 James St, W1   7224 1890   3–1A
256 Muswell Hill Broadway, N10   8815 9292   8–1C
330 Upper St, N1   7359 3026   8–3D
O2 Centre, Finchley Rd, NW3   7433 0700   8–2A
37 Bedford Hill, SW12   8772 0266   10–2C
*"It does what it says on the tin", say fans of this "functional" chain,
who praise its "happy-making" burgers, "rich" shakes and
"top onion rings"; overall, however, ratings for rival GBK are still
a fraction ahead. / www.fineburger.co.uk; 11 pm, Sun 10pm - SW12
Sun-Wed 10pm, Thu-Sat 11pm.*

Fino W1   £52   ❷❷❷
33 Charlotte St   7813 8010   2–1C
*"Outstanding tapas" (plus "an interesting wine and sherry
selection") maintain a formidable reputation – and following –
for the Hart brothers' "buzzy" Spanish restaurant, in a Fitzrovia
basement. / www.finorestaurant.com; 10.30 pm; closed Sat L & Sun; booking:
max 12.*

Fire & Stone WC2   £30   ④④❸
31-32 Maiden Ln   7257 8625   4–3D
*"Out-of-the-ordinary" pizzas come with combos ranging from
"wonderful and exciting" to "plain bizarre", at this "spacious"
central stand-by – a "cool" concrete 'cave', hidden-away in Covent
Garden; service "can take ages". / www.fireandstone.com; 11 pm.*

The Fire Stables SW19   £41   ④❸❸
27-29 Church Rd   8946 3197   10–2B
*"Good food and solid service" make this "bustling" bar and dining
room popular with most Wimbledon reporters; there's some feeling,
however, that "it could be so much more". / www.youngs.co.uk;
10.30 pm, Sun 10 pm; booking: max 8, Sat & Sun.*

Firezza £29 ❷❸⑤
12 All Saints Rd, W11 7221 0020 6–1B
48 Chiswick High Rd, W4 8994 9494 7–2B
276 St Paul's Rd, N1 7359 7400 8–2D
40 Lavender Hill, SW11 7223 5535 10–1C
205 Garrett Ln, SW18 8870 7070 10–2B
"Seriously the best pizza you can ever get" – an oft-heard claim
regarding this *"impressive"* take-away chain; and the worst report?
– the food is *"always well-conceived, and well-executed"*.
/ www.firezza.com; 11 pm, Fri & Sat midnight; no Amex.

First Floor W11 £42 ④❸❶
186 Portobello Rd 7243 0072 6–1A
An *"endearing"* Portobello Market outfit, long liked for its
"gorgeous" and *"eccentric"* décor, rather than the *"very up-and-
down"* realisation of its *"quirky"* menu. / www.firstfloorportobello.co.uk;
11 pm; closed Mon & Sun D.

Fish Central EC1 £27 ❸❷④
149-155 Central St 7253 4970 9–1B
"No City bonus" is needed to enjoy this *"real neighbourhood spot"*,
whose *"excellent-value"* dishes are *"well above the quality of other
chippies locally"*. / www.fishcentral.co.uk; 10.30 pm, Fri & Sat 11 pm; closed
Sun; no Amex.

Fish Club SW11 £31 ❶❷④
189 St John's Hill 7978 7115 10–2C
"A simple thing done very, very well"; this *"unassuming but
fantastic"* Battersea chippy offers *"a really interesting selection
of fish"* encrusted in *"lovely, golden, crispy batter"*, and served with
"seriously chunky home-made chips". / www.thefishclub.com; 10 pm,
Sun 9 pm; closed Mon.

Fish Hook W4 £46 ❷❷④
6-8 Elliott Rd 8742 0766 7–2A
Who cares if it's *"a tight squeeze"*? – fish dishes *"of a very high
and consistent standard"* (as well as some *"first-class wines"*) draw
a big crowd to Michael Nadra's *"plain"* Chiswick spot; a *"great-
value"* lunch is a highlight. / www.fishhook.co.uk; 10.30 pm, Sun 10 pm;
set weekday L £27 (FP).

Fish in a Tie SW11 £23 ④❷❷
105 Falcon Rd 7924 1913 10–1C
"Low ceilings and cramped tables only add to the fun", at this
"always-buzzing" favourite, in a *"dodgy"* backwater, by Clapham
Junction; its *"tasty home-cooked fare"* is *"unremarkable, but great
value"*. / 10.45 pm, Sun 11 pm; no Amex.

Fish Shop EC1 £40 ❸④④
360-362 St John's St 7837 1199 8 3D
"A handy location for Sadlers Wells" is a key selling point of this
Islington spot, which serves *"simple, well-cooked fish"*, sometimes
"chaotically". / www.thefishshop.net; 11 pm; closed Mon & Sun D.

fish! SE1 £40 ❸④❸
Cathedral St 7407 3803 9–4C
By Borough Market, a striking glass shed, offering a *"great range
of fish dishes"*; it's all *"a bit canteen-like"*, though (*"with tables too
close together"*), and service *"varies wildly"*. / www.fishdiner.co.uk;
11pm, Sun 10.30 pm.

Fishworks £43 ❸④④
89 Marylebone High St, W1   7935 9796   2–1A
212 Fulham Rd, SW10   7823 3033   5–3B
177 New King's Rd, SW6   7384 1009   10–1B
188 Westbourne Grove, W11   7229 3366   6–1B
6 Turnham Green Ter, W4   8994 0086   7–2A
134 Upper St, N1   7354 1279   8–3D
57 Regent's Park Rd, NW1   7586 9760   8–3B
54 Northcote Rd, SW11   7228 7893   10–2C
13/19 The Sq, Old Mkt, TW9   8948 5965   1–4A
"Inviting fish counters" set the scene at this ambitious café/fishmonger chain (which has had well-publicised growing pains of late); reporters all agree it serves "wonderful", "fresh" fare – "is it really worth paying through the nose for it", though, "when service is hit-and-miss and the interior is cold and cramped?" / www.fishworks.co.uk; 10 pm; W4 closed Sun D.

5 Cavendish Square W1 £65 ⑤④❸
5 Cavendish Sq   7079 5000   3–1C
This vast, OTT Marylebone townhouse – a bar/club/restaurant – is an ideal venue for those who suffer from delusions of oligarchical grandeur; the food, though, is often a "waste of time". / www.no5ltd.com; 10.30 pm; closed Sat L & Sun D; no trainers; set dinner & weekday L £44 (FP).

Five Hot Chillies HA0 £23 ❷❷⑤
875 Harrow Rd   8908 5900   1–1A
"Authentic, and worth the trip" – this grungy BYO Indian cafeteria, on a busy Sudbury highway, is a "very friendly" place, where the "spicy" and "excellent" scoff offers "great value". / 11.30 pm.

Flâneur EC1 £45 ④④④
41 Farringdon Rd   7404 4422   9–1A
"Good food in an original setting" – you eat amidst the shelves – endears this airy Farringdon deli/diner to some reporters, especially for breakfast; the atmosphere can be "stilted", though, and ratings overall slipped a bit this year. / www.flaneur.com; 10 pm; closed Sun.

The Flask N6 £29 ④④❶
77 Highgate West Hill   8348 7346   1–1C
It's the "fabulous olde worlde building" that makes this famous Highgate coaching inn of note, and it's especially nice on days you can sit outside – the "simple" fare is very much a secondary attraction. / 10pm; no Amex.

Flat White W1 £9 ❶❶❷
17 Berwick St   7734 0370   3–2D
"The best-ever coffee" – "like crack cocaine with froth" – has reporters addicted to this "cramped" Kiwi-run Soho spot; there are also (arguably rather pricey) biscuits and cakes. / www.flat-white.co.uk; L only; no credit cards.

Floridita W1 £57 ⑤⑤❸
100 Wardour St   7314 4000   3–2D
"Go for the ambience", and the "great, live Cuban music" – they are the "only redeeming features" of this huge Soho Latino, which reporters tend to find both "absolutely ghastly" and "absurdly expensive". / www.floriditalondon.com; 2 am, Thu & Fri 3 am; D only, closed Sun.

Foliage
Mandarin Oriental SW1 £82 ❸❷❸
66 Knightsbridge 7201 3723 5–1D
"Get a window table", if you can, at this "elegant" (if arguably
rather dull) Knightsbridge dining room, as there are some "lovely
park views"; Chris Staines's "innovative" cuisine continues to win
high acclaim, but his "culinary high jinks" have, of late, sometimes
fallen a little flat. / www.mandarinoriental.com; 10.30 pm; booking: max 6;
set weekday L £38 (FP).

Food for Thought WC2 £16 ❷❹❹
31 Neal St 7836 0239 4–2C
"One of the last first-wave veggies left" – this "tightly-packed" self-
service basement, in Covent Garden, still offers "brilliant" scoff
at "reasonable prices"; BYO. / 8 pm, Sun 5 pm; no credit cards;
no booking.

Footstool
St Johns SW1 £41
St John's, Smith Sq 7222 2779 2–4C
To be re-launched in late-2008 by the people who do the catering
at the Tate – the café/restaurant in the characterful crypt of this
former church (now a concert hall) in Westminster. / L only
(ex concert evenings), closed Sat & Sun.

The Forge WC2 £45 ❹❷❸
14 Garrick St 7379 1531 4–3C
"Better than many other options" in Covent Garden –
this "humming" yearling wins praise for its "polished" service and
"reasonably-priced" Gallic fare; it's a "perfect pre-theatre" option –
and "good for parties" too – but perhaps a less obvious choice
if you want the focus of the meal to be the food.
/ www.theforgerestaurant.co.uk; midnight; set weekday L & pre-theatre
£27 (FP).

Formosa Dining Room
The Prince Alfred W9 £43 ❹❹❸
5a Formosa St 7286 3287 6–1C
The "comfy" modern dining annex of a fine Victorian pub in Maida
Vale; fans still like its "hearty" cooking, but it seems ever more
"uninspiring", and prices leave some reporters feeling "mugged".
/ www.formosadiningroom.co.uk; 10 pm, Fri & Sat 10.30 pm, Sun 9 pm;
no Amex; set dinner £30 (FP).

(Fountain)
Fortnum & Mason W1 £50 ❹❸❸
181 Piccadilly 7734 8040 3–3D
Refurbishment has brought in a "lighter, brighter" look at the
"vintage" buttery of this famous St James's store; its appeal
remains largely unchanged, though – perfect "for a shopping lunch
with your aunt", a "wonderful breakfast" or a "fabulous afternoon
tea". / www.fortnumandmason.co.uk; 10.45 pm; closed Sun D; no booking
at L.

Four O Nine SW9 £44 ❸❷❶
409 Clapham Rd 7737 0722 10–1D
Behind a "speakeasy-style entrance", this "cosy" and "romantic"
Clapham "gem" (over a pub) offers food that's usually "good",
and occasionally "sublime"; it's beginning to build "quite a local
following". / www.fouronine.co.uk; 10.30 pm; D only.

Four Regions TW9 £36 **❸0❹**

102-104 Kew Rd 8940 9044 1–4A

A Richmond "old favourite" which maintains its popularity in spite of its rather "standard" Chinese food, and a "bright" re-fit that some regulars find "disastrous". / 11.30 pm.

The Four Seasons W2 £27 **❷⑤⑤**

84 Queensway 7229 4320 6–1C

"One of the most authentic Chinese restaurants in London", this "crammed" Bayswater veteran is especially known as "THE place for duck"; service, though, is "even less charming than at the neighbouring establishments", and the queue is "perpetual". / 11 pm; no Amex.

The Fox EC2 £37 **❸❸❷**

28 Paul St 7729 5708 9–1C

"Sustaining old-fashioned charm with solid gastro-fare" – this "panelled" Shoreditch boozer, is a "welcome" antidote to its trendy neighbours, offering a "very short" menu of "always-reliable" British fare, washed down perhaps with a "freshly-pulled pint". / www.thefoxpublichouse.com; 11 pm, Fri & Sat midnight; closed Sat L & Sun D; no Amex.

The Fox & Hounds SW11 £38 **❷❸❷**

66 Latchmere Rd 7924 5483 10–1C

It's "a proper boozer" (with "a top selection of beers"), but this "crammed" Battersea pub also "does everything right" on the food front, offering "unfussy" Mediterranean fare that's "bursting with flavour". / www.thefoxandhoundspub.co.uk; 10.30 pm, Sun 10 pm; Mon-Thu D only, Fri-Sun open L & D.

The Fox and Anchor EC1 🆕 £35 **❸❷❷**

115 Charterhouse St 7250 1300 9–1B

Once celebrated as a "dusty old boozer", this Smithfield spot has been "gloriously restored" by new owners; "rare beers" and "an incomparable selection of whiskies" now accompany some "straight-down-the-line" British fare – not least "legendary" breakfasts, complete with a pint of Guinness. / www.foxandanchor.co.uk; 10 pm; closed Sat & Sun.

The Fox Reformed N16 £34 **❹❸0**

176 Stoke Newington Church St 7254 5975 1–1C

"There are better places to eat in N16", but this offbeat wine bar veteran benefits from a particularly quirky charm, and a cute small garden. / www.fox-reformed.co.uk; 10.30 pm; closed weekday L.

Foxtrot Oscar SW3 £41 **⑤❹⑤**

79 Royal Hospital Rd 7352 4448 5–3D

"Horrifically drab" interior, "sporadic" service, food "not well prepared"... who could possibly be responsible for Chelsea's new Kitchen Nightmare? – step forward Gordon Ramsay, whose first, disastrous, stab at the 'neighbourhood bistro' concept this is. / www.gordonramsay.com/foxtrotoscar/; 10 pm.

Franco Manca SW9 🆕 £12 **0❷❸**

Unit 4 Market Row 7738 3021 10–2D

"A new wood-burning stove, imported from Naples" advertises the seriousness of intent of this recent newcomer, in the atmospheric Brixton Market site that was formerly Eco (RIP); fans already claim it offers "the best pizza outside Italy". / www.francomanca.com; L only, closed Sun; no Amex.

92

Franco's SW1 £51 ④❸④
61 Jermyn St 7499 2211 3–3C
"Such potential", but – despite its "consistent" cooking and
"friendly" service – the Hambro family's St James's Italian still too
often seems "bland" and "uninspiring". / www.francoslondon.com;
10.45 pm; closed Sun; set pre theatre £36 (FP).

Frankie's Italian Bar & Grill £36 ⑤⑤④
3 Yeomans Row, SW3 7590 9999 5–2C
68 Chiswick High Rd, W4 8987 9988 7–2B
263 Putney Bridge Rd, SW15 8780 3366 10–2B
MPW and Franco Dettori's "dire" chain needs to buck up or
"it's one for the knacker's yard"; the problem is not so much the
"gaudy", "glam", "glitter-ball" décor but the "awful" food and
"disinterested" service (although "they are quite nice to kids").
/ www.frankiesitalianbarandgrill.com; 11 pm - SW15 9.45 pm; W4 Mon-Fri L.

Franklins £42 ❸❷❸
205-209 Kennington Ln, SE11 7793 8313 1–3C
157 Lordship Ln, SE22 8299 9598 1–4D
An "interesting", if "limited", British-themed menu wins acclaim for
this South London duo, where the newer Kennington branch –
with "nice courtyard" – is now "a deli/restaurant/farm shop in one";
"the cooking can lack precision, but it is good value".
/ www.franklinsrestaurant.com; SE11 9.30 pm - SE22 10.30pm; set weekday L
£27 (FP).

Frantoio SW10 £42 ❸❶❷
397 King's Rd 7352 4146 5–3B
Transcending its location in a "dreary '60s shopping strip",
this "buzzing" and "friendly" World's Ender is almost invariably
hailed as a "reliable local Italian". / 11.15 pm; set weekday L £27 (FP).

Fratelli la Bufala NW3 £34 ④④❸
45a South End Rd 7435 7814 8–2A
It gets the odd "truly awful" report, but this Hampstead Italian
mostly inspires praise for its "delicious thin-crust pizza"
(from "a wood-fired oven"); "the owner's always swanning around",
though, and "it can feel a bit like Fawlty Towers". / 11 pm; closed
Mon L; no Amex.

Frederick's N1 £54 ❸❸❸
106 Camden Pas 7359 2888 8–3D
An Islington "old favourite", that's "still classy and fun", thanks
in particular to its "wonderful" and "relaxed" garden/conservatory;
even some fans feel it's "not as good as it used to be", though,
and critics dwell on its "wasted potential". / www.fredericks.co.uk;
11 pm; closed Sun; no Amex; set weekday L & pre-theatre £29 (FP).

The Freemasons SW18 £35 ❸④❷
2 Wandsworth Common Northside 7326 8580 10–2C
A "buzzy" Wandsworth gastro-boozer that's "managed to succeed
on a difficult site" – the food may be "nothing exceptional", but it
is "well-executed". / www.freemasonspub.com; 10 pm.

Freemasons Arms NW3 £40 ④④❷
32 Downshire Hill 7433 6811 8–2A
Thanks to its "really good atmosphere" (and "great garden"),
this Hampstead boozer is "always busy"; no-one much mentions
the food. / www.freemasonsarms.com; 10 pm.

French House W1 £47 ❸❷❷

49 Dean St 7437 2477 4–3A

A "tiny, crowded, first-floor room", above a famous old pub, "in the heart of Soho"; it has its own off-beat, "sexy" charm, and serves some "homely" Gallic dishes. / www.frenchhousesoho.com; 11 pm; closed Sun; booking: max 8.

Fresco W2 £15 ❷❷④

25 Westbourne Grove 7221 2355 6–1C

A Bayswater pit stop "gem", notable for its "wonderful juices", "superb salads" and "fresh falafels". / www.frescojuices.co.uk; 11 pm.

Friends SW10 £39 ❸❷❸

6 Hollywood Rd 7376 3890 5–3B

"Welcoming" and "relaxed", this Chelsea "Eurotrash haunt" is known for "the best pizzas in the neighbourhood". / 11.20 pm, Sat & Sun 10.30 pm; closed weekday L; no Amex.

La Fromagerie Café W1 £28 ❶❸❷

2-4 Moxon St 7935 0341 3–1A

"Inventive" breakfasts and "great, freshly-prepared salads" – plus, of course, a "fantastic array of cheeses" – draw a dedicated following to this "cramped" but "special" Marylebone deli/café. / www.lafromagerie.co.uk; 7.30 pm, Sat 7 pm, Sun 6 pm; L only; no booking.

The Frontline Club W2 £42 ④❷❶

13 Norfolk Pl 7479 8960 6–1D

"Fascinating photos" line the walls of this "atmospheric" journos' rendezvous in Paddington; it's not the "variable" food that whets the palate here, however, but rather Malcolm Gluck's "scarily extensive" ("fixed mark-up") wine list. / www.frontlineclub.com; 10.30 pm, Sun 10 pm.

Fryer's Delight WC1 £10 ❸❸④

19 Theobald's Rd 7405 4114 2–1D

Holborn's "legendary" chippy continues to "punch well above its weight"; can it really be true that, despite the "great value" it offers (especially as you can BYO), it's "not as busy as it used to be"? / 10 pm; closed Sun; no credit cards; no booking.

Fujiyama SW9 £21 ❷❸❸

5-7 Vining St 7737 2369 10–2D

"A good range of ramen, curries and sushi" helps make this "brisk" and "cheerful" Brixton Japanese a "very useful local". / www.newfujiyama.com; 11 pm, Fri & Sat midnight; no Amex.

Fung Shing WC2 £35 ❷❸⑤

15 Lisle St 7437 1539 4–3A

A Chinatown "old favourite" whose "interesting" cuisine is still "better than most of the local competition"; not for the first time in its long history, however, it's currently "in need of a facelift". / www.fungshing.co.uk; 11.15 pm.

Furnace N1 £30 ❸❸❸

1 Rufus St 7613 0598 9–1D

"A very pleasant pizza and pasta joint, just off Hoxton Square"; beware though – "when the whole area is busy at Saturday lunchtime, they are inexplicably closed". / 11 pm; closed Sat L & Sun; no Amex.

Fuzzy's Grub £12 ❶❷❸

6 Crown Pas, SW1 7925 2791 3–4D
96 Tooley St, SE1 7089 7590 9–4D **NEW**
15 Basinghall St, Unit 1 Mason's Ave, EC2 7726 6771 9–2C
56-57 Cornhill, EC3 7621 0444 9–2C
58 Houndsditch, EC3 7929 1400 9–2D **NEW**
10 Well Ct, EC4 7236 8400 9–2B
22 Carter Ln, EC4 7248 9795 9–2B **NEW**
62 Fleet St, EC4 7583 6060 9–2A

A "very English" and impeccably "friendly" chain of upmarket caffs, applauded for their "outrageously good sandwiches" ("a full Sunday roast squeezed into a bap") and "heavenly hangover-cure breakfasts". / www.fuzzysgrub.com; 3 pm-4 pm; closed Sat & Sun except SE1 & EC4; no credit cards; no booking.

Gaby's WC2 £29 ❸❸⑤

30 Charing Cross Rd 7836 4233 4–3B

"Great salt beef sandwiches and pickles", "flavoursome falafels" and "fresh" juices – the menu mainstays of this "unchanging" veteran deli, long known as a "top cheap and cheerful" option in the heart of the West End. / midnight, Sun 10 pm; no credit cards.

Gail's Bread £18 ❷❸❸

138 Portobello Rd, W11 7460 0766 6–1B
64 Hampstead High St, NW3 7794 5700 8–1A

"A creative menu, and fresh, well-prepared food" win praise for this small, modern café/bakery chain – "it's a tad expensive, but worth it". / www.gailsbread.co.uk; W11 8 pm - NW3 9 pm; no booking.

Galicia W10 £30 ④④❷

323 Portobello Rd 8969 3539 6–1A

"The crankiness of the staff just adds to the atmosphere", at this "humming", "so Spanish" North Kensington veteran, which serves "authentic" and "cheap" tapas and raciones. / 11.30 pm; closed Mon; set weekday L £16 (FP), set Sun L £17 (FP).

Gallipoli £25 ④④❸

102 Upper St, N1 7359 0630 8–3D
107 Upper St, N1 7226 5333 8–3D
120 Upper St, N1 7359 1578 8–3D

"Expect birthdays, hen nights, and dancing on the tables", at this "noisy and busy" ("sometimes too busy") trio of budget Turkish bistros, in Islington; their "tasty and filling mezze" are "standard" but "great value". / www.cafegallipoli.com; 11 pm, Fri & Sat midnight; 107 Upper St closed Mon.

Galvin at Windows
Park Lane London Hilton Hotel W1 £81 ④❸❷

22 Park Ln, 28th Floor 7208 4021 3–4A

"You can't fail to be impressed" by the "unforgettable views" from this 28th-floor Mayfair eyrie, which makes it a 'natural' for business or romance; the Galvin brothers' two-year-old régime is rather losing its lustre, though – prices can now seem "astronomical", and the food is "disappointing at times". / www.galvinatwindows.com; 10.45 pm; closed Sat L & Sun D; no trainers; set pre-theatre £38 (FP), set weekday L £48 (FP).

GALVIN BISTROT DE LUXE W1 £44 **❶❶❷**
66 Baker St 7935 4007 2–1A
With its "crisp" service of "gutsy" Gallic fare in an "elegant"
setting, the Galvin brothers' "humming" two-year-old, near Baker
Street tube, is "a class act"; "a very safe bet for most occasions",
it has become a true benchmark, and has an enormous following.
/ www.galvinuk.com; 11 pm, Sun 9. 30 pm; set weekday L £29 (FP), set dinner
£32 (FP).

Ganapati SE15 £29 **❷❸❷**
38 Holly Grove 7277 2928 1–4C
"A hidden treasure in deepest Peckham" – this "funky south Indian
diner" offers "excellent" food, "mostly at communal tables".
/ www.ganapatirestaurant.com; 10.45 pm; closed Mon; no Amex.

Garbo's W1 £41 **❹❸❹**
42 Crawford St 7262 6582 2–1A
"The lunch buffet is still the star", at this long-established and
"reliable" Swedish restaurant in Marylebone; dinner "can be fine"
too. / 10.30 pm; closed Sat L & Sun D.

Garrison SE1 £40 **❸❸❶**
99-101 Bermondsey St 7089 9355 9–4D
"It's worth living in SE1 for", say fans of this "quirky" and
"fabulously atmospheric" Bermondsey boozer; the cooking
is "consistently good" too. / www.thegarrison.co.uk; 10 pm, Sun 9.30 pm.

Gastro SW4 £45 **❹❸❶**
67 Venn St 7627 0222 10–2D
The atmosphere is certainly "très français", and the scrambled eggs
are undoubtedly "great", but otherwise reports on this "romantic"
bistro, near the Clapham Picture House, are rather mixed. / midnight;
no Amex; set weekday L £22 (FP).

The Gate W6 £39 **❶❷❸**
51 Queen Caroline St 8748 6932 7–2C
"Unerringly good" veggie fare – "the best and most imaginative"
of its type in London – again wins accolades for this "pleasant"
venue, in an airy former church hall, near Hammersmith Broadway;
"lovely outdoor seating in summer". / www.thegate.tv; 10.45 pm; closed
Sat L & Sun

Gaucho £38 **❷❸❸**
Chelsea Farmers' Mkt, Sydney St, SW3 7376 8514 5–3C
30 Old Brompton Rd, SW7 7584 8999 5–2B
"Huge hunks of cow" grilled in an "authentic" and "delicious"
fashion make it "hard to beat" these small and "crowded"
Argentinean outfits; the Chelsea Farmer's Market branch has a nice
terrace too. / www.elgaucho.co.uk; SW3 6.30 pm, SW7 11.30 pm;
SW3 L only, SW7 D only; SW3 no booking at weekends, SW7 no bookings
before 7 pm.

Gaucho Grill £50 ❷❸❸
25 Swallow St, W1 7734 4040 3–3D
125 Chancery Ln, WC2 7242 7727 2–1D
89 Sloane Ave, SW3 7584 9901 5–2C
64 Heath St, NW3 7431 8222 8–1A
2 Moore London, Riverside, SE1 7407 5222 9–4D
Tow Path, TW10 8948 2944 1–4A
29 Westferry Circus, E14 7987 9494 11–1B
5 Finsbury Ave, EC2 7256 6877 9–1C
1 Bell Inn Yd, EC3 7626 5180 9–2C
"For the confirmed carnivore", this "very dependable" and highly popular Argentinean chain offers a good all-round formula, including "beautiful" steaks and "interesting" New World wine; as you'd expect, it's a top choice for business. / www.gaucho-grill.com; 11 pm, Fri & Sat 11.30pm; EC3, EC2 & WC2 closed Sat & Sun.

LE GAVROCHE W1 £136 ❷0❷
43 Upper Brook St 7408 0881 3–2A
"Still a winner, after all these years" – Michel Roux Jr's "terrific" Mayfair veteran offers "the ultimate old-school dining experience", with "perfect, classic haute cuisine", "astonishingly competent" staff, and "a wine list second to none"; but "ouch, the bill…". / www.le-gavroche.co.uk; 10.45 pm; closed Sat L & Sun; jacket required; set weekday L £61 (FP).

Gay Hussar W1 £39 ❹❸❷
2 Greek St 7437 0973 4–2A
"Ageing politicos" (traditionally of a leftward persuasion) may continue to haunt this "cosy" Soho legend, but it's "not as much fun as it was" – the "heavy" Hungarian dishes are sometimes "awful", and service is "not exactly slick" either. / www.gayhussar.co.uk; 10.45 pm; closed Sun.

The Gaylord E14 £25 ❸❹❹
141 Manchester Rd 7538 0393 11–2D
Despite the odd 'off' report this year, this Isle of Dogs Indian was once again regularly complimented for its "consistency and quality". / www.gaylordrestaurant.co.uk; midnight.

Gaylord W1 £38 ❸❹❹
79-81 Mortimer St 7580 3615 2–1B
Fans "always have a good meal" at this Indian stalwart, in Fitzrovia – part of a long-established international chain. / www.gaylordlondon.com; 11.30 pm.

Gazette £33 ❸❸❷
79 Riverside Plaza, Chatfield Rd, SW11 7223 0999 10–1C
1 Ramsden Rd, SW12 8772 1232 10–2C **NEW**
"Simple" and "rustic" Gallic fare commends this "buzzy" brasserie, near the south end of Wandsworth Bridge, to nearly all who report on it; a visit to its new Balham sibling, however, left us rather unimpressed all-round – perhaps just 'early days'?

Geale's W8 £41 ❹❹❸
2 Farmer St 7727 7528 6–2B
"Don't let nostalgia put you off", say fans, who vaunt the recently "improved" décor of this old-time chippy, near Notting Hill Gate, and the "posh fish 'n' chips" it now serves; there are many critics, though, who find the place just "too expensive" nowadays. / www.geales.com; 10.30 pm; closed Mon L.

Geeta NW6 £18 ❷❷⑤
57-59 Willesden Ln   7624 1713   1–1B
"Smiley, ever-present family members" add life to the "distinctly low-brow" interior of this Kilburn veteran, still extolled by its small fan club for its "excellent", "home-cooked" Indian scoff at "unbelievable" prices; you can BYO too. / 10.30 pm, Fri & Sat 11.30 pm; no Amex.

Gem N1 £22 ❷❶❷
265 Upper St   7359 0405   8–2D
"It really is a gem!" – this "welcoming" Kurdish outfit, in Islington, offers "always-good" food ("wonderful, fresh bread", especially) at "amazing" prices; service is "excellent" too. / midnight.

George & Vulture EC3 £39 ⑤❸❷
3 Castle Ct   7626 9710   9–3C
"Trading on its traditional décor and classic British menu", this Dickensian (literally) City chophouse "is not expensive, but still overpriced for what it is". / L only, closed Sat & Sun.

Getti £47 ④❸④
16-17 Jermyn St, SW1   7734 7334   3–3D
42 Marylebone High St, W1   7486 3753   2–1A
Fans find them "buzzy and fun", but, all things considered, standards at this West End Italian chain would appear to be "distinctly average". / www.getti.com; 10.45 pm; SW1 closed Sun; set always available £29 (FP).

The Giaconda Dining Room WC2 NEW £30 ❷❷④
9 Denmark St   7240 3334   4–1A
First solo UK venture of Aussie chef Paul Merrony, this small and basic newcomer (right by Centrepoint) is one of those rare places which – in an entirely un-precious way – is really all about the food, offering notably satisfying bistro cooking (and very decent wines) at bargain-basement prices. / Rated on Editors' visit; www.giacondadining.com; 9.30 pm; closed Sat & Sun.

Giardinetto W1 £60 ❸④⑤
39-40 Albemarle St   7493 7091   3–3C
Maurizio Vilona's small restaurant, near the Ritz, offers food that's almost always "decent", and sometimes better; high prices, though, discourage much of a following among reporters, and the room can seem rather "dead". / www.giardinetto.co.uk; 10.30 pm; closed Sat L & Sun.

Gilgamesh NW1 £50 ❸⑤❷
The Stables, Camden Mkt, Chalk Farm Rd   7428 4922   8–2B
"Wow!"... the "intricately-carved" décor of this "vast", "night-clubby" Camden Market venue is nothing if not "impressive", and it's a "fun" place too; "appalling service" makes it easy to dismiss as a "theme park", but its oriental-fusion fare is sometimes surprisingly "tasty". / www.gilgameshbar.com; midnight; no jeans or trainers.

FSA

Giraffe £34 ④❸❸
6-8 Blandford St, W1   7935 2333   2–1A
19-21 The Brunswick Centre, WC1   7812 1336   8–4C NEW
270 Chiswick High Rd, W4   8995 2100   7–2A
7 Kensington High St, W8   7938 1221   5–1A
29-31 Essex Rd, N1   7359 5999   8–3D
46 Rosslyn Hill, NW3   7435 0343   8–2A
Royal Festival Hall, Riverside, SE1   7928 2004   2–3D
27 Battersea Rise, SW11   7223 0933   10–2C
1 Crispin Pl, E1   3116 2000   9–1D NEW
Famously "a fun family brunch place" (till 4 pm daily), this 'world food' chain may offer "nothing fancy" on the menu front, but the cooking is generally "fine". / www.giraffe.net; 10.45 pm, Sun 10.30pm; no booking at weekends between 9am & 5pm.

Giusto W1 NEW £35 ❸❸④
43 Blandford St   7486 7340   2–1A
"Don't be put off by the café-like exterior" – or the basement location – of this Marylebone newcomer, on the site of La Spighetta (RIP); the food – including pizza – is usually at least "decent", and our experience coincides with those who found it "really excellent".

Glaisters SW10 £37 ④④❸
4 Hollywood Rd   7352 0352   5–3B
"It never seems to raise its game", but this well-established Chelsea bistro "remains popular" nonetheless – it is "not unduly expensive" and has a "beautiful" rear conservatory. / www.glaisters.co.uk; 11.30 pm; closed Sun D.

The Glasshouse TW9 £52 ❶❶❸
14 Station Pde   8940 6777   1–3A
"Easily the rival of its siblings, such as Chez Bruce"; this "quietly-situated" destination (right by Kew Gardens Tube) not only offers Anthony Boyd's "supremely flavoursome" cooking, but also "super" service and "fabulous" wine; "a bit more space between tables wouldn't harm", though. / www.glasshouserestaurant.co.uk; 10.30 pm; set weekday L £39 (FP).

Glistening Waters TW8 £29 ❸❷④
5 Ferry Ln, Ferry Quays   8758 1616   1–3A
The small fan club of this riverside Caribbean in Brentford say it's "definitely worth a visit" – its hearty scoff is "lovely" but "put in the shade by the characterful service".

Golden Dragon W1 £28 ❸④❸
28-29 Gerrard St   7734 2763   4–3A
"Service is brisk, and they're eager to move you through", but this "bustling" and "reliable" spot, on Chinatown's main drag, has its fans, not least for "authentic dim sum". / midnight.

Golden Hind W1 £19 ❶❶❸
73 Marylebone Ln   7486 3644   2–1A
For "the best fish 'n' chips in W1", seek out this "basic" but "lovely" Marylebone chippy (which does "proper puds" too); BYO. / 10 pm; closed Sat L & Sun.

Goldfish NW3 £38 ❷❸④
82 Hampstead High St   7794 6666   8–2A
This "interesting" modern Chinese yearling in Hampstead
is something of "a mixed bag" – its "experimental" cuisine, though,
can sometimes be "brilliant". / 10.30 pm.

Good Earth £44 ❷❷❸
233 Brompton Rd, SW3   7584 3658   5–2C
143-145 The Broadway, NW7   8959 7011   1–1B
A "smart" Chinese mini-chain with "professional" service,
"attractive" décor and notably "consistent" food.
/ www.goodearthgroup.co.uk; 10.45 pm.

Gopal's of Soho W1 £28 ❸❷④
12 Bateman St   7434 1621   4–2A
"A great stand-by curry house", in Soho – one of the few such
places in the heart of the West End. / www.gopalsofsoho.co.uk;
11.30 pm.

GORDON RAMSAY SW3 £118 ❶❶❷
68-69 Royal Hospital Rd   7352 4441   5–3D
"Faultless" cooking (from new head chef Clare Smyth) is part of the
"absolutely amazing" dining experience on offer at Gordon
Ramsay's "luxurious" (if slightly "muted") Chelsea HQ; it's a shame,
though, that prices have "shot up" in the year which has seen the
food – for the first time in nine years – clearly beaten by a rival.
/ www.gordonramsay.com; 11 pm; closed Sat & Sun; no jeans or trainers;
booking: max 8; set weekday L £68 (FP).

Gordon Ramsay at Claridge's
Claridge's Hotel W1 £90 ④④❸
55 Brook St   7499 0099   3–2B
This Art Deco Mayfair chamber is "losing it", year after year;
the food is distinctly "pedestrian", service "needs work" and prices
are "very inflated" – "you're just paying for the name".
/ www.gordonramsay.com; 11 pm; no jeans or trainers; booking: max 8;
set weekday L £45 (FP).

Gordon's Wine Bar WC2 £23 ⑤❸❶
47 Villiers St   7930 1408   4–4D
A "murky" and ancient wine bar, near Embankment tube, worth
seeking out for its "excellent" wine and its "amazing" setting –
"cosy" vaults in winter, or the "great" (and ever more vast) summer
terrace; the food is "adequate", but a bit of a side show.
/ www.gordonswinebar.com; 11 pm, Sun 10 pm, no booking.

The Goring Hotel SW1 £75 ❸❶❶
15 Beeston Pl   7396 9000   2–4B
"For a smart lunch with grandpa", nowhere could beat the "calm"
dining room of this "charmingly civilised" and "so very English"
family-owned hotel, near Victoria; it is is also particularly popular
for business (and for "memorable" breakfasts too).
/ www.goringhotel.co.uk; 10 pm; closed Sat L; jacket & tie; booking: max 12.

Gourmet Burger Kitchen £20 ❸④④
15 Frith St, W1 7494 9533 4–2A
13-14 Maiden Ln, WC2 7240 9617 4–4D
163-165 Earl's Court Rd, SW5 7373 3184 5–2A
49 Fulham Broadway, SW6 7381 4242 5–4A
107 Old Brompton Rd, SW7 7581 8942 5–2B
160 Portobello Rd, W11 7243 6597 6–1B
50 Westbourne Grove, W2 7243 4344 6–1B
131 Chiswick High Rd, W4 8995 4548 7–2A
200 Haverstock Hill, NW3 7443 5335 8–2A
44 Northcote Rd, SW11 7228 3309 10–2C
333 Putney Bridge Rd, SW15 8789 1199 10–2B
84 Clapham High St, SW4 7627 5367 10–2D
Condor Hs, St Paul's Churchyard, EC4 7248 9199 9–2B
"The best burgers ever" (with "every imaginable topping") are still winning mega-acclaim for the survey's most talked-about chain, despite its "weak" service and "cattle-pen" ambience; it's "not as good as it was", though, leaving its food rating now only a fraction ahead of its many imitators. / www.gbkinfo.com; 10.45 pm; no booking.

Gourmet Pizza Company £29 ④⑤④
Gabriels Wharf, 56 Upper Ground, SE1 7928 3188 9–3A
18 Mackenzie Walk, E14 7345 9192 11–1C
"Great if you can get a river view" – the SE1 branch of this small chain has some lovely tables; the group's funky pizzas are generally "good", too (but there were also a few "terrible" reports this year). / www.gourmetpizzacompany.co.uk; E14 10.30pm - SE1 10.45pm; E14 closed Sat & Sun; E14 need 6+ to book, SE1 need 7+ to book.

Gow's EC2 £46 ④④④
81 Old Broad St 7920 9645 9–2C
A "reliable, rather than spectacular" fish-specialist, in a City basement; "OK for a business lunch, so long as you have plenty of time". / www.ballsbrothers.co.uk; 9 pm; closed Sat & Sun; booking: max 10.

The Gowlett SE15 £28 ❷❷❷
62 Gowlett Rd 7635 7048 1–4C
Peckham folk don't stint in their praise for this "fantastic" local, and applaud its "excellent" pizza and its "friendly" staff; "plenty of good beers" too. / www.thegowlett.com; 10.30 pm.

Goya SW1 £34 ④④④
34 Lupus St 7976 5309 2–4C
This long-established, tapas bar – of note as one of the few decent places to eat in the heart of Pimlico – has "upped its game" of late; the branch by Victoria Coach Station is no more. / www.goyarestaurant.co.uk; 11.30, snacks midnight.

Grafton House SW4 £40 ④⑤⑤
13-19 Old Town 7498 5559 10–2D
Fans say this large and "trendy" Clapham bar/restaurant serves "surprisingly interesting" scoff – for critics, though, it's just "an overpriced All Bar One". / www.graftonhouseuk.com; 10.30 pm; D only, ex Sun L only.

Gran Paradiso SW1 £41 ④❸❸
52 Wilton Rd 7828 5818 2–4B
*"The menu hasn't changed in 40 years", at this "time-warp"
Pimlico Italian; arguably it's "nothing special", but most reporters
judge it to be a "friendly" and "good-value" destination. / 10.45 pm;
closed Sat L & Sun.*

The Grapes E14 £43 ❸❸❷
76 Narrow St 7987 4396 11–1B
*This "old-fashioned" Docklands pub is "well worth a visit" for its
"simple, but well-cooked" fare (notably "a great choice of fresh
fish"); you can eat in the bar, or there's a fuller menu upstairs
in the dining room – "nab a window table for the river view".
/ 11 pm; closed Sat L & Sun.*

Great Eastern Dining Room EC2 £40 ❷❷❷
54-56 Great Eastern St 7613 4545 9–1D
*Who cares if it sometimes seems "too cool for school"? –
this "buzzy" pan-Asian hang-out, in Shoreditch, "always offers
a great evening out", thanks to its "fantastic" fusion fare
(and "an extensive list of cocktails" too). / www.rickerrestaurants.com;
11 pm; closed Sat L & Sun.*

Great Nepalese NW1 £25 ❷❸④
48 Eversholt St 7388 6737 8–3C
*In looks it's "little more than a standard curry place",
but "superior" cooking – with "unusual" Nepalese specials –
has long given an "edge" to this very "friendly" veteran, alongside
Euston Station. / www.great-nepalese.co.uk; 11.30 pm; closed Sun.*

Great Queen Street WC2 £37 ❷❸❸
32 Great Queen St 7242 0622 4–1D
*"Robust", "no-nonsense" British fare helps this "down-to-earth"
Covent Garden yearling win wide acclaim as a "real foodie
location"; its style can be so "unnecessarily basic", though, as to
seem "verging on pretentious". / 10.30 pm; closed Mon L & Sun D;
no Amex.*

Green & Blue SE22 £23 ④❷❷
38 Lordship Ln 8693 9250 1–4D
*"The wine list is nothing short of fabulous", at this bar attached
to an East Dulwich wine shop – the "simple meat, fish, or cheese
platters" are just there "as an accompaniment".
/ www.greenandbluewines.com; 11 pm, Fri & Sat midnight, Sun 10.30 pm;
no Amex.*

Green & Red Bar & Cantina E1 £38 ❷❸❷
51 Bethnal Green Rd 7749 9670 1–2D
*"All the fun of the real Mexico" is to be found at this funky
bar/cantina, near Brick Lane, where the "surprisingly good" dishes
(from a "limited" menu) are some of London's most "authentic";
the occasional reporter, though, senses a slight drift in standards
since the early days. / www.greenred.co.uk; 10.30 pm; closed L.*

Green Chilli W6 £29 ❸❸④
220 King St 8748 0111 7–2B
*"It looks nothing special", but this year-old Hammersmith Indian
is still "trying hard", and offers a menu that's "different from the
usual". / www.greenchilliltd.co.uk; midnight.*

Green Door Bar & Grill £38 ❸❸④
152 Gloucester Rd, SW7 7373 2010 5–2B **NEW**
33 Cornhill, EC3 7929 1378 9–2C
Not what you'd call a chic destination, but this new steakhouse,
by Bank, does what it does pretty well; there's also a longer-
established and horribly brash branch, near Gloucester Road tube,
which reporters never bother to comment on.
/ www.greendoorsteakhouse.co.uk.

The Green Olive W9 £44 ❸❷❸
5 Warwick Pl 7289 2469 8–4A
"Right back on form", say fans of this smartish Maida Vale Italian –
after ups and downs in recent times, it was this year mainly judged
"well above average, for a local". / 10 pm; D only, ex Fri & Sat open
L & D, closed Sun; booking: max 20.

Green's SW1 £67 ❸❷❷
36 Duke St 7930 4566 3–3D
Simon Parker Bowles's "discreet" and "club-like" St James's bastion
"unfailingly" pleases Establishment types with its "civilised" style
and its "simple" and "well-prepared" cooking; fish is the highlight
of the "nursery-fare" menu. / www.greens.org.uk; 11 pm; May-Sep closed
Sun; no jeans or trainers.

The Greenhouse W1 £90 ❸❸❷
27a Hays Mews 7499 3331 3–3B
Marlon Abela's investment has "worked wonders" on the interior
of this Mayfair veteran, "tucked-away" in a mews; "comical" prices,
though, still dent enthusiasm both for the "fabulous" wine list and
for Antonin Bonnet's "complex" cuisine (though London's chefs,
we're told, see him as 'one to watch'). / www.greenhouserestaurant.co.uk;
10.30 pm; closed Sat L & Sun; booking: max 6-10; set weekday L £55 (FP).

Greig's W1 £54 ❸❸④
26 Bruton Pl 7629 5613 3–2B
Hidden-away just off Bond Street, an "upmarket" steakhouse
of long standing, with a somewhat "different" ambience; feedback
– historically, a little mixed – was all upbeat this year.
/ www.greigs.com; midnight; set weekday L £17 (FP).

Grenadier SW1 £36 ④④❶
18 Wilton Row 7235 3074 5–1D
"Quietly tucked-away" in a cuter-than-cute Belgravia mews,
this picture-book pub is "in all the tourist guides"; the food in the
dining room, however, is generally "bland" – stick to a sausage and
a Bloody Mary at the bar. / www.pubexplorer.co.uk; 9.30 pm.

The Greyhound at Battersea SW11 £45 ❸❸❸
136 Battersea High St 7978 7021 10–1C
A "superb" wine list – including "loads of exciting and interesting
bottles" – is the star of the show at this back street Battersea
gastropub; its "good seasonal menus", though, are generally
"enjoyable" too. / www.thegreyhoundatbattersea.co.uk; 10 pm; closed
Mon & Sun D.

The Grille £30 ④④④
200 Pentonville Rd, N1 7841 0401 8–3D **NEW**
81 Great Eastern St, EC2 7739 9111 9–1D
*Views divide on this chain-brasserie (part of a budget hotel)
in trendy Hoxton, which fans say is "modern and reliable",
and critics feel "is like an upmarket Harvester"; in mid-2008 a new
branch opened in King's Cross.* / www.grillerestaurants.com.

Ground W4 £25 ❷❷❷
219-221 Chiswick High Rd 8747 9113 7–2A
*"It beats GBK anytime!"; even reporters who are "not really into
burgers" still love a visit to this "bright" and "casual" Chiswick café,
where "superb meat" is "cooked to perfection", and "sides and
drinks are excellent" too.* / www.groundrestaurants.com; Sun-Mon 10 pm,
Tue-Thu 10.30 pm, Fri & Sat 11 pm.

Grumbles SW1 £36 ④❷❸
35 Churton St 7834 0149 2–4B
*A "cosy" old Pimlico bistro with "no pretensions" – just "reliable
home cooking" that's "inexpensive" and "enjoyable".*
/ www.grumblesrestaurant.co.uk; 10.45 pm, Sun 10.30 pm; set always available
£24 (FP).

The Guinea Grill W1 £52 ❸❸❸
30 Bruton Pl 7499 1210 3–3B
*"The best steak 'n kidney pies in town", and "great grills" too,
make this "cramped" but "convivial" dining room – "hidden-away"
behind a "proper" Mayfair pub – a "last bastion of Englishness";
it's undoubtedly pricey, though, and critics say it's just "old hat".*
/ www.theguinea.co.uk; 10.30 pm; closed Sat L & Sun; booking: max 8.

The Gun E14 £46 ❸④❷
27 Coldharbour Ln 7515 5222 11–1C
*"A riverside pub with a difference" – this popular Isle of Dogs
"gem" is "well worth the walk from Canary Wharf", thanks not
least to its "lovely" views and its sometimes "excellent" food;
service, though, seems increasingly "lax".* / www.thegundocklands.com;
10.30 pm.

Gung-Ho NW6 £34 ❸❷❷
328-332 West End Ln 7794 1444 1–1B
*"Enjoyable", "consistent" and "popular", this Chinese veteran has
now re-established itself as "one of West Hampstead's
best places"; the staff are "really nice" too.* / www.stir-fry.co.uk;
11.30 pm; no Amex.

Haandi SW3 £35 ❷❸④
7 Cheval Pl 7823 7373 5–1C
*"Rich, spicy, flavoursome and copious" curries make it worth
seeking out this "very good" north Indian; it's reasonably-priced too,
especially given its swanky location, hidden-away in a mews
opposite Harrods.* / www.haandi-restaurants.com; 11 pm, Fri-Sat 11.30 pm.

Haché £30 ❷❸❷
329-331 Fulham Rd, SW10 7823 3515 5–3B **NEW**
24 Inverness St, NW1 7485 9100 8–3B
*The "seriously delicious" burgers at this "funky" duo "knock the
spots off all the Gourmet This & That chains"; as well as the
Camden Town original, there's now a Chelsea outlet (formerly the
site of a Randall & Aubin).*

Haiku W1 £52 ④⑤④
15 New Burlington Pl   7494 4777   3–2C
Given its size and level of ambition, it's striking how little interest this large, pan-oriental yearling, off Regent Street, has inspired; it can seem quite "cool", and the huge menu mostly satisfies, but "unprofessional" service can let the side down quite badly. / www.haikurestaurant.com; 10.30 pm; closed Sun.

HAKKASAN W1 £74 ❷❸❷
8 Hanway Pl   7927 7000   4–1A
"It's impossible not to feel cool", at this "sexy", "NY-style" basement, hidden-away off Oxford Street; prices may be "astronomical", but the "vivid" oriental dishes (including "exceptional" dim sum) generally live up to them; this year saw less "snooty" service too. / www.hakkasan.com; 11.30 pm, Fri-Sat 12.30 am; no jeans or trainers.

Halepi W2 £40 ④❷❸
18 Leinster Ter   7262 1070   6–2C
A "time-warp" Bayswater taverna, whose diehard fan club go a bundle on its "quaint" style and "simple" fare; sceptics, though, just find its standards "bafflingly poor". / www.halepi.co.uk; midnight.

Hamburger Union £23 ❸④④
25 Dean St, W1   7437 6004   4–2A
64 Tottenham Court Rd, W1   7636 0011   2–1C
4-6 Garrick St, WC2   7379 0412   4–3C
Irving St (off Leicester Sq), WC2   7839 8100   4–4B
341 Upper St, N1   7359 4436   8–3D
"Meaty burgers", "lovely shakes" and "great malts" inspire all-round satisfaction with this handy chain – now running neck-and-neck with GBK in terms of survey ratings. / 10.30 pm; no booking, except N1 upstairs room.

Hammersmith Café W6 £17 ④④⑤
1a Studland St   8748 2839   7–2B
For either "a greasy-spoon breakfast, or a Thai dinner", this grungy Hammersmith caff is a "busy" and "reliable" option, and it's certainly "cheap" (especially as you can BYO). / 10.30 pm; closed Sun; no Amex.

Haozhan W1 NEW £32 ❷❷❸
8 Gerrard St   7434 3838   4–3A
This "quality newcomer", in the heart of Chinatown, is "definitely at the upper end of the scale for the area"; the décor may be a bit "bland", but the "unusual" Chinese dishes are usually "skillful", and sometimes "inspired". / www.haozhan.co.uk; 11.30 pm, Fri & Sat midnight, Sun 11 pm.

Harbour City W1 £27 ❷❸④
46 Gerrard St   7439 7859   4–3B
A "Chinatown staple", long renowned for "wonderful dim sum at good prices". / 11.30 pm, Fri & Sat midnight, Sun 10.

Hard Rock Café W1 £42 ④④❷
150 Old Park Ln   7629 0382   3–4B
"It's too noisy" – obviously – but the original Mayfair branch of this worldwide rock 'n' burger franchise is "still good fun", say fans, who find its food "standard" but "dependable". / www.hardrock.com; 12.30 am; need 10+ to book.

Hardy's Brasserie W1 £42 ④❷❸
53 Dorset St 7935 5929 2–1A
*This civilised Marylebone "hide-away" has finally changed its name
(having for years mis-described itself as a wine bar); even if the
food is sometimes "only just satisfactory", it still has fans for whom
it's a "favourite" inexpensive stand-by. / www.hardys-w1.com; 10.30 pm;
closed Sat L & Sun.*

Hare & Tortoise £24 ❸④④
15-17 Brunswick Sq, WC1 7278 4945 2–1D
38 Haven Grn, SW5 8610 7066 1–2A
373 Kensington High St, W14 7603 8887 7–1D
296-298 Upper Richmond Rd, SW15 8394 7666 10–2B
*"Bright and buzzing" orientals, noted for their "incredibly large
portions" of noodles and sushi, and an "excellent price/quality
ratio" – "no wonder there's always a queue".
/ www.hareandtortoise-restaurants.co.uk; 10.45 pm; W14 no bookings.*

Harlem W2 £42 ④④❸
78 Westbourne Grove 7985 0900 6–1B
*Fans tout the "excellent American-style brunch" at this fashionable
Bayswater "soul-food" outfit; critics, however, just write the place off
as "an utter shambles". / www.harlemsoulfood.com; midnight, Wed 1 am,
Sun 10 pm.*

Harrison's SW12 £37 ⑤④⑤
15-19 Bedford Hill 8675 6900 10–2C
*"Stunningly average food at not-so-average prices" is the theme
of too many reports on the re-launch of the former Balham Bar
& Grill by Sam Harrison (of Sam's Brasserie fame); it has been
"a real let-down". / www.harrisonsbalham.co.uk/; 10.30 pm.*

Harry Morgan's NW8 £33 ④④⑤
31 St John's Wood High St 7722 1869 8–3A
*"Excellent chicken soup and salt beef" are the sort of culinary
delights that have made this St John's Wood deli a renowned Jewish
institution; overall the food is "fairly ordinary", though, and rather
"overpriced". / www.harryms.co.uk; 10.30 pm.*

The Hartley SE1 £35 ❸❸❸
64 Tower Bridge Rd 7394 7023 1–3C
*Tasty burgers are the menu highlight at this nice enough
boozer – a handy stand-by a mile or so south of Tower Bridge.
/ www.thehartley.com, 10 pm, Sun 7 pm.*

The Hat & Feathers EC1 £43 ⑤④④
2 Clerkenwell Rd 7490 2244 9–1B
*"It thinks it's a gourmet destination, and it isn't!" – this bland dining
room over a Clerkenwell boozer sometimes seems "a find",
but rather too many reporters feel it offers "disappointing" food
at "cheeky" prices. / www.hatandfeathers.com; 10.30 pm; closed
Sat L & Sun.*

The Havelock Tavern W14 £36 ❷⑤❸
57 Masbro Rd   7603 5374   7–1C
"Mouthwatering" food, "famously disinterested staff" and
a "convivial" vibe regularly feature in reports on this famous
Olympia backstreet gastroboozer; a slight slip in ratings boosts
those who say it's "not as exceptional since it changed hands",
but others insist that: "after a wobble, it's back on form".
/ www.thehavelocktavern.co.uk; 10 pm, Sun 9.30 pm; no credit cards;
no booking.

The Haven N20 £40 ❸❷❸
1363 High Rd   8445 7419   1–1B
"West End quality in NW London" has made this Whetstone spot
"very popular"; there's the odd gripe about "turning tables",
though, and about food that's "competent rather than interesting".
/ www.haven-bistro.co.uk; 11 pm; no Amex.

Hawksmoor E1 £52 ❷④④
157 Commercial St   7247 7392   9–1D
This "clubby" and "noisy" Spitalfields steakhouse is getting a bit
cocky; fans still say it offers "the best steak and chips in town"
(and "magnificent cocktails"), but service is increasingly
"disappointing", and critics think prices are "taking the p***".
/ www.thehawksmoor.co.uk; 10.30 pm; closed Sat L & Sun.

Haz £32 ❸❸❸
9 Cutler St, E1   7929 7923   9–2D
6 Mincing Ln, EC3   7929 3173   9–3D
These large and "noisy" Turkish operations in the City are "always
busy", thanks to their "reliable" food at "value-for-money" prices.
/ www.hazrestaurant.co.uk; 11.30 pm.

Hazuki WC2 £33 ❸④④
43 Chandos Pl   7240 2530   4–4C
"Perfect for simple Japanese, and central too" – this small spot,
near the Coliseum, continues to please most reporters; service can
sometimes prove elusive though (especially if you sit upstairs).
/ www.hazukilondon.co.uk; 10.30 pm, Sun 9.30 pm; closed Sun L;
set weekday L £20 (FP).

Hélène Darroze
The Connaught Hotel W1 NEW £78
Carlos Pl   7499 7070   3–3B
This grand Mayfair dining room, formerly occupied by the Ramsay
group's Angela Hartnett, re-opened as this guide was going
to press, with a star Parisian chef at the helm; we did try to bring
you a first-week review, but arrived for lunch to find that the hotel
had managed to lose our booking... / www.the-connaught.co.uk;
10.30 pm; closed Sat & Sun; jacket & tie.

Hellenik W1 £34 ❸❶❸
30 Thayer St   7935 1257   2–1A
A "time-warp classic" where the dishes are "outstanding", or a
"grubby" place serving "uninspired" fare? – both schools of thought
are well represented in feedback on this Greek taverna,
in Marylebone; either way, it's "packed every lunchtime". / 10.45 pm;
closed Sun; no Amex.

Henry J Beans SW3 £35 ④④❸
195-197 King's Rd 7352 9255 5–3C
A small fan club hails this veteran Chelsea dive as a "great burger joint"; it does also take flak though – "how can they screw up salad?" – making the 'surprise' garden the most reliable attraction. / www.henryjbeans.com; 10 pm.

Hereford Road W2 £40 ❸❸④
3 Hereford Rd 7727 1144 6–1B
An "interesting" and "uncompromising" menu (à la St John) wins praise – from some quarters – for this Bayswater spot as a "fabulous newcomer"; its décor is "chilly", though, and sceptical reporters think its arrival has generally been "over-hyped". / www.herefordroad.org; 10.30 pm.

Hibiscus W1 £83 ❸❷④
29 Maddox St 7629 2999 3–2C
"Ludlow's finest arrives in Mayfair"; "after all the hype", though, Claude Bosi's début has proved "not fully convincing" – many reporters do hail its "massively accomplished" cuisine, but others find the food "unfashionably fussy", and the "luxurious" décor seems rather uninspired. / www.hibiscusrestaurant.co.uk; 10.30 pm; closed Sat & Sun; set weekday L £38 (FP).

High Road Brasserie W4 £47 ④④❸
162-166 Chiswick High Rd 8742 7474 7–2A
In classic Nick ('Soho House') Jones style, this "animated" Chiswick brasserie is an "always-bustling" neighbourhood linchpin, usually much-populated with "media folk"; after a fair start, however, the food is now "distinctly average" – "breakfast is what they do best". / www.highroadhouse.co.uk; 10.45 pm, Fri & Sat 11.45 pm.

Hilliard EC4 £26 ❶❷❷
26a Tudor St 7353 8150 9–3A
"It does a roaring take-away trade with the local lawyers", but you can also eat-in, at this "upmarket, 'gastro'-snack bar", by the Temple; it does "really clever and well-produced sarnies, salads and cakes", and decent wines too. / 7 pm; closed Sat & Sun.

Hix Oyster & Chop House EC1 NEW £48 ❷⑤❸
35-37 Greenhill Rents, Cowcross St 7017 1930 9–1A
Ex-Caprice supremo Mark Hix's much-hyped, no-frills Farringdon newcomer – on the former site of Rudland & Stubbs (RIP) – offers sometimes "excellent", plainly-British cooking; "you'd have thought he'd have got some better staff, though" (and not "stand there all evening gassing to his mates"). / www.restaurantsetcltd.com; 11 pm; closed Sat L & Sun D; set Sun L £36 (FP).

Hokkien Chan EC2 £36 ❸❸❸
85 London Wall 7628 5772 9–2C
"Reinvented, with new branding" a year ago, the former Sri Siam City (RIP) is a similarly "good" oriental "all-rounder", and similarly "a little dull". / www.orientalrestaurantgroup.co.uk; 10.30 pm; closed Sat & Sun.

Hole in the Wall W4 £39 ❸❸❸
12 Sutton Lane North 8742 7185 7–2A
"A great garden for warm evenings" is the stand-out attraction of this "good gastropub", hidden-away in a cute back street south of Turnham Green. / 9.45 pm, Sun 9.15 pm; no Amex.

Holly Bush NW3 £36 ④④❶
22 Holly Mount 7435 2892 8–1A
The food is "nothing special" – "pies", "sausages", "excellent
cheese", "well-kept ales" – but this "lovely" Hampstead hostelry
makes an ideal pit stop for those "who prefer a pub to be a pub".
/ www.hollybushpub.com; 10 pm, Sun 9 pm; no Amex.

Holy Cow SW11 £20 ❷❷–
166 Battersea Pk Rd 7498 2000 10–1C
"I'm afraid it's only a delivery service, but this is the BEST", say fans
of this "delicious" Indian take-away, in Battersea.
/ www.holycowfineindianfood.com; 11 pm, Sun 10.30 pm; D only.

Homage
Waldorf Hilton WC2 £40 ④❸④
22 Aldwych 7759 4080 2–2D
Hidden-away inside an Aldwych hotel, this "grand" and "ornate"
former ballroom has never really made many waves – shame,
as the British food is "decent" enough, if arguably on the "pricey"
side. / www.hilton.com/waldorf; 10.30 pm; closed Sat L & Sun L; booking:
max 6.

The Horseshoe NW3 £35 ④④❸
28 Heath St 7431 7206 8–2A
The dreaded 'Hampstead effect' already seems to be nobbling this
"light" and "cheerful" boozer; only a year into its new incarnation,
its "simple and tasty" cooking has already gone "slightly off the
boil". / www.thehorseshoehampstead.com; 10 pm; no Amex.

Hot Stuff SW8 £22 ❶❶❷
19 Wilcox Rd 7720 1480 10–1D
Brave the "dodgy" Vauxhall location – film buffs may recognise the
streetscape from 'My Beautiful Launderette' – to truffle out this
"tiny" but "awesome" BYO caff; "the guy who runs it is a star",
and he serves up some "fabulous" curries at "incredible" prices.
/ www.eathotstuff.com; 10 pm; closed Sun.

The House N1 £45 ④④❸
63-69 Canonbury Rd 7704 7410 8–2D
"Not cheap, but chilled" – this Canonbury bar/restaurant is a
popular hang-out for the (affluent) locals, but service can
be "patchy", and the food has "slipped" of late. / www.inthehouse.biz;
10.30 pm; closed Mon L.

Hoxton Apprentice N1 £39 ④④④
16 Hoxton Sq 7749 2828 9–1D
Though often-compared to Fifteen, this charitable Hoxton training-
venture aims to produce much simpler fare; fans like its "well-
executed" fodder and "always-enthusiastic" approach... but, on a
bad day, results can be "hopeless". / www.hoxtonapprentice.com; 11 pm.

Hudson's SW15 £32 ④❸❷
113 Lower Richmond Rd 8785 4522 10–1A
"A friendly and busy local", in Putney, that's most popular as a
breakfast stop (and also does "fantastic" happy-hour deals);
its "overly varied" food, however, is "not always successful".
/ 10.30 pm, Sun 10 pm.

Hugo's NW6 £39 ④④❸
25 Lonsdale Rd 7372 1232 1–2B
"Healthy and tasty" organic fare – particularly a "huge and delicious" breakfast – wins praise for this cute and "family-friendly" Queen's Park café; (its South Kensington branch is no more). / 10.30 pm; no Amex.

Hummus Bros £15 ❸❷❸
88 Wardour St, W1 7734 1311 3–2D
36-67 Southampton Row, WC1 7404 7079 2–1D
"The best place for cheap and filling food... if you like hummus that is!" – these "easy-going" canteens are "a fantastic simple concept, executed well". / www.hbros.co.uk; 10 pm, Thu Fri Sat 11pm; WC1 closed Sat & Sun; no bookings.

Hunan SW1 £54 ❶❷④
51 Pimlico Rd 7730 5712 5–2D
"Just do as Mr Peng tells you and you will eat very well", at this "very plain and crammed" Pimlico Chinese; as Peng Sr takes over from Peng Jr, though, "touchy" service has occasionally been an issue (especially "if you go off-piste, and actually want to see a menu"). / www.hunanlondon.com; 11 pm; closed Sun.

Huong-Viet
An Viet House N1 £20 ❸⑤④
12-14 Englefield Rd 7249 0877 1–1C
For "authentic Vietnamese food at a great price", this "chaotic" De Beauvoir Town BYO canteen still draws fans from far and wide; the "friendly" service, though, is "so slow" – "the next table ordered on a mobile". / www.huongviet.co.uk; 11 pm; closed Sun; no Amex.

Hush W1 £55 ⑤⑤④
8 Lancashire Ct 7659 1500 3–2B
It may have "a lovely, discreet setting", just off Bond Street, but the best advice at this "Eurotrash" favourite is to "stick to the bar" – "apart from the shocking bill", the restaurant is "stunningly average" all-round. / www.hush.co.uk; 10.30 pm; closed Sun; booking: max 12.

Las Iguanas
Royal Festival Hall SE1 £35 ④⑤④
Unit 14, Festival Walk, Belvedere Rd 7620 1328 2–3D
"A good location" – with nice sunny-day tables, by the Festival Hall – is the main draw to this "noisy" South American chain outlet; its style is a bit "formulaic", though – to some "horribly" so. / www.iguanas.co.uk; 11 pm.

Ikeda W1 £70 ❶❶⑤
30 Brook St 7629 2730 3–2B
Little-known but "top-notch", this Japanese Mayfair veteran may have "no atmosphere", but – especially "for sushi" – it's a "pricey-but-worth-it" destination. / 10.30 pm; closed Sat L & Sun; set weekday L £55 (FP).

Imli W1 £29 ❸❸❸
167-169 Wardour St 7287 4243 3–1D
A "canteen-style" Soho subcontinental whose "tapas-style" approach is widely hailed as "a good concept" – "fun", "tasty" and "good value". / www.imli.co.uk; 11 pm, Sat 11.30 pm, Sun 10 pm.

Imperial China WC2 £37 ❸❸❸
25a Lisle St   7734 3388   4–3B
"Hidden-away off the beaten track", a "solid performer" that offers "a slightly upmarket Chinatown experience"; "good dim sum" too. / www.imperial-china.co.uk; 11.30 pm.

Imperial City EC3 £41 ❸❸❷
Royal Exchange, Cornhill   7626 3437   9–2C
"Beautiful" décor, "fast and efficient" service and "consistently good" Chinese food maintain the solid popularity of this smart all-rounder, in the cellars of the Royal Exchange. / www.orientalrestaurantgroup.co.uk; 11 pm; closed Sat & Sun.

Inaho W2 £33 ❶⑤⑤
4 Hereford Rd   7221 8495   6–1B
"Flawless" sushi (and other "delicious" Japanese fare) makes this "tiny" and "eccentric" Bayswater shack "one of London's best unsung heros"; "service is very poor – only one person for the whole place – but maybe that's how they keep prices low". / 11 pm; closed Sat L & Sun; no Amex or Maestro; set weekday L £20 (FP).

Inamo W1 NEW
134-136 Wardour St   7287 7265   3–1D
Ever wished you could project better? – at this Soho Japanese, scheduled to open in autumn 2008, you get to adjust the image projected on your table, and to order electronically too; it sounds as if the food is going to be hard pressed to live up to the technology… / www.inamo-restaurant.com.

Incognico WC2 £52 ④❸④
117 Shaftesbury Ave   7836 8866   4–2B
This "comfy" brasserie, by Cambridge Circus, is undoubtedly "a very good place to know pre-theatre"; the food, though, is "unspectacular". / www.incognico.com; 11 pm; closed Sun; set weekday L & pre-theatre £37 (FP).

L'Incontro SW1 £59 ④❸❸
87 Pimlico Rd   7730 6327   5–2D
A slick Pimlico Italian still hailed as "the best in town" by a handful of ardent fans; even they agree "you pay for it", though, and critics just find the place "average, and ridiculously overpriced". / www.lincontro-restaurant.com; 11.30 pm, Sat & Sun 10.30 pm; set weekday L £38 (FP).

India Club
Strand Continental Hotel WC2 £21 ❸⑤⑤
143 Strand   7836 0650   2–2D
"With its old lino and worn furniture", this Indian "museum-piece" is still held dear by those who love its quirky style and its "good curry at very good prices" (and BYO too); some former fans, though, now think it "past its sell-by date". / 10.45 pm; no credit cards; booking: max 6.

Indian Ocean SW17 £26 ❸❶④
216 Trinity Rd   8672 7740   10–2C
A notably "reliable" and popular Wandsworth curry house; the cooking is "not the most adventurous", but "the friendly service is pitched just right". / 11.30 pm.

Indian Zing W6 £34 ❷⓪❷
236 King St 8748 5959 7–2B
Manog Vasaikar's "zesty" and "creative" subcontinental cooking
makes it "really worth a trek" to this "bustling" and very
"welcoming" Hammersmith two-year-old. / www.indianzing.co.uk;
10.30 pm.

Indigo
One Aldwych WC2 £58 ④❸❸
1 Aldwych 7300 0400 2–2D
A "calm" mezzanine overlooking the lobby of a sleek Covent
Garden hotel; "solid" cooking makes it a handy option – especially
for a "relaxed" business breakfast or lunch, or pre-theatre – but it's
far from being the destination it once was. / www.onealdwych.com;
11.15 pm; set pre theatre £39 (FP).

The Inn at Kew Gardens
Kew Gardens Hotel TW9 £35 ④④❸
292 Sandycombe Ln 8940 2220 1–4A
An "atmospheric" refurbished pub, not far from Kew Gardens tube;
the food can be "really quite good", but the whole operation seems
to get "over-stressed" at busy times. / www.theinnatkewgardens.com;
10 pm.

Inn the Park SW1 £47 ⑤⑤❸
St James's Pk 7451 9999 2–3C
This beautifully-designed venture has "the best location ever", in the
heart of St James's Park, but sadly its "hit-and-miss" service and
"regularly poor" food reduce it to being nothing more than
a "tourist trap". / www.innthepark.co.uk; 10 pm, Winter 9 pm.

Inshoku SE1 £26 ❸④⑤
23-24 Lower Marsh 7928 2311 9–4A
"In a somewhat decayed street, near Waterloo", a Japanese haunt
known for its "scrumptious and good-value" set lunch menus,
and "enjoyable sushi" too. / 10.30 pm; closed Sat L & Sun.

Inside SE10 £41 ❷❸④
19 Greenwich South St 8265 5060 1–3D
"Pity about the cramped conditions", at Guy Awford's
"unpretentious" dining room – his "assured" cooking is "easily the
best in the Greenwich desert". / www.insiderestaurant.co.uk; 10.30 pm,
Fri-Sat 11pm; closed Mon & Sun D.

Isarn N1 £35 ❷⓪❸
119 Upper St 7424 5153 8–3D
"Staff couldn't be more helpful", at this "small but perfectly-
formed" Islington Thai – a "clean, modern" venture serving food
that's "delicate, flavour-packed and fragrant". / www.isarn.co.uk;
11 pm.

Ishbilia SW1 £38 ❷❷❸
9 William St 7235 7788 5–1D
"A tasteful refurbishment" has improved the all-round appeal
of this Knightsbridge oasis, and its mezze and other Lebanese fare
are just as "good" as ever. / www.ishbilia.com; 11.30 pm.

The Island NW10 £37 ❸❷❸
123 College Rd   8960 0693   1–2B
"In the middle of the gastro-desert that is Kensal Green",
a "friendly" and "unpretentious" gastropub serving "decent" fare.
/ www.islandpubco.com; 10 pm, Thu-Sat 10.30 pm; closed Mon L; no Amex;
no booking Sat L.

Isola del Sole SW15 £36 ❷❶❸
16 Lacy Rd   8785 9962   10–2B
"A hidden gem in a Putney sidestreet" – "a great local",
with "very friendly" service and "surprising and tasty" Sardinian
fare. / www.isoladelsole.co.uk; 10.30 pm; closed Sun; no Amex.

Itsu £27 ❸❸❸
103 Wardour St, W1   7479 4790   3–2D
118 Draycott Ave, SW3   7590 2400   5–2C
Level 2, Cabot Place East, E14   7512 5790   11–1C
These "buzzing" conveyor-cafés are "a good bet for a quick bite" –
"the sushi's not the best, but good enough and so consistent".
/ www.itsu.co.uk; 11 pm, E14 10 pm; Cabot Pl closed Sun; no booking.

THE IVY WC2 £56 ❸❷❷
1 West St   7836 4751   4–3B
"Don't knock it!", says fans of this Theatreland legend, for whom –
despite increasingly "ho-hum" cooking – it remains an "always-
buzzing" favourite; nowadays, however, it can seem a bit
of "cliché" – "is it really worth paying through the nose
just to rubberneck the odd soap star?" / www.the-ivy.co.uk; midnight;
booking: max 6; set Sun L £44 (FP).

Izgara N3 £25 ❸❸④
11 Hendon Lane   8371 8282   1–1B
"Tasty Turkish cuisine" that "doesn't dent your wallet" maintains
this café/take-away as one of Finchley's more popular locals;
service, though, has seemed a little "patchy" of late. / midnight;
no Amex.

Iznik Kaftan SW3 NEW £37 ❸④❸
99-103 Fulham Rd   7581 6699   5–2C
Offshoot of a quirky little outfit in Highbury Park, this "upmarket"
and ornately-furnished Brompton Cross newcomer has impressed
early-days reporters with its "interesting" Turkish fare.
/ www.iznik.co.uk/kaftan/; midnight.

Jade Garden W1 £28 ❸❸❸
15 Wardour St   7437 5065   4–3A
"All the dim sum classics are done well", at this long-serving "cheap
and cheerful" Chinatown veteran. / www.londonjadegarden.co.uk; 11 pm.

Jashan HA0 £25 ❷❷④
1-2 Coronet Pde, Ealing Rd   8900 9800   1–1A
"A top-notch meal for the money" is to be had at this friendly
canteen, which serves a "varied" south Indian menu. / 10.30 pm;
no Amex; need 6+ to book, Sat & Sun.

Jenny Lo's Tea House SW1 £25 ❸❸④
14 Eccleston St   7259 0399   2–4B
"Great-value" stir-frys and noodles – "all freshly cooked up in front
of you" – are served up in a "bustling, school-canteen-like
atmosphere" at this "friendly" Belgravian; "at lunch, be prepared
to queue". / 10 pm; closed Sat L & Sun; no credit cards; no booking.

Jimmy's SW3 NEW £45 ④❷❸
386 King's Rd 7351 9999 5–3B
Mixed early reports on this Chelsea newcomer (on the site of Bacio, RIP) – fans extol its "elegant, casual and charming" style and its "simple" dishes "done to a turn" (by an ex-Ramsay group chef), but sceptics just "can't see the point". / www.jimmyschelsea.com; 11 pm.

Jin Kichi NW3 £35 ❶❷⑤
73 Heath St 7794 6158 8–1A
"Nothing changes (thankfully!)" – "great-value, fresh sushi, sashimi and yakitori" still pack 'em in at this "firm-favourite" Hampstead Japanese veteran; it's a "welcoming" place too. / www.jinkichi.com; 11 pm, Sun 10 pm; closed Mon, Tue-Fri D only, Sat & Sun open L & D.

Joanna's SE19 £43 ❸❸❷
56 Westow Hill 8670 4052 1–4D
Crystal Palace's only "comfortable, grown-up eatery" is still "hard to beat", say fans, thanks to its "reliable" Gallic fare; reports, however, are more up-and-down than they were. / www.joannas.uk.com; 11 pm.

Joe Allen WC2 £40 ④④❶
13 Exeter St 7836 0651 4–3D
A "tremendous" ambience has long made this "fun" American basement, in Covent Garden, a "favourite post-theatre haunt"; the food – including the famous off-menu burger – is "patchy" though, and service sometimes "couldn't care less". / www.joeallen.co.uk; 12.45 am, Sun 11.45 pm; booking: max 10 Fri & Sat; set brunch £25 (FP), set weekday L & pre-theatre £30 (FP).

Joe's Brasserie SW6 £37 ❸❷❷
130 Wandsworth Bridge Rd 7731 7835 10–1B
John Brinkley's "crowded but fun" hang-out has long been a "buzzing" linchpin of deepest Fulham; with its "well-cooked brasserie fare" and "fabulous low cost wine", it has seemed "even better of late". / www.brinkleys.com; 11 pm, Sat 11.30 pm, Sun 10.30 pm.

Jom Makan SW1 NEW £27 ④④④
5-7 Pall Mall East 7925 2402 2–2C
Almost on Trafalgar Square itself, you can't fault this new Malaysian for location, and it's an airy and serene sort of place to escape from the mêlée; on our early-days visit, however, it was otherwise eminently missable. / Rated on Editors' visit; www.jommakan.co.uk; 11 pm, Sun 10 pm.

Joy King Lau WC2 £27 ❸④❸
3 Leicester St 7437 1132 4–3A
A "Chinatown old-timer", with a reputation for "awesome" dim sum, as well as for "classic" Cantonese fare that's "reliably a cut above". / 11.30 pm.

Julie's W11 £50 ④④❶
135 Portland Rd 7229 8331 6–2A
An "absolutely charming, subterranean rabbit warren"; this "secret hide-away", in Holland Park, "hasn't changed in 30 years", and is still "probably the most romantic venue in all of west London"; the food, though, is "from the Dark Ages". / www.juliesrestaurant.com; 11 pm.

FSA

The Junction Tavern NW5 £34 ❸❷❷
101 Fortess Rd 7485 9400 8–2B
An "always-busy" (and "rather noisy") Kentish Town local, praised for its "always-decent" food. / www.junctiontavern.co.uk; 10.30 pm; no Amex.

Just Falafs £16 ❷❹❹
155 Wardour St, W1 7734 1914 3–1D
27b Covent Garden Piazza, WC2 7240 3838 4–3D
"Fantastic, super-healthy wraps" are the stock-in-trade of this small chain; generally they offer "brilliant food and brilliant value", but it's our experience that – even at the same branch – standards can vary widely. / www.justfalafs.com; WC2 8 pm; W1 9 pm; W1 closed Sun; no Amex.

Just St James SW1
12 St James's St 7976 2222 3–4D
The marbled interior of this former St James's banking hall is "magnificent", but the rest of the experience "doesn't match up" – plans for a major re-launch were announced as this guide was going to press. / www.juststjames.com; 10.45 pm; closed Sat L & Sun.

K10 EC2 £31 ❷❸❸
20 Copthall Ave 7562 8510 9–2C
"Reliable" sushi rotates alongside "more experimental, westernised dishes", at this "hectic" City operation – still sometimes tipped as "the best of the conveyor-sushi operations". / www.k10.net; L only, closed Sat & Sun; no booking.

Kai Mayfair W1 £70 ❶❷❸
65 South Audley St 7493 8988 3–3A
"Stunning" and "beautifully-presented" food, backed up by a "premium" wine list, inspires the highest acclaim for this "top-quality" Mayfair Chinese; it's equally suited "to business or romance". / www.kaimayfair.com; 10.45 pm; set weekday L £44 (FP).

Kaifeng NW4 £47 ❹❺❹
51 Church Rd 8203 7888 1–1B
"At its best", this rare kosher-Chinese, in Harrow, offers "vibrant" and "elegant" fare; at its worst, however, it can just seem "disappointing" and "overpriced". / www.kaifeng.co.uk; 10.30 pm; closed Fri & Sat.

Kandoo W2 £24 ❸❹❹
458 Edgware Rd 7724 2428 8–4A
You get "well-cooked food – and at a reasonable price" – at this BYO Persian, near Lords. / www.kandoorestaurant.co.uk; midnight.

kare kare SW5 £36 ❸❷❷
152 Old Brompton Rd 7373 0024 5–2B
This "solid" South Kensington Indian tends to be eclipsed by its more famous neighbours, but it – similarly – is "better than your average curry house". / www.karekare.co.uk; 11 pm.

Karma W14 £28 ❷❷❺
44 Blythe Rd 7602 9333 7–1D
This "posh" but "welcoming" Olympia Indian offers some "great" and "different" dishes – the sole problem seems to be that "they never have enough customers to create a buzzy ambience". / www.k-a-r-m-a.co.uk; 11.30 pm; no Amex.

Kastoori SW17 £26 ❶❷④
188 Upper Tooting Rd 8767 7027 10–2C
"An explosion of tastes" awaits visitors to this "dingy" family-run
Tooting stalwart, which offers "simply stunning" east African/south
Indian cuisine – the survey's best vegetarian fare – at "ridiculously
low" prices. / 10.30 pm; closed Mon L & Tue L; no Amex or Maestro;
booking: max 12.

Kasturi EC3 £35 ❷❸❸
57 Aldgate High St 7480 7402 9–2D
A good standard Indian all-rounder, preferable in many respects
to most of the offerings on nearby Brick Lane.
/ www.kasturi-restaurant.co.uk; 11 pm, Sat 9.30 pm.

Kazan £34 ❷❷❸
93-94 Wilton Rd, SW1 7233 7100 2–4B
34-36 Houndsditch, EC3 7626 2222 9–2D **NEW**
Pimlico's "local marvel" is building an ever-growing following, thanks
to its "tasty" Turkish dishes, its "very knowledgeable" service and
its "fun" atmosphere; mid-2008 saw the opening of a City offshoot.

Ken Lo's Memories SW1 £54 ❷❷❸
67-69 Ebury St 7730 7734 2–4B
An "upmarket" and "charming" Belgravia "stalwart" which
continues to offer "traditional" Chinese food that –
more consistently that its Kensington sibling's nowadays – is "always
of a high standard". / www.memories-of-china.co.uk; 11 pm; closed Sun L.

Ken Lo's Memories of China W8 £48 ❸❸④
353 Kensington High St 7603 6951 7–1D
Reports on this "pricey" Kensington Chinese were unusually up-and-
down this year – part of the general decline in standards afflicting
most members of the London Fine Dining Group (formerly A-Z
Restaurants) since its 2007 sale. / www.memories-of-china.co.uk; 11 pm.

Kennington Tandoori SE11 £30 ❸❸❷
313 Kennington Rd 7735 9247 1–3C
"Very dependable" dishes make this smart and "welcoming"
neighbourhood curry house something of a "delicious local secret".
/ midnight, Fri & Sat 12.30 am.

Kensington Place W8 £54 ④⑤⑤
201-209 Kensington Church St 7727 3184 6–2B
"What have they done?" – new owners D&D London have sent
this well-known, "noisy" 'goldfish bowl' of a restaurant into full-scale
decline; the food picture is slightly complicated by the recent arrival
of a hopeful new chef, but, on other fronts, "little charm" is evident.
/ www.danddlondon.com; 10.45 pm; set always available £37 (FP).

Kensington Square Kitchen W8 £30 ❸❷❸
9 Kensington Sq 7938 2598 5–1A
Wildly over-hyped on launch as some sort of 'destination',
this "friendly" little café is actually just an ideal refuge for
Kensington shoppers and locals; the menu "is not incredibly
exciting, but doesn't aim to be", and includes some "incredible
cakes and puds". / www.kensingtonsquarekitchen.co.uk; 6 pm; closed Sun.

(Brew House)
Kenwood House NW3 £24 ④④❷
Hampstead Heath 8341 5384 8–1A
*"After a walk on Hampstead Heath", this "beautifully-located" café
– with a smashing garden – fits the bill perfectly for "a hearty
organic English breakfast", "a light lunch", or tea and a bun.*
/ www.companyofcooks.com; 6 pm (summer), 4 pm (winter).

Kenza EC2 £55 ④④❷
10 Devonshire Sq 7929 5533 9–2D
*"One of the few City venues you'd consider in the evening" –
this "beautifully-decorated" new operation, in a cellar near Liverpool
Street, is a 'party-Moroccan' of a type not often found in the
Square Mile; "the food's decent-enough, but they charge for it like
a wounded bull".* / www.kenza-restaurant.com; Mon-Wed 10 pm, Thu-Fri
11 pm, Sat 11.30pm; closed Sun.

Kettners W1 £40 ④④❷
29 Romilly St 7734 6112 4–2A
*"A bit bizarre" – this Soho institution (dating from 1867) offers
a "PizzaExpress+" menu (including grills) in "opulent" but "faded"
surroundings reminiscent of a "gentleman's club", and complete
with a champagne bar; the food is "very average".*
/ www.kettners.com; midnight, Thu-Sat 1am; need 7+ to book.

Kew Grill TW9 £50 ❸④❸
10b Kew Grn 8948 4433 1–3A
*It's "not cheap", but AWT's "tightly-packed" Kew venture pleases
most people most of the time with its "wholesome" grills, its "cosy"
ambience and its "obliging" – if not always "sure-footed" – service.*
/ www.awtonline.co.uk; 10.30 pm, Fri - Sat 11.30pm, Sun 10 pm; closed
Mon L.

Khan's W2 £16 ❷④④
13-15 Westbourne Grove 7727 5420 6–1C
*"For a great cheap 'n' cheerful curry", it's hard to beat this
cavernous but ever more "dependable" Bayswater institution;
"sadly, no alcohol".* / www.khansrestaurant.com; 11.45 pm.

Khan's of Kensington SW7 £32 ❸❷④
3 Harrington Rd 7584 4114 5–2B
*"Reliable" – still the key word in reports on this veteran curry
house, near South Kensington tube.* / www.khansofkensington.co.uk;
11 pm.

Khoai £24 ❷❸④
362 Ballards Ln, N12 8445 2039 1–1B **NEW**
6 Topsfield Pde, N8 8341 2120 1–1C
*In Crouch End and, more recently, North Finchley – a dynamic duo
of cafés that are consistently praised for their "delicious"
Vietnamese fare, "friendly" staff and "very cheap" prices.*

Kiasu W2 £30 ❸⑤⑤
48 Queensway 7727 8810 6–2C
*Fans again hail the "brilliant" and "extremely authentic"
Singapore/Malaysian street food on offer at this decidedly "no-frills"
Bayswater yearling; sceptics, though, say it's just a "hit-and-miss"
place, that's been unduly "hyped".* / www.kiasu.co.uk; 11 pm; no Amex
or Maestro.

Kiku W1 £52 ❷④⑤
17 Half Moon St 7499 4208 3–4B
"Even the décor is authentic." (*"which means that it could
be improved!"*), at this *"high-quality"* Mayfair Japanese; *"excellent"*
sushi and sashimi are the culinary high points – they do a *"bargain
set lunch"* too. / www.kikurestaurant.co.uk; 10.15 pm; closed Sun L;
set weekday L £31 (FP).

Kipferl EC1 £14 ❸❸④
70 Long Ln 7796 2229 9–1B
"Fantastic Sachertorte", *"wicked chocolate"*, *"top coffee"* –
such are the attractions of this superior deli/café, handy for the
Barbican. / www.kipferl.co.uk; L only, closed Sun.

Knaypa W6 NEW £35 ④❷④
268 King St 8563 2887 7–2B
"Smartly-dressed" staff and off-beat décor add character to this
Polish shop-conversion newcomer, near Ravenscourt Park tube;
its hearty scoff is certainly inexpensive, but unlikely to dispel any
prejudices you may have about Central European cuisine. / Rated
on Editors' visit; www.theknaypa.co.uk; 11 pm.

Koba W1 £44 ❸❶❸
11 Rathbone St 7580 8825 2–1C
"Helpful staff maintain a watchful eye", at this *"buzzy"* Fitzrovia
Korean, where first-timers enjoy the *"novel"* experience of a
tabletop BBQ, and regulars praise the *"fresh"* cooking and *"lovely"*
sauces. / 11 pm; closed Sun L.

Kolossi Grill EC1 £24 ④❶❷
56-60 Rosebery Ave 7278 5758 9–1A
*"Old-fashioned, dotty and not entirely reliable, but to be supported
for old times' sake"* – this *"'60s throw-back"* taverna maintains
a dedicated Clerkenwell following (not least for its *"unbeatable-
value"* lunches). / www.kolossigrill.com; 11 pm; closed Sat L & Sun;
set weekday L £15 (FP).

Konditor & Cook £20 ❷❸❸
Curzon Soho, 99 Shaftesbury Ave, W1 7292 1684 4–3A
46 Gray's Inn Rd, WC1 7404 6300 9–1A
30 St Mary Axe, EC3 0845 262 3030 9–2D NEW
"Remarkable" cakes are not the only *"tantalising"* treats on offer
at this small café/pâtisserie chain – it also serves *"the freshest"*
soups, sarnies and salads. / www.konditorandcook.com; W1 11 pm,
Sun 10.30 pm, Cornwall Rd & Stoney St SE1 6pm, WC1 7pm; Cornwall
Rd & Stoney St SE1 closed Sun; no booking.

Konstam at the Prince Albert WC1 £43 ❷❷❸
2 Acton St 7833 5040 8–3D
Having *"all food sourced within the M25"* sounds *"like a gimmick"*,
but *"it seems to work"* at Oliver Rowe's *"funky"* King's Cross pub-
conversion, which offers *"interesting"* dishes in a *"relaxed"*,
if *"rather odd"*, setting. / www.konstam.co.uk; 10.30 pm; closed
Sat L & Sun.

Kovalam NW6 £22 ❷❷④
12 Willesden Ln 7625 4761 1–2B
"Very good" and *"authentic"* south Indian dishes again win praise
for this hidden-away Kilburn-fringe spot. / www.kovalamrestaurant.co.uk;
11 pm.

Kulu Kulu £25 ❷④⑤
76 Brewer St, W1   7734 7316   3–2D
51-53 Shelton St, WC2   7240 5687   4–2C
39 Thurloe Pl, SW7   7589 2225   5–2C
"For a quick fix" of "fab" and "fresh" sushi, these "crowded" Kaiten-Zushi cafés are "always satisfying" and "sometimes brilliant"; all the branches, though, look "a bit grotty". / 10 pm, SW7 10.30 pm; closed Sun; no Amex; no booking.

Kurumaya EC4 £31 ❷❷❸
76-77 Watling St   7236 0236   9–2B
*"One of the rare, reliable cheap eateries in the City" – this Kaiten-Zushi outfit near Mansion house is often "first-class".
/ www.kurumaya.co.uk; 9.30 pm; closed Sat & Sun.*

Kyashii
The Kingly Club WC2 NEW £70
4 Upper St Martin's Ln   7836 5211   4–3B
*On the fringe of Covent Garden, a blingy basement newcomer; unfortunately, we didn't have the chance to check out its mega-pricey Japanese fare before this guide went off to the printers, but press reviews have not all been kind.
/ www.kinglyclub.com/sml/kyashii.htm; 10.30 pm, Thu-Sat 11.30 pm; closed Sun; no trainers.*

L-Restaurant & Bar W8 £44 ❸❷④
2 Abingdon Rd   7795 6969   5–1A
Slightly "odd", and certainly "little-known" – this Kensington two-year-old is nonetheless tipped by locals as "a delightful little hide-away"; staff are "great", and the "Spanish-biased" fare is "original" and "delicious". / www.l-restaurant.co.uk; 10.30 pm, Sun 9 pm; closed Mon L; set dinner £32 (FP).

The Ladbroke Arms W11 £38 ❷④❷
54 Ladbroke Rd   7727 6648   6–2B
A "top" Notting Hill boozer with "lots of charm", and offering "simple" but "scrummy" cooking that "never fails to live up to expectations"; "arrive early", if you want a seat on the sunny terrace. / www.capitalpubcompany.com; 9.30 pm; no booking after 7.30 pm.

Ladurée £64 ❷④❸
Harrods, 87-135 Brompton Rd, SW1   7730 1234   5–1D
71-72 Burlington Arc, Piccadilly, W1   7491 9155   3–3C
"Delightful, decadent and oh-so-French" – the famous Parisian tearoom's London offshoots inspire rapturous reports; the 'signature' macarons are of course "to die for", but more substantial dishes (Harrods only) are "delicious" – if, naturally, "pricey" – too. / W1 6 pm, SW1 9 pm, Sun 6 pm.

Lahore Kebab House E1 £22 ❶④④
2-4 Umberston St   7488 2551   11–1A
*"Legendary kebabs" and "brilliant lamb chops" headline the "exceptional-value" Pakistani grub on offer at this "hectic", "no-frills" East Ender – "rough and ready", but a "classic"; BYO.
/ midnight; need 8+ to book.*

Lamberts SW12 £44 **❶❶❷**
2 Station Pde 8675 2233 10–2C
"Top local recommendation after Chez Bruce!"; this "special" but "unpretentious" all-rounder, near Balham tube, makes "a great find", thanks to its "imaginatively-constructed food" and "fantastic" service – and all at "brilliant-value-for-money" prices.
/ www.lambertsrestaurant.com; 10.30 pm, Sun 9 pm; closed weekday L & Sun; no Amex; set dinner £27 (FP).

The Landau
The Langham W1 NEW £75 **❸❷❸**
1c, Portland Pl, Regent Street 7965 0165 2–1B
"Liveried, super-attentive staff" are but one part of the formula that makes this "sumptuous" ("glitzy'") new hotel dining room a fine-dining "beacon" in the purlieus of Oxford Circus; Andrew Turner's menus are certainly on the "fiddly" side, but fans say results are "divine". / www.thelandau.com; 11 pm, Sun 10 pm; no trainers; set pre-theatre £48 (FP), set weekday L £54 (FP).

(Winter Garden)
The Landmark NW1 £75 **❸❸❶**
222 Marylebone Rd 7631 8000 8–4A
An "impressive" atrium provides the "stunning" setting for dining at this Marylebone hotel; prices can seem "outrageous", but the place is still nominated for "peaceful" business meals, or for the "memorable Sunday champagne brunch". / www.landmarklondon.co.uk; 10.30 pm; no trainers; booking: max 12; set weekday L £58 (FP).

Lanes
East India House E1 £52
109-117 Middlesex St 7247 5050 9–2D
The year which saw a relaunch of this east-City basement inspired wildly varying reports, so we don't think a rating appropriate; let's hope history bears out the reporter who says: "the greatly improved room now matches the consistently excellent and unpretentious food". / www.lanesrestaurant.co.uk; 10 pm; closed Sat L & Sun.

Langan's Bistro W1 £38 **❹❸❸**
26 Devonshire St 7935 4531 2–1A
Fans of this "cosy" old Marylebone bistro like its "sociable" and "old-fashioned" style, and say its "familiar" repertoire of dishes is "always good"; for sceptics, though, it's just "disappointing".
/ www.langansrestaurants.co.uk; 11 pm; closed Sat L & Sun.

Langan's Brasserie W1 £51 **❹❸❷**
Stratton St 7491 8822 3–3C
This '80s icon, near the Ritz, maintains an ardent fan club, who say it's "still the place for celebrity-spotting", or for "a boozy business lunch"; critics, though, just find it "well past its sell-by date, and getting worse". / www.langansrestaurants.co.uk; midnight; closed Sun.

Langan's Coq d'Or Bar & Grill SW5 £44 **❹❷❸**
254-260 Old Brompton Rd 7259 2599 5–3A
"Reliable" and "good value" – "especially for lunch" – it may be, but this spacious, art-filled and rather elegant Earl's Court fixture has only a modest following among reporters; on the upside, you "rarely need to book". / www.langansrestaurants.co.uk; 11 pm.

The Lansdowne NW1 £46 ❸❹❸
90 Gloucester Ave 7483 0409 8–3B
A Primrose Hill "gastropub favourite", which retains a big following for its "simple but satisfying" scoff (majoring in "great pizza"); the food, though, is "not exceptional" nowadays, and service can be "lax". / www.thelansdownepub.co.uk; 10 pm; no Amex.

La Lanterna SE1 £36 ❸❷❸
6-8 Mill St 7252 2420 11–2A
A "popular" Italian "stand-by", with great staff, and "reasonable" prices, just over Tower Bridge; it has a courtyard for the summer. / www.pizzerialalanterna.co.uk; 11 pm; closed Sat L.

The Larder EC1 £41 ❸❹❹
91-93 St John St 7608 1558 9–1A
A "buzzy", if "cavernous", Clerkenwell yearling comprising a brasserie and adjoining sandwich bar; both win praise – but particularly the latter – for their "decent" fare, but service can be "slow". / www.thelarderrestaurant.com; 10.30 pm; closed Sat L & Sun.

Latium W1 £44 ❶❶❸
21 Berners St 7323 9123 3–1D
"Assured cooking with real flair", "passionate" service and "excellent prices" make Maurizio Morelli's slightly "hard-edged" five-year-old, just north of Oxford Street, "one of the best Italians in town". / www.latiumrestaurant.com; 10.30 pm, Fri-Sat 11pm; closed Sat L & Sun.

Latymers W6 £24 ❷❸❹
157 Hammersmith Rd 8741 2507 7–2C
No one doubts the quality of the "reasonably-priced" scoff in the rear dining room of this Hammersmith gin palace, even if "Thai-style, they do pack 'em in, and pack 'em out again". / 10 pm; closed Sun D; no Amex; no booking at L.

Laughing Gravy SE1 £41
154 Blackfriars Rd 7721 7055 9–4A
It's early days for the new management of this Southwark stand-by (so we've passed on a rating); an early-days report, however, suggests the food is "still good". / www.thelaughinggravy.com; 10 pm; closed Sat & Sun.

Launceston Place W8 £53 ❶❷❷
1a Launceston Pl 7937 6912 5–1B
"Tucked-away in Kensington", this discreet townhouse was re-launched by D&D London in early-2008, with ex-Pétrus chef Tristan Welch at the stove; our visit was is in-line with a few adulatory early reports, which hail a "great" and "classy" make-over. / www.danddlondon.com; 11 pm; closed Mon L; set weekday L £41 (FP).

Lavender £33 ❹❸❷
112 Vauxhall Walk, SE11 7735 4440 2–4D
171 Lavender Hill, SW11 7978 5242 10–2C
A relaxed South London chain of bar/bistro stand-bys, generally praised for their "no-nonsense" fare. / 10.45 pm; SW11 closed Mon L, SE11 closed Sat L & Sun, SW9 closed Mon-Wed L.

The Ledbury W11   £75   ❶❷❷
127 Ledbury Rd   7792 9090   6–1B
*Brett Graham's "subtly inventive" cuisine is "absolutely top-drawer",
and it's served "with ease and efficiency", at this increasingly high-
profile Notting Hill destination; the "intimate" room is "beautifully
decorated" too.* / www.theledbury.com; 10.30 pm; set weekday L £42
(FP), set Sun L £54 (FP).

Lemonia NW1   £34   ❹❷❶
89 Regent's Park Rd   7586 7454   8–3B
*Perpetually "jam-packed" with "happy people", this landmark
Primrose Hill taverna has an "unbeatable" atmosphere; the food
seems ever more "ordinary", though, and "expensive for what it is".*
/ 11.30 pm; closed Sat L & Sun D; no Amex.

Leon   £20   ❸❸❸
275 Regent St, W1   7495 1514   3–1C
35-36 Gt Marlborough St, W1   7437 5280   3–2C
73-76 The Strand, WC2   7240 3070   4–4D
136 Old Brompton Rd, SW3   7589 7330   5–1D
7 Canvey St, SE1   7620 0035   9–4B **NEW**
Cabot Place West, E14   7719 6200   11–1C **NEW**
3 Crispin Pl, E1   7247 4369   9–1D
12 Ludgate Circus, EC4   7489 1580   9–2A
86 Cannon St, EC4   7623 9699   9–3C **NEW**
*"A great idea being sacrificed on the altar of expansion"? –
this "funky" chain has rightly "taken London by storm" with its
"non-junk fast food", but its ratings continue to slide – "they put
less effort in now than they used to".* / www.leonrestaurants.co.uk;
10 pm; EC4 closed Sat & Sun, W1 closed Sun D; D only.

Levant W1   £48   ❹❹❶
Jason Ct, 76 Wigmore St   7224 1111   3–1A
*"Still a great night out" – however, the attractions of this
nightclubby and romantic Lebanese, in a Marylebone basement,
have nothing at all to do with the food.* / www.levant.co.uk; 11.30 pm.

Levantine W2   £39   ❸❸❸
26 London St   7262 1111   6–1D
*"A stylish hide-away on a boring street in Paddington"; its Lebanese
fare – particularly the mezze – generally satisfies, but views on the
belly dancing are more mixed.* / www.levant.co.uk; 11.30 pm.

The Light House SW19   £45   ❸❸❸
75-77 Ridgway   8944 6338   10–2B
*"The best of an average bunch" – this Wimbledon fixture offers
"modish fusion fare" in an agreeably "light and airy" setting; while
"everything is OK, though, nothing really shines".*
/ www.lighthousewimbledon.com; 10.30 pm, Fri-Sat 10.45 pm; closed Sun D.

Lilly's E1   £39   ❸❸❸
75 Wapping High St   7702 2040   11–1A
*A useful Wapping brasserie, where burgers are a highlight of the
"good but rather limited" menu; snaffle a booth if you can.*
/ www.lillysrestaurant.co.uk; 11 pm.

Lindsay House W1 £84 ④❸❸
11-15 Swallow St 7439 0450 4–3A
This "lovely old Soho townhouse" is losing the "special" charm
that's long made it "perfect for business or romance"; it doesn't
help that the food – overseen by Richard Corrigan – seems ever
more "underwhelming" and "overpriced". / www.lindsayhouse.co.uk;
10.30 pm; closed Sat L & Sun; set pre theatre £52 (FP).

Lisboa Pâtisserie W10 £6 ❶④④
57 Golborne Rd 8968 5242 6–1A
This "unique" North Kensington institution – "a wonderful,
authentic Portuguese pâtisserie" – is always mobbed, and for good
reason: "my Lisbon friend swears the cakes are almost as good
as his mother's". / 7.30 pm; L & early evening only; no booking.

Little Bay £27 ❸❷❷
140 Wandsworth Bridge Rd, SW6 7751 3133 10–1B
228 Belsize Rd, NW6 7372 4699 1–2B
228 York Rd, SW11 7223 4080 10–2B
171 Farringdon Rd, EC1 7278 1234 9–1A
"Gloriously OTT" décor helps spice up these "mad" but
"entertaining" budget bistros; that's not all, though – the food
is "significantly better than it deserves to be at the price".
/ www.little-bay.co.uk; 11.30 pm; no Amex, NW6 no credit cards.

Little Italy W1 £50 ④❸❸
21 Frith St 7734 4737 4–2A
A "lively" late-night Italian for those in search of 'La Dolce Vita',
Soho-style; shame it's "ludicrously overpriced".
/ www.littleitalysoho.co.uk; 4 am, Sun midnight; set weekday L £33 (FP).

The Little Square W1 £40 ④❸❸
3 Shepherd Mkt 7355 2101 3–4B
With its "lovely location", on a corner of Shepherd Market,
this "friendly" little bistro offers food that's "acceptable,
if unspectacular". / 11 pm.

Livebait £46 ④④⑤
21 Wellington St, WC2 7836 7161 4–3D
43 The Cut, SE1 7928 7211 9–4A
These "stark", white-tiled fish "refectories" make some reporters
think of "eating in a Victorian public loo" – fans don't mind, tipping
them as "reliable" stand-bys, but critics just find them "dull and
predictable". / www.santeonline.co.uk; 11 pm, SE1 Sun 9 pm;
WC2 closed Sun.

LMNT E8 £30 ⑤❸❶
316 Queensbridge Rd 7249 6727 1–2D
A Hackney "Aladdin's Cave" of "crazy" décor, where the booths
in particular are "great for hiding away"; fans say the food
is "tasty" too – others think it's "cheap, but not particularly
pleasant". / www.lmnt.co.uk; 10.45 pm; no Amex.

Lobster Pot SE11 £49 ❸❸❷
3 Kennington Ln 7582 5556 1–3C
"Sounds of the sea piped through a loudspeaker" add to the
kitschly "fabulous" experience of a meal at the Régent family's
"eccentric" Gallic fish restaurant, in a "grim" bit of Kennington;
of late, however, the cooking has been a touch more up-and-down
than usual. / www.lobsterpotrestaurant.co.uk; 10.30 pm; closed Mon & Sun;
booking: max 8.

LOCANDA LOCATELLI
CHURCHILL INTERCONT'L W1   £60   ❷❷❷
8 Seymour St   7935 9088   2–2A
"A good whiff of glamour" adds to the allure of Giorgio Locatelli's
"de luxe" Marylebone Italian, where most (if not quite all) reporters
find *"real heart"* shines through in the *"inspiring"* but *"unfussy"*
cooking. / www.locandalocatelli.com; 11 pm, Fri & Sat 11.30 pm; booking:
max 8.

Locanda Ottomezzo W8   £55   ❸❷❸
2-4 Thackeray St   7937 2200   5–1B
Fans praise the *"really superb Italian food"* on offer at this *"lovely
little neighbourhood restaurant"*, in Kensington; standards aren't
entirely consistent, though, and some reporters find
it *"very overpriced"*. / www.locandaottoemezzo.co.uk; 10.30 pm; closed
Sat L & Sun; set weekday L £41 (FP).

Loch Fyne   £36   ❹❸❹
2-4 Catherine St, WC2   7240 4999   2–2D
175 Hampton Rd, TW2   8255 6222   1–4A
"Nothing special, but a useful fall-back" – seems the fairest verdict
on this *"accommodating"* national seafood chain; *"sometimes they
surprise and are very good"*. / www.lochfyne.com; 11 pm, IG10 10 pm.

The Lock Dining Bar N17   £41   ❸❶❸
Heron Hs, Hale Wharf, Ferry Ln   8885 2829   1–1C
"West End-quality" cooking and a *"superb front-of-house team"*
make it worth truffling out this *"off-the-beaten-track"* Tottenham
two-year-old; *"once inside, you forget you're on a main road, in a
disused office block"*. / www.thelock-diningbar.com; 10.30 pm; closed Mon,
Sat L & Sun D.

Lola Rojo SW11   £25   ❸❷❷
78 Northcote Rd   7350 2262   10–2C
"Very lush" tapas – *"way above average"* and *"with a modern
twist"* – again win ecstatic praise for this *"buzzing"* Battersea
yearling; avoid the *"hard-edged"* back room if you can. / 10.30 pm.

The Lord Palmerston NW5   £38   ⑤⑤④
33 Dartmouth Park Hill   7485 1578   8–1B
"Such a shame" – as a number of reports confirm, this *"noisy"* and
"busy" pub *"has truly slipped since it was taken over by a chain"*
(Geronimo Inns). / www.geronimo-inns.co.uk; 10 pm; no booking.

Lots Road SW10   £36   ❸❸❸
114 Lots Rd   7352 6645   5–4B
"In the wasteland by Chelsea Harbour", this *"unadventurous"* but
"very dependable" gastropub makes a good find – *"a great way
to spend a lazy Sunday"*. / www.lotsroadpub.com; 10 pm.

Lotus Chinese Floating Restaurant E14   £35   ④④❸
38 Limeharbour   7515 6445   11–2C
"Great dim sum at very reasonable prices" are a highlight at this
large, floating fixture, near the London Arena. / www.lotusfloating.co.uk;
10.30 pm.

Luc's Brasserie EC3 £45 ④❷❸
17-22 Leadenhall Mkt 7621 0666 9–2D
Some say it's "a typical, lazy City venue", but this "genuine"-seeming first-floor bistro is generally found an "efficient" sort of place, offering "well-executed" Gallic staples.
/ www.lucsbrasserie.com; 8.30 pm; closed Sat & Sun.

Luciano SW1 £61 ④⑤④
72-73 St James's St 7408 1440 3–4D
Fans of Marco Pierre White's "understated" grand Italian, near St James's Palace, hail its "exquisite" food and "calm" atmosphere; there are quite a few critics, though, who dismiss it as a "pompous" and "pretentious" place, with "inattentive" service and "bland" cooking. / www.lucianorestaurant.co.uk; 10.30 pm; closed Sun.

Lucio SW3 £50 ❸❷❸
257 Fulham Rd 7823 3007 5–3B
"Solid" Italian cooking and "attentive" service make this Chelsea "favourite" a "charming" sort of place, for most reporters; critics, though, says it's gone "off the boil". / 11 pm; set weekday L £33 (FP).

Lucky Seven
Tom Conran Restaurants W2 £30 ❷❸❶
127 Westbourne Park Rd 7727 6771 6–1B
A tiny, "funky-retro" Bayswater diner that's the spitting image of "a Lower East Side burger joint"; "you may have to share your booth with strangers", but it's worth it for the "killer burgers" and "excellent milkshakes". / www.tomconranrestaurants.com; 11 pm; no Amex; no booking.

Luna Rossa W11 £37 ④⑤④
192 Kensington Park Rd 7229 0482 6–1A
The pizza may be "decent" but service is "tolerable at best", at this "noisy" Notting Hill Italian. / www.madeinitalygroup.co.uk; 11.30 pm; closed Mon L.

Ma Cuisine £36 ❸❸④
7 White Hart Ln, SW13 8878 4092 10–1A **NEW**
6 Whitton Rd, TW1 8607 9849 1–4A
9 Station Approach, TW9 8332 1923 1–3A
At best, John McClement's "old-fashioned French bistros" are "everything a neighbourhood place should be" – "cheap", "buzzy", and offering "classic" dishes; ratings dipped a little this year, though – perhaps the strain of the new SW13 branch that's been "a most welcome addition to the area". / 10 pm, Fri & Sat 10.30 pm; TW1 closed Sun & Mon; no Amex.

Ma Goa SW15 £33 ❶❷❷
244 Upper Richmond Rd 8780 1767 10–2B
"Beautiful" Goan dishes "bursting with flavour" are served with "understated charm and efficiency" at this "homely" family-run Putney fixture. / www.ma-goa.com; 11 pm, Sun 10 pm; closed Mon, Tue–Sat D only, Sun open L & D.

Made in China SW10 £37 ❸❸⑤
351 Fulham Rd 7351 2939 5–3B
A Chelsea Chinese that may look "unexciting", but which dispenses "fresh and tasty" fare, and quite efficiently too. / 11.30 pm.

Made in Italy SW3 £34 ❸④❸
249 King's Rd 7352 1880 5–3C
"Fab pizza" draws many fans to this "chaotic" Chelsea institution;
satisfaction is sapped, though, by a general feeling that it's
"becoming rather arrogant". / www.madeinitalyrestaurant.co.uk;
11.30 pm, Sun 10.30 pm; closed weekday L; no Amex.

Madhu's UB1 £37 ❶❶❷
39 South Rd 8574 1897 1–3A
This "top-notch" Indian is "well worth a trip to Southall";
"the owners' Kenyan origins show through in the unusual spicing"
of the "sublime" dishes, which are served by "smiling" staff in quite
a "smart" setting. / www.madhusonline.com; 11.30 pm; closed Tue,
Sat L & Sun L.

Magdalen SE1 £46 ❷❷❸
152 Tooley St 7403 1342 9–4D
"The pedigree of the kitchen shines through", in the "superb" and
"gutsy" cooking on offer at this British yearling, not far from Tower
Bridge; the interior is "unatmospheric" or "calming", to taste.
/ www.magdalenrestaurants.co.uk; 10.30 pm; closed Sat L & Sun.

Maggie Jones's W8 £48 ④❸❶
6 Old Court Pl 7937 6462 5–1A
"On a cold day, hole up" at this "cosy" Kensington veteran, where
the "quirky" and "seductive" rustic décor is perfect for a "smoochy"
dinner; the "hearty" comfort food, though, is "very average"
nowadays. / 11 pm.

Magic Wok W2 £25 ❸❷④
100 Queensway 7792 9767 6–2C
"More welcoming" than most orientals locally, this Bayswater
Chinese does much of its "fairly standard" repertoire "really well".
/ 11 pm.

Maison Bertaux W1 £9 ❸❸❶
28 Greek St 7437 6007 4–2A
A "timeless magic" envelops this "rickety" but "charming" Soho
"institution" – serving "good pastries" since 1871. / 11 pm, Sun 7 pm;
no credit cards; no booking.

Malabar W8 £32 ❷❷❷
27 Uxbridge St 7727 8800 6–2B
For a "good-value posh curry", the "skillfully blended" cuisine at this
"friendly" neighbourhood "favourite", near Notting Hill Gate,
"always hits the spot". / www.malabar-restaurant.co.uk; 11.30 pm.

Malabar Junction WC1 £40 ❷❷❷
107 Gt Russell St 7580 5230 2–1C
A "spacious" and "uncrowded" spot, with "wonderfully laid-back
service" and "consistently great south Indian food"; only its obscure
Bloomsbury location discourages a wider following.
/ www.malabarjunction.com; 11 pm.

Malmaison Brasserie EC1 £49 ❸❸④
18-21 Charterhouse St 7012 3700 9–1B
"You could take your mum or your boss" to this "not outstanding
but very reasonable" basement, in an hotel near Smithfield Market;
burgers come especially recommended. / www.malmaison.com;
10.30 pm.

La Mancha SW15   £37   ④④❸
32 Putney High St   8780 1022   10–2B
*"For when you're more focussed on the company than the food",
this large tapas bar on Putney's main drag offers an "always-
buzzing and very reliable" option.* / www.lamancha.co.uk; 11 pm;
need 6+ to book.

Mandalay W2   £25   ❷❸⑤
444 Edgware Rd   7258 3696   8–4A
*The Ally brothers' "cramped" Bayswater shop-conversion has seen
a "return to form" – it can still be a bit "hit-and-miss", but is again
winning acclaim for its "outstanding" Burmese food at "incredibly
low prices".* / 11 pm; closed Sun; set weekday L £13 (FP).

Mandarin Kitchen W2   £36   ❶④⑤
14-16 Queensway   7727 9012   6–2C
*"An amazing choice" of "absolutely stunning" Chinese seafood
(most famously, "divine lobster noodles") makes it "worth the
aggravation" of a visit to this ultra-"seedy", but always "bustling",
Bayswater institution.* / 11.30 pm.

Mangal Ocakbasi E8   £20   ❶❸❸
10 Arcola St   7275 8981   1–1C
*"Almost unbelievable value" is to be had at this "simple but
sensational" Turkish grill, in Dalston, where specialities include
"the best lamb cutlets ever"; BYO.* / www.mangal1.com; midnight;
no credit cards.

Mango & Silk SW14 NEW   £28
199 Upper Richmond Rd   8876 6220   1–4A
*Initial feedback on Udit Sarkhel's new Sheen venture is limited
(so we've left it un-rated); such as there is, though, says his "subtle"
cooking is just as "excellent" as it was at his long-running
Southfields property (now RIP).* / www.mangoandsilk.co.uk/; 10 pm, Fri &
Sat 10.30 pm; closed weekday L.

Mango Room NW1   £37   ❸❸❷
10-12 Kentish Town Rd   7482 5065   8–3B
*"A clever modern take on Caribbean cuisine" adds to the all-round
appeal of this "cool", "fun" and "lively" Camden Town spot; "top-
flight cocktails" too.* / www.mangoroom.co.uk; 11 pm.

Mango Tree SW1   £50   ❸④④
46 Grosvenor Pl   7823 1888   2–4B
*A "massive", "bustling" and "incredibly noisy" space at the foot of a
Belgravia office building – fans say the Thai food is "excellent",
but even they admit "it's on the pricey side".* / www.mangotree.org.uk;
11 pm, Thu-Sat 11.30 pm.

Mango Tree SE1 NEW   £27   ❷❸④
5-6 Cromwell Buildings, Red Cross Way   7407 0333   9–4C
*"Always busy" (and noisy too), this straight-down-the-line modern
Indian is a very handy stand-by, right by Borough Market.*
/ www.justmangotree.co.uk; 11 pm.

Manicomio £48 ④④④
85 Duke of York Sq, SW3 7730 3366 5–2D
Gutter Ln, EC2 7726 5010 9–2B **NEW**
A large terrace, not far from the King's Road, is the stand out attraction of this "upmarket" Italian deli/restaurant – a popular place, though the food is "nothing special" and you "pay for the location"; the new City branch, then, should feel right at home!

Manna NW3 £40 ❸④④
4 Erskine Rd 7722 8028 8–3B
A recent re-fit to this veteran veggie (the UK's oldest), in Primrose Hill, has left it "nicely updated" but little changed; fans say the food has "remained excellent" – sceptics that it's "still over-ambitious".
/ www.manna-veg.com; 11 pm; closed Mon L; no Amex.

Mao Tai SW6 £45 ❷❸❸
58 New King's Rd 7731 2520 10–1B
"Consistently fine" pan-Asian food still makes this smart Fulham veteran a strong local favourite; there are sceptics, though, who say it "doesn't justify the price". / www.maotai.co.uk; 11.30 pm; D only, ex Sun open L & D.

Marco
Stamford Bridge SW6 **NEW** £62 ④❶❸
Fulham Rd 7915 2929 5–4A
MPW's grand newcomer, bizarrely located adjacent to Stamford Bridge, is oddly decked-out in '90s-nightclub style; it's praised by some reporters for its "fantastic", classic Gallic cuisine and its "great" (if "expensive") wine list, but there have also been some "woeful" meals recorded. / www.marcorestaurant.co.uk; closed Mon & Sun.

Marine Ices NW3 £32 ❸❷❷
8 Haverstock Hill 7482 9003 8–2B
"Save room for the ice creams", if you take the family to this North London veteran (est. 1930), which is "great for children of all ages"; pizza and pasta are "reliable" too. / www.marineices.co.uk; 11 pm; closed Mon; no Amex.

Market NW1 **NEW** £37 ❷❸④
43 Parkway 7267 9700 8–3B
"A great addition to Camden Town"; this "informal" (and often "noisy") newcomer offers "heart-warming" British bistro fare – from a daily-changing menu – at very "tempting" prices. / 10.30 pm; closed Sun D.

Marouch £45 ❷①①
I) 21 Edgware Rd, W2 7723 0773 6–1D
II) 38 Beauchamp Pl, SW3 7581 5434 5–1C
III) 62 Seymour St, W1 7724 5024 2–2A
IV) 68 Edgware Rd, W2 7724 9339 6–1D
V) 3-4 Vere St, W1 7493 3030 3–1B
'Garden') 1 Connaught St, W2 7262 0222 6–1D
This "real Lebanese" chain is "great at the bar, late at night" (there are café/takeaways at I, II and V) for a kebab or salad; the plusher restaurants are OK, but "have deteriorated a bit over the years", not least on the hospitableness front. / www.maroush.com; 12.30 am-5 am.

The Marquess Tavern N1 £41 ❷④❸
32 Canonbury St 7354 2975 8–2D
"Proper British cooking" – with "awesome roasts and remarkable beef" – makes this "successfully gentrified" Canonbury boozer a big hit locally; the odd misfire, however, is not unknown.
/ www.marquesstavern.co.uk; 10.30 pm; closed weekday L.

Masala Zone £27 ④❸❸
9 Marshall St, W1 7287 9966 3–2D
147 Earl's Court Rd, SW5 7373 0220 5–2A
71-75 Bishop's Bridge Rd, W2 no tel 6–1C **NEW**
80 Upper St, N1 7359 3399 8–3D
For a "speedy, good-value and strongly-flavoured" meal, these "bustling" Indian canteens still fit the bill (with "fresh and interesting thalis" as top menu choice); standards "have fallen from the early days", though, and continue to do so.
/ www.realindianfood.com; 11 pm; no Amex; no booking unless over 10.

The Mason's Arms SW8 £39 ❷❸❸
169 Battersea Park Rd 7622 2007 10–1C
"An interesting gastropub in a surprising location" (near Battersea Park BR); its "honest" food has waxed and waned over the years, but is currently often "excellent". / www.london-gastros.co.uk; 10 pm.

Matsuba TW9 £41 ❸④④
10 Red Lion St 8605 3513 1–4A
A "small" and "welcoming", but "quite expensive" Japanese, near Richmond town centre; the cooking "varies" – "sometimes it's very good" (especially sushi and sashimi), but "at other times it's just pedestrian". / 11 pm; closed Sun.

Matsuri £63 ❸❸⑤
15 Bury St, SW1 7839 1101 3–3D
Mid City Place, 71 High Holborn, WC1 7430 1970 2–1D
"Excellent sushi", "very good teppan-yaki" and "impeccable" service are hallmarks of this business-friendly Japanese duo, in St James's and Holborn; their ambience is getting ever more "clinical", though, and there's a growing feel that they're "rather overpriced". / www.matsuri-restaurant.com; SW1 10.30 pm, WC1 10 pm; WC1 closed Sun.

Maxwell's WC2 £37 ❸❸④
8-9 James St 7836 0303 4–2D
It looks "brash", but this large burger joint, opposite Covent Garden tube, is a pleasant "surprise" for some reporters, thanks to a menu that's more "varied" than you might expect. / www.maxwells.co.uk; midnight.

MAZE W1 £70 ❷❷❸
10-13 Grosvenor Sq 7107 0000 3–2A
Jason Atherton's "meticulous" preparation of "daring" but "dainty" dishes wins enthusiastic acclaim for this Ramsay-group hot spot in Mayfair; most reporters find it a "lively" place too, but there's also a slight feeling it "lacks personality".
/ www.gordonramsay.com/maze; 10.30 pm.

maze Grill W1 NEW £72 ❷❸❸
10-13 Grosvenor Sq   7107 0000   3–2A
"Perfectly-cooked steaks" – with the help of an American broiler
that's unique in this country – have helped this bright,
new extension to maze make a "very strong start", sometimes
"patchy" service notwithstanding. / www.gordonramsay.com; 10 pm;
no trainers; set weekday L £46 (FP).

Medcalf EC1 £41 ❸❸❸
40 Exmouth Mkt   7833 3533   9–1A
"Lovely comfort food and a nice atmosphere" commend this
"relaxed" Clerkenwell spot to most reporters; to its detractors,
that's another way of saying it's a touch "unmemorable".
/ www.medcalfbar.co.uk; 10 pm, Sat 10.30 pm; closed Sun D; no Amex.

Mediterraneo W11 £44 ❸❸❸
37 Kensington Park Rd   7792 3131   6–1A
A "homely" and "bustling" atmosphere helps attract a dressed-
down but "glamorous" crowd to this "perennial-favourite" Notting
Hill Italian; the food's "very competent", but it's hard not to feel
that it "could do better". / www.mediterraneo-restaurant.co.uk; 11.30 pm;
booking: max 10.

Mekong SW1 £23 ④④④
46 Churton St   7630 9568   2–4B
A "reliable", if dated, Vietnamese of over 20 years' standing –
it makes a handy stand-by in still thinly-provided Pimlico. / 11.30 pm.

Mela £35 ❸④④
152-156 Shaftesbury Ave, WC2   7836 8635   4–2B
136-140 Herne Hill, SE24   7738 5500   10–2D NEW
It's "over-crowded", "noisy", and increasingly "drab", and yet this
Theatreland Indian can still be very handy "for a quick bite",
thanks to its "good, freshly baked breads and filling curries";
a branch opened in Herne Hill in the summer of 2008, and further
expansion is mooted.

Melati W1 £34 ④❷④
21 Gt Windmill St   7437 2745   3–2D
A crowded canteen of long standing, near Piccadilly Circus, serving
up "hot and spicy" Malay/Indonesian dishes that still please
most reporters most of the time. / 11.30 pm.

Mem & Laz N1 £26 ④❸❸
8 Theberton St   7704 9089   8–3D
"Lively and entertaining", this Islington spot makes an "excellent
cheap and cheerful" stand-by, thanks to its "jolly" service and its
"good-value" Mediterranean/Turkish cuisine. / www.memlaz.com;
11.30 pm, Fri & Sat midnight.

Memories of India SW7 £33 ❸❸④
18 Gloucester Rd   7581 3734   5–1B
An "unassuming" South Kensington stalwart almost invariably rated
somewhere between "consistent" and "better than average".
/ 11.30 pm.

Memsaheb on Thames E14 £24 ❷❷❸
65/67 Amsterdam Rd   7538 3008   11–2D
"Views of the Thames add to the experience", at this local Indian
"gem", on the Isle of Dogs. / www.memsaheb.com; 11.30 pm; closed
Sat L.

Menier Chocolate Factory SE1 £36 ④❷❷
51-53 Southwark St 7407 4411 9–4B
*Whether you're off to a show or not, the dining option attached
to this Southwark theatre offers a "buzzy" and "Boho-cool"
experience, and its "basic" scoff is sometimes "great value" too.
/ www.menierchocolatefactory.com; 11 pm; closed Mon & Sun D.*

The Mercer EC2 NEW £50 ❸❸❸
34 Threadneedle St 7628 0001 9–2C
*"Safe" brasserie fare, "above-average" décor and an "unusually
long" wine list ensure this "welcome", "NY-style" City-central
newcomer "hits all the right notes for a business lunch".
/ www.themercer.co.uk; 9.30 pm; closed Sat & Sun.*

Le Mercury N1 £24 ④④❷
140a Upper St 7354 4088 8–2D
*This "typical French bistro" has long been an Islington "institution",
and its "cramped, noisy and fun" quarters have hosted many
a "romantic evening"; "the food varies", but at the "unbelievable"
prices, there are "absolutely no complaints". / www.lemercury.co.uk;
1 am.*

Meson don Felipe SE1 £30 ④④❷
53 The Cut 7928 3237 9–4A
*What's happened to this "authentic" and "friendly" tapas veteran,
near the Old Vic? – it's still always "crowded", but even some
"staunch" supporters think it has felt rather "tired" of late. / 11 pm;
closed Sun; no Amex; no booking after 8 pm.*

Mestizo NW1 £35 ❸④④
103 Hampstead Rd 7387 4064 8–4C
*"It's not the nicest area" – near Warren Street tube – but this
"casual" hang-out (with a well-stocked bar) serves
a "comprehensive range" of Mexican dishes that fans say are
"very authentic"; not all reporters, however, are equally impressed.
/ www.mestizomx.com; 11.30 pm.*

Le Metro SW3 £40 ④④④
28 Basil St 7591 1213 5–1D
*In a basement right by Harrods, "a good, post-shopping hide-
away", with "interesting" wine and "passable" snacks; in no sense,
however, was it improved by last year's major refurb'.
/ www.lemetro.co.uk; 9.30 pm; closed Sun D; need 5+ to book.*

Metro SW4 £42 ④④④
9a Clapham Common S'side 7627 0632 10–2D
*The garden is "lovely" ("especially with the fairy lights on"), at this
otherwise "ordinary-looking" venture, by Clapham Common;
the food gets mixed reports, but the set menus are undoubtedly
"good value". / www.metromotel.co.uk; 11 pm; closed weekday L; no Amex.*

Metrogusto N1 £44 ④❷❷
13 Theberton St 7226 9400 8–3D
*Fans praise the "authentic" cuisine, the "fantastic range of wines"
and the "excellent" service at this Islington Italian; for critics,
though, the food simply "tries too hard". / www.metrogusto.co.uk;
10.30 pm, Thu-Sat 11-30 pm; Mon-Fri D only; booking: max 8, Sat & Sun.*

Mews of Mayfair W1 £60 ❸❸❸
10-11 Lancashire Ct, New Bond St 7518 9388 3–2B
"A good-looking room sited above a buzzy bar, in a small alley in the heart of Mayfair"; fans say its ambitious fare is "invariably beautifully cooked" – critics that it's "confused" or "lacking sparkle". / www.mewsofmayfair.com; 11 pm; closed Sun; booking: max 8.

Mezzanine
Royal National Theatre SE1 £40 ❺❸④
Southbank Centre, Belvedere Rd 7452 3600 2–3D
"What a wasted opportunity"; the RNT's in-house restaurant may be "very convenient" if you're going to a show, but it "continues to charge well over the odds" for food that's "not very exciting". / www.nationaltheatre.co.uk; 11 pm; closed Mon L, Fri L & Sun.

Michael Moore W1 £52 ❷❶❸
19 Blandford St 7224 1898 2–1A
Mr Moore's Marylebone dining room may be "cramped", but he is a "passionate" and "inventive" chef, whose dishes can be a "revelation"; his staff are "absolutely charming" too. / www.michaelmoorerestaurant.com; 10.30 pm; closed Sat L & Sun; set weekday L £33 (FP).

Mildred's W1 £32 ❸④❷
45 Lexington St 7494 1634 3–2D
"Innovative and exciting vegetarian dishes in a buzzing 'diner' atmosphere" – this hidden-away Soho spot is a "complete delight" for most (if not quite all) reporters. / www.mildreds.co.uk; 11 pm; closed Sun; only Maestro; no booking.

Mimmo d'Ischia SW1 £56 ❺④④
61 Elizabeth St 7730 5406 2–4A
A "dated" Belgravia Italian which "needs to shape up" – "living on a reputation earned in the '60s", it can seem "horrendously expensive" nowadays. / www.mimmodischia.co.uk; 11.30 pm; closed Sun.

Min Jiang
The Royal Garden Hotel W8 NEW
2-24 Kensington High St 7937 8000 5–1A
In the old days, the former Tenth restaurant (RIP) – named after its top-floor location – was one of the better hotel dining rooms in town; when it re-launches as a swanky Chinese operation in late-2008, it will still have knock-out views of Kensington Gardens – let's hope the food lives up. / www.royalgardenhotel.co.uk.

Mini Mundus SW17 £36 ❸❶❷
218 Trinity Rd 8767 5810 10–2C
"They don't rush you", at this "lovely" family-run local, in Wandsworth, where the "good-value" Gallic cooking "always makes for a good outing"; (they "also now do take-away"). / www.mini-mundus.co.uk; 10.30 pm; closed Mon L.

Mint Leaf £58 ❸④❸
Suffolk Pl, Haymarket, SW1 7930 9020 2–2C
Angel Ct, Lothbury, EC2 7930 9020 9–2C NEW
A "classy" vibe permeates this "dark" and "clubby" West End basement Indian, which – even if it can seem a bit "pretentious" – mostly wins the thumbs-up for its "inventive, if pricey", cuisine; in mid-2008, a long-awaited City sibling opened, near Bank. / www.mintleafrestaurant.com; set weekday L £42 (FP).

Mirabelle W1
56 Curzon St   7499 4636   3–4B
*Having languished in recent years under the management of MPW,
this Mayfair dowager is scheduled to re-open in 2009 after a major
refurbishment by new owners (including design-guru Joseph
Ettedgui); much glamour is promised.*

Mirch Masala   £26   ❶❸④
171-173 The Broadway, UB1   8867 9222   1–3A
3 Hammersmith Rd, W14   6702 4555   7–1D **NEW**
1416 London Rd, SW16   8679 1828   10–2C
213 Upper Tooting Rd, SW17   8767 8638   10–2D
111 Commercial Rd, E1   7247 9992   9–2D
*"Amaze your palate", with a trip to one of these "Formica-table",
BYO Pakistani caffs – they serve "simply amazing" curries at "dirt-
cheap" prices; "there's now one opposite Olympia too". / midnight.*

Misato W1   £26   ❸④⑤
11 Wardour St   7734 0808   4–3A
*"Prices are rock bottom", at this Japanese pit stop in Soho, and it's
"always good for a quick bite"; "mind the queues, though…"
/ 10.30 pm; no credit cards.*

Missouri Angel EC3 **NEW**   £50   ④❸④
14 Cross Wall   7481 8422   9–3D
*An early-days visitor insists this east-City pub-conversion offers
"London's best steak and crab cakes"; in our view, that's overdoing
it, but it's certainly a handy business venue in a thinly-served part
of town. / www.missourigrill.com; 10.30 pm; closed Sat & Sun.*

Missouri Grill EC3   £46   ❸❸❸
76 Aldgate High St   7481 4010   9–2D
*A useful business restaurant, in the poorly-provided area near
Aldgate tube; feedback is modest, but suggests the American fare
can be "interesting". / www.missourigrill.com; 11 pm; closed Sat & Sun;
set dinner £28 (FP).*

Mitsukoshi SW1   £50   ❷❸⑤
Dorland Hs, 14-20 Lower Regent St   7930 0317   3–3D
*The "drab" basement of a department store near Piccadilly Circus,
redeemed by the "dependable" quality of its Japanese fare – a key
asset is the "good, but under-used sushi bar", presided over by an
"amusing chef". / www.mitsukoshi-restaurant.co.uk; 10 pm.*

Miyama W1   £60   ❶❷⑤
38 Clarges St   7499 2443   3–4B
*What it "lacks in atmosphere" – quite a lot! – this Mayfair
Japanese veteran makes up for, in spades, with its "gracious"
service and its "excellent" (if undoubtedly "expensive") food.
/ www.miyama.co.uk; 10.15 pm; closed Sat L & Sun L.*

The Modern Pantry EC1 **NEW**
47-48 St Johns Sq   no tel   9–1A
*Scheduled to open around publication date of this guide –
a Clerkenwell co-venture between the D&D London group and
Providores co-founder Anna Hansen; its inspiration? – 'the crazy
ingredients you can find these days'…*

Mohsen W14 £26 ②③⑤
152 Warwick Rd 7602 9888 7–1D
*"Fast and honest Persian food in generous portions" attracts
a surprisingly broad following to this "friendly" but "canteen-like"
spot, opposite the Olympia Homebase; you can BYO too. / midnight;
no credit cards.*

Momo W1 £58 ④④②
25 Heddon St 7434 4040 3–2C
*Dark and "sexy", it may be, but Mourad Mazouz's "fun" West End
Moroccan is sadly also "a triumph of style over substance" –
the food is "average", and service is sometimes "shocking".
/ www.momoresto.com; 11 pm; closed Sun L; set weekday L £34 (FP).*

Mon Plaisir WC2 £50 ④③②
19-21 Monmouth St 7836 7243 4–2B
*This "lovely", rambling Covent Garden "old-favourite" has long been
a natural choice for either a "speedy pre-theatre supper" or a
"romantic" dinner; its whole approach, though –
not least to cooking – seems ever more "formulaic".
/ www.monplaisir.co.uk; 11.15 pm; closed Sat L & Sun; set pre theatre
£27 (FP).*

Mona Lisa SW10 £21 ③②④
417 King's Rd 7376 5447 5–3B
*A "friendly" and "unbelievably cheap" Italian greasy spoon,
near World's End, where "an eclectic mix of customers adds to the
charm". / 11 pm; closed Sun D; no Amex.*

Monmouth Coffee Company £10 ①②②
27 Monmouth St, WC2 7379 3516 4–2B
2 Park St, SE1 7645 3585 9–4C
*"A simple formula that works to perfection"; it comprises "quite
simply, the best coffee" and a small selection of "superb" baked
goods, served in characterful premises near Borough Market;
(the Covent Garden original branch is drinks-only).
/ www.monmouthcoffee.co.uk; L & afternoon tea only; closed Sun; no Amex;
no booking.*

Montpeliano SW7 £62 ④④④
13 Montpelier St 7589 0032 5–1C
*Fans "love the food", and discern a "great 'Dolce Vita' vibe" at this
"time-warp" Knightsbridge Italian; critics, however, say it's
"not worth it at any price... and especially at their prices".
/ midnight.*

Monty's £29 ③③④
692 Fulham Rd, SW6 0872 148 1291 10–1B **NEW**
54 Northfield Ave, W13 8566 1442 1–2A
1 The Mall, W5 8567 8122 1–2A
224 South Ealing Rd, W5 8560 2619 1–3A
*"They do you proud on the hot stuff", at these "dependable"
Nepaleses – an Ealing-based 'chain' (not all under precisely the
same ownership), which has recently sprouted a deepest-Fulham
offshoot.*

Mooli SW4 £39 ④④④
36a Old Town 7627 1166 10–2D
*This Clapham Italian "should be a great neighbourhood spot",
but it sometimes misses the mark; it can be "ridiculously noisy" too.
/ www.moolirestaurant.com; 11 pm.*

The Morgan Arms E3 £41 ❸❸❷
43 Morgan St   8980 6389   1–2D
Fans of this "buzzing" Bow boozer say it's "busy, and justifiably so";
one or two black marks were also recorded, though, not least for
Sunday lunches that turned out "average". / www.geronimo-inns.co.uk;
10 pm; closed Sun D; no Amex; booking: max 10.

Morgan M N7 £53 ❶❶❸
489 Liverpool Rd   7609 3560   8–2D
Morgan Meunier's "brilliant" restaurant showcases his "theatrical"
Gallic cuisine that's amongst London's very best – it doesn't really
matter that the décor of this pub-conversion is somewhat "plain",
or its Holloway location rather "dodgy". / www.morganm.com; 9.30 pm;
closed Mon, Tue L, Sat L & Sun D; no Amex; booking: max 6; set weekday L
£39 (FP).

MORO EC1 £46 ❶❷❸
34-36 Exmouth Mkt   7833 8336   9–1A
A dozen years on, there's still "a real buzz" about Sam and
Samantha Clarke's Exmouth Market "gem", where "punchy"
Spanish/Moorish cuisine and "brilliant" wines are served up by
"lovely" staff in a "relaxed" (if sometimes "deafening") setting.
/ www.moro.co.uk; 10.30 pm; closed Sun.

Mosaica
The Chocolate Factory N22 £40 ❷❶❷
Unit C005, Clarendon Rd   8889 2400   1–1C
A "very quirky" Wood Green dining room, located "behind
a factory"; it's a "fun" and "atmospheric" setting in which to enjoy
some "interesting" and "seasonal" cooking.
/ www.mosaicarestaurants.com; 9.30 pm; closed Mon, Sat L & Sun D.

Mosaico W1 £64 ❸❸❸
13 Albemarle St   7409 1011   3–3C
This "stylish" Mayfair basement Italian wins praise as a "reliable"
choice, especially on business; even those who think the food
"very good", though, may conclude that "it doesn't justify the bill".
/ www.mosaicorestaurant.co.uk; 10.30 pm; closed Sat L & Sun; set weekday L
£47 (FP).

Motcombs SW1 £55 ④④④
26 Motcomb St   7235 6382   5–1D
A veteran Belgravia wine bar/restaurant that's finding a younger
crowd as that part of town gets busier (and slightly more groovy);
standards remain somewhere between "OK" and "unimpressive".
/ www.motcombs.co.uk; 11 pm; closed Sun D.

Moti Mahal WC2 £47 ❷❸❸
45 Gt Queen St   7240 9329   4–2D
"Creative, modern Indian food" has won ever-greater acclaim for
this "solid" and pricey, Covent Garden spot; it's the
first outpost of a subcontinental restaurant empire, now planning
a major (£25m) UK expansion. / www.motimahal-uk.com; 11.30 pm;
closed Sun; set weekday L £30 (FP).

Mr Chow SW1 £73 ❸④④
151 Knightsbridge   7589 7347   5–1D
It was madly fashionable back in the '60s, and this Knightsbridge
Chinese is still, for fans, "one of the best"; sceptics, though,
are more inclined to notice its "extortionate" prices.
/ www.mrchow.com; midnight.

Mr Kong WC2　　　　　　　£26　②③④
21 Lisle St　7437 7341　4–3A
*"They've made a good 'un, even better" – this "very handy"
Chinatown "old favourite" has emerged from its revamp with
a "much improved interior", and food that's "as reliable as ever".
/ 2.45 am, Sun 1.45 am.*

Mr Wing SW5　　　　　　　£40　③②❶
242-244 Old Brompton Rd　7370 4450　5–2A
*"After a bit of a dip, Mr Wing is back on form"; this Earl's Court
veteran – with its "jazz, fish tanks and great Chinese food" – is a
"spot-on" all-rounder (especially for a party, or romance).
/ www.mrwing.com; midnight.*

Mugen EC4　　　　　　　　£40　❸❸❸
26 King William St　7929 7879　9–3C
*An "affordable" City stand-by, with a handy location, by London
Bridge; "the place is always full of Japanese people, and the food
is fairly authentic". / 10.30 pm; closed Sat & Sun.*

Mulberry Street W2　　　　£31　④④❸
84 Westbourne Grove　7313 6789　6–1B
*"Enormous", "NY-style" pizzas are the star at this "slightly rowdy,
US sports-bar type of place", in Bayswater; fans find the formula
"authentic" and "good value", but not all reporters are convinced;
"don't order by the slice – it doesn't seem as fresh".
/ www.mulberrystreet.co.uk; midnight, Sun 11 pm.*

Murano W1　NEW
20-22 Queen St　7629 8089　3–3B
*On the site which was long known as Zen Central (RIP), Angela
Hartnett launches her new fine-dining Italian restaurant in late-
2008 – not far from the Connaught, over whose dining room she
lately presided; Gordon Ramsay's group could do with having
an undoubted new hit on its hands – let's hope this is it.*

Nahm
Halkin Hotel SW1　　　　£80　❸④⑤
5 Halkin St　7333 1234　2–3A
*David Thompson's Belgravia Thai is revered by foodies for its
"passionate and challenging" cuisine – even they generally concede,
however, that it comes at "outrageous" prices, and that the "stark"
chamber in which it is served has all the atmosphere "of the
moon". / www.nahm.como.bz; 10.30 pm; closed Sat L & Sun L; set weekday L
£49 (FP).*

Namo E9　　　　　　　　　£29　❷❷❷
178 Victoria Park Rd　8533 0639　1–2D
*"Owner Lynne really does know what she's doing", at this "friendly"
Vietnamese near Victoria Park, which serves "excellent dishes
at reasonable prices". / www.namo.co.uk; 11 pm; closed Mon, Tue L,
Wed L & Thu L; no Amex.*

Nancy Lam's Enak Enak SW11　£35　❸❷❸
56 Lavender Hill　7924 3148　10–1C
*"Service is bonkers if Nancy is on" (more typically you get her
daughters), at the TV-chef's Battersea restaurant; its "yummy
oriental home cooking" may be "a touch pricey", but fans say it's
"worth it". / www.nancylam.com; 10.30 pm; D only, closed Sun.*

Nando's £22 ④④④
Branches throughout London
"Healthy junk food" – this "lively" Portuguese peri-peri chicken chain offer a "cheap" and "simple" formula, which fans proclaim "a better alternative to a burger". / www.nandos.co.uk; 11.30 pm; no Amex; no booking.

Nanglo SW12 £27 ❷❷❷
88 Balham High Rd 8673 4160 10–2C
"As good a local Indian as you'll find"; this "bastion" of Balham (recently refurbished) is a "friendly" place, with a reputation for "first-class" Nepalese food. / 11.30 pm; D only.

Napket £12 ❸❷❷
5 Vigo St, W1 7734 4387 3–3D NEW
6 Brook St, W1 7495 5862 3–2B NEW
342 King's Rd, SW3 7352 9832 5–3C
For an "über-cool sandwich" (or a salad, cake or coffee), this "slick" ("pretentious") chain is worth checking out; undoubtedly, however, it is "rather expensive".

Napulé SW6 £37 ❸❸❸
585 Fulham Rd 7381 1122 5–4A
"Fantastic, authentic pizza" (served "by the foot") is the highlight at this "vibrant" local, off Fulham Broadway. / 11.30 pm; closed weekday L; no Amex.

The Narrow E14 £37 ❸❸❸
44 Narrow St 7592 7950 11–1B
Thanks to the "Ramsay effect", it's "hard to get a table" at his Limehouse boozer; apart from the "beautiful Thames views", however, this is a fairly standard gastropub – indeed, not a few reporters leave disappointed at finding everything "so very average". / www.gordonramsay.com; 10 pm.

The National Dining Rooms
National Gallery WC2 £45 ④⑤④
Sainsbury Wing, Trafalgar Sq 7747 2525 2–2C
The tables "overlooking the bustle of Trafalgar Square" are the best perches at this Oliver Peyton-managed venue; "only go if you just can't stand any more art", though – the "dreary" food, "sketchy" service and "gloomy" ambience don't make a pretty picture. / www.thenationaldiningrooms.co.uk; Wed 8.30 pm; Thu-Tue closed D; no Amex.

National Gallery Café
National Gallery WC2 £42 ④④❸
East Wing, Trafalgar Sq 7747 5942 4–4B
This year-old parlour is proving "a good addition to the National", although that's more down to its "good-looking" traditional styling and ultra-handy location than its very middling food and service. / www.thenationaldiningrooms.co.uk; 11 pm; no Amex.

Natural Burger Co & Grill NW8 £32 ❷❸④
12 Blenheim Terrace 7372 9065 8–3A
A new burger joint that gets a warm ripple of applause from St John's Wood locals; "they could do with offering a bit more choice though". / 11 pm; no Amex.

Nautilus NW6 £30 ②②⑤
27-29 Fortune Green Rd 7435 2532 1–1B
"For a fish 'n' chips fix" – especially a kosher one, using matzo meal batter – it's hard to beat this "brightly-lit" and "old-fashioned" West Hampstead caff. / 10 pm; closed Sun; no Amex.

Navarro's W1 £29 ❸❸❷
67 Charlotte St 7637 7713 2–1C
"You feel like you're in Seville", at this "family-run" Fitzrovia tapas bar; the attraction, though, is the "beautiful" tiled interior and "fun" vibe, rather than the food ("OK, but sometimes bland") or service ("patchy"). / www.navarros.co.uk; 10 pm; closed Sat L & Sun.

Nazmins Balti House SW18 £28 ❷❸④
398 Garratt Ln 8944 1463 10–2B
It looks "inauspicious", but this age-old Earlsfield veteran still offers curry that's "a cut above". / www.nazmins.com; midnight.

New Culture Revolution £22 ④❸④
305 King's Rd, SW3 7352 9281 5–3C
157-159 Notting Hill Gate, W11 7313 9688 6–2B
42 Duncan St, N1 7833 9083 8–3D
"For a fresh bowl of noodles and dumplings", these basic oriental chow-houses have their fans; sceptics, though, say they just serve "tasteless bowls of goo". / www.newculturerevolution.co.uk; 10.30 pm; need 4+ to book.

New Mayflower W1 £28 ❷⑤⑤
68-70 Shaftesbury Ave 7734 9207 4–3A
A "hugely busy" and "authentic" oriental on the fringe of Chinatown; it "justifies its popularity" with its "diverse" and "very unusual" menu, and very "late opening" – not its "manner- less" service or "bright" interior. / 4 am; D only; no Amex.

New Tayyabs E1 £23 ❶④❸
83 Fieldgate St 7247 9543 9–2D
"Bloody brilliant curries and lamb chops to die for" – at "how-do- they-do-it" prices – ensure this "basic" BYO East End Pakistani is always "insanely busy"; "book, or risk standing in a mile-long queue". / www.tayyabs.co.uk; 11.30 pm.

New World W1 £28 ❸④❸
1 Gerrard Pl 7734 0396 4–3A
"The novelty of trolley dim sum never tires", at this "busy" Chinatown landmark (where there's "a superb array of dishes from which to pick 'n' mix"); "brusque" service "only adds to the experience". / 11.45 pm; no booking, Sun L.

Nicole's W1 £59 ④④④
158 New Bond St 7499 8408 3–3C
A fashion store basement offering "fresh" but "pricey" fare, mainly to Mayfair shoppers; the high quotient of "distracting eye-candy", however, also makes it "a good place for hedgies to tell clients about their under-performing funds". / www.nicolefarhi.com; 5.30 pm; L & afternoon tea only, closed Sun.

1901

Andaz Hotel EC2 NEW £62 ❸❷❸
40 Liverpool St 7618 7000 9–2D
*This large and "beautiful" (if slightly "soulless") City dining room –
formerly called Aurora – is much more "impressive" in its new
incarnation; with its "top-notch" cuisine, and its "knowledgeable
and friendly service", it's "perfect for a formal business lunch".*
/ www.andaz.com; 10 pm; closed Sat & Sun; booking: max 8; set weekday L
£44 (FP).

Nobu
Metropolitan Hotel W1 £82 ❷❹❹
Old Park Ln 7447 4747 3–4A
*"Orgasmic" Japanese-fusion dishes still win acclaim for this Mayfair
legend, but it's far from being London's No.1 oriental nowadays –
service can be "horrendous", and even fans can feel the prices
"leave a bitter taste in the mouth".* / www.noburestaurants.com;
10.15 pm; booking: max 12.

Nobu Berkeley W1 £80 ❸❺❸
15-16 Berkeley St 7290 9222 3–3C
*Entered via a "loud" and "clubby" bar, the younger and brasher
of the Mayfair Nobus can seem "way more fun" than Park Lane;
just like the original, though, its cuisine seems ever more "over-
rated", not helped by "rip-off" prices and staff who "seem to be on
work experience".* / www.noburestaurants.com; 1.30 am; closed
Sat L & Sun L.

Noodle Noodle £24 ❹❺❺
18 Buckingham Palace Rd, SW1 7931 9911 2–4B
Vauxhall Bridge Rd, SW1 7630 1778 2–4B
*A handy, "plain and simple" noodle bar duo by Victoria Station,
where the nosh is "fresh" and "reasonably priced".*
/ www.noodle-noodle.co.uk; 10.30 pm; Buckingham Palace Rd closed Sun.

Noor Jahan £35 ❷❷❹
2a Bina Gdns, SW5 7373 6522 5–2B
26 Sussex Pl, W2 7402 2332 6–1D
*It looks "very average", but this "stalwart" South Kensington Indian
is a "classic" of its kind; "very well-prepared" curries
at "inexpensive" prices ensure that both it and its Bayswater spin-
off are "always buzzing".* / 11.30 pm.

Nordic Bakery W1 £12 ❸❷❸
14 Golden Sq 3230 1077 3–2D
*"Minimalist Scandinavian design and healthy Scandinavian snacks"
make a winning combination at this "airy" coffee shop and
sandwich bar – "possibly the most peaceful place in Soho".*
/ www.nordicbakery.com; 10 pm, Sat 7 pm; closed Sat D & Sun; no booking.

The Norfolk Arms WC1 £34 ❸❸❷
28 Leigh St 7388 3937 8–4C
*"Is it a tapas bar? Is it a gastropub? Who cares? It's a great place!"
– this "nice boozer-with-a-twist", in Bloomsbury, has a
"fab atmosphere", and offers an unusual mix of dishes, and some
"good English beer" to wash 'em down.* / www.norfolkarms.co.uk;
10.15 pm.

The Normanby SW15 NEW   £32   ❷❸❷
231 Putney Bridge Rd   8874 1555   10–2B
Early reports are few, but all hail this "high-class" gastropub as a "magic addition to the Putney scene", thanks to its "original" cooking – it "beats the pants off most of the competition".
/ www.thenormanby.co.uk; 10 pm.

North China W3   £27   ❷❷❸
305 Uxbridge Rd   8992 9183   7–1A
"You battle with the locals" to get into this "ordinary-looking" neighbourhood Chinese, in a "grotty" bit of Acton – an "unlikely" find, with "delightful" staff and "mouth-watering" food.
/ www.northchina.co.uk; 11 pm.

The North London Tavern NW6   £38   ❸❸❸
375 Kilburn High Rd   7625 6634   1–2B
A Kilburn gastropub yearling that wins all-round praise from the locals for its "thoroughly enjoyable" food and its "bubbly" atmosphere. / www.realpubs.co.uk; 10.30 pm; closed Mon L; no Amex.

North Sea Fish WC1   £28   ❷❷④
7-8 Leigh St   7387 5892   8–4C
It may look "faded", but this "traditional" Bloomsbury chippy is one of the best-known near the centre of town, thanks to its "amazing fresh fish". / 10.30 pm; closed Sun.

Northbank EC4   £45   ❸④❸
1 Paul's Walk   7329 9299   9–3B
With its "lovely Thames-side location", "delicious" British food and "friendly" service, this new operation on the former Just the Bridge (RIP) site can deliver some "very good City dining"; slightly up-and-down feedback, however, puts overall satisfaction somewhere round: "decent". / www.northbankrestaurant.com/; 10.30 pm.

The Northgate N1   £35   ④④❸
113 Southgate Rd   7359 7392   1–1C
Even critics of this "out-of-the-way" De Beauvoir Town boozer concede it's a "buzzy" and "atmospheric" place, and, on most accounts, it offers a "well-executed gastropub experience". / www.thenorthgate.co.uk; 10.30 pm; closed Mon L; no Amex.

Nosh TW1   £35   ❸❷❷
139 St Margarets Rd   8891 4188   1–4A
A "no-nonsense" St Margaret's bistro, with a "nice local feel" and a "loyal local clientele". / www.noshrestaurant.co.uk; 10.30 pm.

Notting Grill W11   £55   ⑤⑤④
123a Clarendon Rd   7229 1500   6–2A
"Come on AWT: what's happened?" – this year, the TV chef's Holland Park pub-conversion has too often been "a waste of time and money", with "terrible" burgers and grills and "rude" staff; it can seem "extremely overpriced" too. / www.awtonline.co.uk; 10.30 pm, Fri & Sat 11.30 pm, Sun 10 pm; closed Mon L; set weekday L £32 (FP).

Notting Hill Brasserie W11   £59   ❷❷❷

92 Kensington Park Rd   7229 4481   6–2B

A "delightful" townhouse-restaurant offering a "pretty much faultless" mix of "spectacular" food, "excellent" service and a "lovely vibe (often enhanced by a jazz trio)"; "it's far from cheap, but worth every penny". / www.nottinghillbrasserie.co.uk; 11 pm; closed Sun D; set weekday L £37 (FP), set Sun L £45 (FP).

Noura   £49   ④❸❸

122 Jermyn St, SW1   7839 2020   3–3D
16 Hobart Pl, SW1   7235 9444   2–4B
16 Curzon St, W1   7495 1050   3–4B

A "consistent" Lebanese chain that wins praise for its "spacious" branches and "attentive" service; its cooking can seem a bit "dull and stodgy", though, "especially at the price". / www.noura.co.uk; 11.30 pm, SW1 10.30 pm; set always available £31 (FP).

Nozomi SW3   £60   ⑤⑤⑤

15 Beauchamp Pl   7838 1500   5–1C

A "look-at-me" Knightsbridge oriental where many reporters feel "everything is tasteless" – "from the décor, to the food, to the clientele" – and service can be both "pretentious" and "inept"; the prices, naturally, are "ridiculous" too. / www.nozomi.co.uk; 11.30 pm; D only.

Number Twelve WC1 NEW   £45   ❸❸④

12 Upper Woburn Pl   7693 5425   8–4C

Santino Busciglio's cooking has created a ripple of interest in this new, but "rather '90s", hotel dining room, near Euston; sceptical reporters feel his food is "fine, but far from impressive", but others like his "combination of Italian heritage, seasonal British ingredients and superb wine". / www.numbertwelverestaurant.co.uk; 10.15 pm; closed Sat L & Sun D.

Numero Uno SW11   £40   ❸❷❷

139 Northcote Rd   7978 5837   10–2C

"Real Italians serve up real Italian food", at this "always-full" and "wonderfully buzzing local" – a "trusty" Battersea favourite. / 11.30 pm; no Amex.

Nuovi Sapori SW6   £38   ❸❸④

295 New King's Rd   7736 3363   10–1B

It's "easily overlooked", but this Fulham Italian is "trying hard", and maintains a strong fan club, thanks to its "personal" service and its "good food at reasonable prices"; not everyone's mad on the "bright" décor, though. / 11 pm; closed Sun.

Nyonya W11   £30   ❸❸④

2a Kensington Park Rd   7243 1800   6–2B

A Malaysian menu that's "a little different" distinguishes this "good-value" canteen, just off Notting Hill Gate; fans esteem it as "an under-rated gem". / www.nyonya.co.uk; 10.30 pm.

O'Zon TW1   £26   ❸❶④

33-35 London Rd   8891 3611   1–4A

An "efficient" operation, offering "good oriental food in the heart of Twickenham", and "good value" too; "don't try it on a match day". / www.ozon.co.uk; 11 pm.

The Oak W2 £40 ❷❸❶
137 Westbourne Park Rd 7221 3355 6–1B
A "gorgeous" and "laid-back" ambience with tons of "buzz" makes this former boozer – recently re-launched, after a fire – the "perfect local" for Notting Hillbillies; "outstanding" thin-crust pizzas are the house speciality. / www.theoaklondon.com; 10.30 pm, Sun 9 pm; Mon-Thu closed L; no booking.

Odette's NW1 £70 ❸❸❸
130 Regent's Park Rd 7586 8569 8–3B
Last year's lavish (and slightly "weird") refurb of this famously "romantic" Primrose Hill veteran divides reporters – supporters find it "delightful", but to critics it's plain "off-putting", and even fans of Bryn Williams's "top-class" cuisine caution that it's "very, very expensive". / www.odettesprimrosehill.com; 10.30 pm; closed Mon & Sun D.

Odin's W1 £52 ❸❶❶
27 Devonshire St 7935 7296 2–1A
This "elegant" and "civilised" Marylebone dining room is "one of the few that still do the starched-linen thing properly"; even some fans fear its "old-school" cooking risks becoming "tired", but when on form it's still "first-rate". / www.langansrestaurants.co.uk; 11 pm; closed Sat L & Sun; booking: max 10.

Okawari W5 £22 ❸❷❸
13 Bond St 8566 0466 1–3A
"A great local Japanese", bang in the centre of Ealing – "it's just very pleasant, and offers some super, cheap food". / www.okawari.co.uk; 11 pm, Fri & Sat 11.30 pm.

The Old Bull & Bush NW3 £35 ❸❸❷
North End Rd 8905 5456 8–1A
Near the entrance to Golder's Hill Park, this celebrated "traditional" pub had a "very pleasant" revamp two years ago, and serves "well-cooked and plentiful fare". / www.thebullandbush.co.uk; 9.30 pm.

Old Parr's Head W14 £19 ❸❷④
120 Blythe Rd 7371 4561 7–1C
It may have "the smallest kitchen you'll ever see", but no-one doubts the "excellent value" offered by this Olympia boozer's "great, cheap Thai food". / 10 pm, Sat & Sun 10.30 pm; no Amex.

Ye Olde Cheshire Cheese EC4 £35 ⑤❶❶
145 Fleet St 7353 6170 9–2A
Just off the Strand, this perfect Dickensian relic – complete with "roaring fire" – is in all the tourist guides; its "typical pub fare", however, could usefully be brought a little more up-to-date. / 9.30 pm; closed Sun D; no booking, Sat & Sun.

Oliveto SW1 £44 ❷❷❸
49 Elizabeth St 7730 0074 2–4A
"The best, thinnest pizza in London", say fans, is to be had at this "cramped" and "noisy" Belgravia Sardinian. / www.olivorestaurants.com; 11 pm; booking: max 7 at D.

Olivo SW1 £47 ❷❷❷
21 Eccleston St 7730 2505 2–4B
"Lots of regulars" frequent this "attractive" and "tightly-packed"
Belgravia favourite, noted for its "friendly" service and its "genuine
Sardinian home-cooking". / www.olivorestaurants.com; 11 pm; closed
Sat L & Sun L.

Olivomare SW1 £51 ❷❷❸
10 Lower Belgrave St 7730 9022 2–4B
"Perfectly cooked" Sardinian dishes – not least "really interesting
fish" – is helping to carve out quite a reputation for this "über-chic"
("sterile") Belgravia yearling. / www.olivorestaurants.com; 11 pm;
closed Sun.

Olley's SE24 £32 ❷❷④
65-67 Norwood Rd 8671 8259 10–2D
Offering "probably the best fish 'n' chips in South London",
this "cross between a chippy and a bistro", in Brockwell Park,
makes "a pleasant surprise in a culinary desert". / www.olleys.info;
10.30 pm; closed Mon.

Olympus Fish N3 £26 ❸❸⑤
140-142 Ballards Ln 8371 8666 1–1B
"Fantastic char-grilled fish" is served alongside "the usual fish 'n'
chips" at this "unsophisticated" Finchley bistro.
/ olympusfishrestaurant.co.uk; 11 pm; closed Mon.

1 Blossom Street E1 £49 ❸④④
1 Blossom St 7247 6530 9–1D
The garden – "a delight" – is the special feature of this "hidden-
away" City-fringe Italian, but fans say it has an "intimate"
atmosphere at any time of year; the food is generally "good" too,
though service is "slow". / www.1blossomstreet.com; 9 pm; closed
Sat & Sun.

1 Lombard Street EC3 £80 ④⑤④
1 Lombard St 7929 6611 9–3C
A "great location for business entertaining", opposite Bank,
has helped make this former banking hall a top City rendezvous,
if one priced firmly for "expense-accounters"; this year, however,
saw a bizarre dive in standards across the board (and in both the
brasserie and the restaurant). / www.1lombardstreet.com; 9.45 pm; closed
Sat & Sun.

One-O-One
Sheraton Park Tower SW1 £70 ❶❷④
101 Knightsbridge 7290 7101 5–1D
Pascal Proyart's "blissful" seafood cooking – now served "tapas"-
style – remains "unrivalled" in London; it's a shame, then, that –
although a recent revamp has somewhat improved this previously
dire Knightsbridge chamber – it still feels rather "cold".
/ www.oneoonerestaurant.com; 10 pm; set weekday L £36 (FP).

The Only Running Footman W1 £45 ❸❸④
5 Charles St 7499 2988 3–3B
On a handy Mayfair corner, this gastropub newcomer (sibling
to The House and The Bull) is "a welcome addition to the area",
offering "un-fancy" food at "decent" prices – both in the bar and
the upstairs dining room. / www.themeredithgroup.co.uk; 10.30 pm.

Ooze W1 £34 ④❸④
62 Goodge St 7436 9444 2–1B
"The focus on risotto" certainly makes this Fitzrovia yearling
an *"interesting"* concept – fans say they are *"masters of the art"*,
but others find the results *"nothing to write home about"*.
/ www.ooze.biz; 11 pm; closed Sun.

Orange Tree N20 £37 ④⑤④
7 Totteridge Ln 8343 7031 1–1B
With its *"village-pub"* atmosphere (and location), this *"tarted-up"*
Totteridge fixture could easily be a north London 'destination';
too often, though, service is *"muddled"*, and the overall impression
"expensive and average". / www.theorangetreetotteridge.co.uk; 10 pm,
Sun 9 pm.

L'Oranger SW1 £85 ④❸❸
5 St James's St 7839 3774 3–4D
"Luxurious" and classically Gallic, this St James's restaurant has
long been viewed as a *"class act"* (for either business or romance);
as at most other members of the London Fine Dining Group,
however, standards have been notably unsettled after the recent
change of ownership. / www.loranger.co.uk; 11 pm; closed Sat L & Sun;
booking: max 8; set weekday L £60 (FP).

Oriel SW1 £36 ④④④
50-51 Sloane Sq 7730 2804 5–2D
"Go for coffee" (or breakfast) best to savour the *"prime location"*
of this *"constantly busy"* Parisian-style corner-brasserie – otherwise,
the food is likely to be *"average or worse"*. / www.tragusholdings.com;
11 pm, Sun 10.30 pm; no booking.

Origin Asia TW9 £35 ❷❷④
100 Kew Rd 8948 0509 1–4A
"Not your standard curry house"; this *"accommodating"* Richmond
venture wins praise for its *"delicious"* and *"imaginative"* Indian fare.
/ www.originasia.co.uk; 11 pm.

Original Tajines W1 £32 ❸❷❸
7a Dorset St 7935 1545 2–1A
With its *"wholesome"*, *"warming"* tagines and *"helpful"* service,
this tucked-away café in Marylebone offers something of a
"bargain". / 11 pm; closed Sat L & Sun; no Amex.

Orrery W1 £72 ❸❷❸
55 Marylebone High St 7616 8000 2–1A
This *"gracious"* dining room – overlooking a churchyard,
and serving up some *"classy"* Gallic cuisine – has long been
acclaimed as the D&D group's *"crown jewel"*; standards drifted this
year, though, but prices remain *"astronomical"*.
/ www.orreryrestaurant.co.uk; 10.30 pm, Thu-Sat 11 pm; booking: max 12;
set weekday L £45 (FP).

Orso WC2 £47 ④❸④
27 Wellington St 7240 5269 4–3D
"Never disappointed" / *"never understand what the fuss is about"*
– as ever, this *"cosy"* (*"gloomy"*) Covent Garden basement Italian
of long standing totally divides reporters; few would dispute,
however, that it makes an *"efficient post-opera stand-by"*.
/ www.orsorestaurant.co.uk; midnight; set pre-theatre £31 (FP), set brunch
£34 (FP).

Oscar
Charlotte Street Hotel W1   £62   ④④❸
15 Charlotte St   7806 2000   2–1C
*"A lively breakfast" and a fun bar are the best points of this
"bustling" Fitzrovia "media-land hang-out"; otherwise, "at this price
point", it "should be better". / www.charlottestreethotel.com; midnight;
closed Sun L; set always available £40 (FP).*

Oslo Court NW8   £52   ❷0❷
Charlbert St, off Prince Albert Rd   7722 8795   8–3A
*This "restaurant time forgot", near Regent's Park, attracts
an appropriately mature clientele – "we were the only table under
80!"; its "always-friendly" staff serve up "gigantic" dishes that are
"surprisingly good... if you like '70s-Italian food" (save space for
a pudding from the groaning trolley). / 11 pm; closed Sun; set weekday L
£39 (FP).*

Osteria Basilico W11   £43   ❷④❷
29 Kensington Park Rd   7727 9957   6–1A
*"Always loud and busy", this Italian "favourite" in the heart
of Notting Hill is still cranking out "great pizza" and "excellent
pastas" in a "fun" and "cosy" setting; service, however, seems
entirely random – by turns, "über-friendly", "surly", "slow" and
"attentive". / www.osteriabasilico.co.uk; 11.30 pm, Sun 10.30 pm;
no booking, Sat L.*

Osteria dell'Arancio SW10   £54   ❸❸④
383 King's Rd   7349 8111   5–3B
*"Great regional Italian wines" add interest to this "cramped" and
"noisy" World's End trattoria, where the "straightforward" cooking
is sometimes "very good"; it's "not always consistent", though,
and "quite pricey for what it is". / www.osteriadellarancio.co.uk; 11 pm.*

Osteria Emilia NW3 **NEW**   £38   ❸❸❸
85b, Fleet Rd   7433 3317   8–2A
*"A welcome addition to the generally grim Hampstead restaurant
scene"; the former Zamoyski (RIP) premises were re-launched
all'italiana in early-2008, by the owners of the "excellent" deli
opposite; early reports are all encouraging. / www.osteriaemilia.com;
10 pm; closed Mon L, Sat L & Sun.*

Osteria Stecca NW8 **NEW**   £46   ❸④❸
1 Bleinham Ter   7328 5014   8–3A
*"Finally they put some vibe into one of London's best-looking
Italians" – this St John's Wood newcomer (formerly called
Rosmarino, RIP) has won instant praise for its "fresh" cooking and
"great mix of wines"; iffy press reviews, however, suggest success
may be going to their heads. / www.osteriastecca.com; 10.30 pm,
Sat 11 pm, Sun 10 pm.*

Ottolenghi
£37   **❶❸❸**

13 Motcomb St, SW1   7823 2707   5–1D **NEW**
63 Ledbury Rd, W11   7727 1121   6–1B
1 Holland St, W8   7937 0003   5–1A
287 Upper St, N1   7288 1454   8–2D

"Amazingly, the food is just as scrumptious as it looks", at these "seriously posy" café/delis (whose communal tables are "besieged" for weekend brunch); they charge "a small fortune" for "couture" tapas, "phenomenal" salads and "sublime" cakes. / www.ottolenghi.co.uk; 10.15 pm; W11 8pm, Sun 6 pm; N1 closed Sun D, Holland St takeaway only; W11 & SW1 no booking, N1 booking for D only; set always available £25 (FP).

(RESTAURANT)
OXO TOWER SE1
£72   **❺❺❹**

Barge House St   7803 3888   9–3A

The "marvellous" views "may make you forget the food, but not the bill", at this "somewhat embarrassing" 8th-floor South Bank landmark, which continues to trade shamelessly on its location, and offers "dire" cooking and "dismal" service at "crazy" prices. / www.harveynichols.com; 11 pm, Sun 10 pm; booking: max 14; set weekday L £50 (FP).

(BRASSERIE)
OXO TOWER SE1
£60   **❺❹❸**

Barge House St   7803 3888   9–3A

"There's no reason to go to the restaurant, as the view from the brasserie is just as good" – even in the cheaper part of this South Bank operation, however, the food is still "expensive and average". / www.harveynichols.com; 11 pm, Sun 10 pm; booking: max 8; set weekday L & pre-theatre £37 (FP).

Ozer W1
£35   **❹❺❺**

5 Langham Pl   7323 0505   3–1C

This "grand"-looking – but "cheap and cheerful" – Turkish restaurant, just north of Oxford Circus, has quite a following; it suffers from a "lack of consistency", though – "abominable" service attracts particular brickbats, and the room can be "incredibly noisy" too. / www.sofra.co.uk; 11 pm.

Pacific Bar and Grill W6
£38   **❹❸❸**

320 Goldhawk Rd   8741 1994   7–1B

A "good atmosphere" draws locals, especially for brunch, to this boothed hang-out, on the Hammersmith/Chiswick borders; it has "slow service and variable food" though – "it could be so much better". / 11.30 pm, Sun 10.30 pm.

Pacific Oriental EC2
£40   **❸❸❷**

52 Threadneedle St   0871 704 4000   9–2C

In its new, more elegant setting, this big bar/brasserie/restaurant is again producing "flavoursome" pan-Oriental fare; its styling is "fun, for the City", but the "cavernous" interior can seem "quiet" at off-peak times. / www.orientalrestaurantgroup.co.uk; 11 pm; closed Sat & Sun.

Il Pagliaccio SW6
£33   **❹❸❷**

182-184 Wandsworth Bridge Rd   7371 5253   10–1B

A "gloriously mad" Fulham Italian offering "chaotic fun" ("for young families", in particular); the "basic" food – mostly pizza 'n' pasta – is rather variable. / www.paggs.co.uk; midnight; no Amex.

Le Pain Quotidien £35 ❸④❸
18 Great Marlborough St, W1   7486 6154   3–2C
72-75 Marylebone High St, W1   7486 6154   2–1A
174 High Holborn, WC1   7486 6154   4–1C **NEW**
201-203A Kings Rd, SW3   7486 6154   5–3C
15-17 Exhibition Rd, SW7   7486 6154   5–2C **NEW**
9 Young St, W8   7486 6154   5–1A
St Pancras, NW1   7486 6154   8–3C **NEW**
Royal Festival Hall, SE1   7486 6154   2–3D
Breakfast – with "huge bowls of flavoursome coffee, and a fantastic
bread basket" – is a top draw to these "buzzy" communal-table
bakeries, which benefit from some "good locations".
/ www.painquotidien.com; W1 9 pm, Sun 8 pm; SW3 10 pm, Sun 7 pm;
W8 8 pm, Sun & Mon 7 pm; SE1 11 pm, Sun 10 pm; W1F 10 pm, Sun 7 pm;
no bookings at some branches, especially at weekends.

The Painted Heron SW10 £45 ❶❷❸
112 Cheyne Walk   7351 5232   5–3B
"So original" – the "exquisite" cooking at this "upmarket but
unpretentious" Indian is bettered by few others in the capital;
it's "a bit hard to find", though, just off Chelsea Embankment.
/ www.thepaintedheron.com; 11 pm; closed Sat L & Sun.

The Palmerston SE22 £37 ❷❷❸
91 Lordship Ln   8693 1629   1–4D
"One of the very few seriously good gastropubs in south London",
this "friendly" East Dulwich boozer is "still going strong", offering
food that's "good, simple and well-executed". / www.thepalmerston.net;
10 pm, Sun 9.30 pm; no Amex; set weekday L £22 (FP).

Pampa £41 ❸④④
4 Northcote Rd, SW11   7924 1167   10–2C
60 Battersea Rise, SW11   7924 4774   10–2C
A duo of Argentinean steakhouses, in Battersea; they offer
"fabulous" steaks, and "great atmosphere" too (if in a low rent sort
of way). / 11 pm; D only; Battersea Rise closed Sun.

Pantechnicon Rooms SW1 **NEW** £51 ❸❸❷
10 Motcomb St   7730 6074   5–1D
From the Thos. Cubitt team, an even smarter new Belgravia
gastropub, with an upstairs dining room whose restrained grandeur
wouldn't look out of place in a gentleman's club; it offers a wide-
ranging menu, well realised, at prices which – assuming you steer
clear of the caviar and so on – needn't break the bank. / Rated
on Editors' visit; www.thepantechnicon.com; 11 pm, Sun 10.30 pm.

Paolina Café WC1 £18 ❷❷④
181 Kings Cross Rd   7278 8176   8–3D
For "very good value" around King's Cross, you won't do much
better than this "tasty" Thai café; "BYO is a bonus" too. / 10 pm;
closed Sun; no credit cards.

Papageno WC2 £38 ⑤⑤❷
29-31 Wellington St   7836 4444   4–3D
The atmosphere – "something out of 'Moulin Rouge'" – is the point
of this "fun" but "touristy" Covent Garden extravaganza; as at
stablemate Sarastro, however, the food is often "terrible".
/ www.papagenorestaurant.com; 11.45 pm.

Papillon SW3 £50 ❸❷❷
96 Draycott Ave 7225 2555 5–2C
Soren Jessen's "professional" Chelsea two-year-old has a "classy" Belle Époque style particularly suiting dîners-à-deux; it offers "straightforward" (but somewhat "uneven") cooking and "incredible" wines – "the list is more like a book".
/ www.papillonchelsea.co.uk; midnight; closed Sun D; set weekday L £30 (FP).

Pappa Ciccia £28 ❷❷❷
105-107 Munster Rd, SW6 7384 1884 10–1B
41 Fulham High St, SW6 7736 0900 10–1B
90 Lower Richmond Rd, SW15 8789 9040 10–1A
With their "great thin-crust pizza" and "fresh" pasta, these "squashed" and "fun" Italian locals win much praise; prices are "very reasonable", and you can BYO too (modest corkage).
/ www.pappaciccia.com; 11 pm, Sat & Sun 11.30 pm; SW6 no credit cards.

Paradise by Way of Kensal Green W10 £43 ❷❸❶
19 Kilburn Ln 8969 0098 1–2B
This big, "buzzing", "beautiful" and vaguely Gothic favourite has long been a "real find" in a still-unlikely area, thanks not least to its "imaginative" cuisine; other attractions include a bar, dance-floor, garden, roof terrace... / www.theparadise.co.uk; 10.30 pm, Sun 8 pm; closed weekday L.

Paradiso Olivelli £31 ④④④
9 St Christopher's Pl, W1 7486 3196 3–1A
35 Store St, WC1 7255 2554 2–1C
61 The Cut, SE1 7261 1221 9–4A
Fans of this small chain find its branches "pleasant" places that "turn out a good pizza"; mediocre ratings, though, support those who say it's "gone downhill". / www.ristoranteparadiso.co.uk; midnight; W1 11pm; WC1 11.30 pm; WC1 Sun.

El Parador NW1 £28 ❸❷④
245 Eversholt St 7387 2789 8–3C
"A great little authentic tapas bar" – a "friendly" place in an "unexpected" location, near Euston. / www.elparadorlondon.com; 11 pm, Fri & Sat 11.30 pm, Sun 9.30 pm; closed Sat L & Sun L; no Amex.

The Parsee N19 £36 ❷❷⑤
34 Highgate Hill 7272 9091 8–1C
"Unusual" and "lovely" Parsee food never seems to win this Highgate Indian the following it deserves – thanks, we suspect, to its atmosphere-free interior, it can be surprisingly "empty". / www.the-parsee.com; 10.45 pm; D only, closed Sun.

Pasha SW7 £48 ④④❶
1 Gloucester Rd 7589 7969 5–1B
"Rose petals sprinkled on the stairs" and belly dancing help set the ultra-"romantic" scene at this South Kensington townhouse-Moroccan; the food, though, "leaves much to be desired", and sometimes just seems a "rip-off". / www.pasha-restaurant.co.uk; midnight, Thu-Sat 1 am; booking: max 10 at weekends.

Passione W1 £58 ❸❷④
10 Charlotte St 7636 2833 2–1C
Gennaro Contaldo's Fitzrovia HQ wins continuing praise for "simple" but "very well-executed" Italian cooking; especially given its "atmosphere-free" interior, though, it often seems "ridiculously overpriced". / www.passione.co.uk; 10.15 pm; closed Sat L & Sun.

Pasta Brown £42 ④④⑤
31-32 Bedford St, WC2   7836 7486   4–3C
35-36 Bow St, WC2   7379 5775   4–2D
*"The formula   decent enough pasta in large portions – ought
to work", so "it's a pity" that feedback on this Theatreland mini-
chain suggests it is so "persistently ordinary".* / www.pastabrown.com;
11 pm, Fri & Sat 11.30 pm, Sun 7 pm; closed Sun D; no Sat booking.

Patara £45 ❷❷❸
15 Greek St, W1   7437 1071   4–2A
3-7 Maddox St, W1   7499 6008   3–2C
181 Fulham Rd, SW3   7351 5692   5–2C
9 Beauchamp Pl, SW3   7581 8820   5–1C
*This "smart" Thai group remains an utter paragon of consistency –
"courteous" and "lovely" staff dish up "flawless" and "delicate"
dishes in each of its "extremely pleasant" branches.*
/ www.pataralondon.com; 10.30 pm.

Paternoster Chop House EC4 £62 ④④⑤
Warwick Ct, Paternoster Sq   7029 9400   9–2B
*Even a reporter who finds "decent food and service" at this D&D-
group outfit, near St Paul's, notes that it's "noisy", "crowded" and
"expensive" – harsher critics use adjectives like "dreadful",
"mediocre" and "unpleasant".* / www.danddlondon.com; 10.30 pm; closed
Sat & Sun D; set Sun L £41 (FP).

Patio W12 £30 ④❸❸
5 Goldhawk Rd   8743 5194   7–1C
*The Polish "stodge" is "not about to win any prizes", but this
"comfy" Shepherd's Bush venue provides a top "cheap and
cheerful" night out, thanks to its "hospitable" staff, "jolly"
atmosphere, and "excellent-value set menu".* / 11.30 pm; closed
Sat L & Sun L.

Pâtisserie Valerie £25 ④④❸
17 Motcomb St, SW1   7245 6161   5–1D
32-44 Hans Cr, SW1   7590 0905   5–1D
105 Marylebone High St, W1   7935 6240   2–1A
15 Great Cumberland Pl, W1   7724 8542   2–2A **NEW**
162 Piccadilly, W1   7491 1717   3–3C
44 Old Compton St, W1   7437 3466   4–2A
15 Bedford St, WC2   7379 6428   4–4C **NEW**
215 Brompton Rd, SW3   7823 9971   5–1C
Duke of York Sq, SW3   7730 7094   5–2D
174 Queensway, W2   7243 9069   6–1C **NEW**
27 Kensington Church St, W8   7937 9574   5–1A
37 Brushfield St, E1   7247 4906   9–2D
*It may be an "institution" for "flaky croissants and coffee" –
and some branches retain their "lovely ambience" – but Luke
Johnson's régime is wrecking this long-established group;
it's becoming "just another bland chain", offering "predictable"
menus, "unevenly" realised.* / www.patisserie-valerie.co.uk; 7 pm,
Old Compton St 7.30 pm, 10.30 pm Wed-Sat, Brushfield St 8 pm, Hans Cr
11.30 pm; Check each branch as they are all different; minimum £5 for all
cards; no booking.

Patterson's W1 £61 ❷❸④
4 Mill St 7499 1308 3–2C
"Inventive" dishes are pulled off with "flair", if "sometimes unevenly", at this family-run Mayfair establishment – it makes an "enjoyable all-rounder", despite its "understated" going-on "bland" interior; "bargain" prix-fixe lunch.
/ www.pattersonsrestaurant.com; 11 pm; closed Sat L & Sun; set weekday L £39 (FP).

Paul £28 ❸④❸
115 Marylebone High St, W1 7224 5615 2–1A
29-30 Bedford St, WC2 7836 3304 4–3C
73 Gloucester Rd, SW7 7373 1232 5–2B
43 Hampstead High St, NW3 7794 8657 8–1A
147 Fleet St, EC4 7353 5874 9–2A
Leaving aside true 'artisan' operations, these London outposts of France's biggest 'high street' bakers are "hard to beat" for a "tasty" baguette, a "gorgeous" pastry, or a light lunch; the "erratic" Gallic service, though, "can be so bad you have to smile". / www.paul-uk.com; 7 pm-8.30 pm; no Amex; no booking.

Pearl WC1 £71 ❸❷❸
252 High Holborn 7829 7000 2–1D
"The room is spectacular or sterile, depending on your point of view", but – thanks to Jan Tanaka's "complex" and "unexpectedly good" cuisine – this former Holborn banking hall often impresses; in a different way, the "insane" wine mark-ups do too. / www.pearl-restaurant.com; 10 pm; closed Sat L & Sun; set weekday L £48 (FP).

Pearl Liang W2 £34 ❷❸❷
8 Sheldon Sq 7289 7000 6–1C
This "stylish" and "eclectic" Chinese yearling – "tucked-away" in an "obscure" Paddington Basin basement – is widely tipped as well "worth searching out" for its "excellent dim sum" (and other "interesting" dishes). / www.pearlliang.co.uk; 11 pm.

The Peasant EC1 £42 ❸④❸
240 St John St 7336 7726 8–3D
An 'early-wave' Clerkenwell gastropub, with a "homely" upstairs dining room and "great" terrace; foodwise, it's long been an "up-and-down" performer, but recently the emphasis has been on 'up'. / www.thepeasant.co.uk; 11 pm, Sun 10.30 pm.

Pellicano SW3 £44 ❸❷④
19-21 Elystan St 7589 3718 5–2C
This "cramped" and "noisy" Italian has a "useful" Chelsea location, and "operates to a consistently high standard"; even some fans, though, concede that it "lacks distinctive features". / www.pellicanorestaurant.co.uk; 11 pm, Sat 10.30 pm.

E Pellicci E2 £14 ❸❶❶
332 Bethnal Green Rd 7739 4873 1–2D
"An amazing experience in an unexpected situation" – "one of the last proper East End caffs", serving up "the best breakfast in London", in (listed) Art Deco splendour. / 5pm; L only, closed Sun; no credit cards.

Peninsular
Holiday Inn Express SE10 £30 ❷④④
85 Bugsbys Way 8858 2028 1–3D
It's a "long trek from anywhere", but this oddly-sited Greenwich oriental serves – according to its small fan club – "some of the best Chinese food outside Chinatown"; "the room is authentic, in that it looks like a banqueting suite with TVs".
/ www.mychinesefood.co.uk/; 11.30 pm, Sun 11 pm.

The Pepper Tree SW4 £20 ❸❷❷
19 Clapham Common S'side 7622 1758 10–2D
"Fresh-tasting" food, that's "fast" and "cheap-as-chips" wins the usual big thumbs-up for this Thai canteen, by Clapham Common tube. / www.thepeppertree.co.uk; 11 pm, Sun & Mon 10.30 pm; no Amex; no booking at D.

Père Michel W2 £42 ❸❷④
11 Bathurst St 7723 5431 6–2D
"The only thing they've changed in 25 years is the prices", say fans of this "quaint", "traditionally French" Bayswater destination, which – especially for fish-lovers of a certain age – is an ever "reliable" stand-by. / 11 pm; closed Sat L & Sun.

Pescatori £50 ④④④
11 Dover Street, W1 7493 2652 3–3C
55-57 Charlotte St, W1 7580 3289 2–1C
"Quality Italian seafood" and "good service", or "ridiculously pricey" and "rushed"? – reports on this West End chain span quite a range, balancing out somewhere around: "competent enough, but not outstanding". / www.pescatori.co.uk; 11 pm; closed Sat L & Sun.

Petek N4 £28 ❸❶❷
96 Stroud Green Rd 7619 3933 8–1D
An extremely "cheerful" and "upmarket" Finsbury Park "kebab house", which offers "an interesting take on the usual Turkish dishes", and is unsurprisingly "very popular". / 11 pm; Mon-Thu D only, Fri-Sun open L & D.

Petersham Hotel TW10 £52 ④❸❷
Nightingale Ln 8940 7471 3–3B
*"Beautiful views over the Thames" help make this conventional hotel dining room in Richmond "a perfect choice for a swanky Sunday lunch", or for any other "celebratory" meal.
/ www.petershamhotel.co.uk; 9.45 pm, 8.45 pm Sun; –.*

Petersham Nurseries TW10 £61 ❷❸❶
Off Petersham Rd 8605 3627 1–4A
"Sitting amidst roses, pots and plants" ("all for sale") – that's the "unusual" but "fantastic" setting for this glasshouse-café, "in the middle of a garden centre"; Skye Gingall creates some "stunning" dishes from "exceptionally fine produce", but even fans find the prices "horrendous". / www.petershamnurseries.com; L only, closed Mon.

La Petite Auberge N1 £33 ④❷❷
283 Upper St 7359 1046 8–2D
"Reliable and reasonably-priced", this "cosy and dark" French bistro makes a handy Islington "stand-by". / www.petiteauberge.co.uk; 11 pm, Fri-Sat 11.30 pm.

La Petite Maison W1 £63 ❷❸❷
54 Brooks Mews 7495 4774 3–2B
*This "sophisticated", if "outrageously expensive", Mayfair yearling –
a take-off of a fashionable Nice establishment – is always "packed"
with a "chichi" crowd, drawn by its "skillful" dishes (for sharing)
and its "classy" vibe. / www.lpmlondon.co.uk; 10.30 pm; closed Sun D.*

PÉTRUS
THE BERKELEY SW1 £101 ❶❶❷
Wilton Pl 7235 1200 5–1D
*"Better now than Gordon Ramsay!"; Marcus Wareing's
"incomparable" Knightsbridge dining room – with its "sublime"
cuisine, its "immaculate" service and its "stupendous" wine list –
out-scored his ex-boss's across the board this year; the only real
caveat is that ambience loses something if you don't sit in the main
room; NB: by the time you read this, the restaurant's name may
have changed. / www.the-berkeley.co.uk; 10.45 pm; closed Sat L & Sun;
no jeans or trainers; booking: max 10; set weekday L £56 (FP).*

Pham Sushi EC1 £25 ❶❷④
159 Whitecross St 7251 6336 9–1B
*"You can't fault the food" – some of "the best sushi in London" –
at this "excellent", if low-key, destination, near the Barbican.
/ www.phamsushi.co.uk; 10 pm; closed Sat L & Sun.*

Philpotts Mezzaluna NW2 £41 ❷❶❷
424 Finchley Rd 7794 0455 1–1B
*"A north London spot that always hits the mark" – David Philpott's
"intimate" and "reliable" Childs Hill fixture has "very friendly" staff,
and it serves "great-value" Italian cooking too.
/ www.philpotts-mezzaluna.com; 11 pm; closed Mon & Sat L; no Amex.*

Pho £22 ❷❶❷
3 Great Titchfield St, W1 7436 0111 3–1C **NEW**
56 Goodge St, W1 no tel 2–1B **NEW**
126 King's Cross Rd, WC1 7833 9088 8–3D **NEW**
86 St John St, EC1 7253 7624 9–1A
*"You just wish there were more places like 'em" – "busy",
"Formica-table" noodle shops, where "sweet" staff serve
up "consistently delicious Vietnamese street food".*

The Phoenix SW1 £34 ❸❸❸
14 Palace St 7828 8136 2–4B
*"Tucked-away behind the Cardinal Place development", this "buzzy
gastropub" is "surprisingly good" for somewhere so near Victoria
Station; it's "busy during the week" but a "quiet haven"
at weekends. / www.geronimo-inns.co.uk; 10 pm, Sun 9.30 pm; closed Sat.*

The Phoenix SW3 £38 ④❸❸
23 Smith St 7730 9182 5–2D
*Just off the King's Road, this "cosy" pub is "cheap only by Chelsea
standards", but it's praised nonetheless for its "friendly" style and
"dependable" food. / www.geronimo-inns.co.uk; 9.45 pm; closed Sun D.*

Phoenix Bar & Grill SW15 £43 ❷⓪❷
162-164 Lower Richmond Rd 8780 3131 10–1A
This "buzzy" neighbourhood spot in Putney has "steadily improved", to the extent it outperforms its sibling Sonny's nowadays; its all-round formula includes often-"excellent" food and "welcoming" service, and a "pleasant terrace" too.
/ www.sonnys.co.uk; 10.30 pm, 11 pm; set weekday L £27 (FP), set dinner £29 (FP).

Phoenix Palace NW1 £32 ❷④❸
3-5 Glentworth St 7486 3515 2–1A
"Many oriental diners" bespeak the "authenticity" of this "hustling and bustling" Chinese, near Baker Street tube; the service may often be "hopeless", but the dim sum is "consistently excellent".
/ pheonixpalace.uk.com; 11.15 pm.

Picasso's SW3 £32 ④❸❸
127 King's Rd 7352 4921 5–3C
Since the sad demise of the Chelsea Kitchen, this "time-warp" coffee shop is the last hang-over from the 'Swinging Sixties' still occupying prime King's Road real estate; it remains an "essential" breakfasting spot. / www.dinosrestaurants.co.uk; 11 pm.

Piccolino £36 ④④④
21 Heddon St, W1 7287 4029 3–2C
27-29 Bellevue Rd, SW17 8767 1713 10–2C
38 High St, SW19 8946 8019 10–2B
11 Exchange Sq, EC2 7375 2568 9–2D
After a good start in the capital, this "modern and buzzy" Italian chain now attracts mixed reviews; fans still praise its "brisk" service and its "extensive" menu – doubters just feel "processed".
/ www.piccolinorestaurants.co.uk; 11 pm, Sun 10 pm.

Pick More Daisies N8 £32 ❸❸❸
12 Crouch End Hill 8340 2288 8–1C
"A good selection of breakfasts" and "the best burgers in London" (Kobe beef, no less!) are key attractions of this "quirky" and "child-friendly" Crouch End café. / www.pickmoredaisies.com; 10 pm, Fri & Sat 10.30 pm, Sun 9 pm; no Amex.

PIED À TERRE W1 £91 ❷❷❸
34 Charlotte St 7636 1178 2–1C
"An exemplar of quality fine dining"; David Moore's "discreet" Fitzrovian fully shows off Shane Osborn's talent for "foodie fireworks" (without "anything daft or over-wrought"), and the service is "consummately professional" too; most reporters like its "cosy" and "narrow" dining room (but to a few, it's "ambience-free"). / www.pied-a-terre.co.uk; 11 pm; closed Sat L & Sun; booking: max 6; set weekday L £51 (FP).

The Pig's Ear SW3 £43 ❸❸❷
35 Old Church St 7352 2908 5–3C
A "convivial" Chelsea boozer, with a "cosy" upstairs dining room; after a stellar start, its Anglo-French fare has "gone downhill" a bit, but it's still pretty "decent". / www.thepigsear.co.uk; 10.30 pm; closed Sun D.

Pigalle Club W1   £64   ④④❶
215-217 Piccadilly   7734 8142   3–3D
*The food's "incidental", but this supper club right by Piccadilly
Circus is "great for a late-night boogie, and has some fun acts too".*
/ www.thepigalleclub.com; 11.30 pm; D only, closed Sun.

The Pilot W4   £37   ④④❸
56 Wellesley Rd   8994 0828   7–2A
*A "plain and straightforward" pub (with a nice garden) near
Gunnersbury tube; fans say the food's "surprisingly good", but there
were also a couple of "disappointing" reports this year.*
/ www.fullers.co.uk; 10 pm, Sun 9.30 pm.

Pinchito EC1 NEW   £28   ❷❸❸
32 Featherstone St   7490 0121   9–1C
*"Tasty, authentic and nicely-sized tapas in a buzzy bar setting" win
a warm reception for this "really Catalan" newcomer, near Old
Street tube.* / www.pintxopeople.co.uk; midnight; closed Sat L & Sun.

ping pong   £26   ④④❸
10 Paddington St, W1   7009 9600   2–1A
29a James St, W1   7034 3100   3–1A
45 Gt Marlborough St, W1   7851 6969   3–2C
48 Eastcastle St, W1   7079 0550   3–1C
48 Newman St, W1   7291 3080   3–1C
74-76 Westbourne Grove, W2   7313 9832   6–1B
83-84 Hampstead High St, NW3   7433 0930   8–2A NEW
Southbank Centre, SE1   7960 4160   2–3D
St Katharine Docks, E1   7680 7850   9–3D NEW
*Initially so promising, this "buzzing" dim sum chain is often
a "damp squib" on the food front nowadays, and service is often
"scatty" too; "killer cocktails", however, can still help make this
a "fun" option, especially "in a group".* / www.pingpongdimsum.com;
varies; need 8+ to book.

El Pirata W1   £32   ❸❷❷
5-6 Down St   7491 3810   3–4B
*For "unfussy" and "filling" tapas at prices "that seem unusually
sane, by Mayfair standards", this "friendly" and "efficient"
Shepherd Market bar is worth seeking out.* / www.elpirata.co.uk;
11.30 pm; closed Sat L & Sun; set weekday L £17 (FP).

Pissarro's W4   £44   ④④❷
Corney Reach Way   8994 3111   10–1A
*"A beautiful river location" ("ask for a conservatory table") is the
star turn at this "hidden-away" venture, near Chiswick House; it's a
little "pricey", and the food is "slightly variable", but most reporters
find the overall experience "very acceptable".* / www.pissarro.co.uk;
10 pm; closed Sun D; set weekday L £32 (FP).

Pizza Metro SW11   £35   ❷❸❸
64 Battersea Rise   7228 3812   10–2C
*"Great metre-long slabs of traditionally-topped pizzas" –
"the best in London" ("and I'm Italian!") – make this "exuberant",
"crowded" and "noisy" Neapolitan a Battersea hang-out that's well
"worth a detour".* / 11 pm; closed Mon, Tue-Thu D only, Fri-Sun open L & D;
no Amex.

Pizza on the Park SW1   £35   ❸❸❷
11 Knightsbridge   7235 5273   5–1D
A "comfortably metropolitan", upmarket PizzaExpress, near Hyde Park Corner, that makes "an easy and reliable" choice for a "simple but effective" meal; the cellar houses the famous jazz venue (entry charge applies). / www.pizzaonthepark.co.uk; 11 pm, Fri & Sat midnight.

(Ciro's) Pizza Pomodoro   £35   ④④❷
51 Beauchamp Pl, SW3   7589 1278   5–1C
7-8 Bishopsgate Churchyard, EC2   7920 9207   9–2D
Few, and mixed, reports nowadays on these once well-known pizzerias; the original branch in a Knightsbridge cellar – with its "live music", late opening, and seedy 'charm' – can still be "fun", though. / www.pomodoro.co.uk; SW3 1 am, EC2 midnight; EC2 closed Sat/Sun; need 4+ to book.

PizzaExpress   £27   ④❸❸
Branches throughout London
A "fresher" menu (with "new, thin-crust options") and better ("less cookie-cutter") décor are driving a general perception of "improvement" at this benchmark chain, which is regaining its crown for serving "the best high-street pizza" – especially, of course, to families. / www.pizzaexpress.co.uk; 11.30 pm-midnight; most City branches closed all or part of weekend; no booking at most branches.

Pizzeria Oregano N1   £29   ❸❷❸
19 St Albans Pl   7288 1123   8–3D
"Transformed, now the largely Italian clientele can't smoke between courses!" – this "well-loved" Islington local offers "huge" and "tasty" pizzas (in particular), at "good prices". / 11.30 pm, Sun 10.30 pm; closed Mon, Tue-Fri D only, Sat & Sun open L & D; no Amex.

PJ's SW3   £48   ⑤④❷
52 Fulham Rd   7581 0025   5–2C
"Too popular for its own good", this Chelsea Euro-crowd "hang-out" is a "noisy" sort of place where the American fare often disappoints; for a "lazy" brunch, though, it's still a pretty safe bet. / www.pjsbarandgrill.co.uk; 11.45 pm, Sun 11.15 pm.

The Place Below EC2   £18   ❷④❸
St Mary-le-Bow, Cheapside   7329 0789   9–2C
This "hidden gem" has long been "unlike anything else in the Square Mile" – a self-service canteen in a church crypt, offering "very good-quality" veggie and organic fare; BYO.
/ www.theplacebelow.co.uk; L only, closed Sat & Sun; no Amex; need 15+ to book.

Planet Hollywood W1   £45   ⑤⑤⑤
13 Coventry St   7437 7639   4–4A
"Not even worth it for the nostalgia any more"; most of the (few) reports on this Tinseltown-themed West End landmark say it's "dreadful". / www.planethollywoodlondon.com; 1 am.

Plateau E14 £70 ④④④
Canada Pl 7715 7100 11–1C
The interior may be "functional", but this fourth-floor Canary Wharf business favourite has a vista of a "fabulous cityscape, especially at night"; "as at other D&D operations", though, the food is "not exciting" and "very pricey for what you get"; NB: "the bistro is better than the restaurant".
/ www.plateaurestaurant.co.uk; 10.30 pm; closed Sat L & Sun D; set dinner £45 (FP).

Poissonnerie de l'Avenue SW3 £58 ❷❷❷
82 Sloane Ave 7589 2457 5–2C
"Excellent" fish and seafood dishes are often reported at this Brompton Cross veteran; it's infamously associated with a "purple-rinse" crowd… but then "old people often know best".
/ www.poissonneriedelavenue.co.uk; 11.15 pm; closed Sun; set weekday L £43 (FP).

(Ognisko Polskie)
The Polish Club SW7 £39 ④❸❸
55 Prince's Gate, Exhibition Rd 7589 4635 5–1C
With its "fabulous", "old-fashioned" dining room (and "delightful summer terrace"), this "time-warp" émigrés' club can come as "a surprise" in fashionable South Kensington; "the food isn't haute cuisine, but nor are the prices". / www.ognisko.com; 11 pm; set always available £21 (FP).

Pomegranates SW1 £53 ④❷❸
94 Grosvenor Rd 7828 6560 2–4C
In a Pimlico cellar, Patrick Gwynn-Jones's "unique '70s den" has offered a world-fusion menu since long before it became fashionable; perhaps owing to its elevated prices, the place is "never busy" nowadays, but fans find this only contributes to its "private club"-style charm. / 11.15 pm; closed Sat L & Sun.

Le Pont de la Tour SE1 £60 ④④❸
36d Shad Thames 7403 8403 9–4D
Trading, as ever, on its "lovely" riverside location (and "amazing" Tower Bridge view), this "arrogant" D&D-group operation charges "high prices for very average food", and its service is often "slow" and "confused". / www.lepontdelatour.co.uk; 11 pm, Sun 10 pm; closed Sat L; no trainers; set always available £41 (FP).

Popeseye £41 ❷❸❸
108 Blythe Rd, W14 7610 4578 7–1C
277 Upper Richmond Rd, SW15 8788 7733 10–2A
"Boy are those steaks good", at this "cramped" and "convivial" bistro – "hidden-away in Brook Green" – where supporting attractions include great wine and "incredible home-made puds"; hardly anyone mentions Putney. / www.popeseye.com; 10.30 pm; D only, closed Sun; no credit cards.

La Porchetta Pizzeria £26 ❸❸❸
33 Boswell St, WC1   7242 2434   2–1D
141-142 Upper St, N1   7288 2488   8–2D
147 Stroud Green Rd, N4   7281 2892   8–1D
74-77 Chalk Farm Rd, NW1   7267 6822   8–2B
84-86 Rosebery Ave, EC1   7837 6060   9–1A
A "bouncing and bustling" north London chain, where "each branch
has its own character"; in common, though, they have: a "friendly"
but hectic style, "pizzas the size of wagon wheels" and "vast"
portions of pasta at "cheap, cheap" prices. / varies; WC1 closed
Sat L & Sun, N1 Mon-Thu closed L, N4 closed weekday L; no Amex.

Portal EC1 £57 ❸❸❷
88 St John St   7253 6950   9–1B
This modern-Portuguese venture, in Clerkenwell has "interesting"
cuisine, a notable wine list and a "lovely" setting – "especially
at the back", in the "airy conservatory"; "occasional lapses",
though, continue to undercut its ratings. / www.portalrestaurant.com;
10.15 pm; closed Sun.

La Porte des Indes W1 £56 ❸❷❶
32 Bryanston St   7224 0055   2–2A
"A spectacular, two-floor setting, complete with indoor waterfall"
helps make a visit to this "Tardis-like" basement, near Marble Arch,
a "special" experience; the "pricey" Indian cuisine is "unusual"
(in that it's Frenchified) and it's "good" too – "especially for those
who don't like fiery food". / www.pilondon.net; 11.30 pm, Sun 10.30 pm;
closed Sat L.

Porters English Restaurant WC2 £30 ⑤⑤④
17 Henrietta St   7836 6466   4–3D
Supporters claim the menu of this rather touristy Covent Garden
spot includes some "good traditional pies and puddings"; however,
there are as many critics among reporters who just say it's "dire" –
"avoid at all costs!" / www.porters.uk.com; 11.30 pm; no Amex.

Il Portico W8 £40 ❸❶❷
277 Kensington High St   7602 6262   7–1D
An "old-fashioned" Italian (handily located by Kensington's cinema),
that's long been a local "favourite"; the food is "reliable,
not spectacular", but the approach is "very friendly" and "honest".
/ www.ilportico.co.uk; 11.15 pm; closed Sun, & Bank Holidays.

The Portrait
National Portrait Gallery WC2 £50 ④④❷
St Martin's Pl   7312 2490   4–4B
"Go for the wonderful rooftop view across Trafalgar Square",
best to enjoy this "elegant", if "clattery", top-floor venue; there's
an ever-present risk, though, of "overpriced" food and "dreadful"
service. / www.searcys.co.uk; Thu-Fri 8.30 pm; Sat-Wed closed D; set pre
theatre £31 (FP).

Potemkin EC1 £40 ④❸④
144 Clerkenwell Rd   7278 6661   9–1A
"A range of vodkas to satisfy the most discerning connoisseur"
helps win a small but devoted fan club for this (slightly
"atmosphere-free") Russian bar/restaurant, in Clerkenwell;
the food's quite "authentic" too. / www.potemkin.co.uk; 10.30 pm; closed
Sat L & Sun; set weekday L £24 (FP).

LA POULE AU POT SW1 £50 ❸❸❶
231 Ebury St 7730 7763 5–2D
This "quirky" Pimlico "perennial" is – as usual – the survey's
No. 1 romantic tip, thanks to its "so French" mix of "candlelight",
"dark corners", "rustic" décor and "cuisine bourgeoise"; service is a
little "unpredictable", though, and the cooking can seem
"somewhat heavy handed". / 11 pm, Sun 10 pm; set weekday L £33 (FP).

Pret A Manger £11 ❸❷④
Branches throughout London
"Energetic" and "smiley" staff help "make the difference", at these
"über-dependable" pit stops – still many a reporter's "first choice"
for "fresh" sandwiches, salads, soup 'n' sushi, washed down with
"first-class" coffee. / www.pret.com; 4 pm-6 pm, Trafalgar Sq 8 pm,
St. Martin's Ln 9 pm; closed Sun (except some West End branches),
City branches closed Sat & Sun; no credit cards; no booking.

The Prince Arthur E8 £37 ❸❸❸
95 Forest Rd 7249 9996 1–1D
"A fantastic addition to E8"; this "off-the-beaten-track" gastropub
sibling to the famous Gun serves "great food, that's not too
stereotypical". / www.theprincearthurlondonfields.com; 10 pm;
Mon-Thu D only, Fri-Sun open L & D; no Amex.

The Prince Of Wales SW15 NEW £36 ❷❸❸
138 Upper Richmond Rd 8788 1552 10–2B
"A fabulous new Putney gastropub", universally hailed by early
reporters as a "friendly" place, offering "good food at reasonable
prices". / www.princeofwalesputney.co.uk; 10 pm, Sun 9.30 pm.

The Princess EC2 £43 ❸④④
76 Paul St 7729 9270 9–1C
A first-floor Shoreditch dining room which "gets a bit noisy from the
pub downstairs"; service is "a bit haphazard" too, but the "simple"
food can be "surprisingly good". / 10 pm; closed Sat L & Sun.

Princess Garden W1 £50 ❶❷❸
8 North Audley St 7493 3223 3–2A
This "upmarket" Chinese is in "a different class" from most of its
traditional competitors thanks to its "smart" (if "stark") décor and
"smooth" service; the food is "superior" too, and "not too pricey,
for Mayfair". / www.princessgardenofmayfair.com; 11.15 pm.

Princess Victoria W12 NEW £37 ❷④❷
217 Uxbridge Rd 8749 5886 7–1B
A magnificent, newly-revamped Victorian pub, on a lonely bit
of Shepherd's Bush highway; an early visit found brilliantly-realised,
if straightforward, fare served rather sluggishly, but with charm.
/ Rated on Editors' visit; www.princessvictoria.co.uk; 10.30 pm, Sun 9.30 pm.

Priory House W14 £30 ❸④❸
58 Milson Rd 7371 3999 7–1C
A "dimly-lit" and "surprisingly stylish" venue, in the back streets
of Olympia, offering "yummy" tapas and cocktails.
/ www.priorybars.com; 10 pm; no Amex.

Prism EC3 £74 ④④⑤

147 Leadenhall St 7256 3875 9–2D

"Spacious" and "convenient for City clients" – Harvey Nics's converted banking hall, near Leadenhall Market, has obvious advantages for a business rendezvous; the "beautiful" interior is rather dead, however, and the cuisine, though "fine", is "overpriced". / www.harveynichols.com; 10 pm; closed Sat & Sun.

The Providores W1 £61 ❸④④

109 Marylebone High St 7935 6175 2–1A

"It'll dazzle your taste buds", say fans of Peter Gordon's "unique" Pacific Rim cuisine (and there is a "fabulous list of NZ wines" to go with it); doubters find dishes "over-complicated", though, and this first-floor Marylebone dining-room is rather "pokey". / www.theprovidores.co.uk; 10.30 pm; booking: max 12.

(Tapa Room)
The Providores W1 £40 ❸❸❸

109 Marylebone High St 7935 6175 2–1A

An "interesting selection" of light dishes helps make this "funky" and "noisy" Marylebone bar/diner very popular (especially for the "really different, but fabulous" brunch); prices, though, are "on the high side". / www.theprovidores.co.uk; 10.30 pm.

The Pumphouse N8 £38 ④❸④

1 New River Ave 8340 0400 1–1C

"A stunning conversion of an old industrial building", in Hornsey; "standards have plummeted" since it opened, though, and the food – which includes pizza – is "not memorable" nowadays. / www.phn8.co.uk; 9.30 pm; closed Mon, Tue-Fri D only, Sat & Sun open L & D.

Pure California £19 ❸④⑤

102 Wardour St, W1 7287 4008 3–2D
39 Beak St, W1 7287 3708 3–2D
47 Goodge St, W1 7436 3601 2–1C
113 High Holborn, WC1 7242 3533 2–1D
41-43 Ludgate Hill, EC4 7242 3533 9–2A

"Good food that's good for you" – that's the appeal of this small chain, which serves up "a great range of fresh healthy snacks and drinks". / W1T 6 pm; WC1 7 pm, Fri 6 pm, Sat 5 pm; W1F 7 pm, Fri & Sat 6 pm; W1T closed Sat & Sun, WC1 & W1F closed Sun.

Putney Station SW15 £30 ④❷❷

94-98 Upper Richmond Rd 8780 0242 10–2B

It's not just the "incredible value" of John Brinkley's trademark wine list which wins local popularity for his SW15 venture: the food – traditionally rather lacklustre – is "improving" too. / www.brinkleys.com; 11 pm, Tues-Sat midnight.

Quadrato
Four Seasons Hotel E14 £75 ❸❷④

Westferry Circus 7510 1857 11–1B

"In the desert that is Canary Wharf dining", this swish (but "morgue-like") chamber is seen by some reporters as "the best choice for a business lunch", offering "generally good" Italian cuisine; it also does an "amazing" Sunday brunch. / www.fourseasons.com; 10.30 pm.

Quaglino's SW1   £55   ⑤⑤⑤

16 Bury St   7930 6767   3–3D

"Totally embarrassing", "not cooked properly", "the worst meal ever"... – this "cavernous", factory-style former D&D-group outfit, in St James's, has served up even more "expensive rubbish" than usual of late; "how long will it last?" / www.quaglinos.co.uk; midnight, Fri & Sat 1 am, Sun 11 pm; set dinner £34 (FP).

The Quality Chop House EC1   £38   ❷❸❸

94 Farringdon Rd   7837 5093   9–1A

"All the best trappings of a Victorian chophouse" add to the "quirky" charm of Clerkenwell's 'Working Class Caterer', particularly known for the hardness of its benches (they're "sooooo uncomfortable"); its "spectacularly simple, traditional" fare is a touch "hit-and-miss", but at best "heavenly". / www.qualitychophouse.co.uk; 11.30 pm, Sun 10.30 pm; closed Sat L; set always available £26 (FP).

Queen's Head W6   £30   ④④❶

13 Brook Grn   7603 3174   7–1C

A potentially "fantastic" Brook Green tavern, with a "cosy and romantic" beamed interior and a vast and lovely garden; shame about the food, though, which is somewhere between "reliable" and "disappointing". / www.thespiritgroup.com; 10 pm, Sun 9 pm; no booking.

Queen's Head & Artichoke NW1   £38   ❸❸❷

30-32 Albany St   7916 6206   8–4B

"A relaxed gastropub", near Regent's Park, "serving an extensive array of tapas in vintage pub surroundings"; there's a more "formal" dining area upstairs – it attracts fewer reports, but fans say the food is "more assured". / www.theartichoke.net; 10.15 pm.

The Queens Arms SW1 NEW   £35   ❸④④

11 Warwick Way   7834 3313   2–4B

"A welcome newcomer to Pimlico", not least because it's the "first real gastropub" in its immediate vicinity; its "friendly" staff serve up "a good selection of dishes" at "fair prices". / www.thequeensarmspimlico.co.uk; 10 pm.

Le Querce SE23   £31   ❶❷❸

66-68 Brockley Rise   8690 3761   1–4D

This Brockley "hidden gem" certainly "doesn't look much from the outside", but it's of note for its "simple and very genuine Italian food", which includes "wonderful home-made pasta", and "amazing gelati in adventurous flavours" too. / 10.30 pm; closed Mon; no Amex.

Quilon SW1   £57   ❶❷④

41 Buckingham Gate   7821 1899   2–4B

The interior may be "slightly depressing" and "hotel-esque" – no wonder Michelin recently gave this place a star! – but this "posh" Indian, near Buckingham Palace, offers "sophisticated" cuisine which seems to have blossomed even further under the attention directed to it by the tyre men. / www.thequilonrestaurant.com; 11 pm, Sun 10.30 pm; closed Sat L; set weekday L £37 (FP).

Quirinale SW1 £57 ❷❷❸
North Ct, I Gt Peter St 7222 7080 2–4C
"A beacon in the Westminster desert" – this *"light"*, *"quiet"* and *"airy"* basement offers *"imaginative"* and *"varied"* Italian cooking, sometimes of an *"exceptional"* standard. / www.quirinale.co.uk; 10.30 pm; closed Sat & Sun.

Quo Vadis W1 £70 ❸❷❸
26-29 Dean St 7437 9585 4–2A
British hotel grill rooms of times past provide the Hart brothers' inspirations for the relaunch of this '20s Soho classic; that may explain its ultra-straightforward food, and low-key interior design – it all adds up to a quality experience, if one that arguably lacks pizzazz. / Rated on Editors' visit; www.quovadissoho.co.uk; 11 pm; closed Sun.

Racine SW3 £50 ❷❶❷
239 Brompton Rd 7584 4477 5–2C
"A class act"; this *"delightful corner of France, in Knightsbridge"* – notable both for its *"meticulous"* service and for its *"honest-to-goodness"* fare – mercifully suffered no discernible ill effects from last year's departure of co-founder Henry Harris… but as this guide goes to press, we hear he's decided to go back anyway! / 10.30 pm; set always available £33 (FP).

Ragam W1 £28 ❶❶⑤
57 Cleveland St 7636 9098 2–1B
"A dive, but the food is always fantastic"; this *"tiny"* stalwart, near the Telecom Tower, may be *"tatty"*, but its south Indian (mostly veggie) food is *"absolutely the best"*, and *"served with a genuine smile"*; BYO. / www.mcdosa.co.uk; 11 pm, Fri & Sat 11.30 pm, Sun 10.30 pm.

Rajasthan £36 ❸❷④
38-41 Houndsditch, EC3 7626 0033 9–2D
49 Monument St, EC3 7626 1920 9–3C
8 India St, EC3 7488 9777 9–2D
"Dependable and consistent" curries make these *"good-value"* Indians a City *"benchmark"*. / 10.30 pm; closed Sat & Sun.

Randa W8 £36 ❸❷④
23 Kensington Church St 7937 5363 5–1A
"Good-quality Lebanese fare" (much of it from an open grill) is served in a *"bizarre"* interior – a *"steel and glass"* re-fit of a former pub – at this handy Kensington yearling. / www.maroush.com; midnight.

Randall & Aubin W1 £44 ❸❷❶
16 Brewer St 7287 4447 3–2D
"It's fun to watch and be watched", perching on a stool at this *"bustling"* heart-of-sleazy-Soho seafood and champagne bar, which serves up some *"lovely"*, simple fare. / www.randallandaubin.co.uk; 11 pm; no booking.

Rani N3 £26 ❸❷❸
7 Long Ln 8349 4386 1–1B
"Worth the trek, for anyone in search of a great Indian vegetarian meal" – this Finchley veteran please nearly all who comment on it with its *"good value for money"* (the *"fun buffet"* especially). / www.raniuk.com; 10 pm; D only, ex Sun open L & D.

F S A

Ranoush £34 ❸④④

22 Brompton Rd, SW1   7235 6999   5–1D
338 King's Rd, SW3   7352 0044   5–3C
43 Edgware Rd, W2   7723 5929   6–1D
86 Kensington High St, W8   7938 2234   5–1A
"For good fast food without frills", try the "top" mezze, "excellent" kebabs and "yum" juices on offer at this Lebanese chain; service, though, can be "curt". / www.maroush.com; 1 am-3 am.

Ransome's Dock SW11 £47 ④❸❸

35 Parkgate Rd   7223 1611   5–4C
An "incredible, eclectic wine list" (bearing "no comparison" with any other in town) makes Martin & Vanessa Lam's "tucked-away" Battersea fixture well worth seeking out; the food – rather "spasmodic" of late – has always been a bit of a supporting attraction. / www.ransomesdock.co.uk; 11 pm; closed Sun D; set weekday L £36 (FP).

Raoul's Café £38 ④⑤❸

105-107 Talbot Rd, W11   7229 2400   6–1B
13 Clifton Rd, W9   7289 7313   8–4A
A duo of "trendy" and "cramped" deli-cafés in Maida Vale and Notting Hill, notable for their "top brunches" and their "terrible" service. / www.raoulsgourmet.com; 10 pm; no bookings at weekends.

Rapscallion SW4 £40 ❸④④

75 Venn St   7787 6555   10–2D
A "buzzy", "relaxed" and "inexpensive" restaurant, near the Clapham Picture House, which is as suited to a "late-night supper" as it is to brunch; service is generally "efficient" too, though off-days are not unknown. / www.therapscallion.co.uk; 11 pm; no Amex; booking: max 6.

Rasa N16 £26 ❶❶❸

55 Stoke Newington Church St   7249 0344   1–1C
"The original Stokie Rasa" is "always busy… mainly with people coming back"; its "incomparable" veggie Keralan fare "throws all sorts of exotic and wonderful flavours at you", and at "shockingly low prices" too. / www.rasarestaurants.com; 10.45 pm, Fri & Sat 11.30 pm; closed weekday L.

Rasa £33 ❶❶❶

5 Charlotte St, W1   7637 0222   2–1C
6 Dering St, W1   7629 1346   3–2B
Holiday Inn Hotel, 1 Kings Cross, WC1   7833 9787   8–3D
56 Stoke Newington Church St, N16   7249 1340   1–1C
This Indian chain "knocks all others into the shade", thanks to its "phenomenal" Keralan food and its "helpful" staff; it's primarily veggie, but Dering St and N16 (Travancore) also serve meat, while Charlotte St (Samudra) majors in "vivid" fish and seafood; see also Rasa N16. / www.rasarestaurants.com; 10.45 pm; Dering St W1 closed Sun, N16 D only Mon-Sat, N1 L only Mon-Fri, Charlotte St W1 closed Sun L, NW1 Mon - Fri L only, Rathbone St W1 Mon - Fri L only, WC1 closed Sun.

RASOI VINEET BHATIA SW3 £80 ②②③
10 Lincoln St 7225 1881 5–2D
*"Sublime and zingy" spicing creates "1001 intoxicating flavours"
for visitors to Vineet Bhatia's "tucked-away" Chelsea townhouse –
a "bizarre" home for such a pre-eminent "nouvelle-Indian"; prices
are "sky high", though, and – perhaps with the distraction of the
Urban Turban launch? – ratings overall slipped this year.*
/ www.rasoirestaurant.co.uk; 11 pm; closed Sat L & Sun; set weekday L
£46 (FP).

Ratchada SE3 £30 ③④④
129 Lee Rd 8318 0092 1–4D
*"Not a bad little Thai place", in Blackheath, with "simple" food
that's "generally above average".* / www.ratchada.co.uk; 11 pm; closed
Sun; no Amex.

The Real Greek £25 ⑤⑤④
56 Paddington St, W1 7486 0466 2–1A
60/62 Long Acre, WC2 7240 2292 4–2D
15 Hoxton Market, N1 7739 8212 9–1D
1-2 Riverside Hs, Southwark Br Rd, SE1 7620 0162 9–3B
31-33 Putney High St, SW15 8788 3270 10–2B
140-142 St John St, EC1 7253 7234 9–1A
*Is it time this "once-promising chain" was "put out of its misery"? –
thanks to its "terrible" and "overpriced" food and its "poor"
service, you might well be "better off at your local kebab shop";
(note, the original Hoxton branch no longer serves a more
ambitious menu).* / www.therealgreek.com; 10.45 pm; WC2 11 pm;
EC1 & N1 closed Sun; no Amex; WC2 no bookings .

Rebato's SW8 £32 ③①①
169 South Lambeth Rd 7735 6388 10–1D
*Thanks to its "wonderful", "it-could-be-Spain" ambience and
"supremely nice" staff, "people just love" this "unchanging"
Vauxhall "stalwart" – eat "cheap" tapas in the "crowded" bar,
or visit the restaurant and take a "Tardis ride to the '70s".*
/ www.rebatos.com; 10.45 pm; closed Sat L & Sun.

Red Fort W1 £60 ②③③
77 Dean St 7437 2525 4–2A
*For a "very central" Indian, it's hard to beat this "quiet" and
"gracious" veteran (which underwent a "fresh and modern"
revamp a few years ago) – its "excellent" cuisine is up there with
the Tamarinds and Cinnamon Clubs of the world.* / www.redfort.co.uk;
11.30 pm; closed Sat L & Sun; set weekday L £39 (FP), set pre-theatre
£40 (FP).

The Red Pepper W9 £38 ③④④
8 Formosa St 7266 2708 8–4A
*They still do "great pizzas" at this "vibrant" Maida Vale veteran;
"tables are so tightly packed", though, as to risk "spoiling the
ambience".* / 11 pm, Sun 10 pm; closed weekday L; no Amex.

Refettorio
The Crowne Plaza Hotel EC4 £56 ③③⑤
19 New Bridge St 7438 8052 9–3A
*"Wonderful" cheese and meat platters to kick off your meal are
the "authentic" highlight at this "well-spaced" City Italian;
the "bleak" and "sterile" atmosphere, however, makes this very
much a business venue.* / www.refettorio.com; 10.30 pm, Fri & Sat 10 pm;
closed Sat L & Sun; booking: max 8.

Refuel
Soho Hotel W1   £55   ⑤⑤❸
4 Richmond Mews   7559 3007   3–2D
"It's buzzy", "it's bright" and there's "plenty of space", at this
"lovely" design-hotel in the heart of Soho – "how can it let itself
down so badly with very average food and poorly-managed staff?"
/ www.sohohotel.com; midnight, Sun 11 pm; set always available £38 (FP).

Le Relais de Venise L'Entrecôte W1   £35   ❷❸❷
120 Marylebone Ln   7486 0878   2–1A
"Regular queues" attest to the (growing) popularity of this
"crowded" Parisian import, where "the only choice you need make
is the wine" – otherwise it's "steak, steak, steak", plus "proper"
thin cut fries and an "intriguing" secret sauce (and seconds if you
want 'em). / www.relaisdevenise.com; 10.45 pm, Sun 10.30 pm.

Le Rendezvous du Café EC1   £41   ❸❸❸
22 Charterhouse Sq   7336 8836   9–1B
"Great-value French staples" are all part of the classic bistro
formula at this "very cramped" Smithfield favourite.
/ www.cafedumarche.com; 10.30 pm; closed Sat L & Sun; no Amex.

Retsina NW3   £36   ④❷④
48-50 Belsize Ln   7431 5855   8–2A
"Mama's in the kitchen and son's serving", at this Belsize Park
yearling – fans say it's "everything a family-run Greek should be",
but not all reporters are convinced its standards are being
maintained. / 11 pm; no Amex.

Reubens W1   £43   ④④⑤
79 Baker St   7486 0035   2–1A
Being kosher is the only undisputed reason some readers might
wish to seek out this "'80s-style" deli (upstairs) / restaurant
(basement) in Marylebone; fans find it "reliable", but critics feel
it "lacks any finesse". / www.reubensrestaurant.co.uk; 10 pm; closed
Fri D & Sat.

Rhodes 24 EC2   £68   ❸❷❷
25 Old Broad St   7877 7703   9–2C
"Amazing views" ("to impress any client") help create
"a professional environment for business", at Gary Rhodes's 24th-
floor City dining room, where the British grub is "totally consistent",
if "eye-wateringly-priced"; NB: "allow extra time for lifts and
officious security measures". / www.rhodes24.co.uk; 9 pm; closed
Sat & Sun; no shorts; booking essential.

Rhodes W1 Brasserie
Cumberland Hotel W1   £50   ④④⑤
Gt Cumberland Pl   7616 5930   2–2A
"Cavernous", "clinical" and "noisy" – this Oxford Street brasserie
is an object lesson in how not to design a dining room; there are
reporters who say the food has "that Gary Rhodes magic",
but others say it's just "second-rate". / www.rhodesw1.com; 10.30 pm.

Rhodes W1 Restaurant
Cumberland Hotel W1 £87 ④❸❸
Gt Cumberland Pl 7616 5930 2–2A
*"Brilliant and inventive", or "underwhelming in its over-
complication"? – both schools of thought are strongly represented
in feedback on Gary R's "luxurious" and "rather self-conscious"
yearling, near Marble Arch. / www.rhodesw1.com; 10.30 pm; closed Mon,
Sat L & Sun; no trainers; set weekday L £56 (FP).*

Rib Room
Jumeirah Carlton Tower Hotel SW1 £85 ④④④
2 Cadogan Pl 7858 7250 5–1D
*"What must those poor Yanks think, getting charged a hundred
bucks for a grill?" – the roast beef (and steak) may arguably
be "the best in town", but this Knightsbridge dining room is a
"staid" place that critics find "obscenely expensive".
/ www.jumeirah.com; 10.45 pm, Sun 10.15 pm; set weekday L £63 (FP).*

RIBA Café
Royal Ass'n of Brit' Architects W1 £39 ④④❷
66 Portland Pl 7631 0467 2–1B
*The café in the fine '30s HQ of Britain's architects boasts
a most "impressive" and "spacious" setting (and an unexpected
and large roof terrace); the food, though, is "less lovely".
/ www.riba-venues.com; L only, closed Sun.*

Riccardo's SW3
 £42 ❸❷❸
126 Fulham Rd 7370 6656 5–3B
*"A good option for dining with friends" – this "always-buzzing"
Chelsea favourite offers "tapas-style" Italian food that's "ideal for
sharing", and a fair dose of "charm" too. / www.riccardos.it; 11.30 pm.*

Richoux
 £33 ⑤⑤④
172 Piccadilly, W1 7493 2204 3–3C
41a South Audley St, W1 7629 5228 3–3A
86 Brompton Rd, SW3 7584 8300 5–1C
3 Circus Rd, NW8 7483 4001 8–3A
*Fans still tip these "quaint" tea-rooms for "delicious" cakes and
"easy-going" breakfasts – as ever, though, they are drowned out
by critics who attack their "incredibly poor value", and "the worst"
service. / www.richoux.co.uk; 11 pm, SW3 7.30 pm, W1 Sat 11.30 pm,
NW8 10.30 pm.*

Rick's Café SW17
 £34 ❸④❷
122 Mitcham Rd 8767 5219 10–2C
*"Rick has moved on", from this "cramped" Tooting café – most,
in not quite all, reporters, though, think that the "confident"
contemporary cooking has held up well. / 11 pm, Sun 9 pm; closed
Mon; no Amex.*

El Rincón Latino SW4
 £28 ❸⓿⓿
148 Clapham Manor St 7622 0599 10–2D
*"The liveliest and friendliest tapas bar ever"; this little-known
"family-run affair", in Clapham, serves up "traditional" dishes
at "amazingly low prices". / 11.30 pm; closed Mon, Tue L, Wed L, Thu L,
Fri L & Sun D.*

Ristorante Semplice W1 £46 ❷❷❸
10 Blenheim St   7495 1509   3–2B
"You'd never know you were just off Oxford Street", at this "hidden-away" Mayfair yearling – a "caring" (if "somewhat cramped") kind of place, offering some "terrific" modern Italian cuisine.
/ www.ristorantesemplice.com; 10.30 pm; closed Sat L & Sun.

The Ritz Restaurant
The Ritz W1 £100 ④❷❶
150 Piccadilly   7493 8181   3–4C
To visit this "divine" Louis XVI-style chamber, overlooking Green Park, is to enter "a cosseted world of butter-poached lobster and champagne" – "not for modernists", clearly, but a wow for old-fashioned romantics; the food is "much-improved" on a few years ago… but then it had an awfully long way to go.
/ www.theritzlondon.com; 10.30 pm; jacket & tie required; set weekday L £68 (FP).

Riva SW13 £50 ❷❷④
169 Church Rd   8748 0434   10–1A
"Superb, simple, seasonal cooking" and "skilled" service have – despite occasional protests that the place is "over-hyped" – long won approval for Andreas Riva's "smooth" Barnes Venetian; prepare, though, to "make your own atmosphere". / 10.30 pm; closed Sat L.

The River Café W6 £64 ❷❸❷
Thames Wharf, Rainville Rd   7386 4200   7–2C
"Outside, on a warm summer evening" – that's the time to visit Rose Gray and Ruth Rogers' world-famous (but "casual") Hammersmith Italian; the "simple" rustic cooking "continues to be memorable"… but "OMG, the prices are insane".
/ www.rivercafe.co.uk; 9 pm, Sat 9.15 pm; closed Sun D.

The Rivington Grill EC2 £45 ❸④④
28-30 Rivington St   7729 7053   9–1C
Fans salute the traditional British fare (not least, of course, breakfast) on offer at this "enjoyable" Shoreditch brasserie; service is "slapdash", though, and critics say the cuisine has "airs and graces it doesn't live up to". / www.rivingtongrill.co.uk; 11 pm, Sun 10.30 pm.

The Rivington Grill SE10 £43 ④⑤④
178 Greenwich High Rd   8293 9270   1–3D
As an outpost of the Caprice Group, this casual British outfit "should have been a good thing for Greenwich"; it's "expensive for what it is", though, and widely seen as a "poor relation".
/ www.rivingtongrill.co.uk; 11 pm, Sun 10 pm; closed Mon, Tue L & Wed L.

Roast
The Floral Hall SE1 £55 ④⑤❸
Stoney St   7940 1300   9–4C
Only for "gorgeous" breakfasts and brunches can this "fantastic" first-floor space, above Borough Market, be safely recommended – otherwise, its British fare is too often "a waste of ingredients", and the service can be a "nightmare" too. / www.roast-restaurant.com; 10.45 pm; closed Sun D; set Sun L £41 (FP).

Rock & Sole Plaice WC2 £28 ❷④④
47 Endell St 7836 3785 4–1C
"It's the greatest chippy on Earth!"... well in Covent Garden,
anyway; and considering it's in every tourist guide, this "basic but
cosy" veteran is a surprisingly "good-value" destination (especially
for a central meal in a group). / 11 pm; no Amex.

Rock & Rose TW9 NEW £40 ④④❷
106-108 Kew Rd 8948 8008 1–4A
"Funky, upmarket décor, complete with rose wall paper and
chandeliers", helps win acclaim for this "glam" newcomer as a
"great new addition" to Richmond; fans say the food is "good" too
– but sceptics say "they need to focus less on style and more
on cooking". / www.rockandroserestaurant.co.uk; 10.30 pm.

Rocket £42 ❸❸❷
4-6 Lancashire Ct, W1 7629 2889 3–2B
Putney Wharf, Brewhouse Ln, SW15 8789 7875 10–2B
6 Adams Ct, EC2 7628 0808 9–2C
With its "handy branches", "fresh" food and "good prices",
this pizza-to-salads chain is "hard to beat"; the "buzzing" Bond
Street branch and the City one are "great for winter", but "Putney
is a summertime favourite for its outside tables".
/ www.rocketrestaurants.co.uk; 10.45 pm; W1 closed Sun; E6 & EC2 closed
Sat & Sun.

Rodizio Rico £39 ④④④
111 Westbourne Grove, W2 7792 4035 6–1B
77-78 Upper St, N1 7354 1076 8–3D
"Great for groups and office outings" – you get a "grand" BBQ
buffet at these "fun" Brazilian operations; critics, though,
say "quality is lacking". / www.rodiziorico.com; W2 11.30 pm,
N1 midnight; closed weekday L; no Amex.

The Roebuck W4 £38 ❸❸❸
122 Chiswick High Rd 8995 4392 7–2A
A "relaxed" Chiswick gastropub yearling, with "plenty of space" and
a "large garden"; the atmosphere is "jolly", the food "competent"
and staff are "friendly" too ("particularly to those with kids
in tow"). / www.theroebuckchiswick.co.uk; 10.30 pm, Sun 10 pm.

Roka W1 £53 ❶❷❷
37 Charlotte St 7580 6464 2–1C
For "Zuma minus the attitude", seek out its "more relaxed"
Fitzrovia sibling – the latter "oozes cool" and serves up an
"absolutely amazing" mix of "obliging" service and "sublime"
Japanese fare (including "brilliant robata grill dishes");
the basement Shochu bar also offers "a really hip night out".
/ www.rokarestaurant.com; 11.15 pm; booking: max 8.

Ronnie Scott's W1 £44 ⑤④❶
47 Frith St 7439 0747 4–2A
The legendary Soho jazz club may offer a "wonderful" night out,
but it's mainly down to "the atmosphere and the music" – "let's
be honest, you don't come here for the food". / www.ronniescotts.co.uk;
3 am, Sun midnight; D only.

Rooburoo N1 £27 ❸❷❸
21 Chapel Mkt 7278 8100 8–3D
*"A light and fresh approach to curry, deserving success" –
this "interesting" Indian can come as a bit of a "surprise", given its
"backwater" location in Islington's "grotty" Chapel Market.*
/ www.rooburoo.com; 11 pm; closed Mon L.

Rosemary Lane E1 £44 ❷❷④
61 Royal Mint St 7481 2602 11–1A
*This "hidden gem", in a former boozer, lurks in the no-man's-land
just east of Tower Hill; it's a "homely" – some say "romantic" –
place, where the cooking is "seasonal" and "precise".*
*/ www.rosemarylane.btinternet.co.uk; 10 pm; closed Sat L & Sun;
set weekday L £29 (FP).*

The Rosendale SE21 £46 ❷❸④
65 Rosendale Rd 8670 0812 1–4D
*After a year in business, this grand West Dulwich gastropub
is known for "the best pub food in the area" (and an "awesome"
wine list too); while "technically good", though, it can seem
to "lack soul". / www.therosendale.co.uk; 10.30 pm; closed Mon & Sun D;
no Amex.*

Rossopomodoro £33 ④④❸
214 Fulham Rd, SW10 7352 7677 5–3B
184a Kensington Park Rd, W11 7229 9007 6–1A
*"Authentic Neapolitan pizzas made with the freshest ingredients"
make this small chain popular; service can be "dozy", though,
and standards generally are rather up-and-down. / W11 & SW10
midnight.*

The Rôtisserie £37 ④④④
316 Uxbridge Rd, HA5 8421 2878 1–1A
1288 Whetstone High Rd, N20 8343 8585 1–1B
82 Fortune Green Rd, NW6 7435 9923 1–1B
87 Allitsen Rd, NW8 7722 7444 8–3A
*This small steakhouse chain can appear "nothing too special" –
at its best, though, it offers "excellent" grills, "willing" service and
a "neighbourly" vibe. / www.therotisserie.co.uk; 10.30 pm; closed L Mon -
Thurs, NW6 closed L; no Amex (except HA5).*

Rôtisserie Jules £28 ❸⑤⑤
6-8 Bute St, SW7 7584 0600 5–2B
133 Notting Hill Gate, W11 7221 3331 6–2B
*The menu is "limited" – mostly rôtisserie chicken – but results
at these basic pit stops are "always satisfying", and come "at a low
price" (with BYO too); they make "a healthy alternative
to fast food", but brace yourself for sometimes "diabolical" service.*
/ www.rotisseriejules.com; 10.30 pm.

ROUSSILLON SW1 £73 ❶❶❸
16 St Barnabas St 7730 5550 5–2D
*"A great unsung hero of London gastronomy"; Gerard Virolle's
"exceptional" tasting menus – with "beautifully matched" wines –
are the star attraction at this "classy" but perhaps slightly
"sombre" Pimlico fixture, which never quite achieves the profile
it deserves. / www.roussillon.co.uk; 11 pm; closed Sat L & Sun; booking:
max 11; set weekday L £50 (FP).*

Rowley's SW1 £57 ⑤④④
113 Jermyn St 7930 2707 3–3D
*This St James's steakhouse has a wonderfully convenient location,
and a "nice-looking Edwardian interior"; sadly, though, it can also
seem "old-fashioned, average and extremely overpriced".*
/ www.rowleys.co.uk; 11 pm.

Royal Academy W1 £33 ⑤⑤❷
Burlington Hs, Piccadilly 7300 5608 3–3C
*The Academy's café is a civilised spot, whose "ideal" location is not
only handy for art-lovers; the food's not the greatest, however,
and the switch to waiter service for afternoon tea and Friday
evenings hasn't been a step forwards.* / www.royalacademy.org.uk;
8.15 pm; L only, except Fri open L & D; no booking at L.

Royal China £37 ❷❸④
24-26 Baker St, W1 7487 4688 2–1A
805 Fulham Rd, SW6 7731 0081 10–1B
13 Queensway, W2 7221 2535 6–2C
30 Westferry Circus, E14 7719 0888 11–1B
*"Amazing, hectic, in-yer-face, weekend dim sum" is the highlight
of the week at the Bayswater and Marylebone branches of this
"bizarrely glitzy" Cantonese chain; at any time, it offers
an experience "about as close to Hong Kong as you'll get".*
/ 10.45 pm, Fri & Sat 11.15 pm; no bookings Sat & Sun L.

Royal China Club £57 ❷❸④
40-42 Baker St, W1 7486 3898 2–1A
68 Queen's Grove, NW8 7586 4280 8–3A
*"Clattering deep-sea horrors in the aquarium" set the scene at the
fine dining flagship of the well-known Chinese chain, in Marylebone;
it serves "superb dim sum" and other "first-rate" fare ("with a
strong bias to fish"), but even fans can't help noting it's "very,
very expensive"; a St John's Wood twin recently opened.*
/ www.royalchinagroup.co.uk.

Royal China SW15 £35 ❷❸④
3 Chelverton Rd 8788 0907 10–2B
*"The original is still the best", say fans of this Putney oriental, which
– complete with '80s disco décor – spawned (but is no longer part
of) the well-known chain; it's not yet "quite up to the level it was
before its 2007 fire", but "reliable" enough, with still-"excellent"
dim sum.* / 11 pm, Fri & Sat 11.30 pm.

The Royal Exchange Grand Café
The Royal Exchange EC3 £46 ④④❷
Cornhill 7618 2480 9–2C
*It has "a buzzy central location for business lunches", but otherwise
the D&D-group's seafood bar (in the heart of one of the City's
grandest buildings) is "a bland and overpriced venue quite typical
of the former Conran group".* / www.royalexchangegrandcafeandbar.com;
11 pm; closed Sat & Sun; no booking.

RSJ SE1 £40 ❸❷⑤
33 Coin St 7928 4554 9–4A
*A "stunning" Loire wine list underpins the appeal of this "reliable"
South Bank veteran as "a star in a still bleak area"; its enduring
high popularity is particularly impressive in the light of its
formidably "dull" interior.* / www.rsj.uk.com; 11 pm; closed Sat L & Sun.

La Rueda £32 ⑤④❸
642 King's Rd, SW6 7384 2684 5–4A
66-68 Clapham High St, SW4 7627 2173 10–2D
Fans of this old Spanish duo still find them "fun", especially in a group (and they are often "packed"); their performance, though, is "very tired" nowadays, with "bland" tapas served by "off-hand" staff. / www.larueda-restaurant.co.uk; 11 pm, SW6 1 am; no Amex.

Rules WC2 £60 ❸❸❶
35 Maiden Ln 7836 5314 4–3D
"Popular with US tourists, but who cares?" – why shouldn't they like this beautiful Covent Garden veteran (1798), with its "quirky" character and its "honest, traditional fare" (with "great game in season" a highlight); NB: the splendid upstairs rooms are no longer used for private hire. / www.rules.co.uk; 11.30 pm, Sun 10.30 pm; no shorts.

Running Horse W1 £37 ❸❸❷
50 Davies St 7493 1275 3–2A
"A lot cheaper than its near-neighbour, Claridge's", this "pleasant" gastropub makes a useful stand-by for those on tighter Mayfair budgets. / www.therunninghorselondon.co.uk; 9.30 pm; closed Sun D; need 8+ to book.

The Rye SE15 £29 ❸❸❷
31 Peckham Rye 7639 5397 1–4D
"A wonder for Peckham!" – this gastropub near Peckham Rye station wins a big all-round thumbs-up from the locals. / 10 pm, Sun 9 pm; no Amex.

S & M Café £22 ④④④
268 Portobello Rd, W10 8968 8898 6–1A
4-6 Essex Rd, N1 7359 5361 8–3D
48 Brushfield St, E1 7247 2252 9–1D
"Retro" British cafés, praised by fans for a "reliable" sausage-and-mash experience (and an "excellent" crumble too); critics, though, say the food can be "stodgy" and "tasteless". / www.sandmcafe.co.uk; 11 pm; no Amex; W10 no booking for L; E1 no booking Sat & Sun L.

Sabor N1 £35 ❸❸❸
108 Essex Rd 7226 5551 8–3D
A "funky" Latino hang-out, in Islington, with a "colourful" interior, "smiling" staff and an "original" selection of South American dishes; critics, though, complain that "it goes downhill when it's busy", and is "expensive for what it is". / www.sabor.co.uk; 10.45 pm; closed Mon, Tue-Fri D only, Sat & Sun open L & D; no Amex.

Le Sacré-Coeur N1 £34 ④❷❷
18 Theberton St 7354 2618 8–3D
A "crowded" Islington bistro which is "popping with Parisian joie de vivre", and where "you can eat snails and steak-frites at reasonable prices". / www.sacrecoeur.co.uk; 11 pm, Sat 11.30 pm.

Saf EC2 NEW £35
152-154 Curtain Rd 7613 0007 9–1D
We didn't get to visit this trendy new Shoreditch vegan – outpost of an international chain – before we went to press; the sole reporter who did, however, was very impressed, and newspaper reviews have – by and large – been supportive. / www.safrestaurant.co.uk; 11 pm.

Sagar £22 **❶❷④**
17a, Percy St, W1   7631 3319   3–2B **NEW**
157 King St, W6   8741 8563   7–2C
27 York St, TW1   8744 3868   1–4A
Now with a branch in central London, this growing South Indian
veggie chain combines "courteous" and "smiley" service with
"superb" and "subtle" cooking, and all at "incredibly reasonable"
prices. / www.gosagar.com; Sun-Thu 10.45 pm, Fri & Sat 11.30 pm;
set weekday L £12 (FP).

Saigon Saigon W6 £31 **❸❷❸**
313-317 King St   8748 6887   7–2B
Shame it's been rather "uneven" of late – on a good day you get
"authentic" fare at this "value-for-money" Hammersmith
Vietnamese. / www.saigon-saigon.co.uk; 11 pm, Sun 10 pm; closed Mon L;
no Amex.

St Alban SW1 £52 **❸0❸**
4-12 Lower Regent St, Rex Hs   7499 8558   3–3D
Corbin & King's efforts to perfect their "calm" Theatreland yearling
are bearing fruit – the "Med-inspired" cooking is now very "decent"
(if not yet inspired), and the service well up to their trademark
"effortlessly slick" level; perhaps one day everyone will love the
"somewhat weird", "'70s airport lounge" interior too.
/ www.stalban.net; midnight, Sun 11 pm.

St Germain EC1 £40 **④④❸**
89-90 Turnmill St   7336 0949   9–1A
It looks "attractive", but this Farringdon brasserie "could be so
much better" – the food, in particular, "needs improving".
/ www.stgermain.info; 10.30 pm; closed Sat L & Sun D.

St James's Hotel And Club SW1 **NEW**
7-8 Park Pl   7316 1600   3–4C
Dieter Müller is renowned in Germany for his Gallic cuisine,
and two of his acolytes are being installed at the dining room of this
St James's hotel for its re-launch in late-2008; one to watch.
/ www.stjamesclubandhotel.co.uk.

ST JOHN EC1 £48 **❶❷❸**
26 St John St   7251 0848   9–1B
"Take your courage in both teeth, and eat the unthinkable"; Fergus
Henderson's "passionate", "functional"-looking Smithfield shrine
to "nose-to-tail eating" (with much emphasis on the offally bits) has
now achieved international acclaim as a "uniquely British"
institution. / www.stjohnrestaurant.com; 11 pm; closed Sat L & Sun.

St John Bread & Wine E1 £40 **❶❷❸**
94-96 Commercial St   7251 0848   9–1D
"Awesome" (determinedly "unfussy") British dishes and "eclectic"
wine – all at very "affordable" prices – make for a "cool" overall
experience at this "noisy and very plain" Spitalfields Market
canteen; "where else can you just walk in and order brains
on toast?" / www.stjohnbreadandwine.com; 10.30 pm; closed Sun D.

St Johns N19 £39 ❸❷❶
91 Junction Rd 7272 1587 8–1C
A "lovely, high-ceilinged dining room" (built as a music hall) helps
create a "vibey" ambience at this "so popular" Archway gastropub;
as ever, its "delicious", "seasonal" cooking wins high praise,
but there were also a fair few "blips" this year. / 11 pm, Sun 9.30 pm;
Mon-Thu D only, Fri-Sun open L & D; booking: max 12.

Le Saint Julien EC1 £45 ④❸④
62-63 Long Ln 7796 4550 9–1B
"You could be in France", say fans of this "classic" Smithfield bistro;
critics say the cuisine is no more than "reasonable", though,
and service can occasionally be "a bit too authentic". / 10 pm; closed
Sat & Sun.

St Moritz W1 £44 ❸❸❸
161 Wardour St 7734 3324 3–1D
A "Swiss-chalet–kitsch" Soho veteran, whose "delicious fondues"
and "cosy" atmosphere are usually "dependable".
/ www.stmoritz-restaurant.co.uk; 11.30 pm; closed Sat L & Sun.

Sake No Hana SW1 £111 ④④④
23 St James's St 0871 7925 8988 3–4C
"Oh my God, I can't believe how bad it was!"; Alan Yau's
"surprisingly weak" Japanese newcomer (on the former St James's
site of Shumi, RIP) is an out-and-out turkey – it inspires far too
many reports of "clueless" staff, serving up "bland and
disappointing" food at "ridiculous" prices. / 11 pm, Sat 11.30 pm;
closed Sun; no trainers.

Saki Bar & Food Emporium EC1 £44 ❷❷④
4 West Smithfield 7489 7033 9–2A
"A basement Japanese, with a proper sushi bar", and which offers
"amazing oriental cocktails" too; in fact, this "ambitious" Smithfield
operation lacks only one thing – "atmosphere". / www.saki-food.com;
10.30 pm; closed Sat L & Sun.

Sakonis HA0 £18 ❷④⑤
129 Ealing Rd 8903 9601 1–1A
An "excellent-value buffet" remains a top draw to this "cheap and
cheerful" Wembley canteen classic, which offers an "unusual" mix
of Gujarati and Indo-Chinese dishes. / 9.30 pm; no Amex.

Sakura W1 £27 ❷⑤⑤
9 Hanover St 7629 2961 3–2C
"Always being full of Japanese diners" is "the best advertisement"
for this "grim" and "very busy" Mayfair basement; it may have
some of "the rudest waiters in London", but fans "return time and
again" for its "great sushi", "huge bowls of ramen", and so on from
a hugely extensive menu. / 10 pm.

Salaam Namaste WC1 £27 ❸❸④
68 Millman St 7405 3697 2–1D
This Bloomsbury Indian offers "distinctive" dishes, which
most reporters say are "a cut above average"; not everyone
is convinced, though, and the setting is "crowded" and "noisy".
/ www.salaamnamaste.com; 11.30 pm.

Salade £15 ③④⑤
52 Stratton St, W1   7499 6565   3–3C
Paddington Station, W2   7402 5616   6–1C **NEW**
144-146 Fetter Ln, EC4   7242 7972   9–2A **NEW**
3 Old Bailey, EC4   7248 6612   9–2A
"A great place for a DIY salad" with "loads of variety and good portions"; "lovely breakfasts" too. / www.salade.co.uk; L only, W2 7 pm, Sat & Sun 5 pm; closed Sat & Sun; no Amex.

Sale e Pepe SW1 £46 ③②①
9-15 Pavilion Rd   7235 0098   5–1D
"Crazy Italian staff" dish out "a lot of banter" – as well as "ample" and "reliable" classic dishes – at this "fun", "cramped" and "noisy" trattoria, near Harrods. / www.saleepepe.co.uk; 11.30 pm; closed Sun; no shorts.

The Salisbury Tavern SW6 £38 ④③③
21 Sherbrooke Rd   7381 4005   10–1B
Reports on the food at this "stylish" Fulham boozer are not quite consistent, but it usually seems to make a "solid" enough stand-by. / www.thesalisbury.com; 11 pm, Sun 10 pm; closed weekday L.

Salloos SW1 £49 ②③③
62-64 Kinnerton St   7235 4444   5–1D
"Amazing" Pakistani dishes ("renowned lamb chops", in particular) still make this quirky and little-known veteran – hidden-away in a Knightsbridge mews – one of London's top subcontinentals. / 11 pm; closed Sun.

Salt House NW8 £40 ③②②
63 Abbey Rd   7328 6626   8–3A
"Whether inside on a wintery day, or outside 'en terrasse' in summer" – this attractive St John's Wood gastropub offers "enjoyable" food and "friendly" service. / www.thesalthouse.co.uk; 10.30 pm.

Salt Yard W1 £37 ②②③
54 Goodge St   7637 0657   2–1B
"Stunning" tapas – "novel combos" of "well-sourced Spanish and Italian ingredients" – and a "dangerously drinkable" wine list underpin the "mad popularity" of this "casual" and "friendly" Fitzrovian; (beware the "pokey" basement, though). / www.saltyard.co.uk; 11 pm; closed Sat L & Sun.

The Salusbury NW6 £39 ②③③
50-52 Salusbury Rd   7328 3286   1–2B
This "crowded" pub in Queen's Park has the air of a "community hub"; it serves a Mediterranean menu that "rarely disappoints". / 10.15 pm; closed Mon L; no Amex.

Sam's Brasserie W4 £43 ④③④
11 Barley Mow Pas   8987 0555   7–2A
"Sam's a lovely chap", and his "striking" conversion of an old industrial building "brings some urban flair to conservative Chiswick"; the food at this once-promising brasserie has notably slipped though, and the atmosphere can "lack warmth". / www.samsbrasserie.co.uk; 10.30 pm; booking: max 12; set weekday L £27 (FP).

San Carlo N6 £48 ⑤⑤④
2 Highgate High St 8340 5823 8–1B
*Since its "WAG-y" 2007 relaunch, this veteran Italian has divided
opinion – fans say the new régime has done "a great job of reviving
an old institution", but critics say the food "needs more effort",
and really hate this "bit of Poshbeckistan, right here in Highgate".*
/ www.marishasancarlo.co.uk; 11 pm.

San Daniele del Friuli N5 £35 ❸②②
72 Highbury Park 7226 1609 8–1D
*A "good local Italian", in Highbury, offering "authentic" food and
service, and "a gentle buzz"; it's "still popular with the Arsenal
boys, even though their stadium has moved!"* / 10.30 pm; closed
Mon L, Tue L, Sat L & Sun; no Amex.

San Lorenzo SW3 £62 ⑤④④
22 Beauchamp Pl 7584 1074 5–1C
*"The only thing worse than the service is the food", say critics
of this "stale" Knightsbridge icon of the '60s, which fans still see
as something of a "see-and-be-seen" destination.* / 11.30 pm; closed
Sun; no credit cards.

San Lorenzo Fuoriporta SW19 £51 ⑤⑤④
38 Wimbledon Hill Rd 8946 8463 10–2B
*This dated Wimbledon Town Italian is starting to resemble its
Knightsbridge cousin; for too many reporters, nowadays, prices
seem to take customers "for fools", with management apparently
regarding them simply as an "inconvenience" – "there hardly seems
to be anyone in charge, except during Wimbledon fortnight".*
/ www.sanlorenzo.com; 11 pm; set weekday L £29 (FP), set pre-theatre
£30 (FP).

San Remo SW13 £43 ④❷❸
195 Castelnau 8741 5909 7–2C
*A "good, solid Italian" that makes a "comforting" option in the thin
area south of Hammersmith Bridge; "after fifteen years in business,
they must be doing something right".* / 11 pm; closed Sun.

Santa Lucia SW10 £36 ❸②②
2 Hollywood Rd 7352 8484 5–3B
*A "very friendly" Chelsea-fringe fixture that's "usually full
of shouting Italians"; its small fan club says the pizza is "fantastic".*
/ www.madeinitalygroup.co.uk; 11.30 pm; closed weekday L.

Santa Maria del Sur SW8 £38 ❷❷❸
129 Queenstown Rd 7622 2088 10–1C
*"Is there better steak in London?" than at this "brilliant",
if "very basic", Battersea meat-eaters' "haven"; "as we say
in Argentina, que barbaro!"* / www.buenayre.co.uk; 10.30 pm; closed
weekday L.

Santini SW1 £66 ④④❸
29 Ebury St 7730 4094 2–4B
*"Well-spaced tables" help this once-glamorous Belgravia Italian
retain something of a business following among reporters; it's "eye-
wateringly expensive for what it is", though, given the
"disappointingly ordinary" food, and sometimes "appalling" service.*
/ www.santini-restaurant.com; 11 pm; closed Sat L & Sun L.

Sapori WC2 £34 ④❸④
43 Drury Ln 7836 8296 4–2D
*An unpretentious Italian stand-by, near the Royal Opera House;
it's "reasonably priced", and "quick for a pre theatre pasta".
/ 11.30 pm; no Amex.*

Sarastro WC2 £37 ⑤⑤④
126 Drury Ln 7836 0101 2–2D
*This "tacky" OTT-theatrical Covent Garden venue –
with intermittent live opera – is still regularly touted as a "fun"
experience; it's passed its sell-by date, though, and far too many
reports nowadays are of the "never-again" variety.
/ www.sarastro-restaurant.com; 11.30 pm.*

Sardo W1 £44 ❷❸④
45 Grafton Way 7387 2521 2–1B
*For "a real taste of Sardinia" – and "a good selection of wines"
to go with it – this "authentic", if "low key", Fitzrovia back street
operation is well worth seeking out. / www.sardo-restaurant.com; 11 pm;
closed Sat L & Sun.*

Sardo Canale NW1 £44 ④❸❷
42 Gloucester Ave 7722 2800 8–3B
*A "beautiful courtyard" and a "lovely", "semi-subterranean" interior
have helped win this Primrose Hill venture a reputation
as "a wonderful hide-away"; shame, then, that the cooking has
so signally "gone off" in recent times. / www.sardocanale.com; 10 pm;
closed Mon L.*

Sargasso Sea N21 £55 ❷❷❷
10 Station Rd 8360 0990 1–1C
*It's "a little pricey for Winchmore Hill", but this first-rate local offers
"very good" fish cooking, and a "special" all-round experience.
/ www.sargassosea.co.uk; 10.30 pm; closed Mon, Tue L, Wed L, Sat L & Sun D;
set weekday L £31 (FP).*

Sarracino NW6 £38 ❷❷④
186 Broadhurst Gdns 7372 5889 1–1B
*"Baked in a roaring fire in full view" – the pizza (sold "al metro")
is "excellent", and "great-value" too, at this "relaxed, friendly and
tightly-packed" West Hampstead Italian.
/ www.sarracinorestaurant.com/; 11 pm; closed weekday L.*

Sartoria W1 £55 ④④❸
20 Savile Row 7534 7000 3–2C
*"Smart" and "well-spaced" – and also "dull" and "expensive" –
the D&D-group's Mayfair Italian makes a "perfect business venue".
/ www.danddlondon.co.uk; 11 pm; closed Sun.*

Satay House W2 £36 ❸❸④
13 Sale Pl 7723 6763 6–1D
*"Very good satay" is – as you'd hope – the mainstay of this
"friendly" Malaysian Bayswater veteran (recently revamped),
but the rest of the extensive menu is all "genuine" too.
/ www.satay-house.co.uk; 11 pm.*

Satsuma W1 £28 ❸❸④
56 Wardour St 7437 8338 3–2D
*This heart-of-Soho canteen "beats Wagamama hands down"
(not least with its "much more extensive menu") – "the ever-
present queue says it all". / www.osatsuma.com; 10.30 pm; no booking.*

Sauterelle
Royal Exchange EC3 £57 ❸❸❸
Bank 7618 2483 9–2C
"Looking down on the bling-purveyors of the Royal Exchange",
this is one of the better D&D-group operations – "dependable" and
"discreet", it generally makes "a good choice for business lunches".
/ www.restaurantsauterelle.co.uk; 10 pm; closed Sat & Sun; set dinner £36 (FP).

Scalini SW3 £58 ❷❷❷
1-3 Walton St 7225 2301 5–2C
"Not cheap but great fun" – this "tightly-packed" and "noisy"
Italian is "perpetually mobbed" with a well-heeled Knightsbridge
crowd. / midnight.

Scarpetta TW11 £35 ❷❷❷
78 High St 8977 8177 1–4A
"A great local Italian", in downtown Teddington, praised for both its
"authentic" wood-fired pizza and its "delicious fresh pasta";
unsurprisingly, it's "always very busy". / www.scarpetta.co.uk; 11 pm;
no shorts.

The Scarsdale W8 £33 ④❸❶
23a Edwardes Sq 7937 1811 7–1D
A *"fabulous"* Kensington hostelry on one of London's
prettiest squares; it retains the feel of *"a real pub"*, and the menu
hasn't 'gone gastro' either – you get *"good Sunday roasts"*,
"succulent" burgers and so on. / 10 pm.

Scoffers SW11 £37 ❸❸❷
6 Battersea Rise 7978 5542 10–2C
It's not just the greenery ("love the tree growing in the middle")
which wins local acclaim for this "friendly" Battersea veteran –
the food, including "the best brunch in the area", is generally
"good value" too. / www.scoffersrestaurant.co.uk; 11 pm.

SCOTT'S W1 £68 ❷❶❷
20 Mount St 7495 7309 3–3A
"A great revival of a wonderful institution"; just like its sibling
J Sheekey, this "beautifully refurbished" Mayfair veteran offers
"sublime" seafood cooking and "super-slick" service; the more
spacious interior here affords more chances to "see-and-be-seen",
however – perhaps why it's fast becoming the 'new Ivy'.
/ www.scotts-restaurant.com; 10.30 pm.

The Sea Cow SE22 £27 ❸❸❸
37 Lordship Ln 8693 3111 1–4D
Whether you go "grilled or battered", this contemporary-style fish
café, in East Dulwich, is "still tops for fish 'n' chips", according
to fans; it's more "hit-and-miss" than when it opened, though
(and the offshoots it spawned have now closed).
/ www.theseacow.co.uk; 10.30 pm, Sun 8.30 pm.

Seabass £33 ④❸④
40 James St, W1 7486 9540 3–1A
9 Sheldon Sq, Paddington Central, W2 7286 8000 6–1C
On most (if by no means all) accounts, this large fish restaurant has
been a "useful addition" to the Paddington Basin development,
and it certainly has an "extensive" menu; its little-known
Marylebone parent also wins praise as a good option "for a quick
dinner".

Seafresh SW1   £30   ❸❷④
80-81 Wilton Rd   7828 0747   2–4B
"It's not much to look at" (and that's after the revamp!), but this
"clean and comfy" Pimlico chippy still makes a "splendid" choice
for "fresh fish and crisp chips", in "mammoth portions". / 10.30 pm;
closed Sun.

Seaport W1   £43   ❸❸④
24 Seymour Pl   7724 4307   2–2A
"Interesting" and "high-quality" fish dishes wow most – but not all
– who report on this "bland"-looking Mauritian-themed yearling,
"tucked-away" in Marylebone. / 11 pm.

Searcy's Brasserie EC2   £51   ④④④
Level 2, Barbican Centre   7588 3008   9–1B
"In the maze of the Barbican", this "quiet and spacious" brasserie
serves up "acceptable" food to theatre-goers and business types;
it's a "clinical" place, though, and often seems "overpriced".
/ www.searcys.co.uk; 10.30 pm; closed Sat L & Sun.

Seashell NW1   £37   ❷④⑤
49 Lisson Grove   7224 9000   8–4A
"Soft batter, hot chips and yummy mushy peas" all contribute
to some "seriously good" eating at this famous Marylebone chippy;
given the dining room's "miserable" ambience, though, take-away
is arguably the best option. / www.seashellrestaurant.co.uk; 10.30 pm;
closed Sun D.

Serafino W1   £49   ④❷④
8 Mount St   7629 0544   3–3B
An "old-world Italian", near the Connaught, where (especially in its
cheaper basement) fans claim the "standard, but well-cooked fare"
offers "the best value in the area"; sceptics, though, just find
it "boring". / www.finos.co.uk; 10.45 pm; closed Sat L & Sun.

Seven Stars WC2   £28   ❸❸❶
53 Carey St   7242 8521   2–2D
A "quirky" boozer behind the Royal Courts of Justice that's "full of
character", thanks to landlady Roxy Beaujolais's "eccentric,
and sometimes rude" service; the food is "variable, but often good".
/ 11 pm.

Shampers W1   £36   ❸❷❷
4 Kingly St   7437 1692   3–2D
It may look "stuck in the '70s", but this "gem" of a Soho wine bar
– presided over by "ever-helpful owner, Simon" – is "still a fantastic
destination", offering "reliable" bistro fare and "superb vino" in a
"buzzy" atmosphere. / www.shampers.net; 11 pm; closed Sun (& Sat
in Aug).

Shanghai E8   £28   ❸❸❸
41 Kingsland High St   7254 2878   1–1C
In the setting of a "beautiful, old pie 'n' eel shop", in Dalston,
this "better class of local Chinese" makes "a surprise find" for first-
timers, and it's "particularly strong on dim sum"; beware "ear-
splitting Karaoke" sessions. / www.wengwahgroup.com; 11 pm; no Amex.

Shanghai Blues WC1 £53 ❷❸❸
193-197 High Holborn 7404 1668 4–1D
*"Spot-on cocktails" and "chic" décor set the tone of this "pricey"
Holborn yearling, where "great dim sum" is the high point of some
"very good" Chinese cuisine. / www.shanghaiblues.co.uk; 11.30 pm.*

J SHEEKEY WC2 £63 ❶❶❷
28-32 St Martin's Ct 7240 2565 4–3B
*For the sixth year, the survey's most-mentioned destination –
this "very special" Theatreland "classic" offers a "polished" formula
of "simple" but "superlative" fishy fare, served up by "brisk" but
"courteous" staff, in a "gorgeous" "warren" of panelled rooms.
/ www.j-sheekey.co.uk; midnight.*

J Sheekey Oyster Bar WC2 NEW
St Martin's Ct 7240 2565 4–3B
*Opening in late-2008, an oyster-bar neighbour to the survey's
most commented-on restaurant; if they get it half-right, this should
become a key Theatreland rendezvous. / www.j-sheekey.co.uk.*

Shepherd's SW1 £50 ❸❷❸
Marsham Ct, Marsham St 7834 9552 2–4C
*"Simple British fare, done well" commends this "quiet" and
"civilised" stalwart, in a Westminster backstreet, to many peers
and MPs, as well as most reporters who comment on it; sceptics,
though, find the cooking no better than "adequate".
/ www.langansrestaurants.co.uk; 11 pm; closed Sat & Sun.*

Shikara SW3 £29 ❷❷④
87 Sloane Ave 7581 6555 5–2C
*Beware, 'hot' means 'HOT', at this "well-priced" but "under-rated"
curry house, whose straightforward approach is rather at odds with
its chichi Brompton Cross location. / www.shikara.com; 11.30 pm.*

The Ship SW18 £40 ❸❸❸
41 Jews Row 8870 9667 10–2B
*In an unlikely location near Wandsworth Bridge, this popular
boozer offers a "proper menu", "good beer" and "nice river views";
in summer – when they do "fabulous" burgers on the barbecue –
the outside area gets mobbed. / www.theship.co.uk; 10 pm; no booking,
Sun L.*

Shish £30 ④④❸
2-6 Station Pde, NW2 8208 9290 1–1A
313-319 Old St, EC1 7749 0990 9–1D
*Fans say this trendy-looking kebab chain is "a good easy option";
it's "not as good as it was", though, sometimes now seeming
"expensive" for what it is. / www.shish.com; 11.30 pm, Sun 10.30 pm;
need 8+ to book.*

Shogun W1 £61 ❷❷④
Adam's Row 7493 1255 3–3A
*An "easily-missed" Japanese basement, in Mayfair, where the décor
is "poor and tired-looking", but the "wonderful" food and
"excellent" service more than make up for it. / 11 pm; D only,
closed Mon.*

Siam Central W1 £28 ❸❷④
14 Charlotte St 7436 7460 2–1C
*"Great lunchtime deals" are the star turn at this "extremely cheap"
Fitzrovia Thai. / 11 pm.*

Signor Sassi SW1 £44 ❸❷❸
14 Knightsbridge Grn 7584 2277 5–1D
*Near Harrods, a perennially "buzzy" (and cramped) "traditional"
Italian, which remains a "good-but-pricey" favourite, serving
"the usual classics" with "style and friendliness" ("especially when
the waiters start singing"). / 11.30 pm; closed Sun.*

Signor Zilli W1 £48 ④④④
41 Dean St 7734 3924 4–2A
*Aldo Zilli's original venture "used to be a good Soho stand-by",
but few reporters would rate it any more than "OK" nowadays.
/ 11.30 pm; closed Sun.*

Simply Lebanese SW7 £43 ④⑤④
68 Old Brompton Rd 7584 5805 5–2B
*An "authentic" South Kensington Lebanese, which can
be "pleasant" enough, but which can also seem "overpriced";
the "talkative" owner can be "a bit of a challenge" too.
/ www.simplylebanese.com; 10.30 pm.*

Simpson's Tavern EC3 £28 ④❷❶
38 1/2 Ball Ct, Cornhill 7626 9985 9–2C
*Most (if not quite all) reporters love this "jolly good-value" ancient
chophouse, in a City back-alley, where "perfect" waitresses
("all 70+") serve up "traditional British food" in "proper portions".
/ www.simpsonstavern.co.uk; L only, closed Sat & Sun.*

Simpsons-in-the-Strand WC2 £60 ⑤④❸
100 Strand 7836 9112 4–3D
*It retains a good degree of "old worlde" charm (and breakfast is a
highlight), but this Covent Garden temple to roast beef can seem
a "disappointing" sort of place, with "badly-trained" staff and
"leaden" fare; (rather worryingly, the management here are also
in charge of re-launching the neighbouring Savoy in 2009).
/ www.fairmont.com/simpsons; 10.45 pm, Sun 9 pm; no jeans or trainers.*

Singapore Garden NW6 £36 ❷❷❸
83a Fairfax Rd 7624 8233 8–2A
*A "tucked-away" Swiss Cottage favourite; "amusing" staff and
"very reliable" pan-oriental dishes ensure it's "always packed".
/ www.singaporegarden.co.uk; 11 pm, Fri-Sat 11.30 pm.*

Singapura £34 ❷❸④
78-79 Leadenhall St, EC3 7929 0089 9–2D
1-2 Limeburner Ln, EC4 7329 1133 9–2A
*A veteran, '90s-minimalist Singaporean chain in the City; it doesn't
inspire vast feedback, but all confirms that it's "as reliable as ever".
/ www.singapuras.co.uk; 10.30 pm; closed Sat & Sun, EC2 & EC3 L only.*

Sitaaray WC2 £33 ❷❷❷
167 Drury Ln 7269 6422 4–1C
*A "very kitsch" Bollywood-themed Covent Garden Indian, that can
be "immense fun"; menus are all 'set', making it especially well-
suited to a party. / www.sitaaray.com; 1 am.*

606 Club SW10 £46 ④❸❷
90 Lots Rd 7352 5953 5–4B
*Can it really be true? – some reporters claim the food was "better
than expected" on recent visits to this characterful basement jazz
club, in World's End. / www.606club.co.uk; midnight; D only.*

06 St Chad's Place WC1 £34 ❸❸❷
6 St Chad's Pl 7278 3355 8–3D
An "unlikely" building – a converted industrial unit in a back alley by King's Cross station – houses this "unusual" and "buzzy" spot, where "obliging" staff serve up "bistro-style" dishes.
/ www.6stchadsplace.com; 9.30 pm; closed Sat & Sun; no Amex.

(Lecture Room)
Sketch W1 £101 ❺❺❹
9 Conduit St 0870 777 4488 3–2C
"Full of people with more money than sense"; a "super-value" set lunch aside, few reporters have much nice to say about this "pretentious" and "blindingly expensive" Mayfair dining room, associated with Parisian über-chef Pierre Gagnaire.
/ www.sketch.uk.com; 10.30 pm; closed Mon, Sat L & Sun; booking: max 8; set weekday L £39 (FP).

(Gallery)
Sketch W1 £66 ❹❺❹
9 Conduit St 0870 777 4488 3–2C
"Unless you feel the need 'to be seen'", this "shockingly overpriced" Mayfair fashionista hot spot is "just not worth it" – "rude" service and "crummy" food figure in far too many reports, and even the "quirky" décor is inspiring ever less excitement. / www.sketch.uk.com; 1 am; D only, closed Sun; booking: max 12.

(Parlour)
Sketch W1 £32 ❹❷❷
9 Conduit St 0870 777 4488 3–2C
It can seem "overpriced" for what it is, but fans insist that the pâtisserie section of this trendy Mayfair palazzo makes an "unusual but wonderful" spot for some "perfect sandwiches and cakes".
/ www.sketch.uk.com; 10 pm; closed Sun; no booking.

Skylon
South Bank Centre SE1 £56 ❹❹❸
Southbank Centre, Belvedere Rd 7654 7800 2–3D
"The RFH deserves better" than the year-old D&D-group régime at this vast Thames-side chamber, where "off-hand" staff serve up food that's "average at best" – as so often with the group, the "stunning view" is presumably supposed to compensate for everything else. / www.danddlondon.com; 10.45 pm; set weekday L £43 (FP).

Slurp SW19 £18 ❸❸❹
130 Merton Rd 8513 1141 10–2B
"Large portions to satisfy the hungry" win praise for this "fab" pan-Asian canteen in Wimbledon – it "outstrips Wagamama by a mile".
/ 11 pm; no Amex; no booking.

Smithfield Bar & Grill EC1 £43 ❺❹❸
2-3 West Smithfield 7246 0900 9–2A
The "great bar atmosphere" is the best point of this crowded Farringdon grill; fans still praise its "cheery service and chunky steaks", but feedback overall suggests it "has really gone downhill", and is now noticeably "overpriced". / www.blackhousegrills.com; 11 pm; closed Sat L & Sun.

(Ground Floor)
Smiths of Smithfield EC1   £23   ④④❷
67-77 Charterhouse St   7251 7950   9–1A
*"Get there early at the weekend" (you can't book) for
an "awesome brunch" – complete with a "NY-style, casual vibe" –
in the bar of this large Smithfield warehouse-conversion.*
/ www.smithsofsmithfield.co.uk; L only.

(Dining Room)
Smiths of Smithfield EC1   £37   ④④❸
67-77 Charterhouse St   7251 7950   9–1A
*Fans of the "vibrant" ("so noisy") second-floor brasserie of this
Smithfield complex find it a "fun" location (and also handy for
business); service remains "indifferent", though, and the food is now
becoming "decidedly average" too.* / www.smithsofsmithfield.co.uk;
10.45 pm; closed Sat L & Sun.

(Top Floor)
Smiths of Smithfield EC1   £57   ❸❸❸
67-77 Charterhouse St   7251 7950   9–1A
*"Great meat, great wine, and views of London to keep the clients
happy" – the formula that for years has sustained this rooftop
Smithfield steakhouse (with terrace) as a top "business-friendly"
option; it is, however, "far too expensive for what it is".*
/ www.smithsofsmithfield.co.uk; 10.45 pm; closed Sat L; booking: max 10.

Snazz Sichuan NW1   £32   ❷❸❷
37 Chalton St   7388 0808   8–3C
*"Scarily fiery" Sichuan cuisine, "as authentic as it gets", is the draw
to this "off-the-beaten-track" yearling, near Euston, where
"genuine" staff add to the ambience (and "recent improvements
to the décor" have helped too).* / www.newchinaclub.co.uk; 10.30 pm.

Snows on the Green W6   £47   ❸❸④
166 Shepherd's Bush Rd   7603 2142   7–1C
*Sebastian Snow's long-running fixture is – for most Brook Green
types – the "epitome of a good local", offering "decent" food in a
"pleasant" (rather than exciting) atmosphere.*
/ www.snowsonthegreen.co.uk; 11 pm; closed Sat L & Sun.

So W1   £45   ❸❷❸
3-4 Warwick St   7292 0767   3–2D
*Just off Regent Street, an "airy" and "minimalist" establishment
offering a "modern twist on Japanese cuisine"; the food sometimes
"equals that at better-known places", but it can also be "uneven".*
/ www.sorestaurant.com; 10.30 pm; closed Sun.

Sofra   £31   ④④④
1 St Christopher's Pl, W1   7224 4080   3–1A
18 Shepherd St, W1   7493 3320   3–4B
36 Tavistock St, WC2   7240 3773   4–3D
11 Circus Rd, NW8   7586 9889   8–3A
21 Exmouth Mkt, EC1   7833 1111   9–1A
*Fans still praise their "good value", but these Turkish cafés have
become rather "unexciting" over the years; Tas "beats 'em for
variety, flavour and value for money".* / www.sofra.co.uk;
11 pm-midnight.

Soho Japan W1 £28 ❸❸❸
52 Wells St 7323 4661 2–1B
"Tucked-away", just north of Oxford Street – a basic "gem" with
"mismatched tables and cutlery"; it serves a "good range of well-
prepared Japanese favourites" at "low" prices. / www.sohojapan.co.uk;
10.30 pm; closed Sat L & Sun.

Solly's NW11 £39 ❸④④
146-150 Golders Green Rd 8455 2121 1–1B
A fire in early-2008 left this Golder's Green Israeli linchpin "half its
former self" (as the upstairs restaurant is re-built); its ground floor
café/take-away remains an "authentic" and "reliable" spot,
acclaimed by fans for "the best shawarma in London". / 10.30 pm;
closed Fri D & Sat L; no Amex.

Somerstown Coffee House NW1 £30 ❸❷❸
60 Chalton St 7691 9136 8–3C
An unlikely "gastronomic oasis", in the middle of a public housing
estate, near Euston; it's a true rarity – a French-run boozer –
and offers "good Gallic gastropub food" and "well-chosen" wines
(as well as "excellent beer"). / www.somerstowncoffeehouse.com; 11 pm.

Sông Quê E2 £25 ❷⑤⑤
134 Kingsland Rd 7613 3222 1–2D
The food is "bursting with flavour" and "almost embarrassingly
cheap", at this Vietnamese canteen in Shoreditch; service seldom
rises above "average", though, and "no money has been spent
on the décor". / 11 pm.

Sonny's SW13 £40 ④④④
94 Church Rd 8748 0393 10–1A
A "buzzing" Barnes "institution" it may be, but this long-established
neighbourhood staple really has "gone downhill" – it can seem like
a "tired" and "impersonal" sort of place, nowadays, with cooking
"varying by the day". / www.sonnys.co.uk; 10.30 pm; closed Sun D.

Sophie's Steakhouse SW10 £38 ❸❸❷
311-313 Fulham Rd 7352 0088 5–3B
The wait for a table can be "soul-destroying", but that's largely
because this "always-buzzing" Chelsea hang-out has a particular
name for its "straightforward, no-fooling-about steak"; this year,
though, saw standards drift across the board.
/ www.sophiessteakhouse.com; 11.45 pm; no booking.

Sotheby's Café W1 £46 ❷0❷
34 New Bond St 7293 5077 3–2C
You may eat "cheek by jowl", at this "buzzy" café, off the foyer
of the famous Mayfair auction house, but it offers a "very classy"
experience overall, and the food is "always delicious".
/ www.sothebys.com; L only, closed Sat & Sun.

Souk Medina WC2 £32 ④00
1A Short Gdns 7240 1796 4–2B
"A good place, if you're in a big group who really don't care about
the food" – this Moroccan 'riad'-style joint, on the fringe of Covent
Garden, is tailor-made for parties, thanks to its "fab service and
lovely vibe". / www.soukrestaurant.co.uk; midnight.

Spacca Napoli W1 £29 ❷④❷
101 Dean St   7437 9440   3–1D
This "fun" trattoria, just off Oxford Street, is especially worth
knowing about for its "perfect" pizza-by-the-metre; no wonder it's
"always packed with Italians". / www.spaccanapoli.co.uk; 11 pm.

Spago SW7 £29 ❸❸❸
6 Glendower Pl   7225 2407   5–2B
"A favourite for a quick bite" – this South Kensington fixture offers
"very good Italian food without a huge price tag"; pizza is a
highlight. / www.spagolondon.co.uk; midnight; no Amex.

Spaniard's Inn NW3 £30 ④❺❷
Spaniards Rd, Hampstead Heath   8731 8406   8–1A
This "historic" tavern (with garden), near Hampstead Heath, has a
"great atmosphere"; the package "could be so much better",
though – its "standard pub food" is "too expensive", and service
can be "lousy". / 10 pm.

The Spencer Arms SW15 £38 ❸❸❸
237 Lower Richmond Rd   8788 0640   10–1B
Overlooking Putney Heath, this Shaker-style gastropub has a local
name for its "careful", and quite traditional, British fare, and its
"enjoyable" style; feedback this year, though, also included a couple
of 'bad trips'. / www.thespencerarms.co.uk; 10 pm; no Amex.

Spianata £10 ❷❸④
41 Brushfield St, E1   7655 4411   9–1D
20 Holborn Viaduct, EC1   7236 3666   9–2A
12 Moorfields, EC2   7638 6118   9–2C **NEW**
29-30 Leadenhall Mkt, EC3   7929 1339   9–2C **NEW**
73 Watling St, EC4   7236 3666   9–2B
"A taste of Italy on the run" – this "innovative" toasted sandwich
('spianata') chain offers "a welcome change from the Prets of the
world". / L only; closed Sat & Sun, except E1 open Sun; no credit cards;
no bookings.

La Spiga W1 £45 ④④④
84-86 Wardour St   7734 3444   3–2D
A Soho Italian that still inspires praise for its "large" and "crunchy"
pizzas from a wood-fired oven; it was once so fashionable, though,
that one can't help noticing how few reports it attracts nowadays.
/ www.vpmg.net; 11 pm; closed Sun.

The Spread Eagle SE10 £46 ❸④❸
1-2 Stockwell St   8853 2333   1–3D
With its "upscale" Gallic food, this restaurant in an "olde-worlde"
tavern is probably "the best in Greenwich" nowadays; many reports
come with a catch, though – service, in particular, is "weak",
and the whole approach strikes critics as "pretentious".
/ www.spreadeaglerestaurant.com; 10 pm, Sat & Sun 11 pm; no Amex.

THE SQUARE W1 £88 ❷❷❸
6-10 Bruton St   7495 7100   3–2C
"You're sure to impress your client", at this "very professional" and
"formal" Mayfair venue, thanks to Philip Howard's "fantastically
crafted" dishes and a "stupendous selection of wine"; despite all
this excellence, though, the overall effect can seem a little "dull".
/ www.squarerestaurant.org; 10.45 pm; closed Sat L & Sun L; set weekday L
£48 (FP).

Square Pie Company £15 ❸④⑤
Unit 9, The Brunswick Centre, WC1 7837 6207 8–4C
1 Canada Sq, Jubilee Line Mall, E14 7519 6071 11–1C
16 Horner St, Old Spitalfields Mkt, E1 7377 1114 9–1D
"British fast food how it should be!" – this no-frills chain offers
"fresh and tasty pies" in "good-sized portions". / www.squarepie.com;
E14 4 pm -7 pm; E1 3 pm - 6 pm, W1 6 pm - 8 pm, WC1 10.30 pm;
E1 closed Sat, E14 closed Sun; no bookings.

Sree Krishna SW17 £24 ❷❷④
192-194 Tooting High St 8672 4250 10–2C
You get "loads of flavour for amazing prices", at this "reliable" and
"authentic" south Indian veteran, in Tooting. / www.sreekrishna.co.uk;
10.45 pm, Fri & Sat midnight.

Stanza W1 £43 ❸❸④
93-107 Shaftesbury Ave 7494 3020 4–3A
Despite a handy site on Shaftesbury Avenue, and solid (if fairly
simple) fare, this first-floor dining room has yet to win much of a
following among reporters. / www.stanzalondon.com; 11 pm; closed
Sat L & Sun.

Star Café W1 £25 ④④❸
22 Gt Chapel St 7437 8778 3–1D
"A classic that's a cut above your typical greasy spoon" – some ad
execs say this age-old café is "the only place in Soho for a fry-up".
/ www.thestarcafesoho.com; L only, closed Sat & Sun; no Amex.

Star of India SW5 £40 ❷❸❸
154 Old Brompton Rd 7373 2901 5–2B
"It really is a star"; this "buzzing" Earl's Court veteran is "still
packing in the punters", thanks not least to its "top-notch" curries,
which offer "a good mix of innovation and tradition". / 11.45 pm.

Starbucks £14 ④④④
Branches throughout London
"It's uncool to like Starbucks" – nothing new there – but this "bland
and reassuring chain" put in an (even) weaker-than-usual
performance this year, with rising gripes about "declining" service
and "tacky" branches. / www.starbucks.com; 6.30 pm-11 pm; most City
branches closed all or part of weekend; no booking.

Stein's TW10 £21 ❸④❸
Towpath (Rear of 55 Petersham Rd) 8948 8189 1–4A
"Beer and Wurst by the Thames" – an enjoyable summer option
at this good-value "German Biergarten", near Richmond Bridge.
/ www.stein-s.com; 10 pm; no Amex.

Stick & Bowl W8 £19 ❷❸④
31 Kensington High St 7937 2778 5–1A
You just nip "in-and-out", but this "chaotic and uncomfortable"
Kensington canteen still offers "great Chinese chow at cheap
prices". / 11 pm; no credit cards; no booking.

Sticky Fingers W8 £35 ⑤⑤④
1a Phillimore Gdns 7938 5338 5–1A
"Enough already" – this old Kensington diner, filled with rock
memorabilia, may be "regularly fully-booked", but "service
is particularly bad when it's full", and the food… "oh my God".
/ www.stickyfingers.co.uk; 11.30 pm.

Stock Pot £17 ④❸④
40 Panton St, SW1   7839 5142   4–4A
18 Old Compton St, W1   7287 1066   4–2A
273 King's Rd, SW3   7823 3175   5–3C
"An institution"; the food may be "like school dinners", but these "cramped" and "no-frills" '60s canteens are such "dependable" places, and so "amazingly cheap" too. / 11.30 pm, Sun 10.30 pm; no credit cards.

Stone Mason's Arms W6 £38 ❸❷❸
54 Cambridge Grove   8748 1397   7–2C
A "relaxed" and "reliable" gastropub, on a busy Hammersmith highway, where the food is invariably "well cooked" and "tasty". / 10 pm.

The Stonhouse SW4 £36 ④④❸
165 Stonhouse St   7819 9312   10–1D
An "attractive" year-old Clapham gastropub that's "too too busy, nearly all of the time"; fans say "you can see why", given its "high-quality" pub fare – others just think the place is "trying to punch above its weight". / www.thestonhouse.co.uk; 11 pm.

Story Deli
The Old Truman Brewery E1 £27 ❷❸❶
3 Dray Walk   7247 3137   1–2D
"Scrumptious", "paper-thin" pizzas help fuel the "mad popularity" of this "original" and "very organic" hang-out, in a "converted retail unit off Brick Lane" – "an intimate space with a large communal table and mismatched fixtures and fittings". / 9 pm during summer.

Strada £32 ④④❸
Branches throughout London
"They started off so promisingly", but these "welcoming" pizzerias risk "going the way of all chains" – as the food gets ever more "uninspiring", their challenge to PizzaExpress is fading away. / www.strada.co.uk; 11 pm; some booking restrictions apply.

Stringray Globe Café E2 £23 ❷④❸
109 Columbia Rd   7613 1141   1–2D
A "good-value" East End Italian – "with the size of the pizza you won't go hungry". / www.stingraycafe.co.uk; 11 pm; no Amex.

Sugar Hut SW6 £44 ④④④
374 North End Rd   7386 8950   5–3A
Fans still insist this lavish Fulham Thai makes a "good party venue", and it can seem quite "romantic" too; on too many of this year's (few) reports, though, it has just seemed rather "tired". / www.sugarhutgroup.com; midnight; D only.

Sugar Reef W1 £32 ④④④
42-44 Gt Windmill St   7851 0800   3–2D
This big Soho nitespot is no culinary destination, but its "reasonable, fixed-price menus" – offered at certain times only – attract surprisingly good reports. / www.sugarreef.co.uk; 1 am; D only, closed Sun.

Suk Saran SW19 £36 ❷④④
29 Wimbledon Rd   8947 9199   10–2B
"Excitingly-spiced" Thai dishes – including some "exceptional specials" – have already won local acclaim for this "small and buzzy" spot, near Wimbledon Station. / 11 pm.

Suka
Sanderson W1 £70 ④⑤⑤
50 Berners St 7300 1444 3–1D
Few – and mostly negative – reports on this oh-so-trendy design-hotel dining room, just north of Oxford Street; it can seem "frighteningly expensive", especially for Malaysian food, which "doesn't lend itself well to such a chichi environment". / www.sandersonlondon.com; 12.30 am, Sun 10.30 pm.

Sukho Thai Cuisine SW6 £39 ❶❶❷
855 Fulham Rd 7371 7600 10–1B
"Sparkling" cuisine – "the best Thai food in London", say some reporters – makes this "cramped", but "charming" and "colourful" Fulham gem "very, very popular, so book". / 11 pm.

Sumosan W1 £75 ❷④④
26b Albemarle St 7495 5999 3–3C
Re-establishing itself as a "good alternative to Nobu"; this "trendy" Mayfair Japanese has "a newly-acquired buzz", and serves some "superb" dishes (including "very good sushi"); prices are "extreme", of course, so remember the "incredible-value" lunch deal. / www.sumosan.com; 11.30 pm; closed Sat L & Sun L; set weekday L £37 (FP).

Le Suquet SW3 £53 ❷❸❸
104 Draycott Ave 7581 1785 5–2C
"You still get the best plâteau de fruits-de-mer in town", at this "très français" veteran, near Brompton Cross – it "never changes" ("which, in this case, is a good thing"). / 11.30 pm; set weekday L £36 (FP).

Sushi Hiroba WC2 £26 ④④④
50-54 Kingsway 7430 1888 2–2D
Opinions divide on this two-year-old conveyor-sushi outfit near Holborn tube; to supporters it offers a "good selection" of "amazingly good sushi" – to sceptics it's "inauthentic", and has "desultory" service. / www.sushihiroba.co.uk; 11 pm; closed Sun L.

Sushi-Hiro W5 £39 ❶❷⑤
1 Station Pde 8896 3175 1–3A
"An authentic experience that can be a bit overwhelming for westerners"; "phenomenally fresh" sushi and sashimi that's "a work of genius" come at "incredibly low prices" at this ultra-"utilitarian" diner, near Ealing Common Tube – it's "well worth the trek". / 9 pm; closed Mon; no credit cards.

Sushi-Say NW2 £40 ❶❶④
33b Walm Ln 8459 7512 1–1A
"Forget the West End, and head here for the best sushi in town"; this "family-owned" café is an "amazing find in Willesden Green" – the food is "outstanding", and the service is "so polite" too. / 10 pm, Sat & Sun 10.30 pm; closed Mon; no Amex.

The Swag & Tails SW7 £46 ❸❸❷
10-11 Fairholt St 7584 6926 5–1C
"A cosy nook, away from the hustle" – the dining room of this posh, "traditional" Knightsbridge boozer, which generally pleases with its "somewhat inventive" nosh. / www.swagandtails.com; 10 pm; closed Sat & Sun.

The Swan W4 £37 ❸❷❷
119 Acton Ln 8994 8262 7–1A
"With all the gastropubs there are in Chiswick, to stand out is quite something" – a feat this hidden-away local pulls off, thanks to its "seasonal" food, "smiling" staff and "the bonus of a great garden". / 10.30 pm; closed weekday L; no booking.

The Swan At The Globe SE1 £41 ❹❷⓿
New Globe Walk 7928 9444 9–3B
"Make sure you book a table with a river-view", if you visit the elegant first-floor brasserie of the South Bank tavern by Shakespeare's Globe; the "simple" food is no great shakes, but generally gets a thumbs-up. / www.swanattheglobe.co.uk; 10.30 pm.

Sweetings EC4 £47 ❸❸❷
39 Queen Victoria St 7248 3062 9–3B
A "unique" Victorian "relic" in the City that's "unbeatable" for "old-school types", thanks to its "really first-rate fish" and its "lively" but "Dickensian" atmosphere; the ratings slipped this year, though – hopefully just one of the 'wobbles' it goes through from time to time. / L only, closed Sat & Sun; no booking.

Taberna Etrusca EC4 £43 ❹❷❸
9 Bow Churchyard 7248 5552 9–2C
A "solid" and "reliable" City Italian with a characterful al fresco dining area; its "consistent" standards help make it a popular choice for entertaining. / www.etruscarestaurants.com; L only, closed Sat & Sun.

The Table SE1 £32 ❷❷❸
83 Southwark St 7401 2760 9–4B
Part of the Southwark offices of a prominent firm of architects, this "stylish" canteen can make an "outstanding" destination for breakfast or a "healthy" lunch. / www.thetablecafe.com; 9 pm; Mon-Thu & Sat L only, Fri open L & D, closed Sun.

Taiwan Village SW6 £27 ❷⓿❸
85 Lillie Rd 7381 2900 5–3A
"Choose 'leave it to the chef', and let them entertain you" – that's the way to get the best from this "out-of-the-way" Fulham Chinese, where the food is usually "amazing". / www.taiwanvillage.com; 11.30 pm; closed Mon L.

Tajima Tei EC1 £31 ❷❷❸
9–11 Leather Ln 7404 9665 9–2A
"There's a high percentage of Japanese diners", at this "slightly tatty" and "off-the-beaten-track" oriental, near Hatton Gardens – must have something to do with "authentic" food at "excellent" prices. / www.tajima-tei.co.uk; 10 pm; closed Sat & Sun.

Talad Thai SW15 £26 ❷❸⑤
320 Upper Richmond Rd 8789 8084 10–2A
"Cheap, tasty, and authentic Thai scoff" has made a big a name locally for this "friendly" Putney spot; its food rating, though, is not as dazzling as it once was. / www.taladthai.co.uk; 10.30 pm; no Amex.

Taman Gang W1 £77 ❸⑤❷
141 Park Ln 7518 3160 2–2A
A lavish Mayfair basement hang-out for "oligarchs and Eurotrash";
the oriental food is "very acceptable", but can also – surprise,
surprise – seem "overpriced". / www.tamangang.com; 11.30 pm; D only,
closed Sun; booking: max 6.

Tamarai WC2 £53 ❸④❸
167 Drury Ln 7831 9399 4–1C
The natural thing to do at this "dark" and clubby Covent Garden
basement is "to pile into the cocktails"; however, its "fusion-Indian"
fare – though seemingly "incidental" – is sometimes "superb"
(if undoubtedly on the pricey side). / www.tamarai.co.uk; 11.30 pm;
D only, closed Sun.

Tamarind W1 £58 ❷❷❸
20 Queen St 7629 3561 3–3B
Alfred Prasad's "mouthwatering" and "delicate" cuisine maintains
this "sophisticated" Mayfair venture in the vanguard of the
'nouvelle Indian' movement; for a basement, "it feels quite airy and
spacious" too. / www.tamarindrestaurant.com; 11.15 pm; closed Sat L;
set weekday L & pre-theatre £42 (FP).

tamesa@oxo
Oxo Tower SE1 £43 ⑤⑤④
2nd Fl, Oxo Tower Wharf, Barge House St 7633 0088 9–3A
You get "nice views, but that's about it", at this "overpriced" South
Bank dining room, on the second floor of the landmark Oxo Tower;
it's blasted by reporters for its "below-average food" and "surly
service". / www.oxotower.co.uk/tamesa.html; 10.30 pm; closed Sun D.

Tampopo SW10 £30 ❷❸❸
140 Fulham Rd 7370 5355 5–3B
For "a healthy" bite, this Chelsea noodle-bar, right by a cinema,
makes a "quick" and "good-value" option. / www.tampopo.co.uk;
11 pm, Fri-Sat 11.30 pm.

Tandoori Lane SW6 £26 ❷❷❸
131a Munster Rd 7371 0440 10–1B
"Behind blacked-out windows", in deepest Fulham, this superior
Indian veteran has long been of note for its "friendly" service and
its "good, non-greasy curries". / 11.15 pm; no Amex.

Tandoori Nights SE22 £31 ❷❷❷
73 Lordship Ln 0299 1077 1–4D
"Light and fresh-tasting dishes" have made this "absolutely
excellent" curry house "the default choice in the area" for many
East Dulwich types; unsurprisingly, it gets "very crowded and noisy".
/ 11.30 pm; closed weekday L & Sat L.

Tangawizi TW1 £34 ❸❷❸
406 Richmond Rd 8891 3737 1–4A
"Light and fresh cooking" – Indian with "a nice African twist" –
wins support for this Teddington two-year-old; it's a notably
"friendly" place too (and "good with children"). / www.tangawizi.co.uk;
10.30 pm; D only, closed Sun.

Tapas Brindisa SE1   £37   ❷④❸
18-20 Southwark St 7357 8880 9–4C
*"Basic" Hispanic dining at its "most authentically unglamourous";
this "frenetically-paced" café (run by a firm of importers
at neighbouring Borough Market) "brusquely" serves up "pricey"
tapas that are among "the best in town"; "shame you can't book".
/ www.brindisa.com; 11 pm; closed Sun.*

Taqueria W11   £30   ❸❸❸
139-143 Westbourne Grove 7229 4734 6–1B
*"Anyone looking for a proper Mexican 'fix' will find it", at this
"really fun" and "bustling" Bayswater café, where the array of "light
bites" is "absolutely delicious"; "don't miss the margaritas".
/ www.coolchiletaqueria.co.uk; Mon-Thu 11 pm, Fri & Sat 11.30 pm,
Sun 10.30 pm; no Amex; no booking.*

Taro   £23   ❸❷④
10 Old Compton St, W1 7439 2275 4–2B
61 Brewer St, W1 7734 5826 3–2D
*"Prompt" service helps ensure "very quick" bites at Mr Taro's
"very cheap", "very cheerful" and "very busy" Japanese diners,
in Soho. / www.tarorestaurants.co.uk; 10.30 pm, Sun 9.30 pm; no Amex;
Brewer St only small bookings.*

Tart EC1 NEW   £41
117 Charterhouse 7253 3003 9–1B
*It's as much a bar as a restaurant, but the occasional early-days
report hails this "boudoir-ish" Smithfield Market spot as a
"fantastic new arrival"; too little feedback, though, to make a rating
appropriate. / www.moomedia.co.uk/tart/; 11 pm, Thu midnight, Fri 1 am;
Mon D only, Tue-Fri L only, closed Sat & Sun.*

Tartine SW3   £36   ❸❸❷
114 Draycott Ave 7589 4981 5–2C
*"Packed full of Eurotrash", this "trendy" Brompton Cross spot
makes a "great" and "simple" choice "when you aren't too hungry"
– it serves "high-quality open sandwiches and interesting main
dishes too". / www.tartine.co.uk; 11 pm; need 6+ to book at D.*

Tas   £30   ④❷❸
22 Bloomsbury St, WC1 7637 4555 2–1C
33 The Cut, SE1 7928 2111 9–4A
72 Borough High St, SE1 7403 7200 9–4C
37 Farringdon Rd, EC1 7430 9721 9–1A
*For a "quick", "cheap", "no-frills" meal that "never breaks the
bank", "you can't go wrong" at these "bustling" and "welcoming"
Turkish bistros. / www.tasrestaurant.com; 11.30 pm; set dinner £20 (FP).*

Tas Pide SE1   £30   ④④❷
20-22 New Globe Walk 7928 3300 9–3B
*This "oddly-decorated" Anatolian joint (the effect
is almost "Bavarian") is "a haven of warmth", near Shakespeare's
Globe; its "comforting" fare (majoring in pide, a kind of Turkish
pizza) isn't art, but it is "reliably fresh". / www.tasrestaurant.com;
11.30 pm.*

FSA

La Tasca £29 ⑤④④
23-24 Maiden Ln, WC2   7240 9062   4–4C
404-406 Chiswick High Rd, W4   8994 4545   7–2A
21 Essex Rd, N1   7226 3272   8–3D
West India Quay, E14   7531 9990   11–1C
15-17 Eldon St, EC2   7256 2381   9–2C
Fans do say the UK's largest tapas chain is quite "fun"; to its many 'foes', though, it's just a "uniformly dreary" operation, offering "dreadful British/Spanish food". / www.latasca.co.uk; 11 pm, E14 10.45 pm; need 8+ to book.

(Rex Whistler)
Tate Britain SW1 £47 ④❸❷
Millbank   7887 8825   2–4C
Thanks to its Whistler murals, this Westminster dining room has a "lovely" feel, but it's the "stunning selection of wines from across the globe" that provide the real reason to seek it out; its "simple" fare is "rather formulaic", but generally "appetising". / www.tate.org.uk; L & afternoon tea only.

(Restaurant, Level 7)
Tate Modern SE1 £40 ④⑤❷
Bankside   7887 8888   9–3B
"Book a sunset table with a view of St Paul's", to get best value out of a visit to this seventh-floor South Bank dining room; the simple food "can be good" but it can be "mediocre" too, and you risk "nonsensical waits" to get it. / www.tate.org.uk; 9.30 pm; Sun-Thu closed D.

(Café, Level 2)
Tate Modern SE1 £36 ④❸❸
Bankside   7401 5014   9–3B
You get "great views" – if from a fairly low level – in the window seats of this "buzzy" and "crowded" art gallery canteen; though less-known than its Level 7 sibling, its design is "superb", and its "simple" fare is more highly rated by reporters. / www.tate.org.uk/modern/eatanddrink; Fri 9.30 pm; L & tea only, except Fri open L & D.

Tatsuso EC2 £80 ❸④⑤
32 Broadgate Circle   7638 5863   9–2D
The décor is "naff" (especially in the basement restaurant, less so in the ground-floor teppan-yaki), but this veteran Broadgate Japanese remains a "great business lunch venue", thanks to its "very authentic" cuisine; prices, though, are "breathtaking". / 10.15 pm; closed Sat & Sun.

Tawana W2 £33 ❷❷④
3 Westbourne Grove   7229 3785   6–1C
"Where are all the people?" – despite its "consistently good Thai food", this unpretentious establishment, by the Queensway junction, is "often inexplicably empty". / www.tawana.co.uk; 11 pm.

Ten Ten Tei W1 £35 ❷❷⑤
56 Brewer St   7287 1738   3–2D
A "grotty"-looking Soho dive that's "always filled with Japanese customers", thanks to its "tasty", "quick" and "authentic" scoff that "doesn't cost the earth". / 10 pm; closed Sun; no Amex.

Tendido Cero SW5   £35   ❸❸❸
174 Old Brompton Rd   7370 3685   5–2B
*"Delicious tapas" have won an avid following for the "authentic"
offshoot of star Spanish venture, Cambio de Tercio (across the
road); even fans can find prices "inflated", though, and multiple
seatings are "a drag". / www.cambiodetercio.co.uk; 11 pm.*

Tendido Cuatro SW6 NEW   £38   ❷❷❸
108-110 New King's Rd   7371 5147   10–1B
*Despite the 'Cuatro', this is actually the third venture from the
Cambio de Tercio team; a new Parson's Green tapas bar, it's a
congenial, colourful, spacious sort of place, with food that, on our
early-days visit, was very good indeed. / Rated on Editors' visit; 11 pm.*

Tentazioni SE1   £53   ❷❷❸
2 Mill St   7394 5248   11–2A
*An "eager-to-please" chef/patron cooks up some "rich and
luxurious" Italian dishes at this "intimate" and "un-rushed"
Bermondsey spot; doubters find the food a touch "fussy", though.
/ www.tentazioni.co.uk; 10.45 pm; closed Mon L, Sat L & Sun; set weekday L
£20 (FP).*

The Terrace in the Fields WC2   £43   ❸❹❸
Lincoln's Inn Fields   7430 1234   2–2D
*"On a fine day, it's hard to beat sitting outside", at this "isolated"
hut, by the tennis courts in Lincoln's Inn Fields; some West Indian
dishes spice up what's otherwise a pretty conventional menu.
/ www.theterrace.info; 9 pm; closed Sun; set weekday L £28 (FP).*

Terranostra EC4 NEW   £43   ❸❷❹
27 Old Bailey   3201 0077   9–2A
*A "decent" new Italian, near the Old Bailey, that's "better than
it looks from the outside"; "lovely" staff present Sardinian cooking
that's a "cut above" the norm, and "reasonably priced" too.
/ www.terranostrafood.co.uk; 10 pm; closed Sat L & Sun.*

Texas Embassy Cantina SW1   £36   ⑤⑤⑤
1 Cockspur St   7925 0077   2–2C
*You see "the worst side of Tex/Mex", at this Trafalgar Square
tourist trap – "trading on its location", it serves up food that's too
often simply "rubbish". / www.texasembassy.com; 11 pm, Sat midnight.*

Texture W1   £70   ❷❷❸
34 Portman Sq   7224 0028   2–2A
*An "innovative" Marylebone newcomer, offering "spectacular"
contemporary cooking (albeit in a style ridiculed by critics for its
"smears and foams"); the dining room makes the most elegant
possible use of the difficult space that was formerly Deya (RIP).
/ www.texture-restaurant.co.uk; 11 pm; closed Mon & Sun.*

Thai Café SW1   £28   ❸❸⑤
22 Charlwood St   7592 9584   2–4C
*"Reliable", "inexpensive" and "quite authentic" – this "friendly"
Pimlico oriental is "always busy". / 10.30 pm; closed Sat L & Sun L.*

Thai Corner Café SE22   £24   ❸❹❹
44 North Cross Rd   8299 4041   1–4D
*"Enjoyable for a relaxed midweek supper" – this "charmingly
raucous" but "irritatingly cramped" East Dulwich Thai may have
sometimes "grumpy" service, but its food is "authentic" and
"modestly-priced"; you can BYO too. / 10.30 pm; no credit cards.*

Thai Garden SW11 £27 ❸❸❸
58 Battersea Rise   7738 0380   10–2C
A "consistently good" Thai stand-by, in Battersea; don't sit outside, though – "you'll be engulfed by fumes". / 11 pm; D only.

Thai on the River SW11 £36 ❸❷❷
2 Lombard Rd   7924 6090   5–4B
Living up to the name, this Battersea spot offers "good Thai food in a nice riverside setting", and its "solicitous" staff do nothing to detract from the "romantic" atmosphere. / www.thaiontheriver.com; 11 pm.

Thai Pot WC2 £32 ❹❸❹
1 Bedfordbury   7379 4580   4–4C
Tucked-away behind the Coliseum, a useful Theatreland stand-by offering "reliable Thai food at sensible prices". / www.thaipot.biz; 11.15 pm; closed Sun.

Thai Square £30 ❹❹❸
21-24 Cockspur St, SW1   7839 4000   2–3C
27-28 St Annes Ct, W1   7287 2000   3–1D
148 The Strand, WC2   7497 0904   2–2D
19 Exhibition Rd, SW7   7584 8359   5–2C
347-349 Upper St, N1   7704 2000   8–3D
2-4 Lower Richmond Rd, SW15   8780 1811   10–1A
136-138 Minories, EC3   7680 1111   9–3D
1-7 Great St Thomas Apostle, EC4   7329 0001   9–3B
"Exuberant" décor – and, at the Putney branch, an "amazing river view" – are the most distinctive features of these large traditional orientals, where the food is "rather standard". / www.thaisquare.net; between 10 pm and 11.30 pm, SW1 open till 1am Fri & Sat; EC3 & EC4 closed Sat & Sun, Princess St W1 & 148 The Strand WC2 closed Sun, St Annes Court W1 & 229-230 The Strand WC2 closed Sat & Sun.

Thailand SE14 £29 ❸❷❹
15 Lewisham Way   8691 4040   1–3D
Deep in New Cross, this "unprepossessing" venture has a "hidden-gem" reputation, thanks to its "particularly interesting" Thai/Laotian food; the décor isn't great, though, and there was the odd "disappointing visit" this year. / 11.30 pm.

The Thatched House W6 £34 ❸❸❸
115 Dalling Rd   8748 6174   7–1B
"Copious quantities of good traditional pub dishes at fair prices" – plus a nice big garden – continue to please fans of this "no-fuss" Hammersmith local. / www.thatchedhouse.com; 10 pm; no Amex.

Theo Randall
InterContinental Hotel W1 £78 ❸❸❹
1 Hamilton Pl   7318 8747   3–4A
"OK, the room is dull and windowless", but the "sparkling" Italian food "makes up for it", say fans of this "gloomy" Mayfair yearling (named after its chef, who was formerly top toque at the River Café); critics who find it "over-hyped and over-priced", though, are gaining ground. / www.theorandall.com; 11.15 pm; closed Sat L & Sun; set weekday L & pre-theatre £52 (FP).

Thomas Cubitt SW1 £54 ❸❸❷
44 Elizabeth St 7730 6060 2–4A
In surprisingly "under-served" Belgravia, this "posh" but "lively"
gastropub remains "streets ahead" of other local hang-outs;
upstairs (price given), the "tranquil and relaxing" dining room
serves up some quite "interesting" dishes too.
/ www.thethomascubitt.co.uk; 10 pm; set weekday L £39 (FP).

The Three Bridges SW8 NEW £37 ❸❶❸
153 Battersea Park Rd 7720 0204 10–1C
"Don't be deceived by the modest looks" or the "unpromising"
location of this Italian newcomer, near Battersea Dogs Home;
"exuberant" service and "un-flashy" food in "generous" portions
make it "the perfect local". / www.thethreebridges.com; 11 pm;
closed Sun.

The Three Crowns N16 £39 ❷❹❸
175 Stoke Newington High St 7241 5511 1–1D
An "atmospheric" Stokie gastropub with a big local following for its
"intelligent" and "hearty" fare; service is "earnest and friendly",
but it can be "unreliable" too. / www.threecrowns-n16.com; 10 pm;
no Amex.

3 Monkeys SE24 £31 ❸❸❸
136-140 Herne Hill 7738 5500 1–4C
"Fresh"-tasting food and "agreeable" service continue to win
positive reviews for this large and airy Indian in Herne Hill.
/ www.3monkeysrestaurant.com; 11 pm.

Tiffinbites £26 ❸❹❸
22-23 Jubilee Pl, E14 7719 0333 11–1C
23 Russia Row (off Gresham St), EC2 7600 4899 9–2B
It's "decent and quick" – with "the odd interesting menu item" –
but this attempt to create a major Indian chain has yet to inspire
huge interest among reporters; as this guide was going to press,
Tiffinbites acquired the Bombay Bicycle Club chain.

Timo W8 £51 ❸❷❸
343 Kensington High St 7603 3888 7–1D
A "pricey but excellent" gem is how local fans still describe this low-
key Kensington Italian; it doesn't inspire much feedback nowadays,
however, and not all of it is complimentary. / www.timorestaurant.net;
11 pm; closed Sun; booking: max 8; set weekday L £31 (FP).

Toff's N10 £31 ❷❷❹
38 Muswell Hill Broadway 8883 8656 1–1B
Fans say it's "worth a ticket" – "parking is a nightmare" – to enjoy
the "fantastic" fish 'n' chips served in "vast" portions at this
"friendly" Muswell Hill stalwart. / www.toffsfish.co.uk; 10 pm; closed Sun;
no booking, Sat.

Toku
Japan Centre W1 £32 ❸❹❺
212 Piccadilly 7255 8255 3–3D
Just by Piccadilly Circus, this "crammed", "canteen-style" culture-
centre café is certainly a "convenient" rendezvous; "quality sushi"
is the culinary high point, but all the fare seems "rather pricey",
especially given the sometimes "clueless" service.
/ www.japancentre.com; 11 pm, Sun 10 pm; no Amex.

Tokyo City EC2 £37 ❸❸④
46 Gresham St 7726 0308 9–2B
"Reliable" Japanese fare (including "good sushi") makes this
"unpretentious" spot, near the Guildhall, a handy City stand-by.
/ www.tokyocity.co.uk; 10 pm; closed Sat & Sun.

Tokyo Diner WC2 £19 ④❸④
2 Newport Pl 7287 8777 4–3B
"Basic" and "tasty" Japanese scoff, from a "limited" menu, comes
at "very cheap" prices at this downbeat Chinatown diner; tipping
may be forbidden, but staff are notably "helpful and efficient".
/ www.tokyodiner.com; 11.30 pm; no Amex; no booking, Fri & Sat.

TOM AIKENS SW3 £91 ❸❸❸
43 Elystan St 7584 2003 5–2C
Tom Aikens's "Zen-like" ("cold") Chelsea HQ serves up "elaborate"
– and sometimes "astonishing" – dishes, which critics have always
dismissed as "trying too hard"; as his empire grows, though, results
are becoming ever more "hit-and-miss", and yet prices remain
as "unbelievable" as ever. / www.tomaikens.co.uk; 11 pm; closed
Sat & Sun; jacket and/or tie; booking: max 8; set weekday L £45 (FP).

Tom Ilic SW8 NEW £38 ❶❸⑤
123 Queenstown Rd 7622 0555 10–1C
"Tom Illic is trying very hard", at this Battersea newcomer (on the
former site of the Food Room, RIP), and many reporters already
attest to the "unbelievable value" offered by his "hearty" and
"innovative" cuisine; sometimes "chaotic" service needs work,
though, as does the "dreary" décor. / www.tomilic.com; 10.30 pm; closed
Mon, Tue L, Sat L & Sun D.

Tom's Deli W11 £29 ❸④❷
226 Westbourne Grove 7221 8818 6–1B
"One of THE places for the Notting Hill set" – Conran Jr's "deli-
cum-café" is a perennial favourite for a "good but expensive"
brunch. / www.tomsdelilondon.co.uk; 7.30 pm, Sat & Sun 6.30 pm; L only;
no Amex; no booking.

Tom's Kitchen SW3 £48 ④④④
27 Cale St 7349 0202 5–2C
No question that it can be "fun" or that it remains a key Chelsea
rendezvous, but Tom Aikens's "crushed" and "deafening" pub-
conversion has gone notably backwards in its first full year
of operation – the food is often "surprisingly unremarkable",
and service is ever more "haphazard". / www.tomskitchen.co.uk; 11 pm.

Tom's Place SW3 £30 ④❸④
1 Cale St 7351 1806 5–2C
Tom Aikens fans do hail his new eco-friendly Chelsea café (on the
former Monkeys, RIP, site) as "a great take on the traditional
chippy"; the food, though, often seems "ordinary at best",
and sometimes "wildly overpriced" too. / www.tomsplace.org.uk/; 11 pm,
Thu-Sat 11.30 pm, Sun 10.30 pm.

Tootsies £32 ④④④
35 James St, W1   7486 1611   3–1A
120 Holland Park Ave, W11   7229 8567   6–2A
148 Chiswick High Rd, W4   8747 1869   7–2A
196-198 Haverstock Hill, NW3   7431 3812   8–2A
Putney Wharf, 30 Brewhouse St, SW15   8788 8488   10–2B
48 High St, SW19   8946 4135   10–2B
As a "good place for families", it has its fans, but this salads-to-
burgers chain continues to slip in the ratings – "for this money",
say its critics, "you can eat so much better".
/ www.tootsiesrestaurants.co.uk; 11 pm; some booking restrictions apply.

Tosa W6 £33 ❷❸④
332 King St   8748 0002   7–2B
The "café-style" décor "belies the flair and authenticity" of this
"excellent-value" Japanese, "unglamorously-located" near Stamford
Brook tube; "very good yakitori" is the house speciality. / 11 pm;
no Amex.

Toto's SW1 £66 ❸❷❷
Lennox Gardens Mews   7589 0075   5–2C
"Hidden-away", near Harrods, a "lovely", "professional" and "old-
fashioned" Italian that's always been regarded as quite a "gem";
doubters, though, are beginning to find the approach rather
"dated". / 11 pm, Sun 10.30 pm; set weekday L £50 (FP).

Trader Vics
Hilton Hotel W1 £70 ⑤⑤④
22 Park Ln   7208 4113   3–4A
"Past the sell-by"; this Park Lane basement tikki-bar may still
do "very good cocktails", but service is "uninterested",
food "disgraceful" and prices "astonishing". / www.tradervics.com;
12.30 am; closed Sat L & Sun L.

The Trafalgar Tavern SE10 £40 ⑤⑤④
Park Row   8858 2909   1–3D
A palatial and "fantastically-located" Georgian pub, right on the
river at Greenwich; it "could be brilliant"… if the food weren't
a total "rip-off" – "don't even think about eating" (in either the
dining room or the bar). / www.trafalgartavern.co.uk; 10 pm; closed Sun D;
no Amex; no booking, Sun L.

Tree House SW13 £38 ❸❸❷
73 White Hart Ln   8392 1617   10–1A
"A fab atmosphere" and a "delightful outside area" are highlights
at this "slightly eccentric" Barnes pub-conversion; "the food's OK,
and fair value, but not exciting". / www.treehousepeople.com; 11 pm,
Fri & Sat midnight, Sun 10.30 pm.

Trenta W2 £46 ④④④
30 Connaught St   7262 9623   6–1D
Fans do report "goodish" food at this "intimate" Bayswater Italian
yearling; sometimes "inept" cooking, however, can also make
it "a desperate disappointment". / 10.30 pm; closed Mon L, Sat L & Sun.

Trinity SW4 £51 ❷❸④
4 The Polygon   7622 1199   10–2D
Adam Byatt's "seriously accomplished" cooking makes for some "extraordinary" dining experiences at this "quiet" Clapham yearling; shame that its opening was "over-hyped", though, which led some reporters to visit with unduly lofty expectations.
/ www.trinityrestaurant.co.uk; 10.30 pm; closed Mon L; set weekday L £36 (FP).

Trinity Stores SW12 £18 ❸❷❷
5-6 Balham Station Rd   8673 3773   10–2C
The sort of deli/café "every neighbourhood is crying out for" – this "Balham beacon of hope" has gone "from strength to strength". / www.trinitystores.co.uk; 8pm, Sat 5.30 pm, Sun 4 pm; L only; no Amex.

Les Trois Garçons E1 £73 ④❸❶
1 Club Row   7613 1924   1–2D
It's the "OTT" décor – "stuffed animals in tiaras", and so on – which can make this East End pub-conversion an "absolutely fabulous" destination (especially "for a first date"); its "bistro fare", however, comes at "haute-cuisine prices". / www.lestroisgarcons.com; 9.30 pm; D only, closed Sun; set always available £47 (FP).

Trojka NW1 £29 ④④❷
101 Regent's Park Rd   7483 3765   8–2B
In Primrose Hill, a "relaxed" haunt serving a "vast, cheap menu" of (somewhat "Anglicised") Russian and other Eastern European dishes; on Saturday nights, you get "great" live music too. / www.trojka.co.uk; 10.30 pm.

LA TROMPETTE W4 £55 ❶❶❷
5-7 Devonshire Rd   8747 1836   7–2A
"Sophisticated" yet "very understated" – this Chiswick sidestreet jewel is "well worth the journey", thanks to James Bennington's "dazzling" cuisine ("especially at the price"), the "exceptional" service and a wine list that's "one of the best thought-through and best-value in the capital". / www.latrompette.co.uk; 10.30 pm, Sun 10 pm; booking: max 6; set weekday L £39 (FP).

Troubadour SW5 £32 ⑤④❶
263-267 Old Brompton Rd   7370 1434   5–3A
"The bohemian atmosphere of the '60s" lives on at this "chilled" Earl's Court coffee house (and it has a nice "sun trap" garden too); service is "patchy", though, and the food "below par". / www.troubadour.co.uk; 11.30 pm; no Amex.

La Trouvaille W1 £50 ❷❷❷
12a Newburgh St   7287 8488   3–2C
"An excellent bolt hole, off Carnaby Street", which certainly is a 'find', thanks to its "superior" Gallic fare, "fantastic" wines, "friendly" staff and "elegant and cosy" setting; "downstairs is the more casual wine bar – upstairs the more formal dining room". / www.latrouvaille.co.uk; 11 pm; closed Sun; set weekday L & pre-theatre £33 (FP).

Truc Vert W1 £46 ❸④❸
42 North Audley St   7491 9988   3–2A
An "attractive" (if "slightly basic" and "jam-packed") deli/café, near Selfridges, offering "simple and hearty" fare (including "wonderful" breakfasts), at prices which are too rich for some tastes. / www.trucvert.co.uk; 10 pm; closed Sun D.

Tsunami SW4 £37 ❷④④
5-7 Voltaire Rd 7978 1610 10–1D
*What's up, at this "really quite amazing" Clapham Japanese?;
its "Zuma-quality sushi at local prices" is (mostly) "still up to
scratch", but service has often seemed "inattentive" of late,
and the "dated and tacky" décor now "needs refreshing".
/ www.tsunamirestaurant.co.uk; 10.30 pm, Fri & Sat 11 pm, Sun 9.30 pm;
closed weekday L.*

Tuttons WC2 £43 ⑤⑤④
11-12 Russell St 7257 8625 4–3D
*"Watch the goings-on in Covent Garden", from the "pleasant"
outside tables of this corner bistro; historically it's risen a little above
tourist-trap standards, but this year it sometimes just seemed
an "awful rip-off". / www.tuttons.com; 11.30 pm; set pre theatre £27 (FP).*

2 Amici SW1 £39 ④❷④
48a Rochester Rw 7976 5660 2–4C
*"A bonus for Westminster!" – a rather '80s-style Italian yearling,
where the cooking is of "good quality", and service generally comes
"con gusto". / www.2amici.com; 11 pm; closed Sat L & Sun.*

Two Brothers N3 £30 ❷❷❸
297-303 Regent's Park Rd 8346 0469 1–1B
*"We've been dining here monthly for nearly 20 years, and it never
disappoints!" – this Finchley institution is hailed by its large fan club
as "the best chippy in London"; (the brothers departed this year,
but feedback suggests that standards have been maintained,
and maybe even improved). / www.twobrothers.co.uk; 10.15 pm; closed
Mon & Sun; no booking at D.*

202
Nicole Farhi W11 £37 ❸❸❷
202 Westbourne Grove 7792 6888 6–1B
*"Watch those yummy mummies trying not to eat!" – all part of the
fun of a visit to this diner/fashion store, which is a key feature
of the Notting Hill brunch scene; foodwise, "great scrambled eggs"
are a highlight. / www.nicolefarhi.com; L & afternoon tea only; no booking.*

2 Veneti W1 £54 ❸❶❸
10 Wigmore St 7637 0789 3–1B
*"Impeccable" and "friendly" service is the stand-out feature of this
"authentic" Venetian yearling, near the Wigmore Hall; a "fabulous
wine list" rounds off a "classy" formula that's especially popular for
business. / www.2veneti.com; 10.30 pm; closed Sat L & Sun.*

Ubon E14 £80 ❸④④
34 Westferry Circus 7719 7800 11–1B
*Nobu's "relaxed" Canary Wharf cousin is often preferred to the
Mayfair branches – it's "easier to book", has a "much more
impressive view" and comes "without all the nonsense";
unfortunately, however, bills here are just as "outrageous".
/ www.noburestaurants.com; 10 pm; closed Sat L & Sun.*

Uli W11 £30 ❷❶❸
16 All Saints Rd 7727 7511 6–1B
*This "charming" North Kensington neighbourhood spot has got the
lot – "service with a big smile", a menu offering an "eclectic mix"
of "Thai-influenced, Chinese" dishes, and a "lovely garden";
"let Michael choose for you, and you won't go far wrong".
/ www.uli-oriental.co.uk; 11 pm; D only, closed Sun; no Amex.*

Ultimate Burger £22 ④④❸
127 Tottenham Court Rd, W1 7436 5355 2–1B
334 New Oxford St, WC1 7436 6641 4–1C
"A worthwhile stop for lovers of burgers" – this small central-
London (and Lincoln!) chain serves up "juicy" meat and "decent"
fries. / www.ultimateburger.co.uk; WC1 11.30 pm, Sun 10.45 pm, W1 11pm,
Sun 10.30 pm; no bookings for L.

Umu W1 £120 ❷❸❸
14-16 Bruton Pl 7499 8881 3–2C
"This is simply IT", say fans of Marlon Abela's "chic" Japanese,
in the heart of Mayfair, who extol its "divine" and "beautiful"
Kyoto-style cuisine; prices are "quite extortionate", though,
and service more "variable" than you might hope.
/ www.umurestaurant.com; 10.30 pm; closed Sat L & Sun; no trainers; booking:
max 14.

The Union Café W1 £42 ④❷④
96 Marylebone Ln 7486 4860 3–1A
The "straightforward" food isn't bad, but it's John Brinkley's "varied"
and "terrific-value" wine that particularly maintains the popularity
of this "functional" (and "noisy") Marylebone rendezvous.
/ www.brinkleys.com; 10.30 pm, Sat 11 pm; closed Sun D.

Uno SW1 £45 ❷❷❷
1 Denbigh St 7834 1001 2–4B
Having outgrown its pizzeria origins, this Pimlico corner spot
is nowadays a cool-looking but "friendly", full-service Italian, offering
a "very good" overall experience; it deserves to be more widely
known. / www.uno1.co.uk; 11pm, Sun & Mon 10.30 pm.

Upstairs Bar SW2 £38 ❶❶❷
89b Acre Ln (door on Branksome Rd) 7733 8855 10–2D
"A very French and charming little eyrie above a main Brixton
thoroughfare" – its "delicious" food, "attentive service" and "cosy"
ambience make it "exceptional in every way".
/ www.upstairslondon.com; 9.30 pm, Sat 10.30 pm; D only, closed Mon & Sun.

Urban Turban W2 NEW £36 ④⑤⑤
98 Westbourne Grove 7243 4200 6–1B
An unexpected "disaster", from stellar Indian chef Vineet Bhattia,
offering "mediocre" food and "amateurish" service; how did
he manage to get this "trendy-looking" Bayswater chain-prototype
so desperately wrong? / www.urbanturban.uk.com; 11 pm.

Le Vacherin W4 £42 ❷❷❸
76-77 South Pde 8742 2121 7–1A
Malcolm John's "little sliver of France in Chiswick" was
"much improved by a revamp this year"; other aspects of this
"great, great local" are unchanged, though – not least its "simple
fare", offering "real Gallic flavours". / www.levacherin.co.uk; 10.30 pm,
Fri & Sat 11 pm, Sun 10 pm; closed Mon L.

Vama SW10 £48 ❷❸④
438 King's Rd 7351 4118 5–3B
"Fresh and light" dishes that are way "out of the ordinary" regularly
"impress" visitors to this "very enjoyable modern Indian",
near World's End; even for some diehard fans, though, recent visits
have proved "disappointing". / www.vama.co.uk; 11 pm, Sun 10.30 pm;
closed weekday L.

Vanilla W1 NEW £55 ❷❷❶
131 Great Titchfield St   3008 7763   3–1C
A "cool" and "funky" new basement operation "tucked-away"
in Fitzrovia; newspaper critics lined up to slag it off, but we're with
the numerous thirtysomethings who say it's a "hidden treasure",
with a "great bar", an "inventive menu", and staff "who can't
do enough for you". / www.vanillalondon.com; 10 pm; closed Mon,
Sat L & Sun; no trainers; set weekday L £31 (FP).

Vanilla Black EC4 NEW £44 ❹❸❹
17-18 Tooks Ct   7242 2622   9–2A
Just off Chancery Lane, a brave new transplant (from York) of a
smart, if blandly-furnished, veggie; we'd have to agree with the early
reporter who found the cooking "good", but disliked the "nouvelle-
cuisine tiny" portions – did they really get away with that
in Yorkshire? / www.vanillablack.co.uk; 10 pm; closed Sat & Sun.

Vapiano W1 NEW £25 ❹❹❹
19-21 Great Portland St   7268 0080   3–1C
On the former Mash (RIP) site, near Oxford Circus, the first London
outpost of a (German) pasta, pizza and salad cafeteria chain,
where the gimmick is a charge card you present for each purchase;
it's fine for a one-plate snack – for anything more, the multiple
queuing gets in the way. / Rated on Editors' visit; www.vapiano.co.uk;
11 pm.

Vasco & Piero's Pavilion W1 £47 ❸❸❹
15 Poland St   7437 8774   3–1D
A "crowded" and "friendly" old-time Soho Italian, where the
Umbrian cooking is usually "spot-on"; time moves on, though,
and "it's not as much fun as it was". / www.vascosfood.com; 10.30 pm;
closed Sat L & Sun.

Veeraswamy W1 £52 ❷❷❷
Victory Hs, 99-101 Regent St   7734 1401   3–3D
With its "sophisticated" cuisine and "sensual" décor, "London's
oldest Indian, near Piccadilly Circus, still beats most of the
opposition hands-down"; it manages to be both "traditional and
fun", all at the same time. / www.realindianfood.com; 10.30 pm,
Sun 10 pm; booking: max 12.

El Vergel SE1 £18 ❶❷❷
8 Lant St   7357 0057   9–4B
"Is this the best cheap food in London?"; "zesty" Latino dishes
at "ludicrously low prices" make it well "worth seeking out" this
"cantina-style" joint, "hidden down a backstreet in Borough";
hurry... "you won't get a seat after 1 pm". / www.elvergel.co.uk;
breakfast & L only, closed Sat D & Sun; no credit cards.

Vertigo
Tower 42 EC2 £64 ❹❸❷
25 Old Broad St   7877 7842   9–2C
"The best view of London" – from the 42nd floor – will "make for
a memorable and romantic night out", at this City eyrie (which also
works its magic on business clients); the food, of course, is "not why
you go". / www.vertigo42.co.uk; 11 pm; closed Sat & Sun; no shorts; booking
essential.

Via Condotti W1 £43 ③③④
23 Conduit St 7493 7050 3–2C
Just off Bond Street, this initially-promising Italian two-year-old seems to have settled into a groove that's not much better than "pleasant enough" – the food may be "honest", but portions can be "small", and service is notably up-and-down.
/ www.viacondotti.co.uk; 11 pm; closed Sun.

Vic Naylors EC1 £44 ⑤③③
38 & 42 St John St 7608 2181 9–1B
"Go for the bar, not the food" – this Smithfield veteran is a "perennial favourite" for some reporters, but the grub rarely hits any sorts of heights, and is also "expensive, for what it is".
/ www.vicnaylor.com; 12.30 am; closed Sat L & Sun.

Il Vicolo SW1 £44 ③②④
3-4 Crown Passage 7839 3960 3–4D
"Tucked-away off Pall Mall", this "good-value" spot – with "very helpful" service and "reliable" Sardinian food – is well worth knowing about in a "mega-pricey" part of town; regulars find the décor "improved after the fire" too. / 10 pm; closed Sat & Sun.

The Victoria SW14 £41 ④④④
10 West Temple 8876 4238 10–2A
This potentially "lovely" East Sheen gastropub – complete with large conservatory – put in a "chequered" performance this year, taking flak for "tasteless" food, uneven service and a "cold" ambience; one thing hasn't changed: "weekend lunches feel like a crèche". / www.thevictoria.net; 10 pm.

Viet W1 £18 ②⑤④
34 Greek St 7494 9888 4–3A
You get "a fast turnaround" and "fresh-tasting pho" at this "basic" but "highly addictive" Soho "gem"; "don't expect the staff to do you any favours, though". / 11 pm, Fri 11.30 pm; no Amex.

Viet Garden N1 £26 ③②④
207 Liverpool Rd 7700 6040 8–2D
"So popular, it can be difficult to get a table" – this "basic" Islington joint has quite a name for its "delicious, fresh and flavoursome" Vietnamese fare. / www.vietgarden.co.uk; 11 pm; no Amex.

Viet Hoa E2 £25 ④④④
70-72 Kingsland Rd 7729 8293 1–2D
Supporters still cite this BYO Shoreditch Vietnamese as "a great cheap eat"; a couple of "truly shocking" experiences this year, however, left some former fans asking: "what's happened?"
/ www.viethoarestaurant.co.uk; midnight.

Vijay NW6 £28 ❷❷④
49 Willesden Ln 7328 1087 1–1B
"The décor's stuck in the '60s, but that's part of the quirky charm" of this "friendly" Kilburn veteran, to which fans return "time after time" for "great curries at low prices". / www.vijayindia.com; 10.45 pm, Fri-Sat 11.30 pm.

Vijaya Krishna SW17 £19 ③②④
114 Mitcham Rd 8767 7688 10–2C
"A good-quality Tooting curry house" which stands out, thanks to its "varied and unusual" – and occasionally "amazing" – Keralan cuisine. / 11 pm, Fri & Sat midnight; no Amex.

Villa Bianca NW3 £45 ④④❸
1 Perrins Ct 7435 3131 8–2A
"Tucked away in a little Hampstead lane", this "attractive" Italian
is barely changed since the '70s; to fans it's "an old faithful" that's
"great for all occasions" – cynics just find it "jaded" all-round.
/ www.villabiancanw3.com; 11.30 pm.

Village East SE1 £44 ❸❸❷
171-173 Bermondsey St 7357 6082 9–4D
A "cool" and "friendly" Bermondsey 'scene', where foie-gras burgers
and lobster are the (perhaps surprisingly luxurious) culinary
highlights; there's also a "well-priced and interesting wine list" and
some "fab cocktails". / www.villageeast.co.uk; 10 pm, Sun 9.30 pm;
set Sun L £28 (FP).

Villandry W1 £47 ④⑤④
170 Gt Portland St 7631 3131 2–1B
Oh dear! – this "buzzy" Marylebone deli has lost its way again;
last year's Hush-team relaunch has quickly fizzled, and there are
now once again far too many reports of "mediocre" food and
"distracted" service; it's "so expensive" too. / www.villandry.com;
10.30 pm; closed Sun D; booking: max 12.

Vincent Rooms
Westminster Kingsway College SW1 £25 ④④❸
Vincent Sq 7802 8391 2–4C
"Haphazard service" and "variable" food – all part of the charm
of a visit to this Westminster chef's-school dining room; it's often
"good value", though, and "can be superb... if you're lucky".
/ www.thevincentrooms.com; 9 pm; times vary; only term times; closed Mon D,
Wed D, Fri D, Sat & Sun; no Amex.

Vingt-Quatre SW10 £41 ④❸④
325 Fulham Rd 7376 7224 5–3B
An "invaluable" 24/7 Chelsea café that can be relied upon
to deliver "a great breakfast any time of the day or night"; other
fare, though, can be "indifferent". / www.vingtquatre.co.uk; open 24
hours; no booking.

Vino Rosso W4 £49 ❷❷④
9 Devonshire Rd 8994 5225 7–2A
This "deceptively modest-looking local Italian", in Chiswick, is a
significant "cut above" the norm, and offers "surprisingly high-
quality cooking" and super service. / www.vino-rosso.co.uk; 10.30 pm,
Fri & Sat 11 pm; Sun 9.30 pm; set weekday L £29 (FP).

Vinoteca EC1 £35 ❸❷❶
7 St John St 7253 8786 9–1B
A "fabulous" and "reasonably-priced" wine selection
is "enthusiastically" served at this "always-busy" Clerkenwell two-
year-old; the "sturdy" bistro-fare is "lovely" too – no wonder it's
"a bugger to get a table"! / www.vinoteca.co.uk; 10 pm; closed Sun;
no Amex.

FSA

Vital Ingredient £16 ❸④⑤
18a Maddox St, W1 no tel 3–2C
36 Berwick St, W1 no tel 3–1D
6 Vigo St, W1 no tel 3–3C
1 Garlick Hill, EC4 7248 9822 9–3B **NEW**
"A joyous break from sandwiches" – fans of this small group proclaim the virtues of soups "like your mother would make" and "fresh and yummy" salads. / L only; closed D, closed Sat & Sun; no credit cards; no booking.

Vivat Bacchus £45 ❸❷❸
4 Hay's Ln, SE1 no tel 9–4C **NEW**
47 Farringdon St, EC4 7353 2648 9–2A
"Walk-in wine cellars" – displaying some S African "beauties" – and a "heavenly" cheese room add an "unusual" twist to the format of this popular bar/restaurant, near Holborn Viaduct; in late-2008, a new branch opens in a similarly business-friendly location, by London Bridge. / set weekday L £29 (FP).

Vivezza SW1 £42 ④④④
101 Pimlico Rd 7730 0202 5–2D
This two-year-old Pimlico Italian – sister to local legend Caraffini – still hasn't found a steady stride; supporters find it "simpatico", though, and insist it's "one to watch". / www.vivezza.co.uk; 11 pm, Sun 10 pm.

Volt SW1 £42 ④④❸
17 Hobart Pl 7235 9696 2–4B
For those in search of a "romantic"/clubby venue, this coolly-decorated hang-out, near Victoria, has its uses; the food used to be OK too, but of late has seemed rather "uninspired". / www.voltlounge.com; 11.15 pm; closed Sat L & Sun.

Vrisaki N22 £30 ❷❷❸
73 Myddleton Rd 8889 8760 1–1C
"I dare you to try and finish the mezze!"; the food "just keeps coming", at this "consistently good" Greek taverna – an "institution", in an "unlikely" location, in a Bounds Green sidestreet. / midnight, Sun 9 pm.

202

Wagamama £26 ④④④

8 Norris St, SW1 7321 2755 4–4A
Harvey Nichols, Knightsbridge, SW1 7201 8000 5–1D
101a Wigmore St, W1 7409 0111 3–1A
10a Lexington St, W1 7292 0990 3–2D
4a Streatham St, WC1 7323 9223 2–1C
1 Tavistock St, WC2 7836 3330 4–3D
14a Irving St, WC2 7839 2323 4–4B
26a Kensington High St, W8 7376 1717 5–1A
N1 Centre, 37 Parkfield St, N1 7226 2664 8–3D
11 Jamestown Rd, NW1 7428 0800 8–3B
Royal Festival Hall, Southbank Centre, SE1 7021 0877 2–3D
50-54 Putney High St, SW15 8785 3636 10–2B
46-48 Wimbledon Hill Rd, SW19 8879 7280 10–2B
Jubilee Place, 45 Bank St, E14 7516 9009 11–1C
1a Ropemaker St, EC2 7588 2688 9–1C
22 Old Broad St, EC2 7256 9992 9–2C
Tower Pl, EC3 7283 5897 9–3D
109 Fleet St, EC4 7583 7889 9–2A
30 Queen St, EC4 7248 5766 9–3B
This "ubiquitous" noodle-hall chain – with its "hard" benches, "high-decibel" décor and queues – still seems a "clever" concept, even to its critics; praise for its "quick", "cheap" and "healthy" formula, however, is being drowned out nowadays by gripes about its "bland and samey" fodder. / www.wagamama.com; 10 pm-11 pm; EC4 & EC2 closed Sat & Sun; no booking.

Wahaca WC2 £26 ❸❷❷

66 Chandos Pl 7240 1883 4–4C
"Wagamama meets Mexico", at this "funky" Covent Garden basement yearling, where "cheerful" staff serve up "tasty and authentic Mexican street food" that's "very well-priced" too; on the downside, queues can be "intimidating". / www.wahaca.com; 11 pm, Sun 10.30 pm; need 8+ to book.

The Wallace
The Wallace Collection W1 £46 ④④❶

Hertford Hs, Manchester Sq 7563 9505 3–1A
The "lovely" covered courtyard of this Marylebone palazzo is a setting to "lift the spirits" (and at night, you can even "see the stars"); the food – though "enjoyable" – can seem "overpriced", however, and service is sometimes "non-existent".
/ www.thewallacerestaurant.com; Fri & Sat 9.30 pm; Sun-Thu closed D.

The Walmer Castle W11 £32 ❸❸❷

58 Ledbury Rd 7229 4620 6–1B
On the first floor of "a hipster pub in Notting Hill", a "friendly" and "buzzing" dining room where the Thai fare is "really quite good" (and "reasonably-priced" too). / 10.30 pm; D only, ex Fri & Sat open L & D.

Walnut NW6 £35 ❸❸④

280 West End Ln 7794 7772 1–1B
"Great attention to seasonal food" helps win local acclaim for this eco-conscious West Hampstead favourite, and for its "innovative British menu"; the setting is "not exciting", though, and some critics are unimpressed generally. / www.walnutwalnut.com; 10.30 pm; D only, closed Mon.

Wapping Food E1 £47 ❸❹❶
Wapping Power Station, Wapping Wall 7680 2080 11–1A
"You'll be surprised and impressed", by this "cavernous", "derelict-chic" East End power station – "a bizarre but wonderful" venue that's also surprisingly "romantic"; the food is "reliably imaginative", but is eclipsed by the "superb" Aussie wine list.
/ www.thewappingproject.com; 10.30 pm; closed Sun D.

The Warrington W9 £43 ❹❹❹
93 Warrington Cr 7592 7960 8–4A
"Gordon's f***ing awful pub"; for far too many reporters, a visit to this revamped landmark boozer, in Maida Vale, is a "never-to-be-repeated" experience, thanks to its "dull" décor, "crowded" tables, "faffing" staff and "lazy" food – "each new Ramsay seems worse than the last". / www.gordonramsay.com/thewarrington/; 10 pm, Fri & Sat 10.30 pm; Casual.

Water House N1 NEW £48 ❹❸❸
10 Orsman Rd 7033 0123 1–2C
A "position overlooking the canal" adds to the charm of Acorn House's eco-friendly new sibling, in an obscure bit of Shoreditch; ingredients are "wholesome", but the cooking is "patchy".
/ www.waterhouserestaurant.co.uk; 10 pm; closed Sat D & Sun D.

Waterloo Brasserie SE1 £43 ❺❺❹
119 Waterloo Rd 7960 0202 9–4A
With its "fabulous location", by the railway station, this new Gallic brasserie could have been such a hit… if it hadn't been for the "soulless" design and "patchy" cooking, and the sometimes appallingly "amateurish" service. / www.waterloobrasserie.co.uk; 11 pm.

The Waterway W9 £42 ❹❹❷
54 Formosa St 7266 3557 8–4A
A "wonderful" canal-side location ensures this Maida Vale hang-out is "always busy" (and it's "virtually impossible" to get an outside table on a sunny day); the food is a bit incidental, though, and service can struggle – "don't go if you're hungry!"
/ www.thewaterway.co.uk; 10.30 pm, Sun 10 pm; booking: max 12.

The Well EC1 £38 ❷❹❷
180 St John St 7251 9363 9–1A
"A long-standing Clerkenwell gastropub, with an ever-growing clientele drawn from the apartment blocks sprouting all around"; no complacency, though – the food is now "very good" indeed.
/ www.downthewell.com; 10.30 pm, Sun 10 pm.

The Wells NW3 £44 ❸❸❷
30 Well Walk 7794 3785 8–1A
"Perched next to Hampstead Heath", this "posh gastropub" is "terrific to sit outside in summer" (and also "lovely by the fire in winter"); "consistent and enjoyable" food plays an honourable supporting rôle. / www.thewellshampstead.co.uk; 10.30 pm, Sun 9.45 pm; no Amex; booking: max 8.

Weng Wah House NW3 £32 ❹❹❹
240 Haverstock Hill 7794 5123 8–2A
Fans insist this Belsize Park oriental fixture is still "always consistent", and "buzzing" too; it's "slowly losing direction", though – the "dim sum is no better than average" nowadays, and other fare can be "substandard". / www.wengwahgroup.com; 11.30 pm, Sat midnight, Sun 11.15 pm.

The Westbourne W2 £35 ❸④❸
101 Westbourne Park Villas 7221 1332 6–1B
*"The staff may be grumpy, but if you arrive early for a table on a
sunny day, this place is unbeatable", say fans of this evergreen
Notting Hillbilly hang-out (technically located in Bayswater);
the food isn't bad either. / www.thewestbourne.com; 10 pm, Sun 9.30 pm;
closed Mon L; need 4+ to book.*

The Wet Fish Cafe NW6 £39 ❸❸❶
242 West End Ln 7443 9222 1–1B
*An "unusual and interesting" interior – an old fish shop – provides
the "terrific" setting for this West Hampstead local, whose
"well thought-out" menu is not in fact particularly fishy.
/ www.thewetfishcafe.co.uk; 11 pm; closed Mon; no Amex.*

The Wharf TW11 £45 ④⑤❷
22 Manor Rd 8977 6333 1–4A
*It has an "amazing location" – on the river, near Teddington Lock,
and with a huge terrace – but this big bar-brasserie is too often
"let down" by "unacceptable" food. / www.thewharfteddington.com;
10 pm; closed Mon; set weekday L £29 (FP), set dinner £32 (FP).*

White Horse SW6 £38 ❸④❷
1-3 Parsons Grn 7736 2115 10–1B
*"A great pub that's always buzzing"; Parson's Green's famous
'Sloaney Pony' offers "simple but effective" food, an "interesting
wine list" and an "unbeatable selection of beers".
/ www.whitehorsesw6.com; 10.30 pm.*

The White Swan EC4 £43 ❸❷❸
108 Fetter Ln 7242 9122 9–2A
*This "unexpected" top-floor dining room of a tavern near Chancery
Lane is "much more than a gastropub", offering "proper" cooking
that's sometimes "very fine indeed"; there's also "good but pricey
pub fare in the downstairs bar". / www.thewhiteswanlondon.com; 10 pm;
closed Sat & Sun.*

Whits W8 £47 ❷❶❸
21 Abingdon Rd 7938 1122 5–1A
*"A great find"; this "small but perfectly-formed" Kensington
sidestreet "gem" offers "skillful" food, plus notably "charming" and
"attentive" service. / www.whits.co.uk; 10.30 pm; closed Mon,
Tue–Sat D only, closed Sun D.*

Wild Honey W1 £48 ❷❸❸
12 St George St 7758 9160 3–2C
*"Another hit from the Arbutus team", say fans of this wildly popular
Mayfair yearling, which similarly offers "gutsy" cuisine and "brilliant
wines by the carafe"; doubters sniff a touch of "hype" though,
and find the "crowded" setting rather "boring".
/ www.wildhoneyrestaurant.co.uk; 10.30 pm, Sun 9.30 pm; set weekday L £29
(FP), set pre-theatre £32 (FP).*

William IV NW10 £31 ❷❷❷
786 Harrow Rd 8969 5944 1–2B
*"You feel a million miles from the Harrow Road" – especially in the
"beautiful" garden – at this "airy" (but "noisy") Kensal Green pub;
it makes a "great local", where the fare includes "interesting tapas"
and "gorgeous Sunday roasts". / www.williamivlondon.com; 10.30 pm,
Fri & Sat 11 pm, Sun 9.30 pm.*

Wiltons SW1 £86 ❸❸❷
55 Jermyn St 7629 9955 3–3C
"More gentleman's club than restaurant", this *"classic"* St James's fish specialist is a bastion of the sort of *"stuffy"* and *"old-fashioned"* values rarely seen nowadays – perhaps why riffraff may just find the place an *"utter rip-off"*. / www.wiltons.co.uk; 10.30 pm; closed Sat & Sun; jacket required.

The Windmill W1 £35 ❸❸④
6-8 Mill St 7491 8050 3–2C
"It's the home of 'pie excellence', they say", and the pies are *"just as good as they claim"*, at this traditional boozer, near Savile Row. / www.windmillmayfair.co.uk; 9.30 pm; closed Sat D & Sun.

The Windsor Castle W8 £29 ④④❶
114 Campden Hill Rd 7243 8797 6–2B
With its wonderful *"Olde English setting"* and a *"fantastic beer garden"* (*"if the sun shines"*), it's no surprise that this ancient pub, near Notting Hill Gate, is always busy; in recent times, however, its fairly traditional grub has seemed ever more *"average"*. / www.windsorcastlepub.co.uk; 10 pm; no booking.

Wine Factory W11 £33 ④❷❸
294 Westbourne Grove 7229 1877 6–1B
"The food's nice, but it's the wine I go for" – as usual with John Brinkley's places, it's the *"non-existent wine mark-ups"* which make his Notting Hill bistro a good *"cheap-and-cheerful"* stand-by. / www.brinkleys.com; 11 pm; closed Sun D.

Wine Gallery SW10 £35 ④❸❷
49 Hollywood Rd 7352 7572 5–3B
"Cheap booze" – or, to put it another way, *"an outstanding-value wine list"* – fuels the *"buzzing"* atmosphere at John Brinkley's *"old Chelsea favourite"* (complete with *"pretty garden"*); the food is *"average but reliable"*. / www.brinkleys.com; 11.30 pm; closed Sun D; booking: max 12.

The Wine Library EC3 £26 ⑤❸❶
43 Trinity Sq 7481 0415 9–3D
"The best range of wines at the most affordable prices" (retail, plus modest corkage) draws City oenophiles to this merchant's cellar (where nobody cares that the accompanying pâté and cheese buffet is a bit *"pedestrian"*); thankfully, *"BlackBerries don't work down here…"* / www.winelibrary.co.uk; 8 pm, except Mon 6 pm; L & early evening only, closed Sat & Sun.

Wódka W8 £42 ❸❷❷
12 St Alban's Grove 7937 6513 5–1B
"It's a good laugh working your way through the list of vodkas", at this *"secret"* Kensington back street haunt, which – to the extent possible – serves *"Polish food with flair"*; *"it's hard to come here and not have a fun night"*. / www.wodka.co.uk; 11.15 pm; closed Sat L & Sun L; set weekday L & pre-theatre £26 (FP).

Wolfe's WC2 £37 ④④⑤
30 Gt Queen St 7831 4442 4–1D
On the fringe of Covent Garden, a *"'70s-style eatery"* that rarely incites much excitement nowadays; its *"basic"* food is generally *"well cooked"*, though, with burgers the most *"dependable"* choice. / www.wolfes-grill.net; 11 pm, Fri & Sat midnight, Sun 9 pm.

THE WOLSELEY W1 £54 ❸❷❶
160 Piccadilly 7499 6996 3–3C
"For sheer buzz" – Corbin & King's *"gloriously civilised"* grand café, by the Ritz, is an all-hours *"people-watching heaven"* (and a *"power scene"* too); utterly *"fabulous"* breakfasts aside, though, realisation of its long and varied menu teeters on the brink of *"average"*. / www.thewolseley.com; midnight, Sun 11 pm.

Wong Kei W1 £22 ④⑤⑤
41-43 Wardour St 7437 8408 4–3A
Famous for its *"very curt waiters and crumbling décor"*, this *"bustling"* Chinatown classic serves *"steaming heaps of food"* at *"great-value"* prices; the *"vaguely comical"* staff, though, are sadly *"not as rude"* as once they were. / 11 pm; no credit cards; no booking.

Woodlands £30 ❸❸④
37 Panton St, SW1 7839 7258 4–4A
77 Marylebone Ln, W1 7486 3862 2–1A
12-14 Chiswick High Rd, W4 8994 9333 7–2B
102 Heath St, NW3 7794 3080 8–1A
The decoration may be a mite *"chilling"*, but this stalwart Indian chain consistently serves up *"tasty"* and *"reasonably-priced"* veggie fare. / www.woodlandsrestaurant.co.uk; 10.45 pm; W4 Mon-Thu D only.

Wright Brothers SE1 £40 ❶❷❷
11 Stoney St 7403 9554 9–4C
"The freshest oysters in London" head up the array of *"beautiful, simple seafood"* on offer at this *"cramped"* – but *"unique"*, *"fun"* and *"brilliantly buzzy"* – Borough Market spot.
/ www.wrightbros.eu.com; 10.30 pm; closed Sun.

XO NW3 £41 ❸④❸
29 Belsize Ln 7433 0888 8–2A
Sceptics are still *"not sure about"* Will Ricker's *"über-styled"* Belsize Park yearling, which undoubtedly suffers by comparison with its stellar siblings (such as E&O); acclaim is growing, however, for its *"good fusion cooking"* and *"slick"* atmosphere.
/ www.rickerrestaurants.com; 11 pm, Sun 10.30 pm.

Yakitoria W2 £48 ④④❸
25 Sheldon Sq 3214 3000 6–1C
Conflicting reports on this *"beautifully-designed"* oriental, overlooking the canal in Paddington Basin; fans say it's *"worth tracking down"* for its *"delicious"* Japanese fare – sceptics find the cuisine *"humdrum"*, and service *"absent-minded"*.
/ www.yakitoria.co.uk; 11 pm; closed Sat L & Sun.

YAUATCHA W1 £50 ❶④❷
Broadwick Hs, 15-17 Broadwick St 7494 8888 3–2D
"The best dim sum this side of Hong Kong" (plus *"amazing"* cocktails) draw huge crowds to Alan Yau's *"moody"* Soho basement… which may be why service is sometimes *"surly"*; on the ground floor, they also serve *"the most beautiful cakes"*. / 11.30 pm.

Yelo £24 ❸❷❸
136a Lancaster Rd, W11   7243 2220   6–1A
8-9 Hoxton Sq, N1   7729 4626   9–1D
"For a quick meal or a take-away" – this "good-value" oriental noodle chain hits the spot; its Hoxton branch has especially nice al fresco tables. / www.yelothai.com; N1 11 pm, Sun - Mon 10.30 pm, W1 10.30 pm; need 6+ to book.

Yi-Ban £31 ❷❷❷
Imperial Wharf, Imperial Rd, SW6   7731 6606   5–4B
Regatta Centre, Dockside Rd, E16   7473 6699   11–1D
A "super, first-floor waterside location" – "with great views over to London City Airport" – adds to the appeal of this "huge" Chinese venture, which serves "excellent" food, including "a wide range of dim sum"; (it also has an "expensive but worth-it" Fulham sibling, which is rather under-patronised by virtue of its obscure position). / www.yi-ban.co.uk; 10.45 pm; SW6 closed Sun; minimum £10.

Yming W1 £33 ❷❶❸
35-36 Greek St   7734 2721   4–2A
"Far better than Chinatown" – just on the other side of Shaftesbury Avenue, Christine Lau's "civilised" Soho "secret" offers dishes ranging from "flavoursome" to "exciting", as well as "efficient" service that's full of "friendly charm". / www.yminglondon.com; 11.45 pm; closed Sun.

Yo! Sushi £29 ⑤⑤④
Branches throughout London
"I can't believe we used to call this 'Japanese'!" – the food at this "rip-off" conveyor-sushi chain is now "as tired as the concept". / www.yosushi.co.uk; 10 pm-11 pm; no booking.

The York & Albany NW1 NEW
127-129 Parkway   no tel   8–3B
A former Camden Town pub provides the setting for the latest addition to the Gordon Ramsay empire – a small boutique hotel, set to open in late-2008; it will incorporate a restaurant and deli, presided over by Angela Hartnett (formerly of Connaught fame). / www.gordonramsay.com/yorkandalbany/.

Yoshino W1 £38 ❷❷④
3 Piccadilly Pl   7287 6622   3–3D
"Like a little slice of Tokyo, tucked-away just off Piccadilly" – this Japanese "secret" has "charming" staff, who dish up "super fresh and zesty" sushi and sashimi, in a "peaceful" contemporary setting. / www.yoshino.net; 9 pm; closed Sun.

Yum Yum N16 £29 ❷❸❶
187 Stoke Newington High St   7254 6751   1–1D
"Yum yum indeed!"; this "always-reliable-and-popular Stokie Thai" is now – after its move a couple of years ago – a "huge" place, but it maintains "a brilliant atmosphere", and the food is "consistently delicious" too. / www.yumyum.co.uk; 11 pm, Fri & Sat midnight.

Yumenoki SW10 £42 ④❸⑤
204 Fulham Rd   7351 2777   5–3B
Mixed reports on the first full year of this Fulham Japanese – some applaud "tasty fare" and "super service", but others say the place has really "gone downhill". / www.yumenoki.co.uk; 10.30 pm.

Yuzu NW6 £34 ②⑤❸
102 Fortune Green Rd   7431 6602   1–1B
"The quality of the sushi really shines through", say fans of this tiny
West Hampstead Japanese; just as well – the service can
be "lousy". / www.yuzu-restaurants.com; 10.30 pm, Sun 10 pm; D only,
closed Mon.

Zafferano SW1 £63 ❸②②
15 Lowndes St   7235 5800   5–1D
"Classy, but not uptight", this Belgravia fixture has long been
renowned as a "cracking" Italian; it remains a good all-rounder,
but – like some other members of the London Fine Dining Group –
has suffered a notable decline in ratings since the acquisition
by John De Stefano in 2007. / www.zafferanorestaurant.com; 11 pm,
Sun 10.30 pm.

Zaffrani N1 £33 ❸②②
47 Cross St   7226 5522   8–3D
"Finely-spiced" and "original" dishes, "convivial" surroundings and
"unfailingly attentive" service again win local rave reviews for this
"contemporary" Islington Indian; recent reports, though, have also
included the odd misfire. / www.zaffrani-islington.co.uk; 11 pm.

Zaika W8 £52 ❶❸❸
1 Kensington High St   7795 6533   5–1A
"A wonderful, under-rated Indian restaurant"; Sanjay Dwivedi's
"astonishing" and "innovative" cuisine makes this "upscale"
(if slightly "cavernous") former Kensington banking hall a "truly
gourmet" destination. / www.zaika-restaurant.co.uk; 10.45 pm,
Sun 9.45 pm; set pre theatre £35 (FP).

Zero Degrees SE3 £31 ❸❸②
29-31 Montpelier Vale   8852 5619   1–4D
"Heaving at the weekend" – this industrial-looking Blackheath
bar/microbrewery owes its popularity to "superb" pizzas,
good moules/frites, and, of course, "some great home brews".
/ www.zerodegrees.co.uk; 11.30 pm, Sun 10.30 pm; no trainers.

Zero Quattro SW19 £40 ④❷❸
28 Ridgway   8946 4840   10–2B
"OTT" (and, on occasion, "intrusive") service helps create a "fun"
atmosphere at this "cramped" Wimbledon Italian; its "interesting"
food wins strong local praise, but it can also seem rather "pricey".
/ www.zeroquattro.co.uk; 11.30 pm, Sat midnight, Sun 10.30 pm.

The Zetter EC1 £43 ④④❸
St John's Sq, 86-88 Clerkenwell Rd   7324 4455   9–1A
A *"buzzy, feel-good factor"* is a key feature of this "bright" and
"airy" corner dining room – part of a Farringdon design-hotel;
"splendid" breakfasts aside, though, the food is rather "up-and-
down". / www.thezetter.com; 11 pm, Sun-Wed, 10.30 pm.

Ziani SW3 £42 ❸②②
45 Radnor Walk   7352 2698   5–3C
A pint-size but *"perfect"* neighbourhood Italian – with "loads
of character and buzz" – which continues to please its
cast of Chelsea regulars. / www.ziani.uk.com; 11.30 pm, Sun 10.30 pm.

Zilli Fish W1 £59 ❸❸④
36-40 Brewer St 7734 8649 3–2D
"Wonderful, simple fish dishes" help maintain the allure of Aldo
Zilli's "buzzy" Soho corner site; there are niggles, though –
it's "mildly overpriced", staff can be "off-ish", and the décor
is getting a bit "tired". / www.zillialdo.com; 11.30 pm; closed Sun.

Zizzi £29 ④④❸
Branches throughout London
This "pleasant"-looking pizza 'n' pasta chain has not lived up to its
initial promise; if you're looking for "a reasonable refuelling stop",
it has its uses, but the food's pretty "dull" nowadays.
/ www.askcentral.co.uk; 11 pm; some booking restrictions apply.

Zuccato £31 ④❸④
02 Centre, 255 Finchley Rd, NW3 7431 1799 8–2A
41 Bow Ln, EC4 7329 6364 9–2C
An oddly diverse duo of "basic" pizza/pasta places, in the City and
in Finchley; their style is perhaps a bit "robotic", but –
on most accounts – they make "friendly" and "reliable" stand-bys.
/ www.etruscarestaurants.com; NW3 11pm, Fri & Sat 11.30 pm,
Sun 10.30 pm, EC4 10 pm; EC4 closed Sat & Sun.

ZUMA SW7 £65 ❶❸❷
5 Raphael St 7584 1010 5–1C
With its "mind-blowingly good" Japanese-fusion fare and its
maniacally "buzzing" bar, this "flashy" Knightsbridge hang-out still
"has the edge over Nobu" as London's No. 1 oriental; be warned,
though: "you have to climb over the Lamborghinis to get in".
/ www.zumarestaurant.com; 10.45 pm, Sun 9.45 pm; booking: max 8.

INDEXES

BREAKFAST
(with opening times)

Central

Abokado *(8)*
Acorn House *(8, Sat 10am)*
The Albemarle *(7)*
Amato *(8, Sun 10)*
Apostrophe: *Barrett St W1, Tott' Ct Rd W1, WC2 (7)*
Apsleys *(7)*
Asia de Cuba *(6)*
Atrium *(8.30)*
Aubaine: *W1 (8, Sat 10)*
Automat *(Mon - Fri 7)*
Baker & Spice: *SW1 (7)*
Balans: *all branches (8)*
Bar Italia *(7)*
Benugo: *all central branches (7.30)*
Bistro 1: *Beak St W1 (Sun 11)*
Bord'Eaux *(7)*
The Botanist *(9)*
Brasserie Roux *(6.30, Sat & Sun 7)*
Brasserie St Jacques *(8, Sat & Sun 10)*
Browns: *WC2 (8)*
Café Bohème *(8)*
Café in the Crypt *(Mon-Sat 8)*
Caffè Caldesi *(10 am)*
Caffè Vergnano: *WC2 (8, Sun 11)*
Caramel *(8)*
Cecconi's *(7)*
The Chelsea Brasserie *(7)*
Chez Gérard: *Chancery Ln WC2 (8)*
Christopher's *(Sat & Sun 11.30)*
The Cinnamon Club *(Mon-Fri 7.30)*
City Café *(6.30, Sat & Sun 7)*
The Contented Vine *(Sat & Sun 10)*
Crussh: *W1 (7)*
Daylesford Organics *(8, Sun 11)*
Diner: *W1 (8, Sat & Sun 9)*
Dorchester Grill *(7, Sat & Sun 8)*
Eagle Bar Diner *(Sat 10, Sun 11)*
Eat & Two Veg: *W1 (9, Sun 10)*
The Fifth Floor Café *(Mon-Sat 8, Sun 11)*
Fine Burger Company: *all branches (midday, Sat & Sun 11 am)*
5 Cavendish Square *(8)*
Flat White *(8, Sat & Sun 9)*
Fortnum's, The Fountain *(7.30)*
Franco's *(Mon-Fri 7.30, Sat 9)*
La Fromagerie Café *(Mon 10.30, Tue-Fri 8, Sat 9, Sun 10)*
Fuzzy's Grub: *SW1 (7)*
Galvin at Windows *(7)*
Giraffe: *W1 (7.45, Sat & Sun 9)*
Gordon's Wine Bar *(Mon-Fri 8)*
The Goring Hotel *(7, Sun 7.30)*
Homage *(7)*
Hush *(Mon-Fri 7.30)*
Indigo *(6.30)*
Inn the Park *(8)*
Joe Allen *(8)*
Konditor & Cook: *WC1 (9.30);*

W1 (9.30, Sun 10.30)
Ladurée: *W1 (9); SW1 (Mon - Sat 9, Sun noon - 1.30)*
The Landau *(7)*
Leon: *WC2 (7.30, Sat 9, Sun 10); Gt Marlborough St W1 (9.30, Sat & Sun 10.30)*
Loch Fyne: *WC2 (10)*
Luciano *(8.15)*
Maison Bertaux *(8.30, Sun 9)*
Maxwell's *(Sat & Sun 9.30)*
Monmouth Coffee Company: *WC2 (8)*
The National Dining Rooms *(10)*
National Gallery Café *(8, Sat & Sun 10)*
Nicole's *(10)*
Nordic Bakery *(Mon - Fri 10)*
Number Twelve *(7)*
The Only Running Footman *(7.30, Sat & Sun 9.30)*
Oriel *(8.30, Sun 9)*
Oscar *(7, Sun 8)*
Ottolenghi: *SW1 (8, Sun 9)*
Le Pain Quotidien: *Marylebone High St W1 (7, Sat & Sun 8); Great Marlborough St W1 (8, Sat & Sun 9)*
Pâtisserie Valerie: *Piccadilly W1, Marylebone High St W1, Old Compton St W1 (7.30); Motcomb St SW1 (8); Hans Cr SW1 (8-8.30)*
Paul: *WC2 (7.30); W1 (7.30, Sat & Sun 8)*
The Portrait *(10)*
The Providores *(9, Sat & Sun 10)*
Providores (Tapa Room) *(9, Sat & Sun 10)*
Pure California: *WC1 (7, Sat 8); Goodge St W1 (8); Beak St W1 (8, Sat 10)*
Ranoush: *SW1 (noon)*
Refuel *(7, Sun 8)*
Rhodes W1 Brasserie *(6.30, Sat & Sun 7)*
Rib Room *(7, Sun 8)*
RIBA Café *(8, Sat 9)*
Richoux: *all branches (8)*
The Ritz Restaurant *(7, Sun 8)*
Royal Academy *(10)*
Salade: *W1 (7.30)*
Serafino *(7)*
Simpsons-in-the-Strand *(Mon-Fri 7.30)*
06 St Chad's Place *(8)*
Sketch (Parlour) *(Mon-Fri 8, Sat 10)*
Sotheby's Café *(9.30)*
Star Café *(7)*
Stock Pot: *SW1 (7); W1 (9)*
Tate Britain (Rex Whistler) *(10)*
The Terrace in the Fields *(8)*
Tootsies: *W1 (Sat & Sun 11)*
Truc Vert *(7.30, Sun 9.00)*
Tuttons *(9.30)*
The Union Café *(Sat & Sun 11)*
Vital Ingredient: *all central branches (9)*
The Wallace *(10)*

BRUNCH MENUS

BYO

(Bring your own wine at no or low – less than £3 – corkage. Note for £5-£15 per bottle, you can normally negotiate to take your own wine to many, if not most, places.)

Hot Stuff
Mirch Masala: *all branches*
Thai Corner Café

East
Lahore Kebab House
Mangal Ocakbasi
Mirch Masala: *all branches*
New Tayyabs
The Place Below
Viet Hoa

CHILDREN
*(h – high or special chairs
m – children's menu
p – children's portions
e – weekend entertainments
o – other facilities)*

Central
Aaya *(hm)*
Abeno *(hm)*
Abeno Too *(h)*
Al Duca *(hp)*
Al Hamra *(h)*
Al Sultan *(h)*
The Albemarle *(hmp)*
Amato *(hp)*
Apsleys *(hmp)*
Arbutus *(h)*
Asadal *(h)*
Asia de Cuba *(hp)*
Aubaine: *all branches (h)*
L'Autre Pied *(h)*
Axis *(hm)*
Back to Basics *(hp)*
Bank Westminster *(hmp)*
Bar Italia *(hp)*
Bar Shu *(h)*
Barrafina *(p)*
Beiteddine *(p)*
Belgo Centraal: *all branches (hm)*
Bellamy's *(h)*
Benares *(h)*
Benihana: *W1 (hm)*
Benja *(h)*
Bentley's *(h)*
Beotys *(mp)*
Bodean's: *all branches (ehm)*
Bord'Eaux *(hp)*
Boudin Blanc *(p)*
Boxwood Café *(hmob)*
Brasserie Roux *(hm)*
Brasserie St Jacques *(h)*
Browns: *all branches (hm)*
Café Bohème *(hm)*
Café des Amis *(m)*
Café du Jardin *(p)*
Café Emm *(hp)*
Café España *(h)*
Café in the Crypt *(p)*
Café Lazeez *(hm)*
Café Pacifico *(hm)*
Caffè Caldesi *(hp)*

Caffè Vergnano: *WC2 (p)*
Camerino *(hp)*
Cape Town Fish Market *(h)*
Le Caprice *(hp)*
Caraffini *(h)*
Caramel *(hp)*
Centrepoint Sushi *(h)*
Le Cercle *(p)*
The Chelsea Brasserie *(hm)*
Chez Gérard: *all central branches (em)*
Chicago Rib Shack *(hm)*
Chimes *(p)*
China Tang *(h)*
The Chinese Experience *(h)*
Chisou *(h)*
Chor Bizarre *(h)*
Chowki *(h)*
Christopher's *(hm)*
Chuen Cheng Ku *(h)*
Cigala *(h)*
The Cinnamon Club *(h)*
Cipriani *(hp)*
City Café *(hm)*
Clos Maggiore *(p)*
Cocoon *(h)*
Como Lario *(hp)*
The Contented Vine *(p)*
Cyprus Mangal *(m)*
Daylesford Organics *(h)*
Delfino *(h)*
dim T: *all branches (hmo)*
Diner: *W1 (hmp)*
Dorchester Grill *(hm)*
Eagle Bar Diner *(h)*
Eat & Two Veg: *W1 (hp)*
Ed's Easy Diner: *all branches (hm)*
Efes II: *all branches (h)*
L'Escargot *(p)*
L'Escargot (Picasso Room) *(p)*
Fairuz *(h)*
Fakhreldine *(h)*
The Fifth Floor Café *(hmo)*
Fine Burger Company: *W1 (hm)*
Fino *(h)*
Fire & Stone *(h)*
Fishworks: *W1 (hmo)*
Foliage *(hm)*
Fortnum's, The Fountain *(hp)*
La Fromagerie Café *(p)*
Fung Shing *(h)*
Galvin at Windows *(h)*
Galvin Bistrot de Luxe *(h)*
Garbo's *(hp)*
Gaucho Grill: *all central branches (h)*
Gay Hussar *(hp)*
Gaylord *(hm)*
Getti: *all branches (hp)*
Giardinetto *(p)*
Giraffe: *W1 (ehm)*
Golden Dragon *(h)*
Golden Hind *(hmp)*
Gordon Ramsay at Claridge's *(h)*
The Goring Hotel *(hm)*
Gourmet Burger Kitchen: *all*

219

223

Waterloo Brasserie *(mh)*
The Wharf *(h)*
Zero Degrees *(hp)*
Zero Quattro *(hm)*

East

Alba *(hp)*
Ambassador *(mo)*
L'Anima *(h)*
Ark Fish *(hm)*
Barcelona Tapas: *Beaufort Hs, St Botolph St EC3, EC4 (hp)*
Beach Blanket Babylon: *all branches (h)*
Bistrotheque *(p)*
Bleeding Heart *(h)*
Il Bordello *(h)*
Browns: *all branches (hm)*
Buen Ayre *(h)*
Café du Marché *(p)*
Canteen: *all branches (hmp)*
Catch *(h)*
Cây Tre *(hm)*
The Chancery *(hmp)*
Chez Gérard: *EC4 (ehm); EC2, EC3 (em)*
Chi Noodle & Wine Bar *(p)*
The Clerkenwell Dining Room *(h)*
Club Gascon *(p)*
Club Mangia *(hp)*
Coach & Horses *(hp)*
Comptoir Gascon *(h)*
Coq d'Argent *(h)*
Cottons: *EC1 (h)*
Crussh: *Unit 21 Jubilee Pl E14 (h)*
Curve *(m)*
D Sum 2 *(h)*
The Diner: *EC2 (hmp)*
The Drunken Monkey *(p)*
Eastway *(h)*
The Empress of India *(hm)*
Fabrizio *(h)*
Faulkner's *(hm)*
54 Farringdon Road *(hp)*
La Figa *(hp)*
Fish Central *(m)*
Fish Shop *(p)*
The Fox *(p)*
Gaucho Grill: *E14 (h); EC3 (hp)*
The Gaylord *(p)*
Gourmet Burger Kitchen: *all branches (hp)*
Gourmet Pizza Company: *all branches (h)*
Green Door Bar & Grill: *EC3 (hm)*
The Hoxton Grille: *EC2 (hm)*
The Gun *(h)*
The Hat & Feathers *(h)*
Haz: *all branches (hp)*
Hilliard *(p)*
Itsu: *all branches (h)*
Kasturi *(hm)*
Lahore Kebab House *(h)*
The Larder *(hp)*

Leon: *E1 (h)*
Lilly's *(m)*
Lotus Chinese Floating Restaurant *(h)*
Luc's Brasserie *(h)*
Medcalf *(h)*
Missouri Angel *(hp)*
Missouri Grill *(hp)*
Moro *(h)*
Namo *(ehm)*
The Narrow *(hp)*
New Tayyabs *(h)*
1901 *(h)*
Northbank *(h)*
Paternoster Chop House *(h)*
Pâtisserie Valerie: *all branches (h)*
The Peasant *(hp)*
E Pellicci *(pm)*
Pho: *EC1 (ho)*
(Ciro's) Pizza Pomodoro: *EC2 (h)*
Plateau *(h)*
La Porchetta Pizzeria: *all branches (h)*
The Prince Arthur *(hm)*
Prism *(p)*
Quadrato *(hm)*
The Quality Chop House *(hp)*
The Real Greek: *EC1 (hm)*
Refettorio *(h)*
The Rivington Grill *(hp)*
Royal China: *E14 (h)*
The Royal Exchange Grand Café *(p)*
S & M Café: *E1 (hmp)*
Saf *(hp)*
St John *(h)*
St John Bread & Wine *(h)*
Saki Bar & Food Emporium *(h)*
Sauterelle *(h)*
Searcy's Brasserie *(hp)*
Shish: *all branches (ehm)*
Smithfield Bar & Grill *(hm)*
Smiths (Top Floor) *(h)*
Smiths (Ground Floor) *(hm)*
Sofra: *EC1 (hp)*
Sông Quê *(hp)*
Square Pie Company: *all east branches (m)*
Story Deli *(o)*
Stringray Globe Café *(hm)*
Tas: *EC1 (h)*
La Tasca: *E14 (hm)*
Ubon *(hp)*
Vanilla Black *(p)*
Vic Naylors *(h)*
Viet Hoa *(h)*
Vinoteca *(p)*
Wagamama: *all east branches (hm)*
Wapping Food *(h)*
The Well *(hm)*
Yi-Ban: *E16 (h)*
The Zetter *(h)*

ENTERTAINMENT
(Check times before you go)

Central

All Star Lanes:*WC1*
(bowling, DJ Fri & Sat)

Bank Westminster
(DJ, Fri & Sat)

Boisdale
(jazz, Mon-Sat)

Browns:*WC2*
(live piano)

Café du Jardin
(jazz pianist, Wed-Sat)

Café in the Crypt
(jazz, Wed night)

Le Caprice
(pianist, nightly)

Chez Gérard: *SW1*
(jazz, Sun L)

Ciao Bella
(pianist, nightly)

Dover Street Restaurant & Bar
(live bands and DJ, nightly)

Eagle Bar Diner
(DJ, Wed-Sat)

The Easton
(DJ, Fri)

The Ebury
(jazz, Thu-Sat)

Efes II: *Gt Portland St W1*
(belly dancer, nightly)

The Electric Birdcage
(DJ, percussionist on occasion)

Fakhreldine
(bellydancer, Thu-Sat)

Floridita
(live Cuban music, nightly)

Hakkasan
(DJ, nightly)

Hard Rock Café
(regular live music)

Imperial China
(pianist, Thu-Sat)

Indigo
(dinner and a movie, Fri & Sat. Film
brunches, Sun)

Ishbilia
(live music, Thu-Sat, regular belly dancing)

Joe Allen
(pianist, Mon-Sat)

Kai Mayfair
(harpist, Thu and various other days)

Kettners
(pianist, nightly; live music, Thu-Sat)

Langan's Brasserie
(jazz, nightly)

Levant
(belly dancer, nightly)

Little Italy
(DJ, Mon-Sat)

Maroush:*V: 3-4 Vere St W1*
(music & dancing, nightly)

Mint Leaf: *SW1*

(weekend DJ/jazz, Fri D)

Mirabelle
(pianist, Tue-Sat & Sun L)

Momo
(live world music, Tue & Wed)

Noura: *Jermyn St SW1*
(DJ, Thu-Sat)

Oscar
(film club, Sun)

Pearl
(pianist)

Pigalle Club
(live music, nightly)

Planet Hollywood
(DJ, nightly)

La Porte des Indes
(jazz, Sun brunch)

Quaglino's
(jazz, nightly)

Red Fort
(DJ, Thu-Sat)

Refuel
(film club, Sun)

Rib Room
(pianist, Mon-Sun)

The Ritz Restaurant
(string quartet, Mon-Thu; live music,
Fri & Sat)

Roka
(DJ, Thu-Sat)

Ronnie Scott's
(jazz, nightly)

Royal Academy
(jazz, Fri)

Sarastro
(opera, Sun & Mon D)

Sartoria
(pianist, Fri & Sat)

Simpsons-in-the-Strand
(pianist, nightly)

06 St Chad's Place
(DJ, Thu & Fri)

Sketch (Gallery)
(DJ, Thu-Sat)

Souk Medina
(belly dancer, Thu-Sat)

Stanza
(DJ, Thu-Sat)

Sugar Reef
(live music, Thu-Fri)

Taman Gang
(DJ, Thu [an])

Thai Square: *SW1*
(DJ, Fri & Sat)

Trader Vics
(guitarist, nightly)

Volt
(DJ, Sat)

West

Babylon
(live music, Thu D, magician Sun)

Beach Blanket Babylon: *all branches*
(DJ, Fri & Sat)

Belvedere
(pianist, nightly Sat & Sun all day)
Benugo: *SW7*
(jazz, Wed)
Big Easy
(live music, nightly)
La Bodeguita del Medio
(occasional live music)
Le Café Anglais
(magician Sun lunch)
Chutney Mary
(jazz, Sun L)
The Collection
(DJ, nightly)
The Crown & Sceptre
(quiz night, Mon)
Da Mario
(disco, Wed-Sat; magician, Wed)
Del'Aziz
(belly dancer, Thu-Sat, live jazz Tue in deli)
The Establishment
(Wed night, Jazz)
Frankie's Italian Bar & Grill: *W4*
(magician, Fri & Sat, jazz, Thu-Sat D, Sun L);
SW3
(magician, Wed, Fri & Sat)
Harlem
(DJ, Tue-Sun)
Kensington Square Kitchen
(DJ, occasional weekends)
Levantine
(belly dancer, nightly)
Maroush: *I) 21 Edgware Rd W2*
(music & dancing, nightly)
Mr Wing
(jazz, Fri & Sat)
Notting Hill Brasserie
(jazz, nightly)
Nozomi
(DJ, nightly)
Pacific Bar and Grill
(magician, Sun)
Il Pagliaccio
(magician, Sun, salsa nights, weekly jazz,
opera monthly)
Pasha
(belly dancer, nightly)
(Ciro's) Pizza Pomodoro: *SW3*
(live music, nightly)
La Rueda: *SW6*
(live music Fri & Sat)
606 Club
(live music, nightly)
Spago
(Thu-Sun evening Acoustic Guitar Music)
Sticky Fingers
(face painter, Sat & Sun L)
Sugar Hut
(DJ, Fri & Sat)
Troubadour
(live music, most nights)
William IV
(DJ, Fri-Sat)

North
Camino
(DJ, Fri & Sat)
Cottons: *NW1*
(live music, Sun; DJ, Fri & Sat)
Don Pepe
(singer, Fri & Sat)
Fratelli la Bufala: *NW3*
(opera singers every so often)
Gilgamesh
(DJ, nightly)
The Haven
(jazz, Tue-Thu)
Hoxton Apprentice
(Jazz Tue)
Hugo's
(piano, Thu; jazz, Sun; piano, Mon)
Landmark (Winter Gdn)
(pianist & musicians, daily)
Mestizo
(DJ, Thu-Sat)
The Pumphouse
(DJ, Fri)
Shish: *NW2*
(DJ, Sat; live music Wed)
Thai Square: *N1*
(DJ, Thu-Sat)
The Three Crowns
(DJ, Fri & Sat)
Trojka
(Russian music, Fri & Sat)
Villa Bianca
(guitarist, Mon-Thu, pianist, Sat & Sun)
Weng Wah House
(karaoke, nightly)
Yum Yum
(DJ, Fri)

South
Al Forno: *SW15*
(live music, Sat)
Archduke Wine Bar
(jazz, Mon-Sat)
Baltic
(jazz, Sun D)
Barcelona Tapas: *SE22*
(live music Wed every fortnight)
Bayee Village
(Mon-Wed pianist)
Bengal Clipper
(pianist, nightly)
Dish Dash
(belly dancing, first Wed of month)
Donna Margherita
(live music, weekly)
Ev Restaurant, Bar & Deli
(live music, Mon-Sat)
The Fentiman Arms
(quiz night, Tue)
The Freemasons
(quiz night, Mon)
The Gowlett
(DJ, Sun)
Grafton House

LATE
(open till midnight or later as shown; may be earlier Sunday)

OUTSIDE TABLES
(particularly recommended)*

Galvin Bistrot de Luxe
Getti: *all branches*
Giraffe: *W1*
Golden Hind
Gordon's Wine Bar*
Goya
Greig's
Grumbles
Haiku
Hard Rock Café
Hardy's Brasserie
Hellenik
Hush*
Imperial China
Inn the Park
Ishbilia
Jenny Lo's Tea House
Just Falafs: *all branches*
Kazan: *SW1*
Ladurée: *all branches*
Leon: *Gt Marlborough St W1, WC2*
Little Italy
The Little Square
Luciano
Maxwell's
Mekong
Michael Moore
Mildred's
Mimmo d'Ischia
Mirabelle*
Momo
Motcombs
The Norfolk Arms
Olivomare
L'Oranger
Oriel
Original Tajines
Orrery
Oscar
Ozer
Pantechnicon Rooms
Papageno
Paradiso Olivelli: *all branches*
Passione
Pasta Brown: *all branches*
Pâtisserie Valerie: *Motcomb St SW1, Piccadilly W1, Marylebone High St W1*
Pescatori: *Charlotte St W1*
La Petite Maison
Piccolino: *W1*
ping pong: *Eastcastle St W1*
El Pirata
Pizza on the Park
La Poule au Pot
The Providores
Pure California: *Goodge St W1*
The Queens Arms
Quo Vadis
Le Relais de Venise L'Entrecôte
Reubens
RIBA Café*
Richoux: *South Audley St W1*
Ristorante Semplice
The Ritz Restaurant

Roka
Royal Academy
Running Horse
Salaam Namaste
Salt Yard
Santini
Sapori
Sardo
Seafresh
Serafino
Shampers
Siam Central
Signor Zilli
06 St Chad's Place
So
Sofra: *Shepherd St W1, WC2*
Soho Japan
Stock Pot: *W1*
Suka
Taro: *Brewer St W1*
The Terrace in the Fields
Texas Embassy Cantina
Thomas Cubitt
Tootsies: *W1*
Toto's*
La Trouvaille
Truc Vert
Tuttons
2 Amici
2 Veneti
Uno
Vapiano
Via Condotti
Villandry
Vital Ingredient: *all central branches*
Volt
Wolfe's
Zilli Fish

West
The Abingdon
The Academy
L'Accento Italiano
Admiral Codrington
Al-Waha
Angelus
The Anglesea Arms
The Anglesea Arms
Annie's: *all branches*
Aquasia
The Ark
Arturo
The Atlas*
Aubaine: *all branches*
Babylon*
Baker & Spice: *SW3*
Balans: *W4*
Beach Blanket Babylon: *W11*
Bedlington Café
Belvedere
Benugo: *SW7*
Best Mangal
Bibendum Oyster Bar
Big Easy

Zero Degrees

East
Ambassador
Amerigo Vespucci*
Apostrophe: *EC2*
Benugo: *all east branches*
Bevis Marks
Bleeding Heart
Browns: *E14*
Buen Ayre
Café Spice Namaste
Canteen: *E1*
Carnevale
Cellar Gascon
Chamberlain's
Chop'd: *EC3*
Cicada
Coach & Horses
Comptoir Gascon
Coq d'Argent*
Cottons: *EC1*
Curve
D Sum 2
Devonshire Terrace
$
The Eagle
Elephant Royale*
The Empress of India
El Faro*
La Figa
Fish Shop
The Fox
Gaucho Grill: *E14*
Gourmet Pizza Company: *all branches*
The Hoxton Grille: *EC2*
The Gun
The Hat & Feathers
Hix Oyster & Chop House
Kenza
Kolossi Grill
Leon: *Ludgate Circus EC4*
Lilly's
The Little Bay: *EC1*
LMNT
Medcalf
Memsaheb on Thames
Missouri Angel
The Morgan Arms
Moro
Namo
The Narrow
New Tayyabs
Northbank
1 Blossom Street
Paternoster Chop House
Pâtisserie Valerie: *E1*
The Peasant
The Place Below
Plateau
Portal
The Prince Arthur
Quadrato

The Real Greek: *EC1*
Le Rendezvous du Café
Royal China: *E14*
S & M Café: *all branches*
Saf
Shish: *all branches*
Singapura: *EC4*
Smiths (Top Floor)
Smiths (Ground Floor)
Sofra: *EC1*
Spianata: *E1, EC2, EC3*
Story Deli
Stringray Globe Café
Taberna Etrusca
La Tasca: *E14*
Terranostra
Wapping Food
The Well
Yi-Ban: *all branches*
The Zetter

PRIVATE ROOMS
(for the most comprehensive listing of venues for functions – from palaces to pubs – visit www.hardens.com/party, or buy *Harden's London Party, Event & Conference Guide,* **available in all good bookshops)**
* particularly recommended

Central
About Thyme *(30)*
Adam Street *(60,40,15)*
The Admiralty *(30,60)*
Alain Ducasse *(6,10,24)*
Alastair Little *(25)*
Albannach *(20)*
The Albemarle *(80)*
Alloro *(16)*
Amaya *(14)*
Aperitivo *(30)*
Apsleys *(12)*
L'Artiste Musclé *(25,18)*
Asadal *(8,10)*
Atrium *(12,24)*
Aurora *(18)*
L'Autre Pied *(16)*
The Avenue *(24)*
Axis *(48)*
Bam-Bou *(8,12,14,20)*
Bank Westminster *(20,20)*
Bar Shu *(14)*
Belgo Centraal: *WC2 (25,30)*
Benares *(12,22,28)*
Benihana: *W1 (10)*
Benja *(20)*
Bentley's *(6-60)*
Beotys *(60)*
Bertorelli's Café Italian: *Charlotte St W1 (24,25,44); Frith St W1 (80)*
Bodean's: *W1 (10)*
Boisdale *(22)*
Bord'Eaux *(14)*

The Brackenbury (30,35)
Brasserie St Quentin (16)
Brilliant (120)
Brinkley's (18,20,45)
Britannia (20)
Brunello (50)
Bumpkin: W11 (30,35)
Bush Bar & Grill (50)
Le Café Anglais (1)
Cambio de Tercio (22)
The Capital Restaurant (12,24)
Carpaccio's (40)
Charlotte's Place (20,34)
Chelsea Bun Diner (50)
Cheyne Walk Brasserie (70)
Chez Kristof (40)
Chez Marcelle (40)
Chez Patrick (30)
Chutney Mary (32)
Cibo (12,16)
Clarke's (40-50)
Cochonnet (30)
The Collection (40-70)
Le Colombier (30)
Coopers Arms (40)
Crazy Homies (35-40)
Daphne's (40)
Daquise (20)
De Cecco (20)
Del'Aziz (50)
E&O (20)
Edera (20)
Eight Over Eight (14)
The Establishment (15)
L'Etranger (18)
Il Falconiere (20,35)
Firezza: W11 (25)
First Floor (28,44)
Five Hot Chillies (25)
Foxtrot Oscar (30)
Frankie's Italian Bar
    & Grill: W4 (35,40)
The Frontline Club (50)
Gail's Bread: W11 (15)
Geale's (12)
Ground (45)
Haandi (30)
High Road Brasserie (12)
Iznik Kaftan (75)
Jimmy's (10)
Julie's (12,16,16,24,32,45)
Kandoo (30)
kare kare (20)
Karma (30,40)
Kensington Place (45)
Khan's of Kensington (12)
Kiasu (20)
Knaypa (35)
L-Restaurant & Bar (16)
Langan's Coq d'Or Bar
    & Grill (20)
Launceston Place (12)
Little Bay: SW6 (40)
Locanda Ottomezzo (16,20)

Lucio (20)
Lucky Seven (45)
Made in Italy (40)
Madhu's (35)
Magic Wok (30)
Malabar (30)
Manicomio: SW3 (30,12)
Mao Tai (30)
Masala Zone: SW5 (10)
Memories of India (30)
Monty's: The Mall W5 (50)
Mr Wing (6,6,20)
Mulberry Street (40)
Napulé (15)
Noor Jahan: W2 (16)
North China (30)
Notting Grill (20,60)
Notting Hill Brasserie (44)
Nozomi (30)
Nuovi Sapori (30)
The Oak (16)
Okawari (25)
Osteria dell'Arancio (30)
Il Pagliaccio (60)
Papillon (18)
Paradise by Way of Kensal
    Green (20,50)
Pasha (20)
Patio (50)
Pearl Liang (45)
Pellicano (25)
Père Michel (20)
The Pig's Ear (35)
The Pilot (40)
Pissarro's (78)
Poissonnerie de l'Avenue (20)
Polish Club (Ognisko
    Polskie) (150)
Princess Victoria (60)
Priory House (40)
Raoul's Café & Deli: W11 (25)
Rasoi Vineet Bhatia (8,18)
The Red Pepper (25)
Riccardo's (8)
Rossopomodoro: SW10 (45)
Royal China: W2 (20,20)
La Rueda: SW6 (50)
Saigon Saigon (10)
San Lorenzo (30)
Satay House (40)
Snows on the Green (10,15)
Star of India (10,10)
Stone Mason's Arms (50)
Le Suquet (16,25)
Taiwan Village (17)
Tandoori Lane (16)
Tawana (50)
The Thatched House (70)
Timo (18)
Tom Aikens (10)
Tom's Kitchen (22)
Trenta (14)
Troubadour (70,120)
Urban Turban (75)

dim T: *SE1 (16)*
Dish Dash *(33)*
Dragon Castle *(60)*
The Duke's Head *(50)*
Earl Spencer *(70)*
The East Hill *(12)*
Emile's *(50)*
Enoteca Turi *(22)*
Everest Inn *(12,25)*
The Fentiman Arms *(45)*
Fish in a Tie *(40,20,60)*
The Fox & Hounds *(25)*
Franklins: *SE11 (25); SE22 (34)*
Fujiyama *(40,25)*
Garrison *(25)*
Gazette: *SW11 (12); SW12 (4,14,70)*
The Greyhound at Battersea *(25)*
Harrison's *(24)*
The Hartley *(70)*
Hudson's *(30)*
Joanna's *(6)*
La Lanterna *(50,85)*
The Little Bay: *SW11 (40)*
Lobster Pot *(20,28)*
Lola Rojo *(20)*
Ma Cuisine: *TW1 (30)*
La Mancha *(60)*
Nazmins Balti House *(80)*
Nosh *(24)*
The Palmerston *(32)*
Peninsular *(100)*
Petersham Hotel *(26)*
Le Pont de la Tour *(20)*
Ratchada *(16)*
Rock & Rose *(14)*
Rocket Riverside: *SW15 (28)*
The Rosendale *(30,80)*
RSJ *(24,30)*
The Rye *(36)*
San Lorenzo Fuoriporta *(20,30)*
San Remo *(25)*
Scarpetta *(25)*
Scoffers *(14)*
The Ship *(18)*
Sonny's *(20)*
The Spread Eagle *(12,16)*
Sree Krishna *(50,60)*
The Swan At The
  Globe *(14,70,200)*
tamesa@oxo *(28)*
Tentazioni *(25)*
Thailand *(40)*
3 Monkeys *(35)*
The Trafalgar Tavern *(200)*
Tree House *(60)*
Trinity *(12)*
The Victoria *(45)*
Village East *(18)*
Waterloo Brasserie *(60)*
The Wharf *(80)*
Zero Degrees *(35)*
Zero Quattro *(10,20)*

East
Addendum *(60)*
Alba *(50)*
L'Anima *(14,6)*
Barcelona Tapas: *EC4 (50); Beaufort Hs,
  St Botolph St EC3 (75)*
Bertorelli's: *EC3 (36)*
Bevis Marks *(80)*
Bistrotheque *(54,60)*
Bleeding Heart *(20,35,45)*
Boisdale of Bishopsgate *(42)*
Bonds *(8,8,16)*
Café du Marché *(30,60)*
Café Spice Namaste *(40)*
Cellar Gascon *(20)*
Chamberlain's *(65)*
The Chancery *(25,30)*
Chez Gérard: *EC2 (12); EC3 (45)*
Cicada *(24)*
City Miyama *(4,4,8,10)*
The Clerkenwell Dining
  Room *(40)*
Clifton *(160)*
Club Mangia *(80)*
Cottons: *EC1 (70)*
Curve *(30)*
Dans le Noir *(60)*
Devonshire Terrace *(10)*
$ *(12)*
The Don *(24,12)*
The Drunken Monkey *(10,30)*
Fabrizio *(18)*
El Faro *(60)*
Faulkner's *(18)*
Fish Central *(60)*
The Fox *(10-12)*
George & Vulture *(14,16,24)*
The Hoxton Grille: *EC2 (50,50)*
The Gun *(14,22)*
The Hat & Feathers *(40,30)*
Hawksmoor *(10)*
Imperial City *(12)*
Kenza *(50,15)*
Lanes *(28)*
The Larder *(18)*
Luc's Brasserie *(60)*
Malmaison Brasserie *(14,8)*
Medcalf *(18)*
The Mercer *(6-40)*
Missouri Angel *(14,14,24)*
Missouri Grill *(14)*
Moro *(14)*
Mugen *(8)*
The Narrow *(14)*
New Tayyabs *(40)*
Northbank *(30)*
Ye Olde Cheshire Cheese *(15,50)*
1 Blossom Street *(8,12,26)*
1 Lombard Street *(50)*
Pacific Oriental *(40)*
Paternoster Chop House *(14)*
The Peasant *(20)*
Piccolino: *EC2 (24)*
Plateau *(24)*

ROMANTIC

Polish Club (Ognisko Polskie)
Racine
The River Café
Star of India
Le Suquet
La Trompette
Le Vacherin
Wódka
Zuma

North
Anglo Asian Tandoori
L'Aventure
La Cage Imaginaire
The Engineer
Fig
The Flask
Frederick's
Mango Room
Le Mercury
Odette's
Oslo Court
Sardo Canale
Villa Bianca

South
A Cena
Arancia
Beauberry House
Brula
Champor-Champor
Le Chardon: SE22
Chez Bruce
The Depot
Enoteca Turi
Four O Nine
Gastro
The Glasshouse
Joanna's
Lobster Pot
Metro
Petersham Nurseries
Le Pont de la Tour
Rock & Rose
Scoffers
The Spread Eagle
Thai on the River
Tree House
Upstairs Bar

East
Beach Blanket Babylon: all branches
Bleeding Heart
Café du Marché
Club Gascon
LMNT
Moro
Les Trois Garçons
Vertigo
Wapping Food

ROOMS WITH A VIEW

Central
Fakhreldine
Foliage
Galvin at Windows
The National Dining Rooms
The Portrait
The Terrace in the Fields

West
Aquasia
Babylon
Belvedere
Café Laville
Pissarro's

South
Bincho Yakitori: SE1
Blueprint Café
Butlers Wharf Chop House
The Depot
dim T: SE1
The Duke's Head
Gourmet Pizza Company: SE1
Oxo Tower (Brass')
Oxo Tower (Rest')
Petersham Hotel
Le Pont de la Tour
Rocket Riverside: SW15
The Ship
Skylon
Stein's
The Swan At The Globe
tamesa@oxo
Tate Modern (Level 7)
Tate Modern (Level 2)
Thai Square: SW15
The Trafalgar Tavern
Upstairs Bar

East
Coq d'Argent
Curve
The Grapes
The Gun
The Narrow
Northbank
Rhodes 24
Searcy's Brasserie
Smiths (Top Floor)
Ubon
Vertigo
Yi-Ban: E16

NOTABLE WINE LISTS

Central
Adam Street
Andrew Edmunds
Arbutus
Bedford & Strand
Boisdale
Café des Amis

CUISINES

An asterisk (*) after an entry indicates exceptional or very good cooking

AMERICAN
Central
All Star Lanes *(WC1)*
Automat *(W1)*
Bodean's *(W1)*
Chicago Rib Shack *(SW1)*
Christopher's *(WC2)*
Hard Rock Café *(W1)*
Joe Allen *(WC2)*
Maxwell's *(WC2)*
Planet Hollywood *(W1)*
Pure California *(W1,WC1)*

West
All Star Lanes *(W2)*
Big Easy *(SW3)*
Bodean's *(SW6)*
Harlem *(W2)*
Lucky Seven *(W2)**
Pacific Bar and Grill *(W6)*
PJ's *(SW3)*
Sticky Fingers *(W8)*

North
Pick More Daisies *(N8)*

South
Bodean's *(SW4)*

East
All Star Lanes *(E1)*
Missouri Angel *(EC3)*
Missouri Grill *(EC3)*
Pure California *(EC4)*

BELGIAN
Central
Belgo Centraal *(WC2)*

North
Belgo Noord *(NW1)*

BRITISH, MODERN
Central
About Thyme *(SW1)*
Acorn House *(WC1)*
Adam Street *(WC2)*
Alastair Little *(W1)*
Andrew Edmunds *(W1)*
Arbutus *(W1)**
Atrium *(SW1)*
Aurora *(W1)*
The Avenue *(SW1)*
Axis *(WC2)*
Balfour *(WC1)*
Bank Westminster *(SW1)*
Bellamy's *(W1)*
Bob Bob Ricard *(W1)*
The Botanist *(SW1)*
Café du Jardin *(WC2)*
Café Emm *(W1)*
Le Caprice *(SW1)**
The Contented Vine *(SW1)*

Daylesford Organics *(SW1)*
Le Deuxième *(WC2)*
Dorchester Grill *(W1)*
The Easton *(WC1)*
Ebury Wine Bar *(SW1)*
The Fifth Floor Restaurant *(SW1)*
Footstool *(SW1)*
French House *(W1)*
The Giaconda Dining
  Room *(WC2)**
Giraffe *(WC1)*
Homage *(WC2)*
Hush *(W1)*
Indigo *(WC2)*
Inn the Park *(SW1)*
The Ivy *(WC2)*
Just St James *(SW1)*
Konstam at the Prince
  Albert *(WC1)**
The Landau *(W1)*
Langan's Brasserie *(W1)*
Lindsay House *(W1)*
The Little Square *(W1)*
maze Grill *(W1)**
Mews of Mayfair *(W1)*
Nicole's *(W1)*
The Only Running Footman *(W1)*
Oscar *(W1)*
Pantechnicon Rooms *(SW1)*
Patterson's *(W1)**
The Phoenix *(SW1)*
Pigalle Club *(W1)*
The Portrait *(WC2)*
Quaglino's *(SW1)*
The Queens Arms *(SW1)*
Refuel *(W1)*
Rhodes W1 Brasserie *(W1)*
RIBA Café *(W1)*
Rowley's *(SW1)*
Running Horse *(W1)*
Shampers *(W1)*
Sotheby's Café *(W1)**
Stanza *(W1)*
Tate Britain (Rex Whistler) *(SW1)*
The Terrace in the Fields *(WC2)*
Thomas Cubitt *(SW1)*
Tuttons *(WC2)*
The Union Café *(W1)*
Vanilla *(W1)**
Villandry *(W1)*
Vincent Rooms *(SW1)*
Wild Honey *(W1)**
The Wolseley *(W1)*

West
The Abingdon *(W8)*
Admiral Codrington *(SW3)*
The Anglesea Arms *(W6)**
The Anglesea Arms *(SW7)*
Babylon *(W8)*
Beach Blanket Babylon *(W11)*
Belvedere *(W8)*
Bibendum Oyster Bar *(SW3)*
Bistro 190 *(SW7)*
Bluebird *(SW3)*
Bowler Bar & Grill *(SW3)*
The Brackenbury *(W6)*
Brinkley's *(SW10)*

Britannia *(W8)*
The Builders Arms *(SW3)*
Bush Bar & Grill *(W12)*
Butcher's Hook *(SW6)*
The Carpenter's Arms *(W6)*
Clarke's *(W8)**
The Collection *(SW3)*
Commander *(W2)*
Coopers Arms *(SW3)*
The Cow *(W2)*
The Crown & Sceptre *(W12)*
Devonshire House *(W4)*
Duke Of Sussex *(W4)*
Duke on the Green *(SW6)*
Ealing Park Tavern *(W5)*
11 Abingdon Road *(W8)*
The Establishment *(SW6)*
The Farm *(SW6)*
First Floor *(W11)*
Fish Hook *(W4)**
Formosa Dining Room *(W9)*
The Frontline Club *(W2)*
The Havelock Tavern *(W14)**
High Road Brasserie *(W4)*
Hole in the Wall *(W4)*
Jimmy's *(SW3)*
Joe's Brasserie *(SW6)*
Julie's *(W11)*
Kensington Place *(W8)*
The Ladbroke Arms *(W11)**
Launceston Place *(W8)**
Lots Road *(SW10)*
Marco *(SW6)*
Le Metro *(SW3)*
Notting Hill Brasserie *(W11)**
Paradise by Way of Kensal
   Green *(W10)**
The Phoenix *(SW3)*
The Pilot *(W4)*
Pissarro's *(W4)*
PJ's *(SW3)*
Queen's Head *(W6)*
Raoul's Café *(W9)*
Raoul's Café & Deli *(W11)*
The Roebuck *(W4)*
The Salisbury Tavern *(SW6)*
Sam's Brasserie *(W4)*
Snows on the Green *(W6)*
Sophie's Steakhouse *(SW10)*
Stone Mason's Arms *(W6)*
Tom's Deli *(W11)*
Tom's Kitchen *(SW3)*
Vingt-Quatre *(SW10)*
The Warrington *(W9)*
The Waterway *(W9)*
The Westbourne *(W2)*
White Horse *(SW6)*
Whits *(W8)**

North

The Albion *(N1)*
Bacchus *(N1)**
The Barnsbury *(N1)**
The Betjeman Arms *(NW1)*
Bradley's *(NW3)*
The Bull *(N6)*
Café Med *(NW8)*
The Chapel *(NW1)*

Charles Lamb *(N1)*
The Clissold Arms *(N2)*
Cruse 9 *(N1)*
The Drapers Arms *(N1)*
The Duke of Cambridge *(N1)*
The Elk in the Woods *(N1)*
The Engineer *(NW1)*
Frederick's *(N1)*
Freemasons Arms *(NW3)*
The Haven *(N20)*
The Horseshoe *(NW3)*
The House *(N1)*
The Island *(NW10)*
The Junction Tavern *(NW5)*
Kings Cross Grille *(N1)*
The Lansdowne *(NW1)*
The Lock Dining Bar *(N17)*
The Lord Palmerston *(NW5)*
Mango Room *(NW1)*
Market *(NW1)**
Mosaica *(N22)**
The North London Tavern *(NW6)*
The Northgate *(N1)*
Odette's *(NW1)*
The Old Bull & Bush *(NW3)*
The Pumphouse *(N8)*
The Three Crowns *(N16)**
Walnut *(NW6)*
Water House *(N1)*
The Wells *(NW3)*
The Wet Fish Cafe *(NW6)*
Landmark (Winter Gdn) *(NW1)*

South

The Abbeville *(SW4)*
Alma *(SW18)*
Archduke Wine Bar *(SE1)*
Benugo *(SE1)*
Blueprint Café *(SE1)*
The Bridge *(SW13)*
The Brown Dog *(SW13)*
Buchan's *(SW11)*
Cantina Vinopolis *(SE1)*
Chapter Two *(SE3)**
Chez Bruce *(SW17)**
The Clarence *(SW12)*
The Dartmouth Arms *(SE23)*
The Depot *(SW14)*
The Duke's Head *(SW15)*
Earl Spencer *(SW18)**
The East Hill *(SW18)*
Emile's *(SW15)**
The Fentiman Arms *(SW8)*
The Fire Stables *(SW19)*
Four O Nine *(SW9)*
Franklins *(SE11, SE22)*
The Freemasons *(SW18)*
Garrison *(SE1)*
The Glasshouse *(TW9)**
Grafton House *(SW4)*
The Greyhound at
   Battersea *(SW11)*
Harrison's *(SW12)*
The Hartley *(SE1)*
The Inn at Kew Gardens *(TW9)*
Inside *(SE10)**
Lamberts *(SW12)**
The Lavender *(SE11, SW11)*

The Mason's Arms (SW8)*
Menier Chocolate Factory (SE1)
Mezzanine (SE1)
The Normanby (SW15)*
Oxo Tower (Rest') (SE1)
The Palmerston (SE22)*
Petersham Hotel (TW10)
Petersham Nurseries (TW10)*
Phoenix Bar & Grill (SW15)*
Le Pont de la Tour (SE1)
The Prince Of Wales (SW15)*
Ransome's Dock (SW11)
The Rivington Grill (SE10)
Rock & Rose (TW9)
The Rosendale (SE21)*
RSJ (SE1)
Scoffers (SW11)
Skylon (SE1)
Sonny's (SW13)
The Spencer Arms (SW15)
The Swan At The Globe (SE1)
The Table (SE1)*
tamesa@oxo (SE1)
Tom Ilic (SW8)*
The Trafalgar Tavern (SE10)
Tree House (SW13)
Trinity (SW4)*
The Victoria (SW14)
The Wharf (TW11)

East
Addendum (EC3)
Ambassador (EC1)
Bar Bourse (EC4)
Beach Blanket Babylon (E1)
Bevis Marks (EC3)
Bistrotheque (E2)
The Boundary (E2)
The Chancery (EC4)*
Club Mangia (EC4)
Coach & Horses (EC1)
Devonshire Terrace (EC2)
The Don (EC4)*
Eastway (EC2)
The Empress of India (E9)
The Fox (EC2)
Giraffe (E1)
Gow's (EC2)
Smiths (Ground Floor) (EC1)
The Gun (E14)
The Hat & Feathers (EC1)
Hilliard (EC4)*
The Hoxton Grille (EC2)
Lanes (E1)
The Larder (EC1)
LMNT (E8)
Malmaison Brasserie (EC1)
The Mercer (EC2)
The Modern Pantry (EC1)
The Morgan Arms (E3)
Northbank (EC4)
1 Lombard Street (EC3)
The Peasant (EC1)
The Princess (EC2)
Prism (EC3)
Rhodes 24 (EC2)
The Rivington Grill (EC2)
Saf (EC2)

St Germain (EC1)
Searcy's Brasserie (EC2)
Smithfield Bar & Grill (EC1)
Smiths (Top Floor) (EC1)
Tart (EC1)
Vertigo (EC2)
Vic Naylors (EC1)
Vinoteca (EC1)
Wapping Food (E1)
The Well (EC1)*
The White Swan (EC4)

BRITISH, TRADITIONAL
Central
The Albemarle (W1)
Boisdale (SW1)
Chimes (SW1)
Fortnum's, The Fountain (W1)
Fuzzy's Grub (SW1)
The Goring Hotel (SW1)
Great Queen Street (WC2)*
Green's (SW1)
Greig's (W1)
Grenadier (SW1)
The Guinea Grill (W1)
The National Dining
   Rooms (WC2)
Odin's (W1)
Porters English Restaurant (WC2)
Quo Vadis (W1)
Rib Room (SW1)
Rules (WC2)
Scott's (W1)*
Shepherd's (SW1)
Simpsons-in-the-Strand (WC2)
Square Pie Company (WC1)
Wiltons (SW1)
The Windmill (W1)

West
Bumpkin (SW7,W11)*
The Fat Badger (W10)
Ffiona's (W8)
Hereford Road (W2)
Kensington Square Kitchen (W8)
Maggie Jones's (W8)
Princess Victoria (W12)*
S & M Café (W10)
The Windsor Castle (W8)

North
The Flask (N6)
Holly Bush (NW3)
Kenwood (Brew House) (NW3)
The Marquess Tavern (N1)*
S & M Café (N1)
St Johns (N19)

South
The Anchor & Hope (SE1)*
Butlers Wharf Chop House (SE1)
Canteen (SE1)
Roast (SE1)
The Rye (SE15)
The Trafalgar Tavern (SE10)

East
Boisdale of Bishopsgate (EC2)

Canteen *(E1)*
Cock Tavern *(EC1)*
The Fox and Anchor *(EC1)*
Fuzzy's Grub *(EC2, EC3, EC4)**
George & Vulture *(EC3)*
Hix Oyster & Chop House *(EC1)**
Medcalf *(EC1)*
The Narrow *(E14)*
Ye Olde Cheshire Cheese *(EC4)*
Paternoster Chop House *(EC4)*
The Quality Chop House *(EC1)**
S & M Café *(E1)*
St John *(EC1)**
St John Bread & Wine *(E1)**
Simpson's Tavern *(EC3)*
Square Pie Company *(E1, E14)*
Sweetings *(EC4)*
The Wine Library *(EC3)*

CZECH
North
The Czechoslovak
  Restaurant *(NW6)*

EAST & CENT. EUROPEAN
Central
Gay Hussar *(W1)*
The Wolseley *(W1)*

North
Trojka *(NW1)*

East
Kipferl *(EC1)*

FISH & SEAFOOD
Central
Back to Basics *(W1)**
Belgo Centraal *(WC2)*
Bentley's *(W1)**
Cape Town Fish Market *(W1)*
Fishworks *(W1)*
Fung Shing *(WC2)**
Green's *(SW1)*
Livebait *(WC2)*
Loch Fyne *(WC2)*
Olivomare *(SW1)**
One-O-One *(SW1)**
Pantechnicon Rooms *(SW1)*
Pescatori *(W1)*
Quaglino's *(SW1)*
Randall & Aubin *(W1)*
Rib Room *(SW1)*
Royal China Club *(W1)**
Scott's *(W1)**
Seabass *(W1)*
Seaport *(W1)*
J Sheekey *(WC2)**
J Sheekey Oyster Bar *(WC2)*
Wiltons *(SW1)*
Zilli Fish *(W1)*

West
Bibendum Oyster Bar *(SW3)*
Big Easy *(SW3)*
Chez Patrick *(W8)*
The Cow *(W2)*
Fish Hook *(W4)**

Fishworks *(SW10, SW6, W11, W4)*
Geale's *(W8)*
Mandarin Kitchen *(W2)**
Poissonnerie de l'Avenue *(SW3)**
Seabass *(W2)*
Le Suquet *(SW3)**
Tom's Place *(SW3)*

North
Belgo Noord *(NW1)*
Bradley's *(NW3)*
La Brocca *(NW6)*
Chez Liline *(N4)**
Fishworks *(N1, NW1)*
Nautilus *(NW6)**
Olympus Fish *(N3)*
Royal China Club *(NW8)**
Sargasso Sea *(N21)**
Toff's *(N10)**

South
Ev Restaurant, Bar & Deli *(SE1)*
Fish Club *(SW11)**
fish! *(SE1)*
Fishworks *(SW11, TW9)*
Gastro *(SW4)*
Livebait *(SE1)*
Lobster Pot *(SE11)*
Loch Fyne *(TW2)*
Wright Brothers *(SE1)**

East
Catch *(EC2)*
Chamberlain's *(EC3)*
Curve *(E14)*
Fish Central *(EC1)*
Fish Shop *(EC1)*
Gow's *(EC2)*
The Grapes *(E14)*
The Royal Exchange Grand
  Café *(EC3)*
Sweetings *(EC4)*

FRENCH
Central
The Admiralty *(WC2)*
Alain Ducasse *(W1)*
L'Artiste Musclé *(W1)*
L'Atelier de Joel
  Robuchon *(WC2)**
L'Autre Pied *(W1)**
The Avenue *(SW1)*
Bellamy's *(W1)*
Beotys *(WC2)*
Bord'Eaux *(W1)*
The Botanist *(SW1)*
Boudin Blanc *(W1)**
Brasserie Roux *(SW1)*
Brasserie St Jacques *(SW1)*
Café Bohème *(W1)*
Café des Amis *(WC2)*
Le Cercle *(SW1)**
The Chelsea Brasserie *(SW1)*
Chez Gérard *(SW1, W1, WC2)*
Clos Maggiore *(WC2)**
Côte *(W1)*
Criterion Grill *(W1)*
Drones *(SW1)*

The Ebury *(SW1)*
Elena's L'Étoile *(W1)*
L'Escargot *(W1)**
L'Escargot (Picasso Room) *(W1)*
Foliage *(SW1)*
Galvin at Windows *(W1)*
Galvin Bistrot de Luxe *(W1)**
Le Gavroche *(W1)**
Gordon Ramsay at
   Claridge's *(W1)*
The Greenhouse *(W1)*
Hélène Darroze *(W1)*
Hibiscus *(W1)*
Incognico *(WC2)*
Langan's Bistro *(W1)*
maze *(W1)**
Mirabelle *(W1)*
Mon Plaisir *(WC2)*
Odin's *(W1)*
L'Oranger *(SW1)*
Orrery *(W1)*
Pearl *(WC1)*
La Petite Maison *(W1)**
Pétrus *(SW1)**
Pied à Terre *(W1)**
La Poule au Pot *(SW1)*
Randall & Aubin *(W1)*
Le Relais de Venise
   L'Entrecôte *(W1)**
Rhodes W1 Restaurant *(W1)*
The Ritz Restaurant *(W1)*
Roussillon *(SW1)**
St James's Hotel And Club *(SW1)*
Sketch (Lecture Rm) *(W1)*
Sketch (Gallery) *(W1)*
The Square *(W1)**
Texture *(W1)**
La Trouvaille *(W1)**
Villandry *(W1)*
The Wallace *(W1)*

West
Ambassade de l'Ile *(SW7)*
Angelus *(W2)*
Aubergine *(SW10)*
Belvedere *(W8)*
Bibendum *(SW3)*
La Bouchée *(SW7)*
La Brasserie *(SW3)*
Brasserie St Quentin *(SW3)*
Le Café Anglais *(W2)*
The Capital Restaurant *(SW3)**
Charlotte's Place *(W5)*
Cheyne Walk Brasserie *(SW3)*
Chez Kristof *(W6)*
Chez Patrick *(W8)*
Le Colombier *(SW3)*
L'Etranger *(SW7)*
Gordon Ramsay *(SW3)**
Green Door Bar & Grill *(SW7)*
Langan's Coq d'Or Bar &
   Grill *(SW5)*
The Ledbury *(W11)**
Notting Hill Brasserie *(W11)**
Papillon *(SW3)*
Père Michel *(W2)*
The Pig's Ear *(SW3)*
Poissonnerie de l'Avenue *(SW3)**

Racine *(SW3)**
Rôtisserie Jules *(W11)*
Le Suquet *(SW3)**
Tartine *(SW3)*
Tom Aikens *(SW3)*
La Trompette *(W4)**
202 *(W11)*
Le Vacherin *(W4)**
Whits *(W8)**

North
L'Absinthe *(NW1)*
The Almeida *(N1)*
Les Associés *(N8)*
L'Aventure *(NW8)**
Bistro Aix *(N8)*
Bradley's *(NW3)*
La Cage Imaginaire *(NW3)*
Charles Lamb *(N1)*
Fig *(N1)**
Le Mercury *(N1)*
Morgan M *(N7)**
Oslo Court *(NW8)**
La Petite Auberge *(N1)*
Le Sacré-Coeur *(N1)*
Somerstown Coffee
   House *(NW1)*
The Wells *(NW3)*

South
Le Bouchon Bordelais *(SW11)*
Brasserie James *(SW12)**
Brew Wharf *(SE1)*
Brula *(TW1)*
La Buvette *(TW9)*
Le Chardon *(SE22, SW4)*
Chez Gérard *(SE1)*
Chez Lindsay *(TW10)*
Côte *(SW19, TW9)*
Gastro *(SW4)*
Gazette *(SW11, SW12)*
Lobster Pot *(SE11)*
Ma Cuisine *(SW13, TW1, TW9)*
Magdalen *(SE1)**
Mini Mundus *(SW17)*
Rick's Café *(SW17)*
The Spread Eagle *(SE10)*
Trinity Stores *(SW12)*
Upstairs Bar *(SW2)**
Waterloo Brasserie *(SE1)*

East
Bel Canto *(EC3)*
Bistrotheque *(E2)*
Bleeding Heart *(EC1)**
Le Bouchon Breton *(E1)*
Café du Marché *(EC1)**
Cellar Gascon *(EC1)*
Chez Gérard *(EC2, EC3, EC4)*
Club Gascon *(EC1)**
Comptoir Gascon *(EC1)**
Coq d'Argent *(EC2)*
Dans le Noir *(EC1)*
The Don *(EC4)**
Flâneur *(EC1)*
Green Door Bar & Grill *(EC3)*
The Gun *(E14)*
Luc's Brasserie *(EC3)*

1901 *(EC2)*
Plateau *(E14)*
Le Rendezvous du Café *(EC1)*
Rosemary Lane *(E1)**
The Royal Exchange Grand
   Café *(EC3)*
Le Saint Julien *(EC1)*
Sauterelle *(EC3)*
Les Trois Garçons *(E1)*

FUSION
Central
Archipelago *(W1)**
Asia de Cuba *(WC2)*
Nobu *(W1)**
Nobu Berkeley *(W1)*
The Providores *(W1)*
Providores (Tapa Room) *(W1)*
So *(W1)*

West
Aquasia *(SW10)*

South
Beauberry House *(SE21)*
Champor-Champor *(SE1)**
Tsunami *(SW4)**
Village East *(SE1)*

East
Ubon *(E14)*

GAME
Central
Boisdale *(SW1)*
Rules *(WC2)*
Wiltons *(SW1)*

North
San Daniele del Friuli *(N5)*

East
Boisdale of Bishopsgate *(EC2)*

GERMAN
South
Stein's *(TW10)*

GREEK
Central
Beotys *(WC2)*
Hellenik *(W1)*
Real Greek *(W1,WC2)*

West
Costa's Grill *(W8)*
Halepi *(W2)*

North
Daphne *(NW1)*
Lemonia *(NW1)*
The Real Greek *(N1)*
Retsina *(NW3)*
Vrisaki *(N22)**

South
Real Greek *(SE1, SW15)*

East
Kolossi Grill *(EC1)*
The Real Greek *(EC1)*

HUNGARIAN
Central
Gay Hussar *(W1)*

INTERNATIONAL
Central
The Avenue *(SW1)*
Balans *(W1)*
Bedford & Strand *(WC2)*
Bohème Kitchen & Bar *(W1)*
Boulevard *(WC2)*
Boxwood Café *(SW1)*
Browns *(W1,WC2)*
Café in the Crypt *(WC2)*
Caramel *(SW1)*
City Café *(SW1)*
Cork & Bottle *(WC2)*
Eat & Two Veg *(W1)*
The Forge *(WC2)*
Giraffe *(W1)*
Gordon's Wine Bar *(WC2)*
Grumbles *(SW1)*
Hardy's Brasserie *(W1)*
Michael Moore *(W1)**
Motcombs *(SW1)*
National Gallery Café *(WC2)*
Ooze *(W1)*
Oriel *(SW1)*
Papageno *(WC2)*
Pomegranates *(SW1)*
Ronnie Scott's *(W1)*
Sarastro *(WC2)*
Seven Stars *(WC2)*
Star Café *(W1)*
Stock Pot *(SW1,W1)*
Sugar Reef *(W1)*

West
The Academy *(W11)*
Annie's *(W4)*
Balans West *(SW5,W4,W8)*
Blakes *(SW7)*
Brompton Quarter Café *(SW3)*
The Cabin *(SW6)*
Café Laville *(W2)*
Chelsea Bun Diner *(SW10)*
Coopers Arms *(SW3)*
Electric Brasserie *(W11)*
The Enterprise *(SW3)*
Foxtrot Oscar *(SW3)*
The Gate *(W6)**
Giraffe *(W4,W6)*
Glaisters *(SW10)*
Mona Lisa *(SW10)*
The Scarsdale *(W8)*
606 Club *(SW10)*
Stock Pot *(SW3)*
The Swag & Tails *(SW7)*
The Thatched House *(W6)*
202 *(W11)*
The Windsor Castle *(W8)*
Wine Factory *(W11)*
Wine Gallery *(SW10)*

North
The Arches *(NW6)*
Banners *(N8)*
Browns *(N1)*
Eat & Two Veg *(N10)*
The Fox Reformed *(N16)*
Giraffe *(N1, NW3)*
The Haven *(N20)*
Hoxton Apprentice *(N1)*
The Old Bull & Bush *(NW3)*
Orange Tree *(N20)*
Petek *(N4)*
Spaniard's Inn *(NW3)*

South
Annie's *(SW13)*
Browns *(SE1)*
Tate Modern (Level 2) *(SE1)*
Delfina Studio Café *(SE1)**
Giraffe *(SE1, SW11)*
Green & Blue *(SE22)*
Hudson's *(SW15)*
Joanna's *(SE19)*
Laughing Gravy *(SE1)*
The Light House *(SW19)*
Metro *(SW4)*
Nosh *(TW1)*
Putney Station *(SW15)*
Tate Modern (Level 7) *(SE1)*
The Rye *(SE15)*
The Ship *(SW18)*
The Stonhouse *(SW4)*
Vivat Bacchus *(SE1)*
The Wharf *(TW11)*

East
Browns *(E14, EC2)*
Club Mangia *(EC4)*
Dans le Noir *(EC1)*
$ *(EC1)*
Lilly's *(E1)*
The Prince Arthur *(E8)*
Les Trois Garçons *(E1)*
Vivat Bacchus *(EC4)*

ITALIAN
Central
Al Duca *(SW1)*
Alloro *(W1)**
Amato *(W1)*
Aperitivo *(W1)*
Apsleys *(SW1)*
The Beehive *(W1)**
Bertorelli's *(W1, WC2)*
Caffè Caldesi *(W1)*
Caffé Vergnano *(WC2)**
Caldesi *(W1)*
Camerino *(W1)*
Caraffini *(SW1)*
Cecconi's *(W1)*
Ciao Bella *(WC1)*
Cipriani *(W1)*
Como Lario *(SW1)*
Il Convivio *(SW1)*
Da Scalzo *(SW1)*
Dehesa *(W1)**
Delfino *(W1)**
5 Cavendish Square *(W1)*

Franco's *(SW1)*
Getti *(SW1, W1)*
Giardinetto *(W1)*
Giusto *(W1)*
Gran Paradiso *(SW1)*
Incognico *(WC2)*
L'Incontro *(SW1)*
Latium *(W1)**
Little Italy *(W1)*
Locanda Locatelli *(W1)**
Luciano *(SW1)*
Mimmo d'Ischia *(SW1)*
Mosaico *(W1)*
Murano *(W1)*
Number Twelve *(WC1)*
Oliveto *(SW1)**
Olivo *(SW1)**
Orso *(WC2)*
Ottolenghi *(SW1)**
Paolina Café *(WC1)**
Paradiso Olivelli *(W1)*
Passione *(W1)*
Pasta Brown *(WC2)*
Pescatori *(W1)*
Piccolino *(W1)*
Pizza on the Park *(SW1)*
La Porchetta Pizzeria *(WC1)*
Quirinale *(SW1)**
Ristorante Semplice *(W1)**
Sale e Pepe *(SW1)*
Salt Yard *(W1)**
Santini *(SW1)*
Sapori *(WC2)*
Sardo *(W1)**
Sartoria *(W1)*
Serafino *(W1)*
Signor Sassi *(SW1)*
Signor Zilli *(W1)*
Spacca Napoli *(W1)**
La Spiga *(W1)*
Theo Randall *(W1)*
Toto's *(SW1)*
2 Amici *(SW1)*
2 Veneti *(W1)*
Uno *(SW1)**
Vapiano *(W1)*
Vasco & Piero's Pavilion *(W1)*
Via Condotti *(W1)*
Il Vicolo *(SW1)*
Vivezza *(SW1)*
Volt *(SW1)*
Zafferano *(SW1)*
Zilli Fish *(W1)*

West
L'Accento Italiano *(W2)*
Aglio e Olio *(SW10)**
The Ark *(W8)*
Arturo *(W2)*
Assaggi *(W2)**
Bianco Nero *(W6)*
Brunello *(SW7)*
Buona Sera *(SW3)*
Carpaccio's *(SW3)*
Cibo *(W14)*
Da Mario *(SW7)*
Daphne's *(SW3)**
De Cecco *(SW6)*

La Delizia Limbara (SW3)
Edera (W11)
11 Abingdon Road (W8)
Elistano (SW3)
Esenza (W11)
Il Falconiere (SW7)
La Famiglia (SW10)
Frankie's Italian Bar & Grill (SW3)
Frankie's Italian Bar & Grill (W4)
Frantoio (SW10)
Friends (SW10)
The Green Olive (W9)
Locanda Ottomezzo (W8)
Lucio (SW3)
Luna Rossa (SW3)
Made in Italy (SW3)
Manicomio (SW3)
Mediterraneo (W11)
Montpeliano (SW7)
Mulberry Street (W2)
Napulé (SW6)
Nuovi Sapori (SW6)
The Oak (W2)*
Osteria Basilico (W11)*
Osteria dell'Arancio (SW10)
Ottolenghi (W11,W8)*
Il Pagliaccio (SW6)
Pappa Ciccia (SW6)*
Pellicano (SW3)
Picasso's (SW3)
Il Portico (W8)
The Red Pepper (W9)
Riccardo's (SW3)
The River Café (W6)*
Rossopomodoro (SW10,W11)
San Lorenzo (SW3)
Santa Lucia (SW10)
Scalini (SW3)*
Spago (SW7)
Timo (W8)
Trenta (W2)
Vino Rosso (W4)*
Ziani (SW3)

North

L'Artista (NW11)
Il Bacio (N16, N5)
La Brocca (NW6)
Cantina Italia (N1)
La Collina (NW1)
Fifteen Restaurant (N1)
Fifteen Trattoria (N1)
Fratelli la Bufala (NW3)
Marine Ices (NW3)
Metrogusto (N1)
Osteria Emilia (NW3)
Osteria Stecca (NW8)
Ottolenghi (N1)*
Philpotts Mezzaluna (NW2)*
Pizzeria Oregano (N1)
La Porchetta Pizzeria (N1, N4, NW1)
Salt House (NW8)
The Salusbury (NW6)*
San Carlo (N6)
San Daniele del Friuli (N5)
Sardo Canale (NW1)
Sarracino (NW6)*
Villa Bianca (NW3)

The York & Albany (NW1)
Zuccato (NW3)

South

A Cena (TW1)*
Al Forno (SW15, SW19)
Antipasto & Pasta (SW11)
Arancia (SE16)*
Buona Sera (SW11)
Cantina del Ponte (SE1)
Il Cantuccio di Pulcinella (SW11)
Castello (SE16)
Donna Margherita (SW11)*
Enoteca Turi (SW15)*
Esca (SE16)
Frankie's Italian Bar & Grill (SW15)
Isola del Sole (SW15)*
La Lanterna (SE1)
Mooli (SW4)
Numero Uno (SW11)
Pappa Ciccia (SW15)*
Piccolino (SW17, SW19)
Pizza Metro (SW11)*
Le Querce (SE23)*
Rick's Café (SW17)
Riva (SW13)*
San Lorenzo Fuoriporta (SW19)
San Remo (SW13)
Scarpetta (TW11)*
Tentazioni (SE1)*
The Three Bridges (SW8)
Trinity Stores (SW12)
Zero Quattro (SW19)

East

Alba (EC1)
Amerigo Vespucci (E14)
L'Anima (EC2)*
Bertorelli's (EC3, EC4)
Il Bordello (E1)*
Caravaggio (EC3)
Fabrizio (EC1)*
La Figa (E14)*
Flâneur (EC1)
Manicomio (EC2)
1 Blossom Street (E1)
E Pellicci (E2)
Piccolino (EC2)
La Porchetta Pizzeria (EC1)
Quadrato (E14)
Refettorio (EC4)
Stringray Globe Café (E2)*
Taberna Etrusca (EC4)
Terranostra (EC4)
Zuccato (EC4)

MEDITERRANEAN

Central

About Thyme (SW1)
Bistro 1 (W1,WC2)
Dover Street Restaurant & Bar (W1)
The Fifth Floor Café (SW1)
Hummus Bros (W1,WC1)
The Norfolk Arms (WC1)
Rocket (W1)
St Alban (SW1)

Salt Yard (W1)*
06 St Chad's Place (WC1)
Truc Vert (W1)
Tuttons (WC2)

West
The Atlas (SW6)*
Cochonnet (W9)
Cumberland Arms (W14)
Del'Aziz (SW6)
11 Abingdon Road (W8)
Elistano (SW3)
Little Bay (SW6)
Locanda Ottomezzo (W8)
Made in Italy (SW3)
Mediterraneo (W11)
Priory House (W14)
Raoul's Café (W9)
Raoul's Café & Deli (W11)
Snows on the Green (W6)
The Swan (W4)
Tom's Deli (W11)
Troubadour (SW5)
William IV (NW10)*

North
Café Med (NW8)
Camden Brasserie (NW1)
The Chapel (NW1)
The Little Bay (NW6)
Mem & Laz (N1)
Petek (N4)
The Pumphouse (N8)
Queen's Head & Artichoke (NW1)

South
Bermondsey Kitchen (SE1)
Cantina del Ponte (SE1)
Cantina Vinopolis (SE1)
Fish in a Tie (SW11)
The Fox & Hounds (SW11)*
The Little Bay (SW11)
Oxo Tower (Brass') (SE1)
Rapscallion (SW4)
Rocket Riverside (SW15)
The Wharf (TW11)

East
Ambassador (EC1)
Bonds (EC2)
The Clerkenwell Dining Room (EC1)
The Eagle (EC1)
Eyre Brothers (EC2)*
Flâneur (EC1)
The Little Bay (EC1)
The Peasant (EC1)
Portal (EC1)
Rocket (EC2)
Vinoteca (EC1)
The Zetter (EC1)

ORGANIC
Central
Acorn House (WC1)
Daylesford Organics (SW1)

West
Tom's Place (SW3)

North
The Duke of Cambridge (N1)
Holly Bush (NW3)
Hugo's (NW6)
Walnut (NW6)
Water House (N1)

South
The Hartley (SE1)

East
Smiths (Dining Rm) (EC1)
Saf (EC2)
Story Deli (E1)*

POLISH
West
Daquise (SW7)
Knaypa (W6)
Polish Club (Ognisko Polskie) (SW7)
Patio (W12)
Wódka (W8)

South
Baltic (SE1)

PORTUGUESE
West
Lisboa Pâtisserie (W10)*

South
Bar Estrela (SW8)

East
Portal (EC1)

RUSSIAN
North
Trojka (NW1)

East
Potemkin (EC1)

SCANDINAVIAN
Central
Garbo's (W1)
Nordic Bakery (W1)

SCOTTISH
Central
Albannach (WC2)
Boisdale (SW1)

South
Buchan's (SW11)

East
Boisdale of Bishopsgate (EC2)

SPANISH
Central
Barrafina (W1)*
Café España (W1)
Cigala (WC1)

Dehesa *(W1)**
Fino *(W1)**
Goya *(SW1)*
Navarro's *(W1)*
The Norfolk Arms *(WC1)*
El Pirata *(W1)*
Salt Yard *(W1)**
La Tasca *(WC2)*

West
Cambio de Tercio *(SW5)**
Duke Of Sussex *(W4)*
Galicia *(W10)*
L-Restaurant & Bar *(W8)*
La Rueda *(SW6)*
La Tasca *(W4)*
Tendido Cero *(SW5)*
Tendido Cuatro *(SW6)**

North
Camino *(N1)*
Don Pepe *(NW8)*
The Islington Tapas Bar *(N1)*
El Parador *(NW1)*

South
Barcelona Tapas *(SE22)*
don Fernando's *(TW9)*
Lola Rojo *(SW11)*
La Mancha *(SW15)*
Meson don Felipe *(SE1)*
Rebato's *(SW8)*
Rick's Café *(SW17)*
El Rincón Latino *(SW4)*
La Rueda *(SW4)*
Tapas Brindisa *(SE1)**

East
Barcelona Tapas *(EC3, EC4)*
Eyre Brothers *(EC2)**
El Faro *(E14)**
Moro *(EC1)**
Pinchito *(EC1)**
La Tasca *(E14, EC2)*

STEAKS & GRILLS
Central
Black & Blue *(W1)*
Bodean's *(W1)*
Chez Gérard *(SW1,W1,WC2)*
Christopher's *(WC2)*
Gaucho Grill *(W1,WC2)**
The Guinea Grill *(W1)*
Rowley's *(SW1)*
Wolfe's *(WC2)*

West
Black & Blue *(SW7,W8)*
Bodean's *(SW6)*
Bowler Bar & Grill *(SW3)*
El Gaucho *(SW3, SW7)**
Gaucho Grill *(SW3)**
Haché *(SW10)**
Notting Grill *(W11)**
Popeseye *(W14)**
Rôtisserie Jules *(SW7)*
Sophie's Steakhouse *(SW10)*

North
Black & Blue *(NW3)*
Camden Brasserie *(NW1)*
Gaucho Grill *(NW3)**
Haché *(NW1)**
Rôtisserie *(HA5, N20, NW6, NW8)*

South
Barnes Grill *(SW13)*
Bermondsey Kitchen *(SE1)*
Black & Blue *(SE1)*
Bodean's *(SW4)*
Butcher & Grill *(SW11, SW19)*
Chez Gérard *(SE1)*
Gaucho Grill *(SE1,TW10)**
Kew Grill *(TW9)*
La Pampa *(SW11)*
Popeseye *(SW15)**

East
Buen Ayre *(E8)**
Chez Gérard *(EC2, EC3, EC4)*
Smiths (Dining Rm) *(EC1)*
Gaucho Grill *(E14, EC2, EC3)**
Smiths (Ground Floor) *(EC1)*
Hawksmoor *(E1)**
Lilly's *(E1)*
Missouri Grill *(EC3)*
Simpson's Tavern *(EC3)*
Smithfield Bar & Grill *(EC1)*
Smiths (Top Floor) *(EC1)*

SWISS
Central
St Moritz *(W1)*

VEGETARIAN
Central
Eat & Two Veg *(W1)*
Food for Thought *(WC2)**
India Club *(WC2)*
Malabar Junction *(WC1)**
Masala Zone *(W1)*
Mildred's *(W1)*
Ragam *(W1)**
Rasa *(W1)**
Rasa Maricham *(WC1)**
Roussillon *(SW1)**
Sagar *(W1)**
Woodlands *(SW1,W1)*

West
Blah! Blah! Blah! *(W12)*
Blue Elephant *(SW6)*
The Gate *(W6)**
Masala Zone *(SW5,W2)*
Sagar *(W6)**
Woodlands *(W4)*

North
Chutneys *(NW1)*
Diwana Bhel-Poori House *(NW1)*
Geeta *(NW6)**
Jashan *(HA0)**
Kovalam *(NW6)**
Manna *(NW3)*
Masala Zone *(N1)*
Rani *(N3)*

Rasa (N16)*
Rasa Travancore (N16)*
Sakonis (HA0)*
Vijay (NW6)*
Woodlands (NW3)

South
Ganapati (SE15)*
Kastoori (SW17)*
Le Pont de la Tour (SE1)
Sagar (TW1)*
Sree Krishna (SW17)*

East
Carnevale (EC1)
The Place Below (EC2)*
Saf (EC2)
Vanilla Black (EC4)

AFTERNOON TEA
Central
Brasserie Roux (SW1)
The Fifth Floor Café (SW1)
Fortnum's, The Fountain (W1)
Ladurée (SW1,W1)*
Napket (W1)
Pâtisserie Valerie (SW1,W1)
Richoux (W1)
The Ritz Restaurant (W1)
Royal Academy (W1)
Sketch (Parlour) (W1)
Villandry (W1)
The Wolseley (W1)
Yauatcha (W1)*

West
Daquise (SW7)
Napket (SW3)
Pâtisserie Valerie (SW3,W8)
Richoux (SW3)

North
Richoux (NW8)

BURGERS, ETC
Central
Black & Blue (W1)
Diner (W1)
Eagle Bar Diner (W1)*
Ed's Easy Diner (W1,WC2)
Fine Burger Company (W1)
Gourmet Burger Kitchen (W1, WC2)
Hamburger Union (W1,WC2)
Hard Rock Café (W1)
Joe Allen (WC2)
Kettners (W1)
Maxwell's (WC2)
Planet Hollywood (W1)
Tootsies (W1)
The Ultimate Burger (W1,WC1)
Wolfe's (WC2)

West
Big Easy (SW3)
Black & Blue (SW7,W8)
Byron (W8)
Electric Brasserie (W11)

Gourmet Burger Kitchen (SW5, SW6, SW7,W11,W2,W4)
Ground (W4)*
Haché (SW10)*
Henry J Beans (SW3)
Lucky Seven (W2)*
Notting Grill (W11)
Pacific Bar and Grill (W6)
PJ's (SW3)
Sticky Fingers (W8)
Tootsies (W11,W4)

North
Black & Blue (NW3)
The Diner (NW1)
Fine Burger Company (N1, N10, NW3)
Gourmet Burger Kitchen (NW3)
Haché (NW1)*
Hamburger Union (N1)
Natural Burger Co & Grill (NW8)*
Tootsies (NW3)

South
Black & Blue (SE1)
Dexter's Grill (SW17)
Dexters (SW4)
Fine Burger Company (SW12)
Gourmet Burger Kitchen (SW11, SW15, SW4)
Tootsies (SW15, SW19)

East
The Diner (EC2)
Smiths (Dining Rm) (EC1)
$ (EC1)
Gourmet Burger Kitchen (EC4)
Smithfield Bar & Grill (EC1)

CRÊPES
South
Chez Lindsay (TW10)

FISH & CHIPS
Central
Fryer's Delight (WC1)
Golden Hind (W1)*
North Sea Fish (WC1)*
Rock & Sole Plaice (WC2)*
Seafresh (SW1)

West
Costa's Fish Restaurant (W8)*
Geale's (W8)
Tom's Place (SW3)

North
Nautilus (NW6)*
Seashell (NW1)*
Toff's (N10)*
Two Brothers (N3)*

South
Brady's (SW18)
Fish Club (SW11)*
Olley's (SE24)*
The Sea Cow (SE22)

East
Ark Fish *(E18)**
Faulkner's *(E8)**

ICE CREAM
North
Marine Ices *(NW3)*

PIZZA
Central
Delfino *(W1)**
Fire & Stone *(WC2)*
Giusto *(W1)*
Kettners *(W1)*
Oliveto *(SW1)**
Paradiso Olivelli *(W1,WC1)*
Piccolino *(W1)*
Pizza on the Park *(SW1)*
La Porchetta Pizzeria *(WC1)*
Rocket *(W1)*
Sapori *(WC2)*
La Spiga *(W1)*

West
Basilico *(SW6)**
Buona Sera *(SW3)*
Cochonnet *(W9)*
Da Mario *(SW7)*
La Delizia Limbara *(SW3)*
Eco *(W4)*
Firezza *(W11,W4)**
Frankie's Italian Bar & Grill *(SW3,W4)*
Friends *(SW10)*
Made in Italy *(SW3)*
Mulberry Street *(W2)*
The Oak *(W2)**
Osteria Basilico *(W11)**
(Ciro's) Pizza Pomodoro *(SW3)*
Spago *(SW7)*

North
Il Bacio *(N16,N5)*
Basilico *(N1,NW3)**
Cantina Italia *(N1)*
Firezza *(N1)**
Furnace *(N1)*
Marine Ices *(NW3)*
Pizzeria Oregano *(N1)*
La Porchetta Pizzeria *(N1,N4,NW1)*

South
Al Forno *(SW15,SW19)*
Amano Café *(SE1)**
Basilico *(SW11,SW14)**
Buona Sera *(SW11)*
Castello *(SE16)*
Eco *(SW4)*
Firezza *(SW11,SW18)**
Franco Manca *(SW9)**
Frankie's Italian Bar & Grill *(SW15)*
Gourmet Pizza Company *(SE1)*
The Gowlett *(SE15)**
La Lanterna *(SE1)*
Paradiso Olivelli *(SE1)*
Piccolino *(SW17,SW19)*
Pizza Metro *(SW11)**
Rocket Riverside *(SW15)*

Zero Degrees *(SE3)*

East
Il Bordello *(E1)**
Gourmet Pizza Company *(E14)*
Piccolino *(EC2)*
(Ciro's) Pizza Pomodoro *(EC2)*
La Porchetta Pizzeria *(EC1)*
Rocket *(EC2)*
Story Deli *(E1)**

SANDWICHES, CAKES, ETC
Central
Amato *(W1)*
Apostrophe *(SW1,W1,WC2)**
Aubaine *(W1)*
Baker & Spice *(SW1)**
Bar Italia *(W1)*
Benugo *(W1)*
Crussh *(W1)*
Fernandez & Wells *(W1)**
Flat White *(W1)**
La Fromagerie Café *(W1)**
Fuzzy's Grub *(SW1)**
Just Falafs *(W1,WC2)**
Konditor & Cook *(W1,WC1)**
Ladurée *(SW1,W1)**
Leon *(W1,WC2)*
Maison Bertaux *(W1)*
Monmouth Coffee Company *(WC2)**
Napket *(W1)*
Le Pain Quotidien *(W1)*
Pâtisserie Valerie *(SW1,W1,WC2)*
Paul *(W1,WC2)*
Richoux *(W1)*
Royal Academy *(W1)*
Salade *(W1)*
Sketch (Parlour) *(W1)*

West
Aubaine *(SW3)*
Baker & Spice *(SW3)**
Benugo *(SW7)*
Bluebird Café *(SW3)*
Crussh *(W12,W8)*
Gail's Bread *(W11)**
Leon *(SW3)*
Lisboa Pâtisserie *(W10)**
Napket *(SW3)*
Le Pain Quotidien *(SW3,SW7,W8)*
Pâtisserie Valerie *(SW3,W2,W8)*
Paul *(SW7)*
Richoux *(SW3)*
Salade *(W2)*
Tom's Deli *(W11)*
Troubadour *(SW5)*

North
Baker & Spice *(NW6,W9)**
Chamomile *(NW3)*
Gail's Bread *(NW3)**
Hugo's *(NW6)*
Kenwood (Brew House) *(NW3)*
Le Pain Quotidien *(NW1)*
Paul *(NW3)*
Richoux *(NW8)*

South
 Amano *(SE1)**
Boiled Egg & Soldiers *(SW11)*
Caffè Vergnano *(SE1)**
Fuzzy's Grub *(SE1)**
Leon *(SE1)*
Monmouth Coffee
  Company *(SE1)**
Le Pain Quotidien *(SE1)*

East
Apostrophe *(EC2, EC4)**
Benugo *(EC1)*
Brick Lane Beigel Bake *(E1)**
Crussh *(E14, EC3, EC4)*
Fuzzy's Grub *(EC2, EC3, EC4)**
Konditor & Cook *(EC3)**
Leon *(E1, E14, EC4)*
Pâtisserie Valerie *(E1)*
Paul *(EC4)*
Salade *(EC4)*
Spianata *(E1, EC1, EC2, EC3, EC4)**

SALADS
Central
Just Falafs *(W1, WC2)**
Le Pain Quotidien *(WC1)*
Pure California *(W1, WC1)*
Salade *(W1)*
Vital Ingredient *(W1)*

West
Beirut Express *(SW7, W2)**
Salade *(W2)*

East
Chop'd *(EC3)**
Salade *(EC4)*
Vital Ingredient *(EC4)*

ARGENTINIAN
Central
Gaucho Grill *(W1, WC2)**

West
El Gaucho *(SW3, SW7)**
Gaucho Grill *(SW3)**

North
Gaucho Grill *(NW3)**

South
Gaucho Grill *(SE1, TW10)**
La Pampa *(SW11)*
Santa Maria del Sur *(SW8)**

East
Buen Ayre *(E8)**
Gaucho Grill *(E14, EC2, EC3)**
Green Door Bar & Grill *(EC3)*

BRAZILIAN
West
Rodizio Rico *(W2)*

North
Rodizio Rico *(N1)*

CUBAN
Central
Floridita *(W1)*

West
La Bodeguita del Medio *(W8)*

MEXICAN/TEXMEX
Central
Café Pacifico *(WC2)*
Texas Embassy Cantina *(SW1)*
Wahaca *(WC2)*

West
Crazy Homies *(W2)**
Taqueria *(W11)*

North
Mestizo *(NW1)*

East
Green & Red Bar & Cantina *(E1)**

SOUTH AMERICAN
North
Sabor *(N1)*

South
Las Iguanas *(SE1)*
El Vergel *(SE1)**

AFRO-CARIBBEAN
Central
The Terrace in the Fields *(WC2)*

West
Glistening Waters *(TW8)*

North
Cottons *(NW1)*
Mango Room *(NW1)*

East
Cottons *(EC1)*

MOROCCAN
Central
Momo *(W1)*
Original Tajines *(W1)*
Souk Medina *(WC2)*

West
Adams Café *(W12)*
Pasha *(SW7)*

NORTH AFRICAN
Central
Souk Medina *(WC2)*

West
Del'Aziz *(SW6)*

East
Kenza *(EC2)*

SOUTH AFRICAN
South
Chakalaka *(SW15)*

TUNISIAN
West
Adams Café *(W12)*

EGYPTIAN
North
Ali Baba *(NW1)**

ISRAELI
Central
Gaby's *(WC2)*

North
Harry Morgan's *(NW8)*
Solly's *(NW11)*

KOSHER
Central
Reubens *(W1)*

North
Kaifeng *(NW4)*
Solly's *(NW11)*

East
Bevis Marks *(EC3)*

LEBANESE
Central
Al Hamra *(W1)*
Al Sultan *(W1)**
Beiteddine *(SW1)*
Fairuz *(W1)*
Fakhreldine *(W1)*
Ishbilia *(SW1)**
Levant *(W1)*
Maroush *(W1)*
Noura *(SW1,W1)*
Ranoush *(SW1)*

West
Al-Waha *(W2)**
Beirut Express *(SW7,W2)**
Chez Marcelle *(W14)**
Fresco *(W2)**
Levantine *(W2)*
Maroush *(SW3,W2)*
Randa *(W8)*
Ranoush *(SW3,W2,W8)*
Simply Lebanese *(SW7)*

East
Kenza *(EC2)*

MIDDLE EASTERN
North
Solly's *(NW11)*

South
Esca *(SW4)*

PERSIAN
West
Alounak *(W14,W2)*
Kandoo *(W2)*
Mohsen *(W14)**

South
Dish Dash *(SW12)*

SYRIAN
West
Abu Zaad *(W12)**

TURKISH
Central
Cyprus Mangal *(SW1)**
Efes II *(W1)*
Kazan *(SW1)**
Ozer *(W1)*
Sofra *(W1,WC2)*
Tas *(WC1)*

West
Best Mangal *(W14)**
Iznik Kaftan *(SW3)*

North
Beyoglu *(NW3)*
Gallipoli *(N1)*
Gem *(N1)**
Izgara *(N3)*
Petek *(N4)*
Shish *(NW2)*
Sofra *(NW8)*

South
Ev Restaurant, Bar & Deli *(SE1)*
Tas *(SE1)*
Tas Pide *(SE1)*

East
Haz *(E1, EC3)*
Kazan *(EC3)**
Mangal Ocakbasi *(E8)**
Shish *(EC1)*
Sofra *(EC1)*
Tas *(EC1)*

AFGHANI
North
Afghan Kitchen *(N1)**

BURMESE
West
Mandalay *(W2)**

CHINESE
Central
Baozi Inn *(WC2)*
Bar Shu *(W1)**
China Tang *(W1)*
The Chinese Experience *(W1)*
Chuen Cheng Ku *(W1)*
Fung Shing *(WC2)**
Golden Dragon *(W1)*
Hakkasan *(W1)**
Harbour City *(W1)**
Hunan *(SW1)**
Imperial China *(WC2)*
Jade Garden *(W1)*
Jenny Lo's Tea House *(SW1)*
Joy King Lau *(WC2)*
Kai Mayfair *(W1)**
Ken Lo's Memories *(SW1)**

Mekong *(SW1)*
Mr Chow *(SW1)*
Mr Kong *(WC2)*
New Mayflower *(W1)*
New World *(W1)*
Princess Garden *(W1)*
Royal China *(W1)*
Royal China Club *(W1)*
Shanghai Blues *(WC1)*
Taman Gang *(WC1)*
Wong Kei *(W1)*
Yauatcha *(W1)*
Yming *(W1)*

West
Choys *(SW3)*
The Four Seasons *(W2)*
Good Earth *(SW3)*
Ken Lo's Memories of
   China *(W8)*
Made in China *(SW10)*
Magic Wok *(W2)*
Mandarin Kitchen *(W2)*
Min Jiang *(W8)*
Mr Wing *(SW5)*
New Culture Revolution *(SW3,
   W11)*
North China *(W3)*
Pearl Liang *(W2)*
Royal China *(W2, SW6)*
Stick & Bowl *(W8)*
Taiwan Village *(SW6)*
Yi-Ban *(SW6)*

North
Alisan *(HA9)*
Goldfish *(NW3)*
Good Earth *(NW7)*
Gung-Ho *(NW6)*
Kaifeng *(NW4)*
New Culture Revolution *(N1)*
Phoenix Palace *(NW1)*
Royal China Club *(NW8)*
Sakonis *(HA0)*
Singapore Garden *(NW6)*
Snazz Sichuan *(NW1)*
Weng Wah House *(NW3)*

South
Bayee Village *(SW19)*
China Boulevard *(SW18)*
Dalchini *(SW19)*
Dragon Castle *(SE17)*
Four Regions *(TW9)*
O'Zon *(TW1)*
Peninsular *(SE10)*
Royal China *(SW15)*

East
The Drunken Monkey *(E1)*
Imperial City *(EC3)*
Lotus Chinese Floating
   Restaurant *(E14)*
Royal China *(E14)*
Shanghai *(E8)*
Yi-Ban *(E16)*

CHINESE, DIM SUM
Central
Cha Cha Moon *(W1)*
The Chinese Experience *(W1)*
Chuen Cheng Ku *(W1)*
dim T *(W1)*
The Electric Birdcage *(SW1)*
Golden Dragon *(W1)*
Hakkasan *(W1)*
Harbour City *(W1)*
Imperial China *(WC2)*
Jade Garden *(W1)*
Joy King Lau *(WC2)*
New World *(W1)*
ping pong *(W1)*
Royal China *(W1)*
Royal China Club *(W1)*
Shanghai Blues *(WC1)*
Yauatcha *(W1)*

West
Pearl Liang *(W2)*
ping pong *(W2)*
Royal China *(W2, SW6)*
Yi-Ban *(SW6)*

North
Alisan *(HA9)*
dim T *(N6, NW3)*
Phoenix Palace *(NW1)*
Ping Pong *(NW3)*
Royal China Club *(NW8)*
Weng Wah House *(NW3)*

South
China Boulevard *(SW18)*
dim T *(SE1)*
Dragon Castle *(SE17)*
ping pong *(SE1)*
Royal China *(SW15)*

East
D Sum 2 *(EC4)*
The Drunken Monkey *(E1)*
Lotus Chinese Floating
   Restaurant *(E14)*
Ping Pong *(E1)*
Royal China *(E14)*
Shanghai *(E8)*
Yi-Ban *(E16)*

INDIAN
Central
Amaya *(SW1)*
Benares *(W1)*
Café Lazeez *(W1)*
Chor Bizarre *(W1)*
Chowki *(W1)*
The Cinnamon Club *(SW1)*
Gaylord *(W1)*
Gopal's of Soho *(W1)*
Imli *(W1)*
India Club *(WC2)*
Malabar Junction *(WC1)*
Masala Zone *(W1)*
Mela *(WC2)*
Mint Leaf *(SW1)*
Moti Mahal *(WC2)*

La Porte des Indes *(W1)*
Ragam *(W1)**
Red Fort *(W1)**
Sagar *(W1)**
Salaam Namaste *(WC1)*
Sitaaray *(WC2)**
Tamarind *(W1)**
Veeraswamy *(W1)**
Woodlands *(SW1,W1)*

West

Agni *(W6)**
Anarkali *(W6)**
Bombay Bicycle Club *(W11)**
Bombay Brasserie *(SW7)*
Bombay Palace *(W2)**
Brilliant *(UB2)**
Chutney Mary *(SW10)**
Durbar *(W2)*
Five Hot Chillies *(HA0)**
Green Chilli *(W6)*
Haandi *(SW3)*
Indian Zing *(W6)**
kare kare *(SW5)*
Karma *(W14)**
Khan's *(W2)**
Khan's of Kensington *(SW7)*
Madhu's *(UB1)**
Malabar *(W8)**
Masala Zone *(SW5,W2)*
Memories of India *(SW7)*
Mirch Masala *(UB1,W14)**
Monty's *(SW6,W13,W5)*
Noor Jahan *(SW5,W2)**
The Painted Heron *(SW10)**
Rasoi Vineet Bhatia *(SW3)**
Sagar *(W6)**
Shikara *(SW3)**
Star of India *(SW5)**
Tandoori Lane *(SW6)**
Urban Turban *(W2)*
Vama *(SW10)**
Woodlands *(W4)*
Zaika *(W8)**

North

Anglo Asian Tandoori *(N16)**
Atma *(NW3)**
Bombay Bicycle Club *(NW3)**
Chutneys *(NW1)*
Diwana Bhel-Poori House *(NW1)*
Emni *(N1)*
Eriki *(NW3)**
Geeta *(NW6)**
Great Nepalese *(NW1)**
Jashan *(HA0)**
Kovalam *(NW6)**
Masala Zone *(N1)*
The Parsee *(N19)**
Rani *(N3)*
Rooburoo *(N1)*
Sakonis *(HA0)**
Vijay *(NW6)**
Woodlands *(NW3)*
Zaffrani *(N1)*

South

Babur Brasserie *(SE23)**

Bengal Clipper *(SE1)**
Bombay Bicycle Club *(SW12)**
Chutney *(SW18)**
Dalchini *(SW19)**
Everest Inn *(SE3)*
Ganapati *(SE15)**
Holy Cow *(SW11)**
Hot Stuff *(SW8)**
Indian Ocean *(SW17)*
Kastoori *(SW17)**
Kennington Tandoori *(SE11)*
Ma Goa *(SW15)**
Mango & Silk *(SW14)*
Mango Tree *(SE1)**
Mela *(SE24)*
Mirch Masala *(SW16,SW17)**
Nanglo *(SW12)**
Nazmins Balti House *(SW18)**
Origin Asia *(TW9)**
Sagar *(TW1)**
Sree Krishna *(SW17)**
Tandoori Nights *(SE22)**
Tangawizi *(TW1)*
3 Monkeys *(SE24)*

East

Café Spice Namaste *(E1)**
Cinnamon Kitchen *(EC2)*
Clifton *(E1)**
The Gaylord *(E14)*
Kasturi *(EC3)**
Memsaheb on Thames *(E14)**
Mint Leaf *(EC2)*
Mirch Masala *(E1)**
New Tayyabs *(E1)**
Rajasthan II *(EC3)*
Tiffinbites *(E14,EC2)*

INDIAN, SOUTHERN

Central

India Club *(WC2)*
Malabar Junction *(WC1)**
Quilon *(SW1)**
Ragam *(W1)**
Rasa *(W1)**
Rasa Maricham *(WC1)**
Sagar *(W1)**
Woodlands *(SW1,W1)*

West

Sagar *(W6)**
Woodlands *(W4)*

North

Chutneys *(NW1)*
Geeta *(NW6)**
Jashan *(HAU)**
Kovalam *(NW6)**
Rani *(N3)*
Rasa *(N16)**
Rasa Travancore *(N16)**
Vijay *(NW6)**
Woodlands *(NW3)*

South

Ganapati *(SE15)**
Kastoori *(SW17)**
Sagar *(TW1)**

Sree Krishna (SW17)*
Vijaya Krishna (SW17)

INDONESIAN
Central
Melati (W1)
Trader Vics (W1)

West
Kiasu (W2)

South
Nancy Lam's Enak Enak (SW11)

JAPANESE
Central
Aaya (W1)*
Abeno (WC1)*
Abeno Too (WC2)
Abokado (WC2)*
Atami (SW1)
Benihana (W1)
Bincho Yakitori (W1)*
Centrepoint Sushi (WC2)*
Chisou (W1)*
Defune (W1)*
Dinings (W1)*
Donzoko (W1)*
Edokko (WC1)*
Feng Sushi (SW1)
Hazuki (WC2)
Ikeda (W1)*
Inamo (W1)
Itsu (W1)
Kiku (W1)*
Kulu Kulu (W1,WC2)*
Kyashii (WC2)
Matsuri (SW1,WC1)
Misato (W1)
Mitsukoshi (SW1)*
Miyama (W1)*
Nobu (W1)*
Nobu Berkeley (W1)
Roka (W1)*
Sake No Hana (SW1)
Sakura (W1)*
Satsuma (W1)
Shogun (W1)*
So (W1)
Soho Japan (W1)
Sumosan (W1)*
Sushi Hiroba (WC2)
Taro (W1)
Ten Ten Tei (W1)*
Tuku (W1)
Tokyo Diner (WC2)
Umu (W1)*
Wagamama (SW1,W1,WC1,WC2)
Yoshino (W1)*

West
Benihana (SW3)
Feng Sushi (SW10,W11,W8)
Inaho (W2)*
Itsu (SW3)
Kulu Kulu (SW7)*
Nozomi (SW3)
Okawari (W5)

Sushi-Hiro (W5)*
Tosa (W6)*
Wagamama (W8)
Yakitoria (W2)
Yumenoki (SW10)
Zuma (SW7)*

North
Benihana (NW3)
Bento (NW1)
Café Japan (NW11)*
Feng Sushi (NW3)
Jin Kichi (NW3)*
Sushi-Say (NW2)*
Wagamama (N1, NW1)
Yuzu (NW6)*

South
Bincho Yakitori (SE1)*
Cho-San (SW15)*
Feng Sushi (SE1)
Fujiyama (SW9)*
Inshoku (SE1)
Matsuba (TW9)
Slurp (SW19)
Tsunami (SW4)*
Wagamama (SE1, SW15, SW19)

East
City Miyama (EC4)
Itsu (E14)
K10 (EC2)*
Kurumaya (EC4)*
Mugen (EC4)
Pham Sushi (EC1)*
Saki Bar & Food Emporium (EC1)*
Tajima Tei (EC1)*
Tatsuso (EC2)
Tokyo City (EC2)
Ubon (E14)
Wagamama (E14, EC2, EC3, EC4)

KOREAN
Central
Asadal (WC1)
Koba (W1)

MALAYSIAN
Central
C&R Cafe (W1)*
Jom Makan (SW1)
Melati (W1)
Suka (W1)

West
Awana (SW3)*
Kiasu (W2)
Nyonya (W11)
Satay House (W2)

North
Singapore Garden (NW6)*

South
Champor-Champor (SE1)*
Ekachai (SW18)*

East
Ekachai *(EC2)**
54 Farringdon Road *(EC1)**
Singapura *(EC3, EC4)**

PAKISTANI
Central
Salloos *(SW1)**

West
Mirch Masala *(UB1)**

South
Mirch Masala *(SW16, SW17)**

East
Lahore Kebab House *(E1)**
Mirch Masala *(E1)**
New Tayyabs *(E1)**

PAN-ASIAN
Central
Buddha Bar *(WC2)*
Cocoon *(W1)*
dim T *(W1)*
The Electric Birdcage *(SW1)*
Haiku *(W1)*
Haozhan *(W1)**
Hare & Tortoise *(WC1)*
Noodle Noodle *(SW1)*
Tamarai *(WC2)*

West
E&O *(W11)**
Eight Over Eight *(SW3)**
Hare & Tortoise *(SW5,W14)*
Mao Tai *(SW6)**
Tampopo *(SW10)**
Uli *(W11)**

North
Bacchus *(N1)**
dim T *(N6)*
dim T *(NW3)*
Gilgamesh *(NW1)*
XO *(NW3)*

South
The Banana Leaf Canteen *(SW11)**
dim T *(SE1)*
Hare & Tortoise *(SW15)*
Nancy Lam's Enak Enak *(SW11)*
O'Zon *(TW1)*
Rapscallion *(SW4)*

East
Bar Bourse *(EC4)*
Chi Noodle & Wine Bar *(EC4)*
Cicada *(EC1)**
D Sum 2 *(EC4)*
Great Eastern Dining
  Room *(EC2)**
Pacific Oriental *(EC2)*

THAI
Central
Benja *(W1)**
Blue Jade *(SW1)*

Busaba Eathai *(W1,WC1)**
C&R Cafe *(W1)*
Chiang Mai *(W1)*
Crazy Bear *(W1)**
Mango Tree *(SW1)*
Mekong *(SW1)*
Nahm *(SW1)*
Patara *(W1)**
Siam Central *(W1)*
Thai Café *(SW1)*
Thai Pot *(WC2)*
Thai Square *(SW1,W1,WC2)*

West
Addie's Thai Café *(SW5)**
Bangkok *(SW7)*
Bedlington Café *(W4)*
Blue Elephant *(SW6)*
Café 209 *(SW6)*
Churchill Arms *(W8)**
Esarn Kheaw *(W12)**
Fat Boy's *(W5)*
Hammersmith Café *(W6)*
Latymers *(W6)**
Old Parr's Head *(W14)*
Patara *(SW3)**
Sugar Hut *(SW6)*
Sukho Thai Cuisine *(SW6)**
Tawana *(W2)**
Thai Square *(SW7)*
The Walmer Castle *(W11)*
Yelo Thai Canteen *(W11)*

North
Isarn *(N1)**
Thai Square *(N1)*
Yelo *(N1)*
Yum Yum *(N16)**

South
Amaranth *(SW18)**
Ekachai *(SW18)**
Fat Boy's *(TW1,TW8,W4)*
The Pepper Tree *(SW4)*
Ratchada *(SE3)*
The Rye *(SE15)*
Suk Saran *(SW19)**
Talad Thai *(SW15)**
Thai Corner Café *(SE22)*
Thai Garden *(SW11)*
Thai on the River *(SW11)*
Thai Square *(SW15)*
Thailand *(SE14)*

East
Ekachai *(EC2)**
Elephant Royale *(E14)*
Hokkien Chan *(EC2)*
Thai Square *(EC4)*
Thai Square City *(EC3)*

VIETNAMESE
Central
Bam-Bou *(W1)*
Mekong *(SW1)*
Pho *(W1,WC1)**
Viet *(W1)**

CUISINES | ASIAN

West
Kiasu *(W2)*
Saigon Saigon *(W6)*

North
Huong-Viet *(N1)*
Khoai *(N8)**
Khoai Cafe *(N12)**
Viet Garden *(N1)*

East
Cây Tre *(EC1)**
Namo *(E9)**
Pho *(EC1)**
Sông Quê *(E2)**
Viet Hoa *(E2)*

AREA OVERVIEWS

Soho, Covent Garden & Bloomsbury
(Parts of W1, all WC2 and WC1)

£80+					
	Lindsay House	British, Modern	④	❸	❸
	L'Atelier de Joel Robuchon	French	❷	④	❷
	Asia de Cuba	Fusion	④	④	❷

£70+					
	Quo Vadis	British, Traditional	❸	❷	❸
	Pearl	French	❸	❷	❸
	Kyashii	Japanese	–	–	–

£60+					
	Rules	British, Traditional	❸	❸	❶
	Simpsons-in-the-Strand	"	⑤	④	❸
	J Sheekey	Fish & seafood	❶	❶	❷
	L'Escargot (Picasso Room)	French	❸	❷	❷
	Red Fort	Indian	❷	❸	❸
	Matsuri	Japanese	❸	❸	⑤

£50+					
	Christopher's	American	⑤	④	④
	Adam Street	British, Modern	❸	❸	❷
	Alastair Little	"	④	❸	⑤
	Axis	"	④	❸	④
	Indigo	"	④	❸	❸
	The Ivy	"	❸	❷	❷
	The Portrait	"	④	④	❷
	Refuel	"	⑤	⑤	❸
	Zilli Fish	Fish & seafood	❸	❸	④
	Clos Maggiore	French	❷	❶	❶
	L'Escargot	"	❷	❷	❷
	Incognico	"	④	❸	④
	Mon Plaisir	"	④	❸	❷
	La Trouvaille	"	❷	❷	❷
	Little Italy	Italian	④	❸	❸
	Albannach	Scottish	⑤	⑤	④
	Gaucho Grill	Steaks & grills	❷	❸	❸
	Floridita	Cuban	⑤	⑤	❸
	Shanghai Blues	Chinese	❷	❸	❸
	Yauatcha	"	❶	④	❷
	Tamarai	Pan-Asian	❸	④	❸

£40+					
	Joe Allen	American	④	④	❶
	Acorn House	British, Modern	❸	④	④
	Arbutus	"	❷	❷	❸
	Café du Jardin	"	④	④	④
	Le Deuxième	"	④	❸	④
	French House	"	❸	❷	❷
	Homage	"	④	❶	④
	Konstam	"	❷	❷	❸
	Stanza	"	❸	❸	④
	The Terrace	"	❸	④	❸
	Tuttons	"	⑤	⑤	④
	The National Dining Rooms	British, Traditional	④	⑤	④
	Cape Town Fish Market	Fish & seafood	④	④	⑤
	Livebait	"	④	④	⑤
	The Admiralty	French	⑤	④	④
	Beotys	"	④	❸	④
	Café des Amis	"	④	❸	❸
	Chez Gérard	"	⑤	⑤	④

	Name	Cuisine	Ratings
	Randall & Aubin	"	③②①
	So	Fusion	③②③
	Bedford & Strand	International	③②②
	Bohème Kitchen	"	④④③
	The Forge	"	④②③
	National Gallery Café	"	④④③
	Ronnie Scott's	"	⑤④①
	Bertorelli's	Italian	⑤⑤⑤
	Dehesa	"	②③①
	Number Twelve	"	③③④
	Orso	"	④③④
	Pasta Brown	"	④④⑤
	Signor Zilli	"	④④④
	Vasco & Piero's Pavilion	"	③③④
	Barrafina	Spanish	①①②
	Cigala	"	④③④
	St Moritz	Swiss	③③③
	Planet Hollywood	Burgers, etc	⑤⑤⑤
	Kettners	Pizza	④④②
	La Spiga	"	④④④
	Malabar Junction	Indian	②②②
	Moti Mahal	"	②③③
	Edokko	Japanese	①①③
	Asadal	Korean	③④⑤
	Benja	Thai	②①③
	Patara	"	②②③
£35+	All Star Lanes	American	④⑤④
	Bodean's	"	④④④
	Maxwell's	"	③③④
	Belgo Centraal	Belgian	④④③
	Andrew Edmunds	British, Modern	③②①
	Aurora	"	③②①
	Shampers	"	③②②
	Great Queen Street	British, Traditional	②③③
	Loch Fyne	Fish & seafood	④③④
	Café Bohème	French	④④②
	Côte	"	④③④
	Gay Hussar	Hungarian	④③②
	Boulevard	International	④③③
	Browns	"	④④④
	Cork & Bottle	"	④④①
	Papageno	"	⑤⑤②
	Sarastro	"	⑤⑤④
	Aperitivo	Italian	③②④
	Wolfe's	Burgers, etc	④④⑤
	Le Pain Quotidien	Sandwiches, cakes, etc	③④③
	Pain Quotidien	Salads	③④③
	Café Pacifico	Mexican/TexMex	⑤⑤④
	Bar Shu	Chinese	②④④
	Fung Shing	"	②③⑤
	Imperial China	"	③③③
	Café Lazeez	Indian	③③③
	Mela	"	③④④
	Ten Ten Tei	Japanese	②②⑤
£30+	Balfour	British, Modern	④④③
	The Easton	"	③③②
	The Giaconda	"	②②④
	Giraffe	"	④③③

	Name	Cuisine			
	Porters	British, Traditional	5	5	4
	Balans	International	5	3	2
	Sugar Reef	"	4	4	4
	Ciao Bella	Italian	3	2	0
	Sapori	"	4	3	4
	The Norfolk Arms	Mediterranean	3	3	2
	06 St Chad's Place	"	3	3	2
	Mildred's	Vegetarian	3	4	2
	Fire & Stone	Pizza	4	4	3
	Paradiso Olivelli	"	4	4	4
	Souk Medina	Moroccan	4	0	0
	Sofra	Turkish	4	4	4
	Tas	"	4	2	3
	The Chinese Experience	Chinese	3	3	4
	Chuen Cheng Ku	"	4	4	4
	Yming	"	2	0	3
	Sitaaray	Indian	2	2	2
	Rasa Maricham	Indian, Southern	0	2	3
	Abeno	Japanese	2	3	4
	Abeno Too	"	3	2	3
	Bincho Yakitori	"	2	2	0
	Donzoko	"	2	4	4
	Hazuki	"	3	4	4
	Melati	Malaysian	4	2	4
	Haozhan	Pan-Asian	2	2	3
	Chiang Mai	Thai	3	4	5
	Thai Pot	"	4	3	4
	Thai Square	"	4	4	3
£25+	Café Emm	British, Modern	4	2	2
	Real Greek	Greek	5	5	4
	Seven Stars	International	3	3	0
	Star Café	"	4	4	3
	Amato	Italian	3	3	3
	La Porchetta Pizzeria	"	3	3	3
	Spacca Napoli	"	2	4	2
	Café España	Spanish	4	3	2
	La Tasca	"	5	4	4
	North Sea Fish	Fish & chips	2	2	4
	Rock & Sole Plaice	"	2	4	4
	Fernandez & Wells	Sandwiches, cakes, etc	2	3	3
	Pâtisserie Valerie	"	4	4	3
	Paul	"	3	4	3
	Wahaca	Mexican/TexMex	3	2	2
	Gaby's	Israeli	3	3	5
	Golden Dragon	Chinese	3	4	3
	Harbour City	"	2	3	4
	Jade Garden	"	3	3	3
	Joy King Lau	"	0	0	0
	Mr Kong	"	2	3	4
	New Mayflower	"	2	5	5
	New World	"	3	4	3
	ping pong	Chinese, Dim sum	4	4	3
	Chowki	Indian	4	4	4
	Gopal's of Soho	"	3	2	4
	Imli	"	3	3	3
	Masala Zone	"	4	3	3
	Salaam Namaste	"	3	3	4
	Itsu	Japanese	3	3	3
	Kulu Kulu	"	2	4	5

	Misato	"	③④⑤
	Satsuma	"	③③④
	Sushi Hiroba	"	④④④
	Wagamama	"	④④④
	Busaba Eathai	Thai	❷❸❷
	C&R Cafe	"	❷⑤④
£20+	Café in the Crypt	International	④④❷
	Gordon's Wine Bar	"	⑤❸❶
	Bistro 1	Mediterranean	④❷❸
	Ed's Easy Diner	Burgers, etc	❸❷❷
	Gourmet Burger Kitchen	"	❸④④
	Hamburger Union	"	❸④④
	The Ultimate Burger	"	④④❸
	Konditor & Cook	Sandwiches, cakes, etc	❷❸❸
	Leon	"	❸❸❸
	Wong Kei	Chinese	④⑤⑤
	India Club	Indian	❸⑤⑤
	Centrepoint Sushi	Japanese	❷❷❷
	Taro	"	❸❷④
	Hare & Tortoise	Pan-Asian	❸④④
	Pho	Vietnamese	❷❶❷
£15+	Pure California	American	❸④⑤
	Square Pie Company	British, Traditional	❸④⑤
	Stock Pot	International	④❸④
	Paolina Café	Italian	❷❷④
	Hummus Bros	Mediterranean	❸❷❸
	Food for Thought	Vegetarian	❷④④
	Bar Italia	Sandwiches, cakes, etc	④❸❶
	Just Falafs	Salads	❷④④
	Vital Ingredient	"	❸④⑤
	Baozi Inn	Chinese	④④❸
	Cha Cha Moon	Chinese, Dim sum	❷❷❷
	Abokado	Japanese	❷❸④
	Tokyo Diner	"	④❸④
	Viet	Vietnamese	❷⑤④
£10+	Nordic Bakery	Scandinavian	❸❷❸
	Napket	Afternoon tea	❸❷❷
	Fryer's Delight	Fish & chips	❸❸④
	Apostrophe	Sandwiches, cakes, etc	❷❸❷
	Monmouth Coffee Company	"	❶❷❷
£5+	Caffé Vergnano	Italian	❷❷❷
	Flat White	Sandwiches, cakes, etc	❶❶❷
	Maison Bertaux	"	❸❸❶

Mayfair & St James's (Parts of W1 and SW1)

Price	Restaurant	Cuisine	Rating
£130+	Le Gavroche	*French*	2 1 2
£120+	Umu	*Japanese*	2 3 3
£110+	Sake No Hana	*Japanese*	4 4 4
£100+	Alain Ducasse	*French*	4 3 4
	The Ritz Restaurant	"	4 2 1
	Sketch (Lecture Rm)	"	5 5 4
£90+	G Ramsay at Claridges	*French*	4 4 3
	The Greenhouse	"	3 3 2
£80+	Dorchester Grill	*British, Modern*	4 4 5
	Wiltons	*British, Traditional*	3 3 2
	Galvin at Windows	*French*	4 3 2
	Hibiscus	"	3 2 4
	L'Oranger	"	4 3 3
	The Square	"	2 2 3
	Nobu	*Japanese*	2 4 4
	Nobu Berkeley	"	3 5 3
£70+	maze Grill	*British, Modern*	2 3 3
	Hélène Darroze	*French*	– – –
	maze	"	2 2 3
	Cipriani	*Italian*	5 5 4
	Theo Randall	"	3 3 4
	China Tang	*Chinese*	4 4 3
	Hakkasan	"	2 3 2
	Kai Mayfair	"	1 2 3
	Taman Gang	"	3 5 2
	Trader Vics	*Indonesian*	5 5 4
	Ikeda	*Japanese*	1 3 5
	Sumosan	"	2 4 4
£60+	Bellamy's	*British, Modern*	3 2 3
	Mews of Mayfair	"	3 3 3
	Patterson's	"	2 3 4
	Pigalle Club	"	4 4 1
	The Albemarle	*British, Traditional*	4 4 4
	Green's	"	3 2 2
	Bentley's	*Fish & seafood*	2 3 3
	Scott's	"	2 1 2
	La Petite Maison	*French*	2 3 2
	Sketch (Gallery)	"	4 5 4
	Giardinetto	*Italian*	3 4 5
	Luciano	"	4 5 4
	Mosaico	"	3 3 3
	Ladurée	*Afternoon tea*	2 4 3
	Benares	*Indian*	2 2 3
	Matsuri	*Japanese*	3 3 5
	Miyama	"	1 2 5
	Shogun	"	2 2 4
£50+	The Avenue	*British, Modern*	4 4 4
	Le Caprice	"	2 1 1
	Hush	"	5 5 4
	Langan's Brasserie	"	4 3 2

	Nicole's	"	④④④
	Quaglino's	"	⑤⑤⑤
	Rhodes W1 Brasserie	"	④④⑤
	The Wolseley	"	❸❸❷
	Fortnum's, The Fountain	British, Traditional	④❸❸
	Greig's	"	❸❸④
	Pescatori	Fish & seafood	④④④
	Bord'Eaux	French	❸❷⑤
	Boudin Blanc	"	❷❸❷
	Brasserie Roux	"	❸❸❸
	Criterion Grill	"	④④❷
	Alloro	Italian	❷❷❸
	Cecconi's	"	❸❸❷
	Franco's	"	④❸④
	Sartoria	"	④④❸
	St Alban	Mediterranean	❸❶❸
	Gaucho Grill	Steaks & grills	❷❸❸
	The Guinea Grill	"	❸❸❸
	Rowley's	"	⑤④④
	Momo	Moroccan	④④❷
	Fakhreldine	Lebanese	❸④④
	Princess Garden	Chinese	❶❷❸
	Mint Leaf	Indian	❸④❸
	Tamarind	"	❷❷❸
	Veeraswamy	"	❷❷❷
	Quilon	Indian, Southern	❶❷④
	Benihana	Japanese	④④⑤
	Kiku	"	❷④⑤
	Mitsukoshi	"	❷❸⑤
	Cocoon	Pan-Asian	❸④❷
	Haiku	"	④⑤④
£40+	Automat	American	④④❸
	Inn the Park	British, Modern	⑤⑤❸
	The Little Square	"	④❸❸
	The Only Running Footman	"	❸❸④
	Sotheby's Café	"	❷❶❷
	Wild Honey	"	❷❸❸
	Chez Gérard	French	⑤⑤④
	Al Duca	Italian	④❸④
	Getti	"	④❸④
	Ristorante Semplice	"	❷❷❸
	Serafino	"	④❷④
	Via Condotti	"	❸❸④
	Il Vicolo	"	❸❷④
	Dover Street	Mediterranean	⑤④④
	Rocket	"	❸❸❷
	Truc Vert	"	❸④❸
	Hard Rock Café	Burgers, etc	④④❷
	Aubaine	Sandwiches, cakes, etc	④⑤④
	Al Hamra	Lebanese	④⑤⑤
	Levant	"	④④❶
	Noura	"	④❸❸
	Chor Bizarre	Indian	❷❸❷
	Chisou	Japanese	❷❶④
	Patara	Thai	❷❷❸
£35+	Running Horse	British, Modern	❸❸❷
	The Windmill	British, Traditional	❸❸④
	L'Artiste Musclé	French	④❸❷

271

	Name	Cuisine	Rating
	Browns	International	4 4 4
	Piccolino	Italian	4 4 4
	Delfino	Pizza	2 3 4
	Al Sultan	Lebanese	2 3 5
	Yoshino	Japanese	2 2 4
£30+	El Pirata	Spanish	3 2 2
	Richoux	Sandwiches, cakes, etc	5 5 4
	Royal Academy	"	5 5 2
	Sketch (Parlour)	"	4 2 2
	Sofra	Turkish	4 4 4
	Woodlands	Indian	3 3 4
	Rasa	Indian, Southern	0 2 3
	Toku	Japanese	3 4 5
	Thai Square	Thai	4 4 3
£25+	Diner	Burgers, etc	4 5 2
	Pâtisserie Valerie	Sandwiches, cakes, etc	4 4 3
	Sakura	Japanese	2 5 5
	Wagamama	"	4 4 4
	The Electric Birdcage	Pan-Asian	3 2 3
	Busaba Eathai	Thai	2 3 2
£20+	Noodle Noodle	Pan-Asian	4 5 5
£15+	Stock Pot	International	4 3 4
	Salade	Salads	3 4 5
	Vital Ingredient	"	3 4 5
£10+	Napket	Afternoon tea	3 2 2
	Apostrophe	Sandwiches, cakes, etc	2 3 2
	Benugo	"	4 3 2
	Crussh	"	3 2 4
	Fuzzy's Grub	"	0 2 3

Fitzrovia & Marylebone (Part of W1)

	Name	Cuisine	Rating
£90+	Pied à Terre	French	2 2 3
£80+	Rhodes W1 Restaurant	French	4 3 3
£70+	The Landau	British, Modern	3 2 3
	Orrery	French	3 2 3
	Texture	"	2 2 3
	Suka	Malaysian	4 5 5
£60+	Oscar	British, Modern	4 4 3
	The Providores	Fusion	3 4 4
	5 Cavendish Square	Italian	5 4 3
	Locanda Locatelli	Italian	2 2 2
	Defune	Japanese	0 2 5
£50+	Vanilla	British, Modern	2 2 0
	Odin's	British, Traditional	3 0 0
	Pescatori	Fish & seafood	4 4 4
	L'Autre Pied	French	2 3 4
	Elena's L'Etoile	"	4 3 2
	Michael Moore	International	2 0 3
	Caffè Caldesi	Italian	4 3 4

	Caldesi	"	❸❷④
	Passione	"	❸❷④
	2 Veneti	"	❸❶❸
	Fino	Spanish	❷❷❷
	Royal China Club	Chinese	❷❸④
	La Porte des Indes	Indian	❸❷❶
	Aaya	Japanese	❷❷❷
	Roka	"	❶❷❷
	Crazy Bear	Thai	❷❷❶
£40+	The Union Café	British, Modern	④❷④
	Back to Basics	Fish & seafood	❶❷④
	Fishworks	"	❸④④
	Seaport	"	❸❸④
	Galvin Bistrot de Luxe	French	❶❶❷
	Villandry	"	④⑤④
	The Wallace	"	④④❶
	Archipelago	Fusion	❷❶❶
	Providores (Tapa Room)	"	❸❸❸
	Hardy's Brasserie	International	④❷❸
	Bertorelli's	Italian	⑤⑤⑤
	Camerino	"	❸❸④
	Getti	"	④❸④
	Latium	"	❶❶❸
	Sardo	"	❷❸④
	Garbo's	Scandinavian	④❸④
	Black & Blue	Steaks & grills	❸❸④
	Reubens	Kosher	④④⑤
	Fairuz	Lebanese	❸❸④
	Maroush	"	❸④④
	Koba	Korean	❸❶❸
	Bam-Bou	Vietnamese	❸❸❶
£35+	RIBA Café	British, Modern	④④❷
	Langan's Bistro	French	④❸❸
	Le Relais de Venise	"	❷❸❷
	Giusto	Italian	❸❸④
	Salt Yard	Mediterranean	❷❷❸
	Le Pain Quotidien	Sandwiches, cakes, etc	❸④❸
	Ozer	Turkish	④⑤⑤
	Royal China	Chinese	❷❸④
	Gaylord	Indian	❸④④
£30+	Seabass	Fish & seafood	④❸④
	Hellenik	Greek	❸❶❸
	Eat & Two Veg	International	④④④
	Giraffe	"	④❸❸
	Ooze	"	④❸④
	The Beehive	Italian	❷❸④
	Eagle Bar Diner	Burgers, etc	❷④❷
	Fine Burger Company	"	❸④④
	Tootsies	"	④④④
	Paradiso Olivelli	Pizza	④④④
	Original Tajines	Moroccan	❸❷❸
	Efes II	Turkish	❸❷④
	Sofra	"	④④④
	Woodlands	Indian	❸❸④
	Rasa Samudra	Indian, Southern	❶❷❸
	Dinings	Japanese	❶❷❷

Price	Name	Cuisine	Rating
£25+	Real Greek	Greek	⑤⑤④
	Vapiano	Italian	④④④
	Navarro's	Spanish	❸❸❷
	La Fromagerie Café	Sandwiches, cakes, etc	❶❸❷
	Pâtisserie Valerie	"	④④❸
	Paul	"	❸④❸
	ping pong	Chinese, Dim sum	④④❸
	Ragam	Indian	❶❶⑤
	Soho Japan	Japanese	❸❸❸
	Wagamama	"	④④④
	dim T	Pan-Asian	④④❸
	Siam Central	Thai	❸❷④
£20+	Hamburger Union	Burgers, etc	❸④④
	The Ultimate Burger	"	④④❸
	Leon	Sandwiches, cakes, etc	❸❸❸
	Sagar	Indian	❶❷④
	Pho	Vietnamese	❷❶❷
£15+	Pure California	American	❸④⑤
	Golden Hind	Fish & chips	❶❶❸
£10+	Apostrophe	Sandwiches, cakes, etc	❷❸❷
	Benugo	"	④❸❷

Belgravia, Pimlico, Victoria & Westminster (SW1, except St James's)

Price	Name	Cuisine	Rating
£100+	Pétrus	French	❶❶❷
£80+	Rib Room	British, Traditional	④④④
	Foliage	French	❸❷❸
	Nahm	Thai	❸④⑤
£70+	The Goring Hotel	British, Traditional	❸❶❶
	One-O-One	Fish & seafood	❶❷④
	Roussillon	French	❶❶❸
	Apsleys	Italian	④❷❸
	Mr Chow	Chinese	❸④④
£60+	The Fifth Floor Restaurant	British, Modern	④④④
	Boxwood Café	International	❸❸④
	Il Convivio	Italian	❸❸❸
	Santini	"	④④❸
	Toto's	"	❸❷❷
	Zafferano	"	❸❷❷
	Boisdale	Scottish	④❸❷
	Ladurée	Afternoon tea	❷④❺
	The Cinnamon Club	Indian	❷❸❷
	Atami	Japanese	❸❸④
£50+	Pantechnicon Rooms	British, Modern	❸❸❷
	Thomas Cubitt	"	❸❸❷
	Shepherd's	British, Traditional	❸❷❸
	Olivomare	Fish & seafood	❷❷❸
	La Poule au Pot	French	❸❸❶
	Motcombs	International	④④④
	Pomegranates	"	④❷❸
	L'Incontro	Italian	④❸❸

	Mimmo d'Ischia	"	⑤④④
	Quirinale	"	❷❷❸
	Hunan	Chinese	❶❷④
	Ken Lo's Memories	"	❷❷❸
	Amaya	Indian	❶❷❷
	Mango Tree	Thai	❸④④
£40+	Atrium	British, Modern	⑤⑤⑤
	Bank Westminster	"	⑤④④
	The Botanist	"	④④❸
	The Contented Vine	"	④❸④
	Daylesford Organics	"	④❷❶
	Ebury Wine Bar	"	④❸❸
	Footstool	"	– – –
	Tate Britain (Rex Whistler)	"	④❸❷
	Brasserie St Jacques	French	④④④
	Le Cercle	"	❶❸❷
	The Chelsea Brasserie	"	④④④
	Chez Gérard	"	⑤⑤④
	The Ebury	"	④⑤④
	City Café	International	❸❷④
	Caraffini	Italian	❸❶❷
	Como Lario	"	④❷❷
	Gran Paradiso	"	④❸❸
	Olivo	"	❷❷❷
	Sale e Pepe	"	❸❷❶
	Signor Sassi	"	❸❷❸
	Uno	"	❷❷❷
	Vivezza	"	④④④
	Volt	"	④④❸
	About Thyme	Mediterranean	❸❷④
	The Fifth Floor Café	"	④④④
	Oliveto	Pizza	❷❷❸
	Beiteddine	Lebanese	❸❷④
	Noura	"	④❸❸
	Salloos	Pakistani	❷❸❸
£35+	Chicago Rib Shack	American	⑤⑤④
	The Queens Arms	British, Modern	❸④④
	Grenadier	British, Traditional	④④❶
	Grumbles	International	④❸❸
	Oriel	"	④④④
	Ottolenghi	Italian	❶❸❸
	Pizza on the Park	"	❸❸❷
	2 Amici	"	④❷④
	Baker & Spice	Sandwiches, cakes, etc	❷④④
	Texas Embassy Cantina	Mexican/TexMex	⑤⑤⑤
	Ishbilia	Lebanese	❷❷❸
£30+	The Phoenix	British, Modern	❸❸❸
	Caramel	International	④④❸
	Goya	Spanish	④④④
	Seafresh	Fish & chips	❸❷④
	Ranoush	Lebanese	❸④④
	Kazan	Turkish	❷❷❸
	Feng Sushi	Japanese	④④④
	Blue Jade	Thai	❸❶④
£25+	Vincent Rooms	British, Modern	④④❸
	Chimes	British, Traditional	④❸❸

	Pâtisserie Valerie	*Sandwiches, cakes, etc*	④④❸
	Cyprus Mangal	*Turkish*	❷❸⑤
	Jenny Lo's	*Chinese*	❸❸④
	Wagamama	*Japanese*	④④④
	Jom Makan	*Malaysian*	④④④
	Thai Café	*Thai*	❸❸⑤
£20+	Mekong	*Vietnamese*	④④④
£10+	Apostrophe	*Sandwiches, cakes, etc*	❷❸❷

WEST

Chelsea, South Kensington, Kensington, Earl's Court & Fulham (SW3, SW5, SW6, SW7, SW10 & W8)

Price	Name	Cuisine	Rating
£110+	Gordon Ramsay	French	❶❶❷
£100+	Blakes	International	⑤④❷
£90+	Ambassade de l'Ile	French	④④④
	Aubergine	"	❸❸④
	Tom Aikens	"	❸❸❸
£80+	The Capital Restaurant	French	❷❷④
	Rasoi Vineet Bhatia	Indian	❷❷❸
£70+	Brunello	Italian	④❸❸
£60+	Babylon	British, Modern	④④❶
	Clarke's	"	❷❷❸
	The Collection	"	⑤⑤⑤
	Marco	"	④❶❸
	Bibendum	French	❸❷❷
	Cheyne Walk Bras'	"	❸❸❷
	L'Etranger	"	❸❸④
	Montpeliano	Italian	④④④
	San Lorenzo	"	⑤④④
	Nozomi	Japanese	⑤⑤⑤
	Zuma	"	❶❸❷
£50+	Big Easy	American	❸❸❷
	Bistro 190	British, Modern	④❸❸
	Bluebird	"	⑤⑤⑤
	Kensington Place	"	④⑤⑤
	Launceston Place	"	❶❷❷
	Poissonnerie de l'Av.	Fish & seafood	❷❷❷
	Le Suquet	"	❷❸❸
	Belvedere	French	❸❸❶
	Papillon	"	❸❷❷
	Racine	"	❷❶❷
	Aquasia	Fusion	④❸❸
	Carpaccio's	Italian	⑤④❸
	Lucio	"	❸❷❸
	Osteria dell'Arancio	"	❸❸④
	Scalini	"	❷❷❷
	Timo	"	❸❷❸
	Locanda Ottomezzo	Mediterranean	❸❷❸
	Gaucho Grill	Steaks & grills	❷❸❸
	Bombay Brasserie	Indian	— — —
	Chutney Mary	"	❷❷❷
	Zaika	"	❶❸❸
	Benihana	Japanese	④④⑤
	Awana	Malaysian	❷❷❸
	Blue Elephant	Thai	❸❷❶
£40+	PJ's	American	⑤④❷
	The Abingdon	British, Modern	❸❷❸
	Admiral Codrington	"	④❸❸
	Bibendum Oyster Bar	"	❸❸❷

Name	Cuisine	Ratings
Bowler Bar & Grill	"	❸❸④
Brinkley's	"	④④❸
Duke on the Green	"	❸❸❸
11 Abingdon Road	"	❸❸④
The Establishment	"	④④❸
The Farm	"	④❷❸
Jimmy's	"	④❷❸
Le Metro	"	④④④
Tom's Kitchen	"	④④④
Vingt-Quatre	"	④❸④
Whits	"	❷⓿❸
Bumpkin	British, Traditional	❷❷❷
Ffiona's	"	❸⓿⓿
Maggie Jones's	"	④❸⓿
Fishworks	Fish & seafood	❸④④
La Bouchée	French	❸❸❷
La Brasserie	"	④④❷
Brasserie St Quentin	"	❸❸④
Le Colombier	"	❸⓿❷
Langan's Coq d'Or	"	④❷❸
The Pig's Ear	"	❸❸❷
Brompton Quarter Café	International	⑤⑤④
Coopers Arms	"	❸④❷
The Enterprise	"	❸❷❷
Foxtrot Oscar	"	⑤④⑤
606 Club	"	④❸❷
The Swag & Tails	"	❸❸❷
The Ark	Italian	④④❸
Daphne's	"	❷❷❷
Elistano	"	④④④
La Famiglia	"	❸❷❷
Frantoio	"	❸⓿❷
Manicomio	"	④④④
Pellicano	"	❸❷④
Il Portico	"	❸⓿❷
Riccardo's	"	❸❷❸
Ziani	"	❸❷❷
Wódka	Polish	❸❷❷
Cambio de Tercio	Spanish	⓿⓿❷
L-Restaurant & Bar	"	❸❷④
Black & Blue	Steaks & grills	❸❸④
Geale's	Fish & chips	④④❸
Aubaine	Sandwiches, cakes etc	④⑤④
Pasha	Moroccan	④④⓿
Maroush	Lebanese	❸④④
Simply Lebanese	"	④⑤④
Good Earth	Chinese	❷❷❸
Ken Lo's Memories	"	❸❸④
Mr Wing	"	❸❷⓿
The Painted Heron	Indian	⓿❷❸
Star of India	"	❷❸❸
Vama	"	❷❸④
Yumenoki	Japanese	④❸⑤
Eight Over Eight	Pan-Asian	⓿❷❷
Mao Tai	"	❷❸❸
Patara	Thai	❷❷❸
Sugar Hut	"	④④④

Price	Name	Cuisine	Ratings
£35+	Bodean's	American	④④④
	Sticky Fingers	"	⑤⑤④

	Britannia	British, Modern	④④❸
	The Builders Arms	"	④④❷
	Butcher's Hook	"	❸❷❷
	Joe's Brasserie	"	❸❷❷
	Lots Road	"	❸❸❸
	The Phoenix	"	④❸❸
	The Salisbury Tavern	"	④❸❸
	White Horse	"	❸④❷
	Chez Patrick	Fish & seafood	❸❷❸
	Green Door Bar & Grill	French	❸❸④
	Tartine	"	❸❸❷
	The Cabin	International	❸❷❷
	Glaisters	"	④④❸
	Wine Gallery	"	④❸❷
	Da Mario	Italian	④❸❸
	De Cecco	"	❸❸④
	Il Falconiere	"	④❸⑤
	Frankie's Italian Bar & Grill	"	⑤⑤④
	Napulé	"	❸❸❸
	Nuovi Sapori	"	❸❸④
	Ottolenghi	"	❶❸❸
	Santa Lucia	"	❸❷❷
	Polish Club	Polish	④❸❸
	Tendido Cero	Spanish	❸❸❸
	Tendido Cuatro	"	❷❷❸
	El Gaucho	Steaks & grills	❷❸❸
	Sophie's Steakhouse	"	❸❸❷
	Henry J Beans	Burgers, etc	④④❸
	Friends	Pizza	❸❷❸
	(Ciro's) Pizza Pomodoro	"	④④❷
	Baker & Spice	Sandwiches, cakes, etc	❷④④
	Bluebird Café	"	⑤⑤⑤
	Le Pain Quotidien	"	❸④❸
	La Bodeguita del Medio	Cuban	❸④❶
	Beirut Express	Lebanese	❷④⑤
	Randa	"	❸❷④
	Iznik Kaftan	Turkish	❸④❸
	Choys	Chinese	❸❷④
	Made in China	"	❸❸⑤
	Royal China	"	❷❸④
	Haandi	Indian	❷❸④
	kare kare	"	❸❷❷
	Noor Jahan	"	❷❷④
	Sukho Thai Cuisine	Thai	❶❶❷
£30+	The Anglesea Arms	British, Modern	④④❷
	Kensington Square Kitchen	British, Traditional	❸❷❸
	Tom's Place	Fish & seafood	④❸④
	Balans	International	⑤❸❷
	Giraffe	"	④❸❸
	The Scarsdale	"	④❸❶
	Aglio e Olio	Italian	❷④❸
	Buona Sera	"	④❸❸
	Made in Italy	"	❸④❸
	Il Pagliaccio	"	④❷❷
	Picasso's	"	④❸❸
	Rossopomodoro	"	④④❸
	The Atlas	Mediterranean	❷❷❷
	Del'Aziz	"	❸❸❷
	La Rueda	Spanish	⑤④❸

			Rating
	Haché	Steaks & grills	❷❸❷
	Basilico	Pizza	❷❷④
	Richoux	Sandwiches, cakes, etc	⑤⑤④
	Troubadour	"	⑤④❶
	Ranoush	Lebanese	❸④④
	Yi-Ban	Chinese	❷❷❷
	Khan's of Kensington	Indian	❸❷④
	Malabar	"	❷❷❷
	Memories of India	"	❸❸④
	Feng Sushi	Japanese	④④④
	Tampopo	Pan-Asian	❷❸❸
	Bangkok	Thai	❸❷④
	Thai Square	"	④④❸
£25+	Chelsea Bun Diner	International	❸❸④
	The Windsor Castle	"	④④❶
	Pappa Ciccia	Italian	❷❷❷
	Spago	"	❸❸❸
	Little Bay	Mediterranean	❸❷❷
	Daquise	Polish	④④❸
	Rôtisserie Jules	Steaks & grills	❸⑤⑤
	Byron	Burgers, etc	❸❸❷
	La Delizia Limbara	Pizza	❸④④
	Pâtisserie Valerie	Sandwiches, cakes, etc	④④❸
	Paul	"	❸④❸
	Taiwan Village	Chinese	❷❶❸
	Masala Zone	Indian	④❸❸
	Monty's	"	❸❸④
	Shikara	"	❷❷④
	Tandoori Lane	"	❷❷❸
	Itsu	Japanese	❸❸❸
	Kulu Kulu	"	❷④⑤
	Wagamama	"	④④④
	Addie's Thai Café	Thai	❷❶❷
£20+	Costa's Grill	Greek	④❸④
	Mona Lisa	International	❸❷④
	Gourmet Burger Kitchen	Burgers, etc	❸④④
	Costa's Fish	Fish & chips	❷❷❸
	Leon	Sandwiches, cakes, etc	❸❸❸
	New Culture Rev'n	Chinese	④❸④
	Hare & Tortoise	Pan-Asian	❸④④
	Café 209	Thai	④❷❶
	Churchill Arms	"	❷④❷
£15+	Stock Pot	International	④❸④
	Stick & Bowl	Chinese	❷❸④
£10+	Napket	Afternoon tea	❸④④
	Benugo	Sandwiches, cakes, etc	④❸❷
	Crussh	"	❸❷④

Notting Hill, Holland Park, Bayswater, North Kensington & Maida Vale (W2, W9, W10, W11)

			Rating
£70+	The Ledbury	French	❶❶❷
£60+	Beach Blanket Babylon	British, Modern	⑤⑤❶
	Angelus	French	❸❸④

£50+			
Julie's	British, Modern	④④❶
Notting Hill Brasserie	"	❷❷❷
Assaggi	Italian	❶❶❸
Notting Grill	Steaks & grills	⑤⑤④

£40+			
Harlem	American	④④❸
The Cow	British, Modern	❸④❸
First Floor	"	④❸❶
Formosa Dining Room	"	④④❸
The Frontline Club	"	④❷❶
Paradise, Kensal Green	"	❷❸❶
The Warrington	"	④④④
The Waterway	"	④④❷
Bumpkin	British, Traditional	❷❷❷
The Fat Badger	"	❸④❸
Hereford Road	"	❸❸④
Fishworks	Fish & seafood	❸④④
Le Café Anglais	French	❸④❸
Père Michel	"	❸❷④
Halepi	Greek	④❷❸
Electric Brasserie	International	❸④❷
L'Accento Italiano	Italian	❸④❸
Arturo	"	④❷❸
Edera	"	❸❸④
Esenza	"	❸❸④
The Green Olive	"	❸❷❸
Mediterraneo	"	❸❸❸
The Oak	"	❷❸❶
Osteria Basilico	"	❷④❷
Trenta	"	④④④
Maroush	Lebanese	❸④④
Bombay Palace	Indian	❶❷④
Yakitoria	Japanese	④④❸
E&O	Pan-Asian	❷❷❶

£35+			
All Star Lanes	American	④⑤④
The Ladbroke Arms	British, Modern	❷④❷
Raoul's Café & Deli	"	④⑤❸
The Westbourne	"	❸④❸
The Academy	International	❸❷❸
Café Laville	"	④❸❷
202	"	❸❸❷
Luna Rossa	Italian	④⑤④
Ottolenghi	"	❶❸❸
The Red Pepper	"	❸④④
Baker & Spice	Sandwiches, cakes, etc	❷④④
Rodizio Rico	Brazilian	④④④
Crazy Homies	Mexican/TexMex	❷⑤❷
Beirut Express	Lebanese	❷④⑤
Levantine	"	❸❸❸
Mandarin Kitchen	Chinese	❶④⑤
Royal China	"	❷❸④
Bombay Bicycle Club	Indian	❷❷❸
Noor Jahan	"	❷❷④
Urban Turban	"	④⑤⑤
Satay House	Malaysian	❸❸④

£30+			
Lucky Seven	American	❷❸❶
Seabass	Fish & seafood	④❸④
Wine Factory	International	④❷❸

281

	Rossopomodoro	*Italian*	④④❸
	Galicia	*Spanish*	④④❷
	Tootsies	*Burgers, etc*	④④④
	Mulberry Street	*Pizza*	④④❸
	Taqueria	*Mexican/TexMex*	❸❸❸
	Al-Waha	*Lebanese*	❷❷❸
	Ranoush	*"*	❸④④
	Pearl Liang	*Chinese*	❷❸❷
	Kiasu	*Indonesian*	❸⑤⑤
	Feng Sushi	*Japanese*	④④④
	Inaho	*"*	❶⑤⑤
	Nyonya	*Malaysian*	❸❸④
	Uli	*Pan-Asian*	❷❸❸
	Tawana	*Thai*	❷❷④
	The Walmer Castle	*"*	❸❸❷
£25+	Rôtisserie Jules	*French*	❸⑤⑤
	Cochonnet	*Mediterranean*	❸❸❸
	Firezza	*Pizza*	❷❸⑤
	Pâtisserie Valerie	*Sandwiches, cakes, etc*	④④❸
	Tom's Deli	*"*	❸④❷
	Alounak	*Persian*	❸④④
	Mandalay	*Burmese*	❷❸⑤
	The Four Seasons	*Chinese*	❷⑤⑤
	Magic Wok	*"*	❸❷④
	ping pong	*Chinese, Dim sum*	④④❸
	Durbar	*Indian*	❸④④
	Masala Zone	*"*	④❸❸
£20+	S & M Café	*British, Traditional*	④④④
	Gourmet Burger Kitchen	*Burgers, etc*	❸④④
	Kandoo	*Persian*	❸④④
	New Culture Rev'n	*Chinese*	④❸④
	Yelo Thai Canteen	*Thai*	❸❷❸
£15+	Gail's Bread	*Sandwiches, cakes, etc*	❷❸❸
	Salade	*Salads*	❸④⑤
	Fresco	*Lebanese*	❷❷④
	Khan's	*Indian*	❷④④
£5+	Lisboa Pâtisserie	*Sandwiches, cakes, etc*	❶④④

Hammersmith, Shepherd's Bush, Olympia, Chiswick, Brentford & Ealing (W4, W5, W6, W12, W13, W14, TW8)

			Ratings
£60+	The River Café	*Italian*	❷❸❷
£50+	La Trompette	*French*	❶❶❷
£40+	The Brackenbury	*British, Modern*	④❸❸
	Devonshire House	"	④⑤⑤
	High Road Brasserie	"	④④❸
	Pissarro's	"	④④❷
	Sam's Brasserie	"	④❸④
	Snows on the Green	"	❸❸④
	Fish Hook	*Fish & seafood*	❷❷④
	Fishworks	"	❸④④
	Charlotte's Place	*French*	④❸❸
	Chez Kristof	"	④④❸
	Le Vacherin	"	❷❷❸
	Bianco Nero	*Italian*	④④④
	Cibo	"	❷❷❸
	Vino Rosso	"	❷❷④
	Popeseye	*Steaks & grills*	❷❸❸
£35+	Pacific Bar and Grill	*American*	④❸❸
	The Anglesea Arms	*British, Modern*	❶❸❷
	Bush Bar & Grill	"	⑤④④
	The Carpenter's Arms	"	❸④④
	Duke Of Sussex	"	❸④④
	Ealing Park Tavern	"	– – –
	The Havelock Tavern	"	❷⑤❸
	Hole in the Wall	"	❸❸❸
	The Pilot	"	④④❸
	The Roebuck	"	❸❸❸
	Stone Mason's Arms	"	❸❷❸
	Princess Victoria	*British, Traditional*	❷④❷
	Annie's	*International*	④❸❶
	Frankie's Italian Bar & Grill	*Italian*	⑤⑤④
	Cumberland Arms	*Mediterranean*	❸❷④
	The Swan	"	❸❷❷
	Knaypa	*Polish*	④❷④
	The Gate	*Vegetarian*	❶❷❸
	Brilliant	*Indian*	❷❸④
	Madhu's	"	❶❶❷
	Sushi-Hiro	*Japanese*	❶❷⑤
£30+	The Crown & Sceptre	*British, Modern*	❸❸❷
	Queen's Head	"	④④❶
	Balans	*International*	⑤❸❷
	Giraffe	"	④❶❶
	The Thatched House	"	❸❸❸
	Priory House	*Mediterranean*	❸④❸
	Patio	*Polish*	④❸❸
	Blah! Blah! Blah!	*Vegetarian*	❸❸④
	Tootsies	*Burgers, etc*	④④④
	Indian Zing	*Indian*	❷❶❷
	Woodlands	"	❸❸④
	Tosa	*Japanese*	❷❸④
	Saigon Saigon	*Vietnamese*	❸❷❸

Price	Name	Cuisine	Ratings
£25+	La Tasca	Spanish	⑤④④
	Ground	Burgers, etc	❷❷❷
	Eco	Pizza	❸④❸
	Firezza	"	❷❸⑤
	Glistening Waters	Afro-Caribbean	❸❷④
	Adams Café	Moroccan	❸⓪❸
	Chez Marcelle	Lebanese	⓪④⑤
	Alounak	Persian	❸④④
	Mohsen	"	❷❸⑤
	North China	Chinese	❷❷❸
	Agni	Indian	❷❷④
	Anarkali	"	❷❷④
	Green Chilli	"	❸❸④
	Karma	"	❷❷⑤
	Mirch Masala	"	⓪❸④
	Monty's	"	❸❸④
	Fat Boy's	Thai	④❸④
£20+	Gourmet Burger Kitchen	Burgers, etc	❸④④
	Best Mangal	Turkish	❷❷❷
	Sagar	Indian	⓪❷④
	Okawari	Japanese	❸❷❸
	Hare & Tortoise	Pan-Asian	❸④④
	Bedlington Café	Thai	❸❸④
	Esarn Kheaw	"	⓪❸④
	Latymers	"	❷❸④
£15+	Abu Zaad	Syrian	❷④❸
	Hammersmith Café	Thai	④④⑤
	Old Parr's Head	"	❸❷④
£10+	Crussh	Sandwiches, cakes, etc	❸❷④

Hampstead, West Hampstead, St John's Wood, Regent's Park, Kilburn & Camden Town (NW postcodes)

£70+			
	Odette's	*British, Modern*	❸❸❸
	Landmark (Winter Gdn)	"	❸❸❶
£50+			
	L'Aventure	*French*	❷❷❶
	Oslo Court	"	❷❶❷
	Gaucho Grill	*Steaks & grills*	❷❸❸
	Royal China Club	*Chinese*	❷❸④
	Benihana	*Japanese*	④④⑤
	Gilgamesh	*Pan-Asian*	❸⑤❷
£40+			
	Bradley's	*British, Modern*	④④④
	The Engineer	"	❸④❸
	Freemasons Arms	"	④④❷
	The Lansdowne	"	❸④❸
	The Wells	"	❸❸❷
	Fishworks	*Fish & seafood*	❸④④
	Osteria Stecca	*Italian*	❸④❸
	Philpotts Mezzaluna	"	❷❶❷
	Salt House	"	❸❷❷
	Sardo Canale	"	④❸❷
	Villa Bianca	"	④④❸
	Black & Blue	*Steaks & grills*	❸❸④
	Manna	*Vegetarian*	❸④④
	Good Earth	*Chinese*	❷❷❸
	Kaifeng	"	④⑤④
	Atma	*Indian*	❷❷❸
	Sushi-Say	*Japanese*	❶❶④
	XO	*Pan-Asian*	❸④❸
£35+			
	Belgo Noord	*Belgian*	④④❸
	The Betjeman Arms	*British, Modern*	④④⑤
	Café Med	"	④④④
	The Horseshoe	"	④④❸
	The Island	"	❸❷❸
	The Lord Palmerston	"	⑤⑤④
	Market	"	❷❸④
	The North London Tavern	"	❸❸❸
	The Old Bull & Bush	"	❸❸❷
	Walnut	"	❸❸④
	The Wet Fish Cafe	"	❸❸❶
	Holly Bush	*British, Traditional*	④④❶
	L'Absinthe	*French*	❸❷❷
	La Cage Imaginaire	"	④❸❸
	Retsina	*Greek*	④❷④
	The Arches	*International*	⑤❸❷
	La Collina	*Italian*	❸④④
	Osteria Emilia	"	❸❸❸
	The Salusbury	"	❷❸❸
	Sarracino	"	❷❷④
	Camden Brasserie	*Mediterranean*	④❸⑤
	Queen's Head & Artichoke	"	❸❸❷
	Don Pepe	*Spanish*	❸❸❷
	Rôtisserie	*Steaks & grills*	④④④
	Seashell	*Fish & chips*	❷④⑤

	Baker & Spice	Sandwiches, cakes, etc	2	4	4
	Hugo's	"	4	4	3
	Pain Quotidien	"	3	4	3
	Mestizo	Mexican/TexMex	3	4	4
	Cottons	Afro-Caribbean	4	3	2
	Mango Room	"	3	3	2
	Solly's	Israeli	3	4	4
	Goldfish	Chinese	2	3	4
	Bombay Bicycle Club	Indian	2	2	3
	Eriki	"	0	0	3
	Jin Kichi	Japanese	0	2	5
	Singapore Garden	Malaysian	2	2	3
£30+	The Chapel	British, Modern	3	3	2
	The Junction Tavern	"	3	2	2
	Somerstown Coffee House	French	3	2	3
	Daphne	Greek	3	0	2
	Lemonia	"	4	2	0
	Giraffe	International	4	3	3
	Spaniard's Inn	"	4	5	2
	L'Artista	Italian	3	5	4
	La Brocca	"	3	3	2
	Fratelli la Bufala	"	4	4	3
	Marine Ices	"	3	2	2
	Zuccato	"	4	3	4
	William IV	Mediterranean	2	2	2
	Haché	Steaks & grills	2	3	2
	Fine Burger Company	Burgers, etc	3	4	4
	Natural Burger Co & Grill	"	2	3	4
	Tootsies	"	4	4	4
	Nautilus	Fish & chips	2	2	5
	Basilico	Pizza	2	2	4
	Richoux	Sandwiches, cakes, etc	5	5	4
	Harry Morgan's	Israeli	4	4	5
	Shish	Turkish	4	4	3
	Sofra	"	4	4	4
	Gung-Ho	Chinese	3	0	2
	Phoenix Palace	"	2	4	3
	Snazz Sichuan	"	2	3	2
	Weng Wah House	"	4	4	4
	Woodlands	Indian	3	3	4
	Feng Sushi	Japanese	4	4	4
	Yuzu	"	2	5	3
£25+	La Porchetta Pizzeria	Italian	3	3	3
	The Little Bay	Mediterranean	3	2	2
	Trojka	Russian	4	4	2
	El Parador	Spanish	3	2	4
	The Diner	Burgers, etc	4	5	4
	Paul	Sandwiches, cakes, etc	3	4	3
	Beyoglu	Turkish	3	3	4
	Alisan	Chinese	0	2	4
	Ping Pong	Chinese, Dim sum	4	4	3
	Chutneys	Indian	3	4	4
	Great Nepalese	"	2	3	4
	Jashan	"	2	2	4
	Vijay	"	2	2	4
	Bento	Japanese	3	3	4
	Café Japan	"	0	3	4
	Wagamama	"	4	4	4

	dim T	*Pan-Asian*	④④❸
£20+	The Czech Restaurant	*Czech*	④④④
	Gourmet Burger Kitchen	*Burgers, etc*	❸④④
	Chamomile	*Sandwiches, cakes, etc*	❸❷❸
	Kenwood (Brew House)	"	④④❷
	Ali Baba	*Egyptian*	❷❸④
	Diwana B-P House	*Indian*	④⑤⑤
	Five Hot Chillies	"	❷❷⑤
	Kovalam	"	❷❷④
£15+	Gail's Bread	*Sandwiches, cakes, etc*	❷❸❸
	Geeta	*Indian*	❷❷⑤
	Sakonis	"	❷④⑤

Hoxton, Islington, Highgate, Crouch End, Stoke Newington, Finsbury Park, Muswell Hill & Finchley (N postcodes)

£80+	Bacchus	*British, Modern*	❷❷④
£70+	Fifteen Restaurant	*Italian*	④④④
£50+	Frederick's	*British, Modern*	❸❸❸
	Sargasso Sea	*Fish & seafood*	❷❷❷
	Morgan M	*French*	❶❶❸
	Fifteen Trattoria	*Italian*	❸❷❸
£40+	The Barnsbury	*British, Modern*	❷❸❸
	The Bull	"	④④④
	The Drapers Arms	"	❸❷❷
	The Duke of Cambridge	"	④④❸
	The Haven	"	❸❷❸
	The House	"	④④❸
	The Lock Dining Bar	"	❸❶❸
	Mosaica	"	❷❶❷
	Water House	"	④❸❸
	The Marquess Tavern	*British, Traditional*	❷④❸
	Chez Liline	*Fish & seafood*	❷④⑤
	Fishworks	"	❸④④
	The Almeida	*French*	④❸④
	Bistro Aix	"	❸④❸
	Fig	"	❷❶❶
	Metrogusto	*Italian*	④❶❷
	San Carlo	"	⑤⑤④
	Camino	*Spanish*	❸❸❸
£35+	The Albion	*British, Modern*	④❷❷
	The Clissold Arms	"	❸❸④
	Cruse 9	"	④④④
	The Elk in the Woods	"	❸❸❷
	The Northgate	"	④④❸
	The Pumphouse	"	④❸④
	The Three Crowns	"	❷④❸
	St Johns	*British, Traditional*	❸❷❶
	Browns	*International*	④④④
	Hoxton Apprentice	"	④④④
	Orange Tree	"	④⑤④
	Ottolenghi	*Italian*	❶❸❸

		Food	Service	Ambience
San Daniele	"	③	②	②
Rôtisserie	Steaks & grills	④	④	④
Rodizio Rico	Brazilian	④	④	④
Sabor	South American	③	③	③
Emni	Indian	③	③	③
The Parsee	"	②	②	⑤
Isarn	Thai	②	⓪	③
£30+ Pick More Daisies	American	③	③	③
Kings Cross Grille	British, Modern	④	④	④
Les Associés	French	③	②	②
La Petite Auberge	"	④	②	②
Le Sacré-Coeur	"	④	②	②
Vrisaki	Greek	②	②	③
Banners	International	④	③	⓪
Eat & Two Veg	"	④	④	④
The Fox Reformed	"	④	③	⓪
Giraffe	"	④	③	③
Cantina Italia	Italian	③	③	③
Fine Burger Company	Burgers, etc	③	④	④
Toff's	Fish & chips	②	②	④
Two Brothers	"	②	②	③
Il Bacio	Pizza	③	③	②
Basilico	"	②	②	④
Furnace	"	③	③	③
Zaffrani	Indian	③	②	②
Rasa Travancore	Indian, Southern	⓪	②	③
Thai Square	Thai	④	④	③
£25+ Charles Lamb	British, Modern	③	③	②
The Flask	British, Traditional	④	④	⓪
Olympus Fish	Fish & seafood	③	③	⑤
The Real Greek	Greek	⑤	⑤	④
Pizzeria Oregano	Italian	③	②	③
La Porchetta Pizzeria	"	③	③	③
Mem & Laz	Mediterranean	④	③	③
The Islington Tapas Bar	Spanish	⑤	④	④
Firezza	Pizza	②	③	⑤
Gallipoli	Turkish	④	④	③
Izgara	"	③	③	④
Petek	"	③	⓪	②
Masala Zone	Indian	④	③	③
Rani	"	③	②	③
Rooburoo	"	③	②	③
Rasa	Indian, Southern	⓪	⓪	③
Wagamama	Japanese	④	④	④
dim T	Pan-Asian	④	④	③
Yum Yum	Thai	②	③	⓪
Viet Garden	Vietnamese	⓪	④	④
£20+ S & M Café	British, Traditional	④	④	④
Le Mercury	French	④	④	②
Hamburger Union	Burgers, etc	③	④	④
Gem	Turkish	②	⓪	②
New Culture Rev'n	Chinese	④	③	④
Anglo Asian Tandoori	Indian	②	⓪	④
Yelo	Thai	③	②	③
Huong-Viet	Vietnamese	③	⑤	④
Khoai	"	②	③	④

| £15+ | Afghan Kitchen | *Afghani* | ❷❸④ |

SOUTH

South Bank (SE1)

£70+	Oxo Tower (Rest')	British, Modern	⑤⑤④
£60+	Le Pont de la Tour	British, Modern	④④❸
	Oxo Tower (Brass')	Mediterranean	⑤④❸
£50+	Skylon	British, Modern	④④❸
	Butlers W'f Chop-house	British, Traditional	⑤⑤❸
	Roast	"	④⑤❸
	Tentazioni	Italian	❷❷❸
	Gaucho Grill	Steaks & grills	❷❸❸
£40+	Blueprint Café	British, Modern	④④❷
	Cantina Vinopolis	"	④④❸
	Garrison	"	❸❸❶
	Mezzanine	"	⑤❸④
	RSJ	"	❸❷⑤
	The Swan At The Globe	"	④❷❶
	tamesa@oxo	"	⑤⑤④
	fish!	Fish & seafood	❸④❸
	Livebait	"	④④⑤
	Wright Brothers	"	❶❷❷
	Brew Wharf	French	❸④❶
	Chez Gérard	"	⑤⑤④
	Magdalen	"	❷❷❸
	Waterloo Brasserie	"	⑤⑤④
	Champor-Champor	Fusion	❷❷❶
	Village East	"	❸❸❷
	Delfina Studio Café	International	❷❶❸
	Laughing Gravy	"	– – –
	Tate Modern (Level 7)	"	④⑤❷
	Vivat Bacchus	"	❸❷❸
	Cantina del Ponte	Italian	⑤⑤④
	Bermondsey Kitchen	Mediterranean	❸④④
	Baltic	Polish	❸④❷
	Black & Blue	Steaks & grills	❸❸④
£35+	Archduke Wine Bar	British, Modern	⑤⑤④
	The Hartley	"	❸❸❸
	Menier Chocolate Factory	"	④❷❷
	The Anchor & Hope	British, Traditional	❶❸❸
	Canteen	"	④④④
	Browns	International	④④④
	Tate Modern (Level 2)	"	④❸❸
	La Lanterna	Italian	❸❷❸
	Tapas Brindisa	Spanish	❷④❶
	Le Pain Quotidien	Sandwiches, cakes, etc	❸④❸
	Las Iguanas	South American	④⑤④
	Bengal Clipper	Indian	❷④④
£30+	The Table	British, Modern	❷❷❸
	Giraffe	International	④❸❸
	Meson don Felipe	Spanish	④④❷
	Paradiso Olivelli	Pizza	④④④
	Tas	Turkish	④❷❸
	Tas Pide	"	④④❷
	Bincho Yakitori	Japanese	❷❷❶

	Feng Sushi	"	④④④
£25+	Real Greek	*Greek*	⑤⑤④
	Gourmet Pizza Co.	*Pizza*	④⑤④
	Amano Café	*Sandwiches, cakes, etc*	❷④❸
	Ev Restaurant, Bar & Deli	*Turkish*	④❸❸
	ping pong	*Chinese, Dim sum*	④④❸
	Mango Tree	*Indian*	❷❸④
	Inshoku	*Japanese*	❸④⑤
	Wagamama	"	④④④
	dim T	*Pan-Asian*	④④❸
£20+	Leon	*Sandwiches, cakes, etc*	❸❸❸
£15+	El Vergel	*South American*	❶❷❷
£10+	Benugo	*British, Modern*	④❸❷
	Fuzzy's Grub	*Sandwiches, cakes, etc*	❶❷❸
	Monmouth Coffee Company	"	❶❷❷
£5+	Caffé Vergnano	*Sandwiches, cakes, etc*	❷❷❷

Greenwich, Lewisham & Blackheath
(All SE postcodes, except SE1)

£40+	Chapter Two	*British, Modern*	❷❶❸
	Franklins	"	❸❷❸
	Inside	"	❷❸④
	The Rivington Grill	"	④⑤④
	The Rosendale	"	❷❸④
	The Trafalgar Tavern	*British, Traditional*	⑤⑤④
	Lobster Pot	*Fish & seafood*	❸❸❷
	The Spread Eagle	*French*	❸④❸
	Beauberry House	*Fusion*	⑤④❸
	Joanna's	*International*	❸❸❷
£35+	The Dartmouth Arms	*British, Modern*	❸❸❸
	The Palmerston	"	❷❷❸
	Le Chardon	*French*	④④❸
	Mela	*Indian*	❸④④
£30+	The Lavender	*British, Modern*	④❸❷
	Arancia	*Italian*	❷❷❷
	Le Querce	"	❶❷❸
	Barcelona Tapas	*Spanish*	④④❸
	Olley's	*Fish & chips*	❷❷④
	Zero Degrees	*Pizza*	❸❸❷
	Dragon Castle	*Chinese*	❸❷❸
	Peninsular	"	❷④④
	Babur Brasserie	*Indian*	❶❷❶
	Kennington Tandoori	"	❸❸❷
	Tandoori Nights	"	❷❷❷
	3 Monkeys	"	❸❸❸
	Ratchada	*Thai*	❸④④
£25+	The Rye	*International*	❸❸❷
	The Sea Cow	*Fish & chips*	❸❸❸
	Castello	*Pizza*	– – –
	The Gowlett	"	❷❷❷

	Name	Cuisine	Ratings
	Everest Inn	Indian	❸❸④
	Ganapati	"	❷❸❷
	Thailand	Thai	❸❷④
£20+	Green & Blue	International	④❷❷
	Thai Corner Café	Thai	❸④④

Battersea, Brixton, Clapham, Wandsworth Barnes, Putney & Wimbledon
(All SW postcodes south of the river)

	Name	Cuisine	Ratings
£50+	Chez Bruce	British, Modern	❶❶❷
	Trinity	"	❷❸④
	Riva	Italian	❷❷④
	San Lorenzo Fuoriporta	"	⑤⑤④
£40+	The Brown Dog	British, Modern	❸❸❸
	Buchan's	"	❸④❸
	The Depot	"	④④❷
	The Fire Stables	"	④❸❸
	Four O Nine	"	❸❷❶
	Grafton House	"	④⑤⑤
	The Greyhound at Battersea	"	❸❸❸
	Lamberts	"	❶❶❷
	Phoenix	"	❷❶❷
	Ransome's Dock	"	④❸❸
	Sonny's	"	④④④
	The Victoria	"	④④④
	Fishworks	Fish & seafood	❸④④
	Le Bouchon Bordelais	French	④❸❸
	Gastro	"	④❸❶
	The Light House	International	❸❸❸
	Metro	"	④④④
	The Ship	"	❸❸❸
	Donna Margherita	Italian	❶❸❷
	Enoteca Turi	"	❷❷❸
	Numero Uno	"	❸❶❷
	San Remo	"	④❷❸
	Zero Quattro	"	④❷❸
	Rapscallion	Mediterranean	❸④④
	Rocket Riverside	"	❸❸❷
	Barnes Grill	Steaks & grills	⑤④④
	Butcher & Grill	"	④⑤⑤
	Popeseye	"	❷❸❸
	La Pampa	Argentinian	❸④④
£35+	Bodean's	American	④④④
	Alma	British, Modern	④④④
	The Bridge	"	④④④
	Earl Spencer	"	❷❸❷
	The East Hill	"	❸❸❷
	Emile's	"	❷❶❷
	The Freemasons	"	❸④❷
	Harrison's	"	⑤④⑤
	The Mason's Arms	"	❷❸❸
	The Prince Of Wales	"	❷❸❸
	Scoffers	"	❸❸❷
	The Spencer Arms	"	❸❸❸
	Tom Ilic	"	❶❸⑤

	Tree House	"	❸❸❷
	Brasserie James	French	❷❸❸
	Le Chardon	"	④④❸
	Côte	"	④❸④
	Ma Cuisine	"	❸❸④
	Mini Mundus	"	❸0❷
	Upstairs Bar	"	00❷
	Annie's	International	④❸0
	The Stonhouse	"	④④❸
	Frankie's Italian Bar & Grill	Italian	⑤⑤④
	Isola del Sole	"	❷0❸
	Mooli	"	④④④
	Piccolino	"	④④④
	Pizza Metro	"	❷❸❸
	The Three Bridges	"	❸0❸
	The Fox & Hounds	Mediterranean	❷❸❷
	La Mancha	Spanish	④④❸
	Dexters	Burgers, etc	④④❸
	Santa Maria del Sur	Argentinian	❷❷❸
	Chakalaka	South African	❸❸④
	China Boulevard	Chinese	❷④④
	Royal China	"	❷❸④
	Bombay Bicycle Club	Indian	❷❷❸
	Nancy Lam's Enak Enak	Indonesian	❸❷❸
	Cho-San	Japanese	❷❸④
	Tsunami	"	❷④④
	Suk Saran	Thai	❷④④
	Thai on the River	"	❸❷❷
£30+	The Abbeville	British, Modern	④④❷
	The Duke's Head	"	❸❸0
	The Fentiman Arms	"	④④❷
	The Lavender	"	④❸❷
	The Normanby	"	❷❸❷
	Fish Club	Fish & seafood	0❷④
	Gazette	French	❸❸❷
	Giraffe	International	④❸❸
	Hudson's	"	④❸❷
	Putney Station	"	④❷❷
	Antipasto & Pasta	Italian	❸❸❷
	Buona Sera	"	④❸❸
	Rick's Café	"	❸④❷
	Rebato's	Spanish	❸00
	La Rueda	"	⑤④❸
	Fine Burger Company	Burgers, etc	❸④④
	Tootsies	"	④④④
	Basilico	Pizza	❷❷④
	Dish Dash	Persian	④❸❸
	Bayee Village	Chinese	❸0❸
	Dalchini	"	❷❷❷
	Ma Goa	Indian	❷0❷
	The Banana Leaf Canteen	Pan-Asian	❷❷❷
	Thai Square	Thai	④④❸
£25+	The Clarence	British, Modern	❸④❸
	Real Greek	Greek	⑤⑤④
	Il Cantuccio di Pulcinella	Italian	❸0④
	Esca	"	❸❸❸
	Pappa Ciccia	"	❷❷❷
	The Little Bay	Mediterranean	❸❷❷

	Bar Estrela	Portuguese	④④②
	Lola Rojo	Spanish	❸②②
	El Rincón Latino	"	❸⓪⓪
	Brady's	Fish & chips	❸②❸
	Al Forno	Pizza	④②②
	Eco	"	❸④❸
	Firezza	"	②⓪⑤
	Chutney	Indian	②⓪❸
	Indian Ocean	"	❸⓪④
	Kastoori	"	⓪②④
	Mango & Silk	"	– – –
	Mirch Masala SW17	"	⓪❸④
	Nanglo	"	❷②②
	Nazmins Balti House	"	②❸④
	Wagamama	Japanese	④④④
	Amaranth	Thai	②❸❸
	Ekachai	"	②④④
	Talad Thai	"	②❸⑤
	Thai Garden	"	❸❸❸
£20+	Fish in a Tie	Mediterranean	④②②
	Gourmet Burger Kitchen	Burgers, etc	❸④④
	Boiled Egg & Soldiers	Sandwiches, cakes, etc	❸④④
	Holy Cow	Indian	②②–
	Hot Stuff	"	⓪⓪②
	Sree Krishna	"	②②④
	Fujiyama	Japanese	②❸❸
	Hare & Tortoise	Pan-Asian	❸④④
	The Pepper Tree	Thai	❸②②
£15+	Trinity Stores	Italian	❸②②
	Vijaya Krishna	Indian, Southern	❸②④
	Slurp	Japanese	❸❸④
£10+	Franco Manca	Pizza	⓪②❸

Outer western suburbs
Kew, Richmond, Twickenham, Teddington

£60+	Petersham Nurseries	British, Modern	②❸⓪
£50+	The Glasshouse	British, Modern	⓪⓪❸
	Petersham Hotel	"	④❸②
	Gaucho Grill	Steaks & grills	②❸❸
	Kew Grill	"	❸④❸
£40+	Rock & Rose	British, Modern	④④②
	The Wharf	"	④⑤②
	Fishworks	Fish & seafood	❸④④
	Brula	French	❸⓪②
	La Buvette	"	④②❸
	A Cena	Italian	②⓪②
	Matsuba	Japanese	❸④④
£35+	The Inn at Kew Gardens	British, Modern	④④❸
	Loch Fyne	Fish & seafood	④❸④
	Chez Lindsay	French	❸❸❸
	Côte	"	④❸④
	Ma Cuisine	"	❸❸④

	Nosh	*International*	❸❷❷
	Scarpetta	*Italian*	❷❷❷
	Four Regions	*Chinese*	❸❶④
	Origin Asia	*Indian*	❷❷④
£30+	don Fernando's	*Spanish*	❸❷❷
	Tangawizi	*Indian*	❸❷❸
£25+	O'Zon	*Chinese*	❸❶④
	Fat Boy's	*Thai*	④❸④
£20+	Stein's	*German*	❸④❸
	Sagar	*Indian*	❶❷④

EAST

Smithfield & Farringdon (EC1)

£60+	Club Gascon	French	❷❷❸
£50+	Smiths (Top Floor)	British, Modern	❸❸❸
	Dans le Noir	French	❺❸❹
	Portal	Mediterranean	❸❸❷
£40+	The Hat & Feathers	British, Modern	❺❹❹
	The Larder	"	❸❹❹
	Malmaison Brasserie	"	❸❸❹
	The Peasant	"	❸❹❸
	St Germain	"	❹❹❸
	Smithfield Bar & Grill	"	❺❹❸
	Tart	"	– – –
	Vic Naylors	"	❺❸❸
	Hix	British, Traditional	❷❺❸
	Medcalf	"	❸❸❸
	St John	"	❶❷❸
	Fish Shop	Fish & seafood	❸❹❹
	Bleeding Heart	French	❷❷❷
	Café du Marché	"	❷❷❶
	Comptoir Gascon	"	❶❸❷
	Le Rendezvous du Café	"	❸❸❸
	Le Saint Julien	"	❹❸❹
	Alba	Italian	❸❷❹
	The Clerkenwell Dining Rm	Mediterranean	❸❸❹
	Flâneur	"	❹❹❹
	The Zetter	"	❹❹❸
	Potemkin	Russian	❹❸❹
	Moro	Spanish	❶❷❸
	Saki Bar & Food Emporium	Japanese	❷❷❹
	Cicada	Pan-Asian	❷❸❸
£35+	Ambassador	British, Modern	❸❷❸
	Coach & Horses	"	❸❷❹
	Vinoteca	"	❸❷❶
	The Well	"	❷❹❷
	The Fox and Anchor	British, Traditional	❸❷❷
	The Quality Chop House	"	❷❸❸
	Cellar Gascon	French	❸❷❸
	$	International	❹❺❸
	Fabrizio	Italian	❷❸❺
	Smiths (Dining Rm)	Steaks & grills	❹❹❸
	Cottons	Afro-Caribbean	❹❸❷
£30+	Carnevale	Vegetarian	❶❸❹
	Shish	Turkish	❹❹❸
	Sofra	"	❹❹❹
	Tas	"	❹❷❸
	Tajima Tei	Japanese	❷❷❸
	54 Farringdon Road	Malaysian	❷❷❸
	Cây Tre	Vietnamese	❷❷❹
£25+	Fish Central	Fish & seafood	❸❷❹
	The Real Greek	Greek	❺❺❹
	La Porchetta Pizzeria	Italian	❸❸❸
	The Eagle	Mediterranean	❸❹❷

	The Little Bay	"	❸❷❷
	Pinchito	Spanish	❷❸❸
	Pham Sushi	Japanese	❶❷④
£20+	Smiths (Ground Floor)	British, Modern	④④❷
	Cock Tavern	British, Traditional	❸❷④
	Kolossi Grill	Greek	④❶❷
	Pho	Vietnamese	❷❶❷
£10+	Kipferl	East & Cent. European	❸❸④
	Benugo	Sandwiches, cakes, etc	④❸❷
	Spianata	"	❷❸④

The City (EC2, EC3, EC4)

£80+	1 Lombard Street	British, Modern	④⑤④
	Tatsuso	Japanese	❸④⑤
£70+	Prism	British, Modern	④④⑤
£60+	Rhodes 24	British, Modern	❸❷❷
	Vertigo	"	④❸❷
	Paternoster Chop House	British, Traditional	④④⑤
	Catch	Fish & seafood	④④④
	Chamberlain's	"	④④④
	1901	French	❸❷❸
	Bevis Marks	Kosher	❸❸④
£50+	Missouri Angel	American	④❸④
	Addendum	British, Modern	❸❸④
	Bar Bourse	"	④❸④
	The Mercer	"	❸❸❸
	Searcy's Brasserie	"	④④④
	Coq d'Argent	French	④④❸
	Sauterelle	"	❸❸❸
	L'Anima	Italian	❷❶❷
	Refettorio	"	❸❸⑤
	Bonds	Mediterranean	❸④④
	Eyre Brothers	Spanish	❷❷❸
	Gaucho Grill	Steaks & grills	❷❷❸
	Kenza	Lebanese	④④❷
	Mint Leaf	Indian	❸④❸
£40+	Missouri Grill	American	❸❸❸
	The Chancery	British, Modern	❷❸④
	Devonshire Terrace	"	④❸④
	The Don	"	❷❶❷
	Eastway	"	⑤⑤④
	Northbank	"	❸④❸
	The Princess	"	❸④④
	The Rivington Grill	"	❸④④
	The White Swan	"	❸❷❸
	Gow's	Fish & seafood	④④④
	Sweetings	"	❸❸❷
	Chez Gérard	French	⑤⑤④
	Luc's Brasserie	"	④❷❸
	The Royal Exchange	"	④④❷
	Vivat Bacchus	International	❸❷❸
	Bertorelli's	Italian	⑤⑤⑤

Caravaggio	"	④④⑤
Manicomio	"	④④④
Taberna Etrusca	"	④❷❸
Terranostra	"	❸❷④
Rocket	Mediterranean	❸❸❷
Boisdale of Bishopsgate	Scottish	❸❸❸
Vanilla Black	Vegetarian	④❸④
Imperial City	Chinese	❸❸❷
City Miyama	Japanese	④④⑤
Mugen	"	❸❸❸
D Sum 2	Pan-Asian	❸❸④
Gt Eastern Dining Room	"	❷❷❷
Pacific Oriental	"	❸❸❷

£35+			
The Fox	British, Modern	❸❸❷
George & Vulture	British, Traditional	⑤❸❷
Ye Olde Cheshire Cheese	"	⑤❸❶
Green Door	French	❸❸④
Browns	International	④④④
Piccolino	Italian	④④④
Saf	Vegetarian	– – –
(Ciro's) Pizza Pomodoro	Pizza	④④❷
Kasturi	Indian	❷❸❸
Rajasthan II	"	❸❷④
Tokyo City	Japanese	❸❸④
Hokkien Chan	Thai	❸❸❸

£30+			
The Hoxton Grille	British, Modern	④④④
Zuccato	Italian	④❸④
Barcelona Tapas	Spanish	④④❸
Haz	Turkish	❸❸❸
Kazan	"	❷❷❸
K10	Japanese	❷❸❸
Kurumaya	"	❷❷❸
Singapura	Malaysian	❷❸④
Thai Square	Thai	④④❸

£25+			
Club Mangia	British, Modern	❸❷❷
Hilliard	"	❶❷❷
Simpson's Tavern	British, Traditional	④❷❶
The Wine Library	"	⑤❸❶
La Tasca	Spanish	⑤④④
The Diner	Burgers, etc	④⑤❷
Paul	Sandwiches, cakes, etc	❸④❸
Tiffinbites	Indian	❸④❸
Wagamama	Japanese	④④④
Ekachai	Thai	❷④④

£20+			
Gourmet Burger Kitchen	Burgers, etc	❶④④
Konditor & Cook	Sandwiches, cakes, etc	❷❸❸
Leon	"	❸❸❸
Chi Noodle & Wine Bar	Pan-Asian	❸❷❷

£15+			
Pure California	American	❸④⑤
The Place Below	Vegetarian	❷④❸
Salade	Salads	❸④⑤
Vital Ingredient	"	❸④⑤

£10+			
Apostrophe	Sandwiches, cakes, etc	❷❸❷
Crussh	"	❸❷④

Fuzzy's Grub	"		❶❷❸
Spianata	"		❷❸④
Chop'd	Salads		❷④⑤

East End & Docklands (All E postcodes)

£80+	Ubon	Japanese	❸④④
£70+	Plateau	French	④④④
	Les Trois Garçons	"	④❸❶
	Quadrato	Italian	❸❷④
£60+	Beach Blanket Babylon	British, Modern	⑤⑤❶
£50+	Lanes	British, Modern	– – –
	Curve	Fish & seafood	❸❸⑤
	Gaucho Grill	Steaks & grills	❷❸❸
	Hawksmoor	"	❷④④
£40+	The Gun	British, Modern	❸④❷
	The Morgan Arms	"	❸❸❷
	Wapping Food	"	❸④❶
	St John Bread & Wine	British, Traditional	❶❷❸
	The Grapes	Fish & seafood	❸❸❷
	Bistrotheque	French	❸❷❷
	Rosemary Lane	"	❷❷④
	Amerigo Vespucci	Italian	④❸④
	Il Bordello	"	❷❶❶
	1 Blossom Street	"	❸④④
	El Faro	Spanish	❶❷❸
	Café Spice Namaste	Indian	❶❷❸
£35+	All Star Lanes	American	④⑤④
	The Empress of India	British, Modern	④④④
	Canteen	British, Traditional	④④④
	The Narrow	"	❸❸❸
	Browns	International	④④④
	The Prince Arthur	"	❸❸❸
	La Figa	Italian	❷❷❷
	Lilly's	Steaks & grills	❸❸❸
	Ark Fish	Fish & chips	❷❷④
	Buen Ayre	Argentinian	❷❸❷
	Green & Red Bar & Cantina	Mexican/TexMex	❷❸❷
	Lotus	Chinese	④④❸
	Royal China	"	❷❸④
	Elephant Royale	Thai	❸❸❸
£30+	Giraffe	British, Modern	④❸❸
	LMNI	"	⑤❸❶
	Faulkner's	Fish & chips	❷❸④
	Haz	Turkish	❸❸❸
	Yi-Ban	Chinese	❷❷❷
£25+	Story Deli	Organic	❷❸❶
	La Tasca	Spanish	⑤④④
	Gourmet Pizza Co.	Pizza	④⑤④
	Pâtisserie Valerie	Sandwiches, cakes, etc	④④❸
	The Drunken Monkey	Chinese	❸❸❷
	Shanghai	"	❸❸❸

	Ping Pong	*Chinese, Dim sum*	④④❸
	The Gaylord	*Indian*	❸④④
	Mirch Masala	"	❶❸④
	Tiffinbites	"	❸④❸
	Itsu	*Japanese*	❸❸❸
	Wagamama	"	④④④
	Namo	*Vietnamese*	❷❷❷
	Sông Quê	"	❷⑤⑤
	Viet Hoa	"	④④④
£20+	S & M Café	*British, Traditional*	④④④
	Stringray Globe Café	*Italian*	❷④❸
	Leon	*Sandwiches, cakes, etc*	❸❸❸
	Mangal Ocakbasi	*Turkish*	❶❸❸
	Clifton	*Indian*	❷❷❸
	Memsaheb on Thames	"	❷❷❸
	Lahore Kebab House	*Pakistani*	❶④④
	New Tayyabs	"	❶④❸
£15+	Square Pie Company	*British, Traditional*	❸④⑤
£10+	E Pellicci	*Italian*	❸❶❶
	Crussh	*Sandwiches, cakes, etc*	❸❷④
	Spianata	"	❷❸④
£5+	Brick Lane Beigel Bake	*Sandwiches, cakes, etc*	❷④⑤

MAPS

MAP 1 – LONDON OVERVIEW

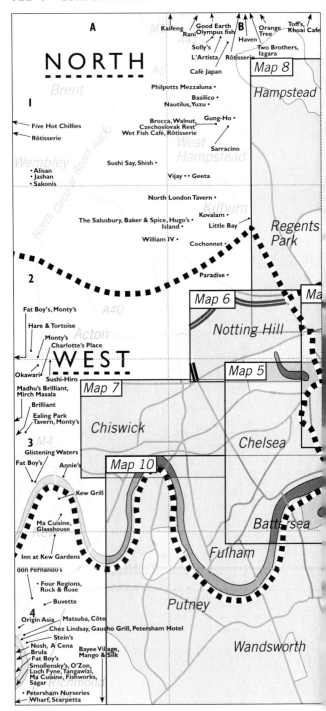

A

NORTH

Brent

1

Kaifeng
Rani
Good Earth
Olympus fish

Solly's
L'Artista
Café Japan

B

Haven

Orange
Tree
Toff's,
Khoai Cafe

Two Brothers,
Izgara

Rôtisserie

Map 8

Hampstead

Philpotts Mezzaluna •

Basilico •
Nautilus, Yuzu •

Brocca, Walnut,   Gung-Ho •
Czechoslovak Rest
Wet Fish Café, Rôtisserie   *West*
Hampstead
Sarracino

Sushi Say, Shish •

Vijay • • Geeta

Five Hot Chillies

Rôtisserie

Wembley

• Alisan
• Jashan
• Sakonis

North London Tavern •

The Salusbury, Baker & Spice, Hugo's •
Island •
William IV •

Kilburn

Kovalam •
Little Bay

*Regents
Park*

Cochonnet •

Paradise •

Map 6

Map 6

Notting Hill

Ma

Map 5

Acton

Fat Boy's, Monty's

Hare & Tortoise

Monty's
Charlotte's Place

WEST

Okawari

Sushi-Hiro

Map 7

Chiswick

Chelsea

Madhu's Brilliant,
Mirch Masala

Brilliant

Ealing Park
Tavern, Monty's

3 *M4*

Glistening Waters

Fat Boy's   Annie's

Kew Grill

Map 10

Ma Cuisine,
Glasshouse

Inn at Kew Gardens

Battersea

Fulham

don Fernando's

• Four Regions,
Rock & Rose

Buvette

Putney

Origin Asia — Matsuba, Côte

Chez Lindsay, Gaucho Grill, Petersham Hotel

Stein's

Nosh, A Cena
Brula
Fat Boy's
Smollensky's, O'Zon, Tangawizi,
Loch Fyne, Fishworks,
Sagar

Bayee Village,
Mango & Silk

Wandsworth

• Petersham Nurseries
— Wharf, Scarpetta

4

MAP I – LONDON OVERVIEW

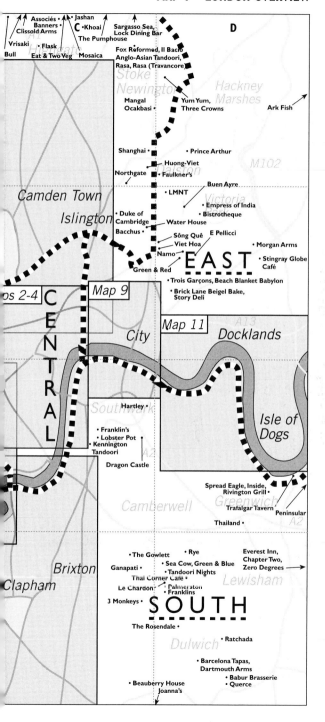

Associés •
Banners •
Clissold Arms •
Vrisaki •
Bull
• Flask
Eat & Two Veg

C • Khoai
• Jashan
The Pumphouse

Mosaica

Sargasso Sea,
Lock Dining Bar

D

Fox Reformed, Il Bacio
Anglo-Asian Tandoori,
Rasa, Rasa (Travancore)

Stoke
Newington

Hackney
Marshes

Mangal
Ocakbasi •

Yum Yum, Three Crowns

Ark Fish

M102

Shanghai •

• Prince Arthur

Huong-Viet

Northgate ■
• Faulkner's

Dalston

Buen Ayre

• LMNT

Victoria

• Empress of India

Camden Town

Islington

• Duke of
Cambridge
Bacchus •

Water House

• Bistrotheque

E Pellicci

• Morgan Arms

Sông Quê
Viet Hoa

Namo •

E A S T

• Stingray Globe
Café

os 2-4

C E N T R A L

Map 9

Green & Red

City

• Trois Garçons, Beach Blanket Babylon

• Brick Lane Beigel Bake,
Story Deli

Map 11

Docklands

A13

Southwark

Hartley

Isle of
Dogs

• Franklin's
• Lobster Pot
• Kennington
Tandoori

A2

Dragon Castle

Camberwell

Greenwich

Spread Eagle, Inside,
Rivington Grill •
Trafalgar Tavern

Peninsular

A2

Thailand •

Brixton

• The Gowlett
Ganapati •

• Rye
• Sea Cow, Green & Blue
• Tandoori Nights

Everest Inn,
Chapter Two,
Zero Degrees

Thai Corner Café •

Lewisham

Clapham

Le Chardon •
3 Monkeys •

• Palmerston
• Franklins

S O U T H

The Rosendale •

Dulwich

• Ratchada

• Barcelona Tapas,
Dartmouth Arms
• Babur Brasserie
• Querce

• Beauberry House
Joanna's

MAP 2 – WEST END OVERVIEW

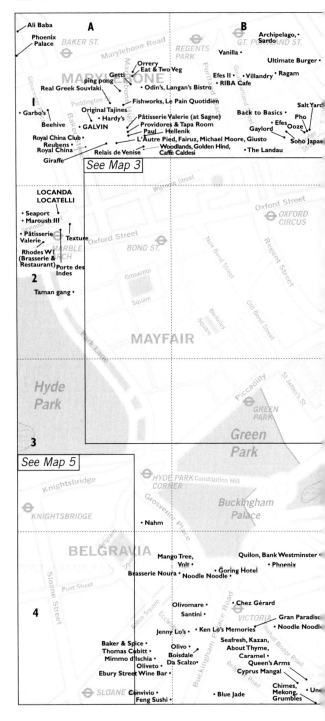

A

Ali Baba
Phoenix Palace

BAKER ST.

Marylebone Road

REGENTS PARK

B

Archipelago,
Sardo

GT. PORTLAND ST.

Vanilla

Ultimate Burger

Orrery
Eat & Two Veg

Getti
ping pong

MARYLEBONE

Efes II
RIBA Cafe

Villandry
Ragam

Real Greek Souvlaki

Odin's, Langan's Bistro

Paddington

Fishworks, Le Pain Quotidien

Original Tajines

Hardy's

Garbo's

Beehive

GALVIN

Pâtisserie Valerie (at Sagne)
Providores & Tapa Room
Paul   Hellenik

Back to Basics

Pho
Efes
Ooze

Salt Yard

Royal China Club
Reubens
Royal China

Giraffe

L'Autre Pied, Fairuz, Michael Moore, Giusto
Relais de Venise

Gaylord

Soho Japan

Woodlands, Golden Hind,
Caffè Caldesi

The Landau

See Map 3

LOCANDA LOCATELLI

Seaport
Maroush III

Pâtisserie Valerie

Rhodes W1
(Brasserie & Restaurant)

Texture

Porte des Indes

Taman gang

Oxford Street

MARBLE ARCH

Oxford Street

BOND ST.

Grosvenor

OXFORD CIRCUS

New Bond Street

Regent Street

2

Seymour

MAYFAIR

Grosvenor Square

Berkeley Square

Old Bond Street

Park Lane

Piccadilly

St James's St.

GREEN PARK

Hyde Park

3

Green Park

See Map 5

Knightsbridge

HYDE PARK CORNER

Constitution Hill

KNIGHTSBRIDGE

Grosvenor Place

Buckingham Palace

Nahm

BELGRAVIA

Mango Tree,
Volt

Brasserie Noura

Noodle Noodle

Goring Hotel

Quilon, Bank Westminster

Phoenix

Sloane Street

Pont Street

Eaton Square

Ebury Street

Olivomare
Santini

Chez Gérard

VICTORIA

Gran Paradiso
Noodle Noodle

4

Jenny Lo's

Ken Lo's Memories

Baker & Spice
Thomas Cubitt
Mimmo d'Ischia
Oliveto

Olivo
Boisdale
Da Scalzo

Seafresh, Kazan,
About Thyme,
Caramel
Queen's Arms

Cyprus Mangal

Ebury Street Wine Bar

Buckingham Palace Road

Belgrave Road

Vauxhall Bridge Road

SLOANE SQUARE

Convivio
Feng Sushi

Blue Jade

Chimes,
Mekong,
Grumbles

Une

MAP 2 – WEST END OVERVIEW

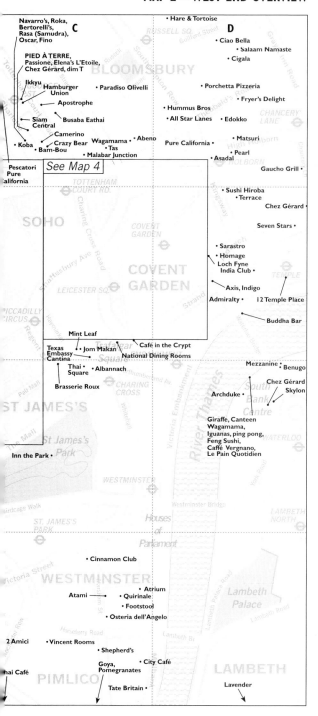

MAP 3 – MAYFAIR, ST JAMES'S & WEST SOHO

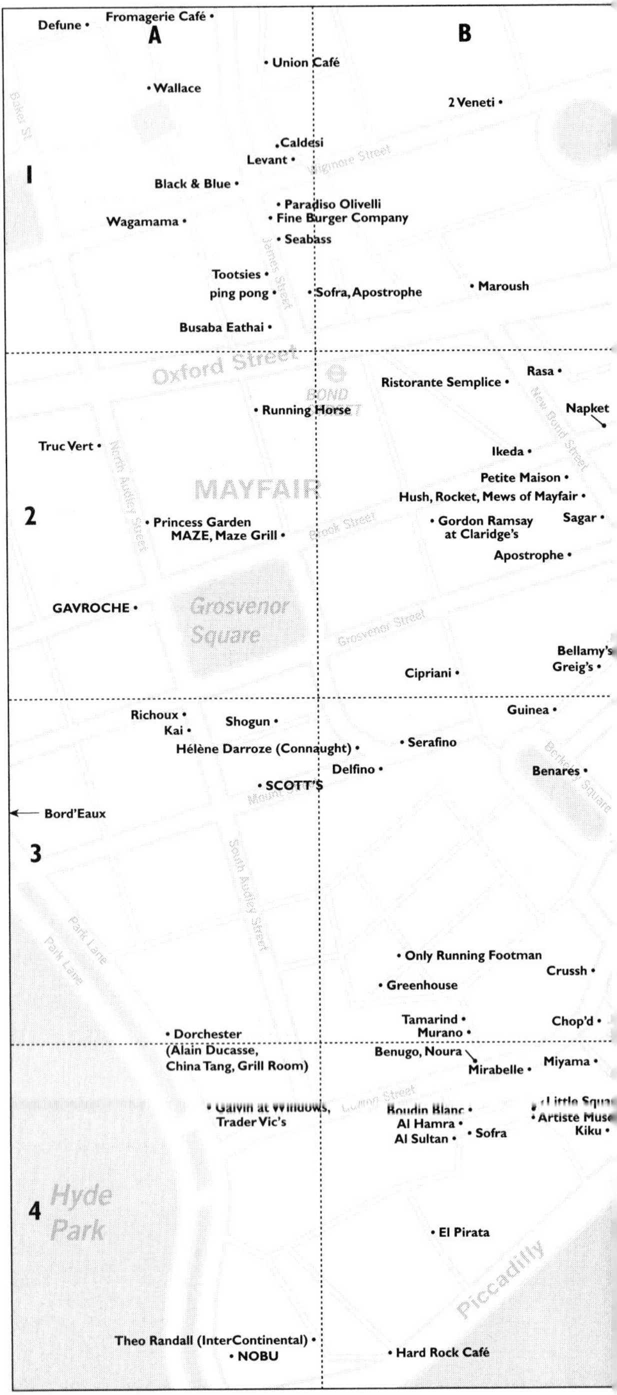

Defune •

Fromagerie Café •

A

B

• Union Café

• Wallace

2 Veneti •

• Caldesi
Levant •

1

Black & Blue •

• Paradiso Olivelli
• Fine Burger Company

Wagamama •

• Seabass

Tootsies •

ping pong •   • Sofra, Apostrophe

• Maroush

Busaba Eathai •

Oxford Street

Rasa •

Ristorante Semplice •

• Running Horse

Napket

BOND

Truc Vert •

Ikeda •

Petite Maison •

MAYFAIR

Hush, Rocket, Mews of Mayfair •

2

• Princess Garden
MAZE, Maze Grill •

• Gordon Ramsay
at Claridge's

Sagar •

Apostrophe •

GAVROCHE •

Grosvenor
Square

Grosvenor Street

Bellamy's

Cipriani •

Greig's •

Richoux •

Guinea •

Kai •   Shogun •

Hélène Darroze (Connaught) •

• Serafino

Benares •

• SCOTT'S

Delfino •

← Bord'Eaux

3

• Only Running Footman

Crussh •

• Greenhouse

Tamarind •

Chop'd •

• Dorchester

Murano •

(Alain Ducasse,

Benugo, Noura •

China Tang, Grill Room)

Mirabelle •   Miyama •

• Galvin at Windows,
Trader Vic's

Boudin Blanc •

• Little Squa

Al Hamra •

• Artiste Muse

Al Sultan •   • Sofra

Kiku •

4

Hyde
Park

• El Pirata

Piccadilly

Theo Randall (InterContinental) •
• NOBU

• Hard Rock Café

MAP 3 – MAYFAIR, ST JAMES'S & WEST SOHO

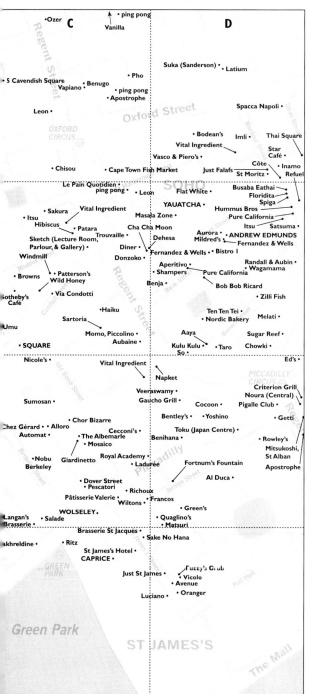

MAP 4 – EAST SOHO, CHINATOWN & COVENT GARDEN

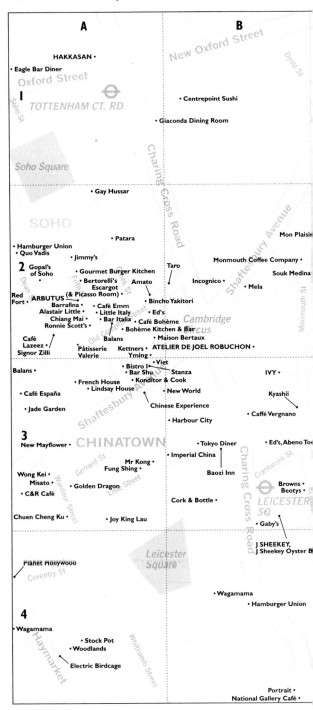

MAP 4 – EAST SOHO, CHINATOWN & COVENT GARDEN

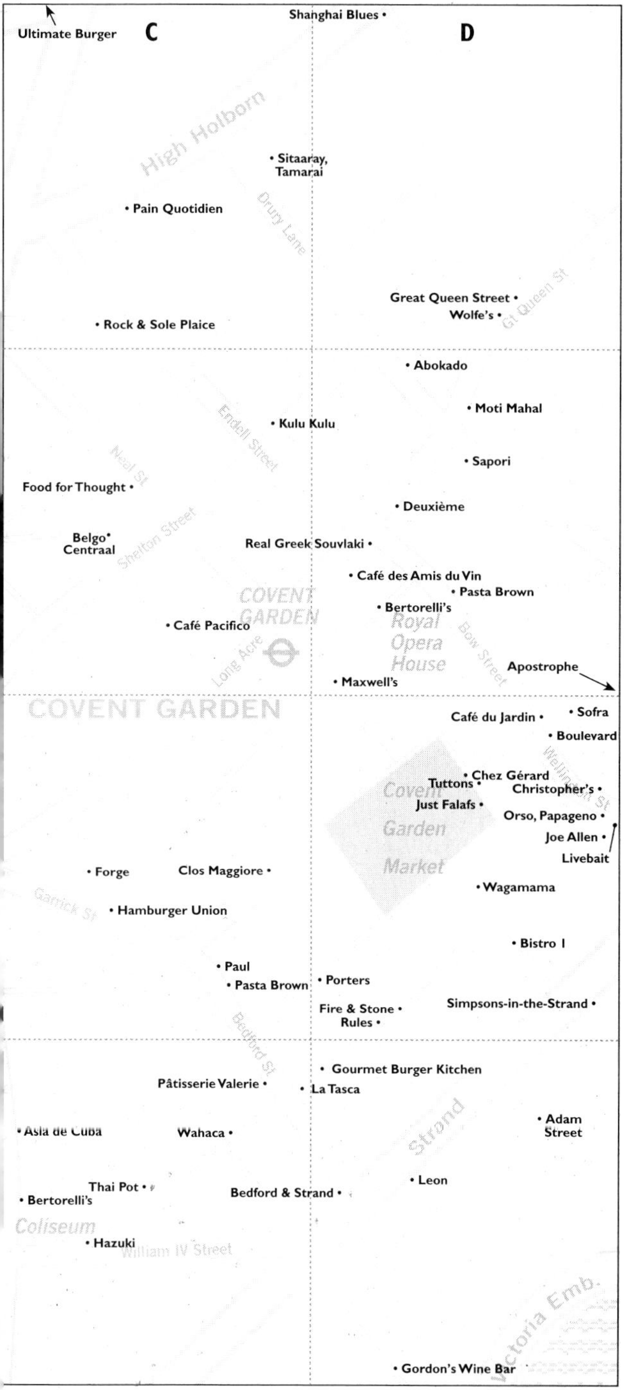

Ultimate Burger   C

Shanghai Blues •   D

High Holborn

• Sitaaray,
  Tamarai

Drury Lane

• Pain Quotidien

Great Queen Street •
Wolfe's •

Gt Queen St

• Rock & Sole Plaice

• Abokado

• Moti Mahal

Endell Street

• Kulu Kulu

• Sapori

Neal St

Food for Thought •

• Deuxième

Shelton Street

Belgo•
Centraal

Real Greek Souvlaki •

• Café des Amis du Vin

• Pasta Brown

COVENT
GARDEN

Royal
Opera
House

• Bertorelli's

Bow Street

• Café Pacifico

Long Acre

• Maxwell's

Apostrophe

COVENT GARDEN

Café du Jardin •   • Sofra

• Boulevard

Coven

• Chez Gérard

Tuttons •

Christopher's •

Just Falafs •

Garden

Orso, Papageno •

Joe Allen •

Market

Livebait

• Forge

Clos Maggiore •

Wellington St

Garrick St

• Hamburger Union

• Wagamama

• Bistro 1

• Paul
• Pasta Brown

• Porters

Fire & Stone •
Rules •

Simpsons-in-the-Strand •

Bedford St

Pâtisserie Valerie •

• Gourmet Burger Kitchen
• La Tasca

•Asia de Cuba

Wahaca •

Strand

• Adam
  Street

Thai Pot •

Bedford & Strand •

• Leon

• Bertorelli's

Coliseum

• Hazuki

William IV Street

Victoria Emb.

• Gordon's Wine Bar

MAP 5 – KNIGHTSBRIDGE, CHELSEA & SOUTH KENSINGTON

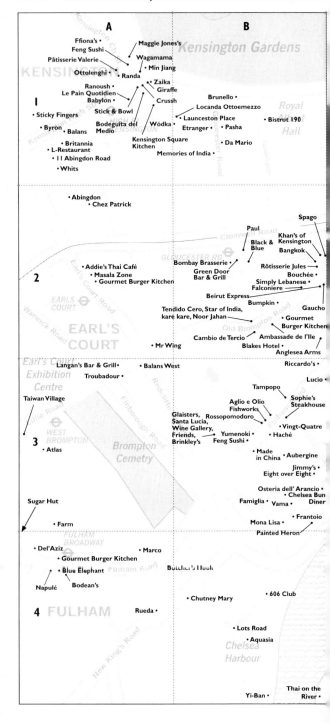

MAP 5 – KNIGHTSBRIDGE, CHELSEA & SOUTH KENSINGTON

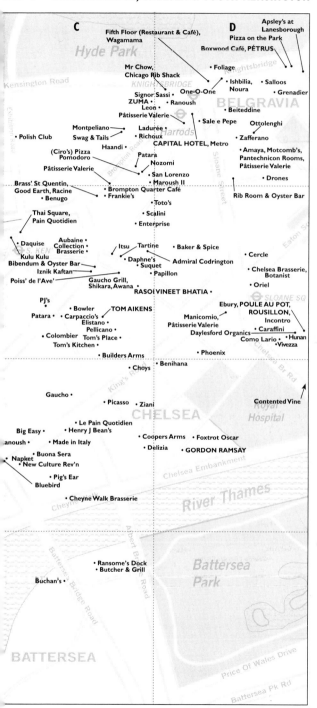

C

D

Hyde Park

Kensington Road

Fifth Floor (Restaurant & Café),
Wagamama

Apsley's at
Lanesborough

Pizza on the Park

Boxwood Café, PÉTRUS

• Foliage

Mr Chow,
Chicago Rib Shack

One-O-One

KNIGHTSBRIDGE

Signor Sassi •
ZUMA •
Leon

• Ranoush

Pâtisserie Valerie

BELGRAVIA

• Ishbilia,
Noura

• Salloos

• Grenadier

• Beiteddine

• Sale e Pepe

Ottolenghi

Montpeliano
Swag & Tails

Ladurée •
• Richoux

CAPITAL HOTEL, Metro

• Zafferano

(Ciro's) Pizza
Pomodoro

Haandi •

Patara
Nozomi

• Amaya, Motcomb's,
Pantechnicon Rooms,
Pâtisserie Valerie

Pâtisserie Valerie

San Lorenzo
• Maroush II

• Drones

Brass' St Quentin,
Good Earth, Racine
• Benugo

• Brompton Quarter Café
• Frankie's

Rib Room & Oyster Bar

• Toto's

Thai Square,
Pain Quotidien

• Scalini

• Enterprise

• Daquise
Kulu Kulu
Bibendum & Oyster Bar
Iznik Kaftan

Aubaine •
Collection •
Brasserie •

Itsu • Tartine

• Baker & Spice

• Cercle

• Daphne's
• Suquet

Admiral Codrington

• Chelsea Brasserie,
Botanist

Poiss' de l'Ave'

• Papillon

Gaucho Grill,
Shikara, Awana

• Oriel

RASOI VINEET BHATIA

PJ's
•

• Bowler

TOM AIKENS

Ebury, POULE AU POT,
ROUSSILLON,

Patara •

• Carpaccio's
Elistano •
Pellicano •

Manicomio,
Pâtisserie Valerie

Incontro

• Colombier

Tom's Place •

Daylesford Organics

• Caraffini

Tom's Kitchen

Como Lario •

• Hunan
•Vivezza

• Builders Arms

• Phoenix

• Choys

• Benihana

Gaucho •

KING'S
• Picasso • Ziani

CHELSEA

Royal
Hospital

Contented Vine

Big Easy •

• Le Pain Quotidien
• Henry J Bean's

• Coopers Arms

• Foxtrot Oscar

-anoush •

• Made in Italy

• Delizia

• GORDON RAMSAY

• Buona Sera

Napket
• New Culture Rev'n

Chelsea Embankment

• Pig's Ear

Bluebird

• Cheyne Walk Brasserie

Cheyne

River Thames

• Ransome's Dock
• Butcher & Grill

Battersea
Park

Buchan's •

BATTERSEA

Price Of Wales Drive

Battersea Pk Rd

MAP 6 – NOTTING HILL & BAYSWATER

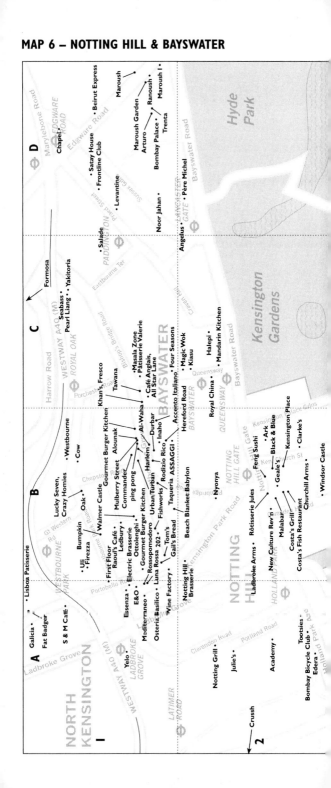

Hyde Park

Kensington Gardens

NORTH KENSINGTON

BAYSWATER

NOTTING HILL GATE

NOTTING HILL

Marbylebone Road
EDGWARE ROAD
Edgware Road
Chapel
Maroush
Beirut Express
Maroush Garden
Ranoush
Satay House
Arturo
Maroush I
Frontline Club
Trenta
Bombay Palace
Levantine
Bayswater Road
Sussex Gardens
Praed Street
Noor Jahan
PADDINGTON
LANCASTER
Angelus
Père Michel
GATE

Formosa
Seabass
Pearl Liang
Yakitoria
WESTWAY A40 (M)
ROYAL OAK
Harrow Road
Porchester Road
Bishop's Bridge Road
Eastbourne Ter
Westbourne Gr
Masala Zone
Pâtisserie Valerie
Khan's, Fresco
Café Anglais,
All Star Lane
Tawana
Urban Turban
Accento Italiano
Four Seasons
Hereford Road
Magic Wok
Kiasu
Queensway
Bayswater Road
Halepi
Mandarin Kitchen

Westway A40 (M)
Gt Western Rd
Lucky Seven,
Crazy Homies
Oak
Westbourne
Cow
Lisboa Patisserie
Bumpkin
Firezza
Ulli
Walmer Castle
Gourmet Burger Kitchen
Alounak
Mulberry Street
Commander
ping pong
Al-Waha
Durbar
Inaho
Chepstow Rd
Harlem
Rodizio Rico
Fishworks
Taqueria
ASSAGGI
Beach Blanket Babylon
Porchester Gdns

Galicia
Fat Badger
S & M Café
WESTBOURNE PARK
Yelo
LADBROKE GROVE
First Floor
Raoul's Café
Ledbury
Electric Brasserie
Ottolenghi
Essenza
E&O
Gourmet Burger Kitchen
Rossopomodoro
Mediterraneo
Luna Rossa 202
Osteria Basilico
Tom's
Gail's Bread
Wine Factory
Notting Hill
Brasserie
Kensington Park Road
Portobello Rd
Gail's Bread
Nyonya
Royal China
QUEENSWAY
Notting Hill Gate
Feng Sushi
Kensington Church St
Black & Blue
Ark
Geale's
Kensington Place
Clarke's
Churchill Arms
Windsor Castle

Ladbroke Grove
Ladbroke Arms
New Culture Rev'n
Rôtisserie Jules
Malabar
Costa's Grill
Costa's Fish Restaurant
HOLLAND PARK
NOTTING HILL
Holland Park Ave
Notting Grill
Julie's
Clarendon Road
Academy
Portland Road
Bombay Bicycle Club
Tootsies
Edera
Holland Park Ave
LATIMER ROAD
Crush

MAP 7 – HAMMERSMITH & CHISWICK

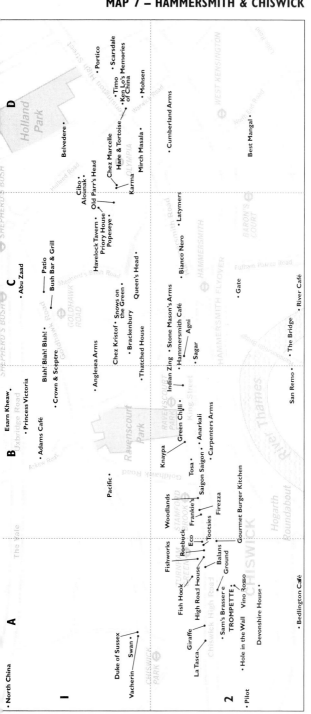

MAP 8 – HAMPSTEAD, CAMDEN TOWN & ISLINGTON

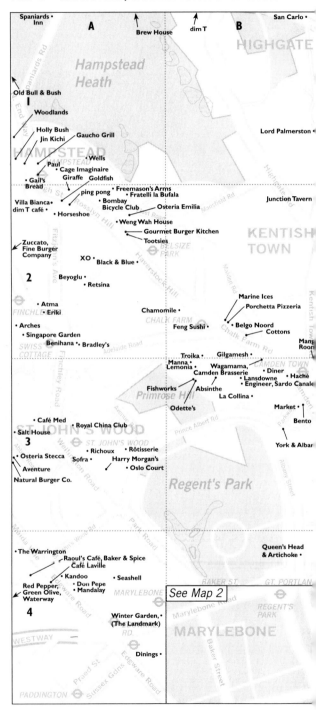

Spaniards Inn

A

Brew House

dim T

B

San Carlo

HIGHGATE

Hampstead Heath

Old Bull & Bush

Woodlands

Holly Bush
Jin Kichi
Gaucho Grill

Lord Palmerston

HAMPSTEAD

Wells

Paul
Cage Imaginaire
Giraffe   Goldfish

Gail's Bread

Villa Bianca
dim T café
Horseshoe

ping pong

Freemason's Arms
Fratelli la Bufala
Bombay
Bicycle Club
Osteria Emilia

Junction Tavern

Weng Wah House

Gourmet Burger Kitchen

Tootsies

BELSIZE PARK

KENTISH TOWN

Zuccato,
Fine Burger Company

XO   Black & Blue

2   Beyoglu

Retsina

Atma
Eriki

Arches

Singapore Garden

Benihana   Bradley's

SWISS COTTAGE

FINCHLEY

Chamomile

CHALK FARM

Feng Sushi

Chalk Farm Rd

Marine Ices

Porchetta Pizzeria

Belgo Noord

Cottons

Mang Room

Troika

Manna
Lemonia

Gilgamesh

Wagamama,
Camden Brasserie

CAMDEN TOWN

Diner

Lansdowne

Engineer, Sardo Canale

Haché

Fishworks

Absinthe

La Collina

Odette's

Primrose Hill

Café Med

Royal China Club

Salt House

3

ST JOHN'S WOOD

Osteria Stecca

Aventure

Natural Burger Co.

Richoux   Rôtisserie
Sofra   Harry Morgan's
Oslo Court

Market

Bento

York & Albar

Regent's Park

The Warrington

Raoul's Café, Baker & Spice
Café Laville
Kandoo
Red Pepper,   Don Pepe
Green Olive,   Mandalay
Waterway

4

Seashell

MARYLEBONE

See Map 2

Queen's Head & Artichoke

BAKER ST   GT. PORTLAN

REGENT'S PARK

Winter Garden,
(The Landmark)

MARYLEBONE

WESTWAY

Dinings

PADDINGTON

MAP 8 – HAMPSTEAD, CAMDEN TOWN & ISLINGTON

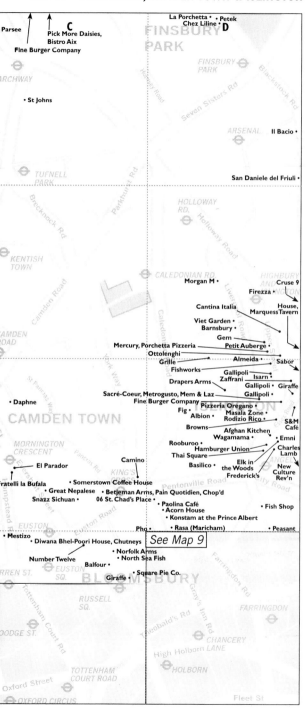

Parsee

C
Pick More Daisies,
Bistro Aix
Fine Burger Company

FINSBURY
PARK

La Porchetta • • Petek
Chez Liline • **D**

FINSBURY
PARK

ARCHWAY

• St Johns

ARSENAL

Il Bacio •

TUFNELL
PARK

San Daniele del Friuli •

HOLLOWAY
RD.

KENTISH
TOWN

CALEDONIAN RD

Morgan M •

HIGHBURY
AND
ISLINGTON

Cruse 9

Firezza •

House,
Marquess Tavern

Cantina Italia

CAMDEN
ROAD

Viet Garden •
Barnsbury •

Gem —

Mercury, Porchetta Pizzeria —
Ottolenghi
Grille —
Fishworks
Drapers Arms •

Petit Auberge •

Almeida •

Gallipoli
Zaffrani

Isarn •

Sabor

Gallipoli •
Gallipoli

Giraffe

Sacré-Coeur, Metrogusto, Mem & Laz •
Fine Burger Company

Fig •
Albion •

Pizzeria Oregano •
Masala Zone •
Rodizio Rico •

S&M
Café

• Daphne

CAMDEN TOWN

Browns
Wagamama •

Afghan Kitchen

Emni

Rooburoo •

Hamburger Union

Charles
Lamb

MORNINGTON
CRESCENT

Thai Square •

Basilico •

Elk in
the Woods

New
Culture
Rev'n

• El Parador

Camino

Frederick's •

Fratelli la Bufala

• Somerstown Coffee House

Pentonville Road

• Great Nepalese
Snazz Sichuan •

KING'S
• Betjeman Arms, Pain Quotidien, Chop'd
06 St. Chad's Place •

• Paolina Café
• Acorn House
• Konstam at the Prince Albert

• Fish Shop

EUSTON

Pho •

• Rasa (Maricham)

• Peasant

• Mestizo

• Diwana Bhel-Poori House, Chutneys

Number Twelve

Balfour •

WARREN ST.

EUSTON
SQ.

BLOOMSBURY

Giraffe •

• Norfolk Arms
• North Sea Fish

• Square Pie Co.

See Map 9

FARRINGDON

RUSSELL
SQ.

GOODGE ST.

Theobald's Rd

CHANCERY

High Holborn LANE

HOLBORN

Oxford Street

TOTTENHAM
COURT ROAD

OXFORD CIRCUS

Fleet St

MAP 9 – THE CITY

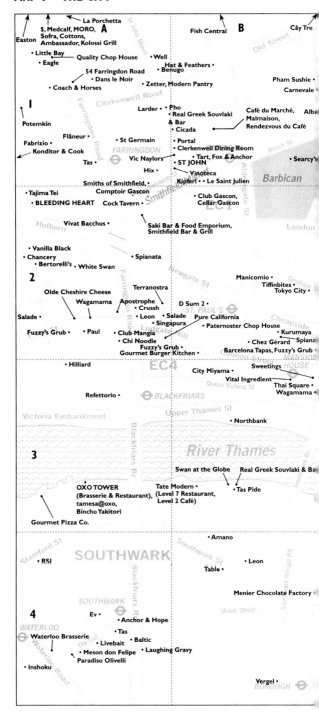

MAP 9 – THE CITY

C

D

Benugo • Pinchito Rivington Grill Apostrophe The Princess

• Boundary

Fifteen
(Restaurant & Trattoria)

Fox •

Real Greek, Yelo,
Furnace, Diner,
Hoxton Apprentice, Shish

FINSBURY

Eyre Brothers •

Drunken Monkey

HAC
(Bunhill
Fields)

Great Eastern
Dining Room,
Hoxton Grille, Saf

All Star Lanes
(Old Truman
Brewery)

Cobwell St

I Blossom St •

St John Bread & Wine •

Hawksmoor •

Anima • • Piccolino

Gaucho Grill •

• Wagamama

Leon, Canteen, Giraffe •

Square Pie Company, Bouchon Breton •
Chop'd, Spianata • • S & M Café

MOORGATE

Broadgate

Tasca •

Tatsuso

LIVERPOOL ST. • Pâtisserie Valerie

Spianata •

Finsbury Circus

Boisdale of Bishopsgate

• Lanes

Gow's •

1901, Catch,
Eastway

• Devonshire Terrace,
Cinnamon Kitchen

EC2

Ekachai

• Hokkien Chan

• Kenza

New Tayyabs •

(Ciro's) Pizza Pomodoro •

Haz •

Clifton

K10 •

• Fuzzy's Grub

Fuzzy's Grub •

• Chez Gérard

Rhodes 24, Vertigo, Wagamama •

Rajasthan III, Kazan City •
Konditor & Cook •

Barcelona Tapas •
Mirch Masala •

Rocket • Pacific Oriental •

Bevis Marks •

Kasturi, Missouri Grill •

Taberna Etrusca
Place Below
• Browns

Mercer
Mint Leaf
• Bonds

Prism

• Caravaggio

• Singapura

• Coq d'Argent
• Zuccato

• Imperial City Fuzzy's Grub •
• Crussh

Chamberlain's,
Luc's Bistro Deluxe,
Barcelona Tapas,
Chop'd, Spianata •

BANK

Cornhill

• Gaucho Grill

• Rajasthan II

Green Door
Bar & Grill

I Lombard
Street

George & Vulture •

• Don

Royal Exchange
Grand Café,
Sauterelle

• Thai Square City

MONUMENT

• Missouri
Angel

Bar Bourse

• Leon

• Haz • Bel Canto

CANNON ST.

FENCHURCH ST.

Mugen •

Eastcheap

Bertorelli's •

• The Wine Library •

Upper Thames St

Gt Tower St

TOWER HILL

Addendum • • Chez Gérard

Rajasthan •

EC3
Lower Thames St

Wagamama •

Tower of
London

ping pong →

River Thames

Cantina Vinopolis

• Amano

Dim T • • Vivat Bacchus

• Gaucho Grill

Roast,
Feng Sushi,
Wright Brothers,
Monmouth Coffee Company,
fish!, Black & Blue, Brew Wharf,
Tapas Brindisa

• Mango
Tree

• Fuzzy's Grub

Magdalen •

Browns •

Butlers Wharf Chop-house,
Cantina del Ponte,
Blueprint Café,
Bengal Clipper,
Pont de la Tour

Tas •

Amano

• Amano

Champor-Champor •

BOROUGH

Delfina Studio Café •

Long Lane

Bermondsey Kitchen, Village East •
↓ • Garrison

MAP 10 – SOUTH LONDON (& FULHAM)

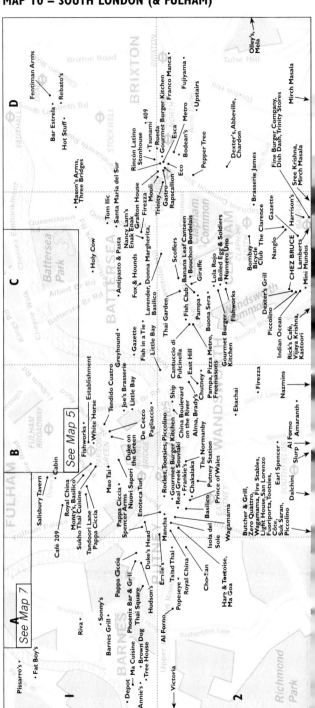

MAP II – EAST END & DOCKLANDS

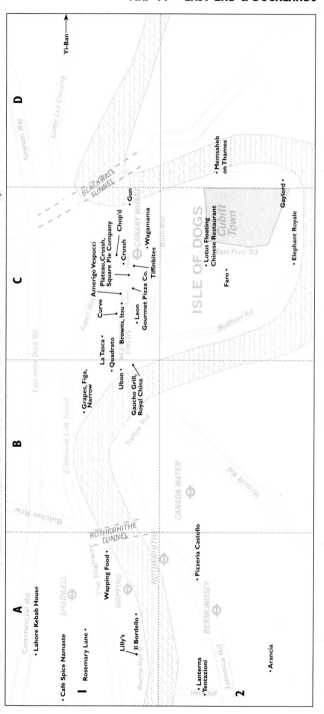

A B C D

Yi-Ban

Newham Way

Lower Lea Crossing

BLACKWALL TUNNEL

• Memsaheb on Thames

• Gun

Amerigo Vespucci • Plateau, Crush, Square Pie Company
• Chop'd

• Crussh

CANARY WHARF

Curve •

• Wagamama

East India Dock Rd

Aspen Way

Tiffinbites

La Tasca •
Quadrato •

• Leon
Browns, Itsu •
Gourmet Pizza Co. •

WEST INDIA QUAY
CIRCUS

ISLE OF DOGS

Cubitt Town

Limehouse Link Tunnel

• Grapes, Figa, Narrow

Ubon •

Gaucho Grill, Royal China •

• Lotus Floating Chinese Restaurant

East Ferry Rd

Faro •

West Ferry Rd

• Elephant Royale

• Gaylord

Salter Rd

Redriff Rd

CANADA WATER

Butcher Row

ROTHERHITHE TUNNEL

The Highway

Wapping Food •

ROTHERHITHE

WAPPING

Rosemary Lane •

Commercial Rd

• Lahore Kebab House

• Café Spice Namaste

Lilly's •
Il Bordello •

Wapping High St

• Pizzeria Castello

BERMONDSEY

Jamaica Rd

• Lanterna
• Tentazioni

Mill St

• Arancia

I

2